Law and Records in Medieval England

Dr Jane E. Sayers

Jane E. Sayers

Law and Records in Medieval England

Studies on the Medieval Papacy,
Monasteries and Records

VARIORUM REPRINTS
London 1988

British Library CIP data   Sayers, Jane E. (Jane Eleanor), *1933-*
                                Law and records in medieval England:
                                studies on the medieval papacy, monasteries
                                and records. — (Collected studies series;
                                CS278)
                                1. England. Christian church. Canon law,
                                1100-1450
                                I. Title
                                262.9'0941

                                ISBN 0-86078-226-3

Published in Great Britain by   Variorum Reprints
                                20 Pembridge Mews London W11 3EQ

Printed in Great Britain by   Galliard (Printers) Ltd
                                Great Yarmouth Norfolk

                                VARIORUM REPRINT CS278

CONTENTS

This volume contains x + 320 pages.

PREFACE

Two themes are represented in this volume — law and records. The first six essays deal with the application and administration of the canon law. England in the medieval period existed under two laws — the law of the state and the law of the church. The law of the state was made up of customary law (of indigenous, native growth), of feudal law and of common (or royal) law. The English common law, dependent on original writs, was in its infancy in the twelfth century. Later it cross-pollinated church law in some areas but its real force was as a land law. The law of the church (or canon law) applied to every Christian country in Western Europe. Canon law covered all cases of marriage (separation), legitimacy, wills, church property and tithes, and defamation. In England these main areas of jurisdiction remained with the ecclesiastical courts until 1857. The Roman or civil law, the other root law of most of Europe, had no hold in England as a legal system (as it did in the Mediterranean countries and in Scotland), but its procedure was adapted to the needs of the developing canon law courts and in this way it exerted an important influence.

Roman law presented the men of the middle ages with an ordered, juristic legacy, but it was fossilized in the sense that it could not be further declared. Canon law, on the other hand, was burgeoning from the mid-twelfth century into a live, sophisticated and written law. The pope interpreted and declared the law, as the Roman emperor had once done. His declarations (decretals) were collected and codified by the lawyers, and studied and commented on in the universities, especially in the the great law university of Bologna. Central to a legal system of such widespread application was the papal curia, the final tribunal of justice. Crucial to the acceptance and growth of the ecclesiastical law were the judges delegate appointed by the curia to deal with many cases in the countries from whence the plaints came. The men who served as administrators, lawyers, legal practitioners and representatives of the parties, the proctors, controlled the working of the law and of justice. The first essay (I) deals with the links between those in the royal and those in the papal service and with the problems of financing the papal judicial and administrative machine. It is followed (II) by a study of the procedure of the courts of the judges delegate, showing how the Roman law was absorbed into the

viii

practice of the courts and how it was interpreted and affected those tribunals in England. The papal court of 'Audientia Litterarum Contradictarum' was essential to the process of delegating cases and this is the subject of the third essay (III), made possible by the discovery of a collection of its documents at Canterbury. Proctors representing British interests at the papal court form the subject of the following essay (IV). The last two essays in the first section, on the judicial and legislative activities of the general chapters and on monastic archdeacons (V and VI), concern specific (or select) areas of jurisdiction developed within the framework of canon law and the church courts. In V, I have attempted to trace the judicial arrangements made by the Cistercians, based on the general chapter, which acted as a miniature papal curia within the order. Its influence spread to the other religious orders in the thirteenth century and suits between religious of different orders might be settled without reference to the pope. The final essay in the first part deals with another area of separate development or exemption — the monastic archdeaconries of the ancient and influential Benedictine houses of Bury St Edmunds, St Albans, Glastonbury and Westminster. These houses exercised archidiaconal rights in their areas, outside the diocesan's control, and sometimes had power over secular or hundredal courts as well.

The second group of essays that have been selected concern records — their compilation, use and retention. They start with an essay (VII) on a procedural treatise, the *Actor et Reus,* of Anglo-Norman origin in the early thirteenth century, but with a wide European circulation, and of use to parties, their advocates and proctors. The manuscript in which it is found contains other legal material and comes from the Benedictine abbey of Evesham in Worcestershire. This essay is followed (VIII) by an edition (with an introduction) of a formulary made for the use of judges delegate or their clerks, now in a St Augustine's Canterbury book — also containing notably the earliest known register of original writs destined for Ireland — but probably originating at Christ Church. The author was working from original charters in his possession c.1227 and he shows the extent to which the Roman procedure had been assimilated by this time. It is not in the general run of formularies so far known (see essay II). Two essays on papal privileges (IX and X) have been chosen next. The Benedictine house of St Alban, England's protomartyr, acquired numerous papal privileges. I have sought to examine the growth, structure and changing use of this section of its archive, concentrating on four phases: the acquisition of privileges to secure exemption from the bishop in the twelfth century; renewal of these and the grant of further contemporarily desirable rights in the thirteenth; the interpretation of these concessions in the fourteenth century; and the changing nature of the grants in an age less tolerant of the autocratic position of the abbot — the indults and personal documents granted to individual monks and the privileges given to the cells in the fifteenth century. The companion article (X) concerns one privilege for a religious community, and one almost as insignificant as St Albans was significant, the leper house of St Giles at Maldon in Essex. It is of interest diplomatically as a hybrid document, having features both of the letter of grace and of the letter of justice. It confirmed in general terms their church and cemetery. A drop in the ocean of privileges, it had its importance to that particular community and was carefully preserved, surviving the Dissolution as a deed of title. English arrangements for the issuing of charters leading up to and during the course of the Third Crusade is the subject of XI. This essay is an incursion into 'secular' diplomatic and considers the cross currents of influence on Richard I's 'crusading chancery' and in particular the charters of two lesser knights drawn up in the Holy Land and now surviving in English cartulary copies. The final article (XII) investigates medieval muniment rooms and especially the arrangements for the safe-keeping and care of the archbishop of Canterbury's archives, their storage, inventories or finding-lists and the whereabouts of the main archive or treasury.

Factual and typographical errors and misidentifications have been rectified in the text and the footnotes, wherever possible. Where an article has served to produce further work, discussion and revision since publication, this is noted at its end.

I am delighted to offer my very sincere thanks to those who originally published these articles and who have given me permission to reproduce them in this selection, namely the Cambridge University Press (I, V, VI, XI), the Oxford University Press (II, IX), the Fordham University Press (III), the Director of the Institute of Medieval Canon Law (IV, VII), and the Director of the Institute of Historical Research (VIII, X, XII). I am also very grateful to Professor Christopher Brooke, the late Professor C.R. Cheney, Dr D.E. Greenway, Professor Peter Herde, Professor Kathleen Major, Professor Winfried Stelzer and Dr P.N.R Zutshi who have corrected errors or caused me to think again. Finally I should like to thank Dr John Smedley of *Variorum* for his care, advice and help in the preparation of this volume.

J.E.S

University College, London
March 1988

PUBLISHER'S NOTE

The articles in this volume, as in all others in the Collected Studies Series, have not been given a new, continuous pagination. In order to avoid confusion, and to facilitate their use where these same studies have been referred to elsewhere, the original pagination has been maintained wherever possible.

Each article has been given a Roman number in order of appearance, as listed in the Contents. This number is repeated on each page and quoted in the index entries.

I

CENTRE AND LOCALITY: ASPECTS OF PAPAL ADMINISTRATION IN ENGLAND IN THE LATER THIRTEENTH CENTURY

LIKE THE ENGLISH ROYAL COURT, the papal court was peripatetic. The restless nature of royal and papal government was partly imposed by the difficulties of staying put in one place. The justices-in-eyre and the judges-delegate were the expedients of the twelfth century – administration on the move – reaching their zenith in the mid-thirteenth century. The new demand was for a settled place of administration and justice, a demand which was met more successfully by the royal government in England (although the baronial activities caused temporary dislocations) with the settlement of the bench and its professional judges at Westminster, than by the papal court of audience which was never able to remain in Rome for long. Rome in the thirteenth century presented a panorama of fortified residences and castellated towers, sheltering barons as turbulent as any in Europe. Many popes spent time in their native cities, where their landed influence provided stability: Innocent IV at Genoa, for example, and Boniface VIII at Anagni. The two French popes, Urban IV (1261–4) and Clement IV (1265–8), never entered the papal city of Rome. Of the thirteenth-century popes, Gregory IX spent much time at Anagni, Innocent IV at Genoa and Lyons, Clement IV at Perugia and Viterbo, and Gregory X at Orvieto and Lyons.

A political elite and a professional civil service were responsible for both the papal and English royal administrations, centring on the household. We do not need Namier to show that it was family connection, rather than any kind of specific party alliance, that determined selection and entry into the household, whether it was the household of pope, king, cardinal, bishop or earl. The paternalistic nature of curial government – papal, royal, episcopal – extended the conception of the family into a wider field. A pope, king or bishop, who did not provide for his own 'especially for those of his own house', as Adam Marsh reminded Grosseteste, citing I Timothy 5.8, 'had denied the faith and was worse than an infidel'.[1] The reliance on family and friends filled an otherwise unsupplied need in the administrative system.

Nowhere is this better shown in the late thirteenth century than by examining the family of Fieschi. The Fieschi were a noble family from Lavagna near Genoa, whose influence on thirteenth-century politics was comparable with that of the Bonapartes in nineteenth-century Europe or the Kennedys in twentieth-century America. In origin the family was probably Germanic (as were the Conti). They were married into most of the royal families of Europe and were connected with the Marquises of Carreti and of Pallavicini and later with the Este, Gonzaga and Visconti families. Their accession to the papal throne in the person of Innocent IV signalised their first major entry into papal politics, although there had been two earlier Fieschi cardinals.[2] The difficulty of staying in Rome meant that Innocent IV had to create his own power base elsewhere and the exile of this pope from the city exalted the house of Fieschi perhaps more than would otherwise have been the case.

There was, indeed, during the years of their influence, scarcely a diocese or cathedral chapter in Europe where the Fieschi were not represented. In Italy, they were, of course, strong in Genoa, and also in other cathedral churches, such as Parma. In France and the Low Countries, they held office in Bayeux, Beauvais, Cambrai, Meaux, Narbonne, Paris, Rheims, Rouen and St Brieuc. In England they had prebends in York, Lincoln, Salisbury and Lichfield, and various benefices. By far the most influential of the Fieschi in touch with England was Innocent IV's nephew, the legate Ottobon, but the family also produced at least two royal clerks – Master Tedisius (who was also a papal scribe) and Master Rowland, who served as a royal proctor – and numerous papal chaplains. Master Rowland of Lavagna, brother of the legate, occurs as a king's clerk between 1258 and 1267, and in 1259 was presented to the church of Steeple Morden by the king, during a vacancy in the see of Winchester. Two other Fieschi were engaged on the king's business – Percival in 1268, and Luke, cardinal deacon of St Mary in Via Lata, who in 1301 was granted a pension of fifty marks at the Exchequer 'in consideration of his good offices in the king's affairs'. Luke was Edward I's kinsman, the son of Nicholas, the elder

---

[1] Cited by C. R. Cheney, *Pope Innocent III and England*, Päpste und Papsttum, IX (Stuttgart, 1976), pp. 82–3.
[2] F. Federici, *Della famiglia Fiesco trattato* (Genoa, ?1650) deals (somewhat inaccurately) with the family.

Papal administration in England

brother of Ottobon, whose sister had married into the house of Savoy.[3] If, indeed, we had to find a parallel for the Fieschi at this period, in filling offices in Church and State, it would surely be the house of Savoy.

Payment of the increasing bureaucracy presented a severe problem. The benefice was the most common reward, for all the officers with whom we are concerned were in orders of some kind, usually deacon's, but there is evidence of a growing shortage of benefices at this time due to increased appropriation by the monasteries. No doubt the payment of a papal civil service had already exercised the mind of Honorius III, as chamberlain and vice-chancellor, before his accession to the papacy. Indeed the pope's letter putting forward a scheme in 1225 refers to an earlier proposal which had been discussed at the Fourth Lateran Council, when it was suggested that a tenth should be levied on the revenues of all cathedral churches. Honorius said that he had heard of complaints about financial excesses in Rome, which he believed to be not wholly warranted because many proctors spent their expenses on good living, and then lied to their employers about the amounts necessary for the conduct of business. However, the pope thought that reform was desirable and therefore he wished to obtain a permanent income for the curial officers. If such a revenue could be assured, he would impose heavy penalties on those in the curia who took bribes, and would eliminate not only the customary gratuities but also all fees, with the one exception of that charged by the chancery for the application of the *bulla*. To provide a fixed income for the curial officials, the pope proposed that the bishops should hand over a prebend in each cathedral and prebendal church, that the monasteries and collegiate churches should provide a sum relative to their resources, and that bishops personally should provide some long-term gift to form a common fund. The plan was not accepted, nor was a renewed form of it in 1244.[4] In the face of such a negative response, the curia was left with no alternative but to continue with the old system of revenue-raising to pay its officers, and to operate the system of provision to foreign benefices for which it was so severely criticised. To understand clearly why the scheme was rejected it is necessary to consider the channels of communication to the papal court.

[3] F. M. Powicke, *King Henry III and the Lord Edward*, 1 vol. edn (Oxford, 1966), p. 526.
[4] *Regesta Honorii Papae III*, ed. P. Pressutti (Rome, 1888–95), no. 5285. For the full text see *Register of S. Osmund*, I, ed. W. H. Rich Jones, R.S. (London, 1883), p. 366; and see W. E. Lunt, *Financial Relations of the Papacy with England to 1327* (Cambridge, Mass., 1939), pp. 178, 213.

Much of the work of papal government operated through the cardinals' households. There was usually one English-born cardinal in the curia: in the latter part of the century, John of Toledo (1244–75), Robert Kilwardby (1278–9) and Hugh of Evesham (1281–7). There were also those whose legations and assignments brought them into touch with England and English affairs, who were the natural targets for English petitioners and placemen in search of provision – Ottobon, cardinal from 1252–76 and legate from 1265–8, and among the cardinals of foreign origin, Cardinal Richard Annibaldi (1238–76).

It is unknown how the English-born John of Toledo, cardinal from 1244–75, entered the curia, but if the chronicler is correct when he states on John's death in 1275 that he had been in the curia for some sixty years some further *curriculum vitae* is necessary for him. So far as is known he was not in Langton's household nor in the royal service, but had, like Adrian IV before him, entered a foreign religious house, in this case Clairvaux, from where he had come to prominence, possibly as a proctor. The influence of the Cistercians within the curia is apparent from the mid-twelfth century, and it had certainly not died by the time of John of Toledo, the 'Cardinal Albus', protector of the Order in all but name. He had in his youth studied medicine at Toledo and another possible channel of his influence is as a doctor. His households as cardinal priest and later as cardinal bishop contained some fifty-eight members, of whom eighteen to nineteen were apparently English, two were Scots, thirteen to fourteen Italian, eight to nine French, one Spanish and one from Tortosa (fourteen unknown).[5] Fourteen were beneficed in England, and two deserve some short comment. William de Lexington, a chaplain of the cardinal, came from the Nottinghamshire family of Laxton, and was a relative of Stephen de Lexington, Abbot of Clairvaux from 1243 to 1255.[6] When, on 16 March 1247, William was authorised to have an additional benefice with cure of souls – the one he already held was probably Whaddon, Cambs. – the letter was endorsed 'To the Abbot of Clairvaux (Stephen de Lexington) at the instance of J(ohn of Toledo) cardinal priest of St Laurence in Lucina by Master William de Buttona, Archdeacon of Wells'. William de Lexington's future was to be identi-

[5] Based on A. Paravicini Bagliani, *Cardinali di curia e 'familiae' cardinalizie dal 1227 al 1254*, Italia Sacra XVIII, XIX (Padua, 1972), pp. 242–55.
[6] On the family see *Rufford Charters*, I, ed. C. J. Holdsworth, Thoroton Soc. Rec. Ser. XXIX (1972), pp. xcii–xcix; and *Rolls and Register of Bishop Oliver Sutton*, III, ed. R. M. T. Hill, LRS, XLVIII (1954), p. xiv.

Papal administration in England

fied with his home region of Lincoln. He was a canon of Lincoln by 1259 and prebendary of Langford manor (this prebend had been held consecutively by Henry de Lexington and Richard Gravesend), precentor, and elected dean in 1262.[7] Master Richard Gravesend who occurs as a chaplain of the cardinal in August 1254 was already treasurer of Hereford cathedral. Nine years earlier, in 1245, he had objected to residence, enforced by a papal bull, in order to draw from the common fund.[8] He was archdeacon of Oxford by 1249, and, on the occasion when he is referred to as chaplain, he was dispensed to hold both the rectory of Ross (Herefordshire) and the deanery of Lincoln.[9] He was consecrated bishop of Lincoln in 1258, on the death of Henry de Lexington.[10] He supported the baronial party and hence was *persona non grata* with the legate, Ottobon.

Through the good offices of the 'Cardinal Albus', during the years of his influence at the curia, especially under Alexander IV (1254–61), many members of his household and others were provided to benefices. His own clerk, the king's clerk and papal chaplain, Roger Lovel, was 'at the cardinal's request' dispensed for plurality, as was Roger's brother Philip, papal chaplain and royal treasurer, while the canonist, Master Roger Marmion, prebendary of York, was appointed papal chaplain on the cardinal's recommendation.[11] There were also dispensations for illegitimacy, issued at John's request, and licences to appropriate livings, for the English Cistercian houses of Newenham and Roche, and the Benedictine nuns of Elstow (Beds.). In 1258, through John's influence, Waverley, and all the English Cistercian houses, were exempted from contributing to the tenth of church revenues, granted by the pope to the king; and the papal registers abound with references to John's activities on behalf of English petitioners and the Cistercian College in Paris.[12]

The two other most influential cardinals at this time, Cardinal Richard Annibaldi and Cardinal Ottobon Fieschi, were both closely attached to the English. Cardinal Richard Annibaldi (1238–76) came from the great Roman family of Annibaldi and was a nephew of Innocent III. Cardinal Richard's household had some thirty-eight members, two of whom were English: John of Somercotes and Roger

[7] BL Harley Ch. III A 7; and see *John Le Neve, Fasti Ecclesiae Anglicanae 1066–1300: III. Lincoln*, comp. D. E. Greenway (London, 1977), pp. 11, 14, 76.
[8] Hereford D. and C. Ch. 2515.
[9] *Les Registres d'Innocent IV*, ed. E. Berger (4 vols., Paris, 1884–1911), no. 7974.
[10] See introduction by A. Hamilton Thompson to *Rotuli Ricardi Gravesend episcopi Lincolniensis*, ed. F. N. Davis, LRS, xx (1925).
[11] CPL pp. 324, 330, 336, 349.　　　[12] *Ibid.*, pp. 331, 348, 351–2, 359–60.

Lovel, who transferred to John of Toledo's household in 1252. Mainly the cardinal's associates were Italian, two at least of whom had English benefices: Roffredus of Ferentino, rector of Holland, and John de Panormo, rector of Wandsworth. Richard's activities in English government were concerned with the candidature of Henry III's son, Edmund, for the *Regno* in 1252 and the election of Richard of Cornwall as senator of Rome in 1261. His support for Edmund was canvassed by John of Toledo, and, in recognition of his activities, the English crown granted him a yearly salary of thirty marks. He was a highly respected papal auditor during nearly forty years of influence, and protector of the Augustinians.[13] His nephew, the papal subdeacon and notary, Richard, held several English benefices, including Dorking, and another nephew, Stephen Surdus, held the prebend of Scamblesby and the living of Kirkby Thore.[14] Both Richard and John Annibaldi, who occur at the turn of the century, beneficed in Lincoln, were probably great-nephews.

Cardinal Ottobon Fieschi, nephew of Innocent IV, and later Pope Adrian V, was legate in England from 1265 to 1268. He had close associations with the royal house – indeed his mission was to provide a political settlement – and, in a stay of two-and-a-half years, his influence was bound to be felt in favour of his family and *familia* on English benefices. He had come to England with Otto's legation in 1237 and had held the churches of Twywell (Northants) (patrons, Thorney), and St Nicholas, Durham, to which he had been presented by the king during a vacancy.[15] In 1257, on his petition to the papal court, William son of Mussus, his cousin, was dispensed to hold another benefice besides St Mary-in-the-castle, Chester, and St Eval (Cornwall).[16] His household included two men provided to prebends in Hereford cathedral – the Englishman John le Berton, canon of Merton, his chaplain, and Ardicio de Comite, his chancellor, from the Conti family, and later papal collector in England.[17] Master James de Portubus, canon of Syracuse, living in England from 1263, was his clerk during the English legation. It also included Alfred the Englishman in 1271, Gilbert of St Léofard, in his service in March 1266, and Geoffrey de

---

[13] F. Roth, 'Cardinal Richard Annibaldi', *Augustiniana*, II (1952), pp. 26–60, 108–49, 283–313; IV (1954), pp. 5–24.

[14] *CPL* pp. 377, 417, 492.

[15] *Rotuli Roberti Grosseteste*, ed. F. N. Davis, LRS, XI (1914), p. 182; and *Register or Rolls of Walter Gray*, ed. J. Raine, Surtees Society, LVI (1870), no. 382.

[16] *CPL* p. 345.

[17] *Diplomatic Documents*, I, ed. P. Chaplais (London, 1964), no. 412.

Papal administration in England

Sancta Agatha (?Easby), rector of Houghton and incumbent of Lazonby (Cumb.) (patrons, Lanercost), chaplain from October 1258. His secretary during the English legation was Benedict Gaetani, the future Boniface VIII.

Finally, Hugh of Evesham, cardinal from 1281 to 1287 ('Anglicus cardinalis'), previously prebendary of Bugthorpe, proctor of the archbishop of York in 1280, and archdeacon of Worcester, deserves some attention. Overtures, softly made to him in those years, speak discreetly from the bishops' registers – thirty marks from Bishop Cantelupe in June 1281,[18] for example – as they had done to others in the 1230s and 1240s. Even Bishop Grosseteste had felt no compunction about writing to Cardinal Robert of Somercotes on his elevation to the cardinalate, congratulating him, and asking his favour in current business in the curia, though he got his name wrong, calling him Cardinal Raymond, and hence perhaps reaped little harvest, but the cardinal after all was beneficed in his diocese, and could be expected to repay those who had sped him on his way).[19] When Archbishop Giffard sent a present to Cardinal Richard Annibaldi, he rather archly apologised for the smallness of it.[20] But a Giffard could at least offer a present to an Annibaldi, without fear of rebuff.

On the promotion of Hugh of Evesham to the cardinalate, indeed, English spirits must have risen, and the papal registers show his activities on behalf of his family, English petitioners and his household. Richard de Duriard, a relative, was to have a prebend of Lichfield when one came vacant,[21] Master Henry of Somerset, rector of Curry Rivel, 'at the request of the cardinal' was to have another benefice. Master Walter of Bath, king's clerk and doctor of civil law, was to be ordained and hold a benefice, although he was illegitimate.[22] With Cardinal Hugh's chaplain, Master Stefano di San Giorgio, who was a papal scribe in 1288,[23] we touch on an important royal clerk of the wardrobe, who first appears in the royal court in 1274, was proctor of Edward I at the papal court in 1283 and was still employed by the king in 1290.[24]

---

[18] *Registrum Thome de Cantilupo*, ed. R. G. Griffiths and W. W. Capes, CYS, II (1907), p. 274.

[19] *Roberti Grosseteste . . . Epistolae*, ed. H. R. Luard, R.S. (London, 1861), no. lxv.

[20] *Register of Walter Giffard*, Surtees Society, CIX (1904), p. 244.

[21] *Les Registres d'Honorius IV*, ed. M. Prou (Paris, 1886–8), no. 342.

[22] *Ibid.*, no. 54.

[23] *CPL* p. 492.

[24] T. F. Tout, *Chapters in . . . Administrative History*, II (Manchester, 1937), pp. 23–4; *CPR* (*1272–81*), pp. 61, 76, 209, 242, 295; and *CPR* (*1281–92*), pp. 86, 374, 447. He had acted as proctor of M. Robert of Lavagna, king's clerk (see below, p. 125).

How easily such men moved between the royal court, the papal court and the cardinals' households! This brings us to new realms of connection in the curia's business, but, before following them, we must consider the extent of provision for curialists in English secular cathedrals and benefices. The bishops, who were expected in Honorius's scheme to make gifts to the Roman church, were doubtless continuing to do so, into the hands of those whom *they* chose. They surrendered prebends for curial officers (sometimes more than the required one) when *they* chose. That way they played their own cards: no faceless Roman pope did it for them and absorbed their contributions into a common sinking fund where none knew from whence they came. When Innocent III appointed his nephew, Leonard, to York, he did not hesitate to point out to the chapter the benefits which might accrue to it, but he was forced to ask and persuade them and explain his action.[25] Bishop Hugh Nonant of Coventry, who assigned prebends in his projected secular chapter to Roman cardinals, is said to have done so with the definite purpose of securing defenders of the new constitution in the curia.[26]

If we look at three out of the nine English secular cathedral chapters in the thirteenth century, the evidence is as follows. Of the thirty-six prebends of York, twenty-one identified prebends, i.e. two-thirds, were in the hands of foreigners (mainly Italians from the great papal families) at some point in the century. Three prebends were occupied by the Fieschi, two by the Savelli, three by the Orsini, two by the Gaetani, one by a Conti and one by a Ceccano. Rufinus, the nephew of the legate Guala, and prebendary of Strensall, who had a multitude of benefices, was forced in 1233 to be content with those to a value of 200 marks, but he kept Cropredy in Lincoln. Eight of the thirty-six prebends had more than one foreign occupant in succession.

Fifteen of the fifty-six prebends of Lincoln had foreign occupants. Lincoln supported five Colonnas, two Fieschi, two Conti, two Savelli, two Annibaldi, and various relatives of these families, such as a Surdi related to the Annibaldi. Cropredy, described by Grosseteste as one of the best prebends, represents the most interesting succession: Rufinus, Master Adenulf dei Conti of Anagni (nephew of Gregory IX, prebendary of Salisbury, canon of St Paul's, and canon and prebendary of

---

[25] *York Minster Fasti*, II, ed. C. T. Clay, Yorks. Archaeol. Soc. Rec. Ser., CXXIV (1958), p. 47.
[26] 'Chronicle of Richard of Devizes', *Chronicles of the Reigns of . . . Stephen, Henry II and Richard I*, III, ed. R. Howlett, R.S. (London, 1886), pp. 440–1.

Papal administration in England

York), Odo de Colonna and John Annibaldi. Pandulph de Savelli, son of Luke, who succeeded Cinthius de Pinea de Urbe in the prebend of Farndon-cum-Balderton, was a papal notary and prebendary of Hereford, Salisbury and York, and of several French cathedrals.

London (St Paul's) had an establishment of thirty canons and twelve minor canons. Five of the prebends were held by eight Italians (nine foreigners) during the thirteenth century. There were two Italian archdeacons of Essex. The prebend of Rugmere invites comparison with Cropredy. Master Cinthius the Roman was followed by the Gascon, Master Rostand, papal nuncio, and in the service of the king, and also beneficed in York, who was succeeded by two further Romans, Jordan Piruntus dei Conti, papal vice-chancellor, and Osbert. Brownswood nurtured Henry de Sarracenis, while Cantlers provided for Antony de Camilla (a branch of the Fieschi family). The church of St Paul was called upon apparently more frequently to supply prebends for distinctly royal, rather than papal, curial servants.[27]

There were heavy losses for both Lincoln and York with Percival of Lavagna, canon of Bayeux, canon of Paris, papal chaplain, and described in 1268 as in the service of the king. He acquired during his brother Ottobon's legation a prebend of Ripon, the sacristy of the chapel of St Mary and the Holy Angels, York (to which belonged thirteen parish churches), the rich prebend of Aylesbury, for which he gladly surrendered Brampton, and in 1270 the archdeaconry of Buckingham.[28] Disenchantment with Percival was apparent at Lincoln by 1269. Bishop Gravesend offered Percival, whom he addressed as 'immensely reverent man', 350 marks for the prebend. Percival, however, took the matter before a papal auditor who decreed 400 marks for the farm, and later in the relations between Percival and Lincoln, the Lincoln clerk described him, now the pope's brother, as the pope's eye.[29] The Lincoln bishop and chapter were not alone in feeling dissatisfied with the lack of services by Percival. Archbishop Giffard, who, having himself collated Percival to the sacristy, doubtless expected his help and intervention on behalf of the church of York, by 1271 was lamenting his action and describing Percival as 'brought up almost

[27] See John Le Neve, Fasti Ecclesiae Anglicanae 1066–1300: I St Paul's, London, comp. D. E. Greenway (London 1968).

[28] Les Registres d'Urbain IV, ed. J. Guiraud, (4 vols., Paris, 1899–1958), nos. 362, 1602; Reg. Walter Giffard, pp. 148–9, 230–1, 233–4; Close Rolls (1256–9), p. 176; and Greenway, Fasti . . . Lincoln, pp. 40–1, 49.

[29] Lincoln, D. & C. Dij 66/2/30, 31, 74.

from infancy on the goods of the Church' and 'like a child that hangs at its mother's breast, living upon the food and doing no good'.[30]

The papal schemes to pay for the activities of the papal court had suggested that each religious house might contribute a benefice, and Innocent IV had proposed one worth not less than forty marks per annum. In refusing the papal request, the monasteries, like the cathedral chapters and the bishops, almost certainly fared worse financially than if they had accepted. But in doing so they retained a direct channel of influence to the papal court, which might be needed in the event of litigation or when some other business was pending, such as the procurement of a privilege or a dispensation. Undoubtedly the cathedral chapters and the monasteries found it advantageous to be able to distribute largesse on the pope's behalf, through which means they might make personal contact with powerful papal officials. It is, of course, impossible actually to see these influences and pressures at work, but we can trace certain benefices which continued in the hands of papal clerks when once a curial person had been presented. Scotter church (Lincs.), of which Peterborough were the patrons, was held by Master John of Ferentino, papal chamberlain, and archdeacon of Norwich, in 1236–7, and then by Richard Annibaldi by papal provision in 1238.[31] Conisbrough vicarage (Yorks.), belonging to Lewes priory, was given to John, cardinal deacon of St Mary in Cosmedin, papal chancellor, and Innocent III's brother, in 1205, and then to Ptolemy, clerk, also a kinsman of Innocent III, in 1213.[32] Sibsey, belonging to the prior and convent of Spalding, passed from Robert of Somercotes to Tedisius of Lavagna in 1251.[33] Ombersley, belonging to Evesham, had been given by the legate Nicholas of Tusculum to one of his clerks before passing to Master Marinus, papal vice-chancellor and chamberlain, and in 1249 to Tedisius of Lavagna.[34] Tedisius's provision to Ombersley took effect before he ceased to be a papal scribe in the chancery of his uncle Innocent IV[35] and in this capacity and as a royal clerk (perhaps as early as 1258) and papal chaplain from 1265 to 1268 – Ottobon's legation[36] – he must have been of use to Evesham. But

---

[30] *Memorials of the Church of . . . Ripon*, ed. J. T. Fowler, Surtees Society, LXXVIII (1884), II, pp. 5–7.

[31] *Rot. Grosseteste*, pp. 136, 137; *Rot. Gravesend*, p. 96.   [32] *York Minster Fasti*, II, p. 47.

[33] *Rot. Grosseteste*, pp. 70, 165; and see *Rot. Gravesend*, p. 51.

[34] BL Harley MS 3763 fo.13r–v.

[35] P. Herde, *Beiträge zum Päpstlichen Kanzlei- und Urkundenwesen im 13. Jahrhundert*, 2nd edn (Kallmünz, 1967), pp. 22, 44–5, 47, 55.

[36] *Close Rolls (1264–8)*, p. 138; *CPR (1266–72)*, pp. 259, 306; and see *CPR (1247–58)*, p. 626.

when the dispute about the ownership of the church broke out in 1284, Tedisius being now in Genoa, the abbot and convent were naturally keen to regain the living.[37]

Strenuous efforts were made in some instances to get the benefices back, particularly when the occupant was no longer useful to the provider. Richard de Burstall got Sibson rectory (patrons, Lyre) probably on the death or retirement of M. Andrew de Mevagna. Master Giles of Spoleto was probably succeeded by Peterborough's clerk, Adam de Bretegat, at Warmington in 1243–4, and Master Gregory, Otto's chancellor, was succeeded in the living of Berkhampstead (patrons, Grestein) by John de Merse. When the future Cardinal Ottobon relinquished Twywell (patrons, Thorney) it was held by John de Hengham.[38] The living of Gainford (patrons, St Mary's, York) was held by Master Godfrey de Trani in 1240 and by Opizo of San Vitale, canon of Parma, and nephew of Innocent IV, in 1245, but the pope promised that when Opizo vacated the living it would return to St Mary's.[39]

The king did not hesitate to squeeze in his own servants during vacancies – and often this right worked in favour of the Church's servants who were also his own – men such as Master Peter de Burdegal, clerk of the legate Otto, who was presented by the king to the church of West Wycombe during a vacancy in the see of Winchester. Master Peter had been on the king's business in 1242. The church of Kirkby Thore (Westmorland) in the patronage of the Vipont family, is found in the possession of Master Peter de Piperno, papal chaplain, and chancellor of Percival of Lavagna.[40] On the death of Master Peter, Urban IV provided Stephen Surdus, nephew of Cardinal Richard Annibaldi, to the church, and a dispute about possession ensued between Stephen and a clerk who was probably Master Robert of Lavagna, king's clerk, and a member of the Fieschi family, presented by the king on behalf of Roger de Clifford (husband of one of the Vipont heiresses) whose heir and lands were in the king's hands.[41]

[37] *Register of Bishop Godfrey Giffard*, ed. J. W. Willis Bund, Worcestershire Historical Society (1902), II, pp. 264, 284, 299; and *Les Registres de Boniface VIII*, ed. G. Digard and R. Fawtier, (4 vols., Paris, 1904–39), no. 1758. There were persistent rumours that he was dead by 1272 but he was in fact at Bologna from 1270.

[38] *Rot. Grosseteste*, p. 182; *Rot. Gravesend*, p. 136.

[39] *Les Registres de Grégoire IX*, ed. L. Auvray (Paris, 1896–1910), no. 5250; *Reg. Walter Gray*, p. 77; and *Reg. Inn. IV*, p. 1460.

[40] See G. F. Nüske, 'Untersuchungen über das Personal der päpstlichen Kanzlei 1254–1304', *Archiv für Diplomatik*, xx (1974), p. 74, and *CPL* pp. 369, 382.

[41] *CPL* pp. 492, 588; and see *CPR* (*1272–81*), pp. 427, 456; *CPR* (*1280–92*), p. 56.

I

Much work remains to be done on the king's clerks – their powers and position. Many who were in the king's service, both Englishmen and foreigners, were also papal chaplains – Henry of Wingham, Philip Lovel, king's treasurer, and Albert, chancellor of Milan, beneficed in Salisbury cathedral, who as such made requests for petitioners (for plurality, for example)[42] and effected provisions. Some were (besides being papal chaplains and royal clerks) royal proctors, such as Roger Lovel and Master Rostand. There were legists, too, such as the canonist, Master Roger Marmion, and the civilian, William Arnaldi de Mota, against whom apparently, amongst the counsellors and royal clerks of Henry III, the bishops and chapters felt most dislike. Matthew Paris says that of these the king had a 'large pack which he uncoupled as a huntsman uncouples his dogs, and let loose upon the electors of prelates'.[43]

The advantages of a confidential royal clerk being also in the papal service were apparent to king and pope. Such dual appointments allowed the wheels of government to turn. A common identity for many of the royal servants and papal officers and provisees meant less friction between crown and papacy than between national Church (bishops, deans and chapters and monasteries) and papacy at this time. Rights of advowson were dear to all parties, but often king and pope might be mutually suited in the appointment of candidates to benefices, for the personnel of the papal and of the royal service frequently overlapped.

[42] E.g. *CPL* p. 349: William de Wendling, dispensed for plurality in 1257 at the request of Master Nicholas, archdeacon of Ely and papal chaplain.
[43] Powicke, *King Henry III*, p. 297.

II

THE PROCEDURE OF THE COURTS
OF THE JUDGES DELEGATE

ABBREVIATIONS

A.N.C.	S. Kuttner and E. Rathbone, 'Anglo-Norman Canonists of the Twelfth Century', *Traditio*, vii.
Ann. Mon.	*Annales Monastici*, ed. H. R. Luard.
App. A (ii)	See below, 284-96.
App. A (iv)	*P.J.D.* (see below).
App. B (ii)	*P.J.D.* (see below).
App. B (iv)	*P.J.D.* (see below).
Arnulphus	'Summa Minorum', *Quellen zur Geschichte*, i, pt. ii, ed. L. Wahrmund.
Bresslau	H. Bresslau, *Handbuch der Urkundenlehre*, 2nd. edn.
C.	'Code', *Corpus Iuris Civilis*, ii, ed. P. Krueger.
'Canterbury Proctors'	See Study III below.
C.F.	'A Judge Delegate Formulary from Canterbury', ed. Jane E. Sayers, *Bulletin of the Institute of Historical Research*, xxxv (Study VIII below).
Chertsey Cart.	*Chertsey Abbey Cartularies* (all references are to pt. i).
C.P.L.	*Calendar of Entries in the Papal Registers*, ed. W. H. Bliss and others.
C.R.R.	*Curia Regis Rolls.*
C.S.	*Councils and Synods*, ii, ed. F. M. Powicke and C. R. Cheney.
D.	'Digest', *Corpus Iuris Civilis*, i, ed. T. Mommsen and P. Krueger.

ABBREVIATIONS

D.D.C.	*Dictionnaire de Droit Canonique.*
Drogheda	'Summa Aurea', *Quellen zur Geschichte*, ii, pt. ii, ed. L. Wahrmund.
Dunstable Cart.	*A Digest of the Charters preserved in the Cartulary of the Priory of Dunstable*, comp. G. H. Fowler.
E.H.R.	*English Historical Review.*
Emden, *Oxf. Reg.*	A. B. Emden, *A Biographical Register of the University of Oxford.*
Eubel	C. Eubel, *Hierarchia Catholica Medii Aevi* (all references are to vol. i).
Fournier	P. Fournier, *Les Officialités au Moyen Âge.*
Glos. Cart.	*Historia et Cartularium monasterii Sancti Petri Gloucestriae*, ed. W. H. Hart.
Godstow Reg.	*The English Register of Godstow Nunnery near Oxford*, ed. A. Clark.
J.S.L.	*The Letters of John of Salisbury*, i (1153–61), ed. W. J. Millor and H. E. Butler, revsd. C. N. L. Brooke.
Letters of Inn. III	*The Letters of Pope Innocent III (1198–1216) concerning England and Wales*, cal. C. R. and Mary G. Cheney.
Lewes Cart. N.P.	*The Norfolk Portion of the Chartulary of the Priory of St. Pancras of Lewes*, cal. J. H. Bullock.
Lewes Cart. S.P.	*The Chartulary of the Priory of St. Pancras of Lewes*, cal. L. F. Salzman.
Malmesbury Reg.	*The Register of Malmesbury Abbey*, ed. J. S. Brewer and C. T. Martin.
N.L.C.	*Newington Longeville Charters*, ed. H. E. Salter.
Oseney Cart.	*The Cartulary of Oseney Abbey*, ed. H. E. Salter.
P.J.D.	Jane E. Sayers, *Papal Judges Delegate in the Province of Canterbury 1198-1254* (Oxford 1971).
P.U.E.	*Papsturkunden in England*, ed. W. Holtzmann.
Reg. Antiq. Linc.	*The Registrum Antiquissimum of the Cathedral Church of Lincoln*, ed. C. W. Foster and K. Major.
Reg. Greg. IX	*Les Registres de Grégoire IX*, ed. L. Auvray.
Reg. Hon. III	*Regesta Honorii Papae III*, cal. P. Pressutti.
Reg. Inn. IV	*Les Registres d'Innocent IV*, ed. E. Berger.
R.S.	Rolls Series.
Russell	J. C. Russell, *A Dictionary of Thirteenth Century Writers.*
St. Frideswide's Cart.	*The Cartulary of the Monastery of St. Frideswide at Oxford*, ed. S. R. Wigram.
Stickler	A.-M. Stickler, 'Ordines Judiciarii', *D.D.C.* vi.

ABBREVIATIONS

Tancred	'Tancredi Bononiensis Ordo Iudiciarius', *Pillii, Tancredi Gratiae Libri de Iudiciorum Ordine*, ed. F. Bergmann.
V.C.H.	*Victoria County Histories.*
W.P.	G. B. Flahiff, 'The Writ of Prohibition to Court Christian in the Thirteenth Century', *Mediaeval Studies*, vi and vii.
X.	'Decretales', *Corpus Iuris Canonici*, ii, ed. E. Friedberg.
6.	'Liber Sextus Decretalium D. Bonifacii Papae VIII', *Corpus Iuris Canonici*, ii, ed. E. Friedberg.

UNPRINTED SOURCES

A	Lambeth Palace Library MS. 105
Abingdon Cart.	Bodleian MS. Lyell 15
Alvingham Cart.	Bodleian MS. Laud Misc. 642
B	Baltimore, Walters Art Gallery MS. W 15
Bardney Cart.	B.M. Cotton MS. Vesp. E xx
Bayham Cart.	B.M. Cotton MS. Otho A ii
Beaulieu Cart.	B.M. MS. Loans 29/330
Belvoir	Archives belonging to the Duke of Rutland at Belvoir Castle
Biddlesden Cart.	B.M. Harley MS. 4714
Binham Cart.	B.M. Cotton MS. Claudius D xiii
Blythburgh Cart.	B.M. Add. MS. 40725
B.M.	MSS. and charters in the British Museum, London
Bodleian	MSS. and charters in the Bodleian Library, Oxford
Boxgrove Cart.	B.M. Cotton MS. Claudius A vi
Bradenstoke Cart.	B.M. Stowe MS. 925
Bromholm Cart.	C.U.L. MS. Mm 2. 20
Burton Cart.	B.M. MS. Loans 30
Byland Cart.	B.M. Egerton MS. 2823
C	Cambridge, Gonville and Caius College MS. 150 (44)
Canons Ashby Cart.	B.M. Egerton MS. 3033
Canterbury	Dean and Chapter Archives at Canterbury
Carisbrooke Cart.	B.M. Egerton MS. 3667
Castle Acre Cart.	B.M. Harley MS. 2110
Chatteris Cart.	B.M. Cotton MS. Julius A i

ABBREVIATIONS

Christchurch (Twynham) Cart.	B.M. Cotton MS. Tiberius D vi (all references are to vol. i)
Combe Cart.	B.M. Cotton MS. Vitellius A i
Crowland Cart.	Spalding Gentlemen's Society. Transcripts and rotographs in the Lincoln Archives Office
Croxton Transcript	B.M. Stowe MS. 928
C.U.L.	MSS. in the Cambridge University Library
Daventry Cart.	B.M. Cotton MS. Claudius D xii
Dover Cart.	Lambeth Palace Library MS. 241
Dunmow, Little, Cart.	B.M. Harley MS. 662
Dunstable Cart.	B.M. Harley MS. 1885 (cal. *Dunstable Cart.*, see Abbreviations (ii), Printed Books, etc.)
Easby Cart.	B.M. Egerton MS. 2827
Eton	Archives at Eton College, Bucks.
Exeter Exeter Cart.	Dean and Chapter Archives at Exeter Exeter, MS. 3672 (paginated)
Eye Cart.	Essex Record Office, Chelmsford, D/D By Q 19
Godsfield Transcript	B.M. Harley MS. 6603
Kenilworth Cart.	B.M. Harley MS. 3650
Kirkham Cart.	Bodleian MS. Fairfax 7
Kirkstead Cart.	B.M. Cotton MS. Vesp. E xviii
L	B.M. Royal MS. 10 B iv
Lambeth	MSS. and charters in Lambeth Palace Library, London
Langdon Cart.	P.R.O. E 164/29
Lanthony Cart. A 1, etc.	P.R.O. C 115/A 1—
Leeds Cart.	Kent Record Office, Maidstone, U/120 Q/13
Lewes Cart.	B.M. Cotton MS. Vesp. F xv (cal. *Lewes Cart.*, see Abbreviations (ii), Printed Books, etc.)
Lichfield Cart.	Bodleian MS. Ashmole 1527
Northampton, St. Andrew's Cart. (A) (B) St. James's Cart.	B.M. Cotton MS. Vesp. E xvii B.M. Royal MS. 11 B ix B.M. Cotton MS. Tiberius E v
Norwich	Dean and Chapter Archives at Norwich
Nun Cotham Cart.	Bodleian MS. Top. Lincs. d 1
O	Bodleian MS. Laud Lat. 17

ABBREVIATIONS

Oxford, Magdalen, New College, St John's	MSS. and charters in the college libraries
Pershore Cart.	P.R.O. E 315/61
Peterborough	Dean and Chapter Archives at Peterborough
Pipewell Cart. (A)	B.M. Cotton MS. Caligula A xii
(B)	B.M. Add. MS. 37022
(C)	B.M. Stowe MS. 937
P.R.O.	MSS. and charters in the Public Record Office, London
Ramsey Cart.	B.M. Cotton MS. Vesp. E ii
Reading Cart.	B.M. Cotton MS. Vesp. E xxv
St. Albans Cart. (A)	MS. belonging to the Duke of Devonshire at Chatsworth
(B)	B.M. Cotton MS. Otho D iii
Almoner's Cart.	B.M. Lansdowne MS. 375
St. Augustine's Cart.	B.M. Cotton MS. Julius D ii
Red Book	B.M. Cotton MS. Claudius D x
White Book	P.R.O. E 164/27
St. Neots Cart.	B.M. Cotton MS. Faustina A iv
St. Paul's	Dean and Chapter Archives at St. Paul's Cathedral, London
St. Radegund's (Bradsole) Cart.	Bodleian MS. Rawlinson B 336
Shaftesbury Cart.	B.M. Harley MS. 61
Sibton Cart.	B.M. Arundel MS. 221
Spalding Cart.	B.M. Add. MS. 35296
Stixwould Cart.	B.M. Add. MS. 46701
Thorney Cart.	C.U.L. Add. MS. 3020
Tintern Cart.	B.M. Arundel MS. 19
Torre Cart.	P.R.O. E 164/19
Walden Cart.	B.M. Harley MS. 3697
Walsingham Cart.	Bodleian MS. Top. Norfolk b 1
Waltham Cart.	B.M. Cotton MS. Tiberius C ix
Warter Cart.	Bodleian MS. Fairfax 9
Welbeck Cart.	B.M. Harley MS. 3640
Wells	Dean and Chapter Archives at Wells
West Dereham Cart.	B.M. Add. MS. 46353
Westminster	Dean and Chapter Archives at Westminster

ABBREVIATIONS

Whalley Cart.	B.M. Add. MS. 10374
Wherwell Cart.	B.M. Egerton MS. 2104A
Windsor	Dean and Chapter Archives at St. George's Chapel, Windsor
Wymondham Cart.	B.M. Cotton MS. Titus C viii

1. *Procedural Books*

THE procedure of the Church courts, and consequently of the delegated tribunals, derived from the form of extraordinary procedure by *libellus conventionis* of the late Roman Empire, which divided the suit into three parts, *jus, litis contestatio,* and *judicium*.[1] The Roman law had not entirely died out in the lay and Church courts of Rome and North Italy, especially in the commercial centres, and at the end of the eleventh century an increasing interest in it brought to light better and fuller texts of Justinian's compilation, the *Corpus Iuris Civilis*. But that the practical application of its procedure was crude and far from uniform is attested by the eagerness with which the lawyers set to work on the new texts.

The process of digesting, expounding, and explaining the founts of the old Roman law began with Irnerius and the school of glossators at Bologna. The Novels[2] and Digest were newly discovered; the Code and the Institutes were more fully used than ever before. These books were to form the basis of the procedure of the ecclesiastical courts. Recent research has shown, however, that the Roman law sources were not used in the first redaction of the *Decretum* (or compilation of the canons) in 1139–40. But before the book began to circulate they were fed into the text by Gratian's followers, who were attracted increasingly towards the civil law procedure for standardizing and improving the machinery

---

[1] For a general sketch of canonical procedure see C. Lefebvre, 'Procédure', *D.D.C.* vii (1959), cols. 285–96, and for a detailed consideration of procedure by libel, P. Collinet, *La Procédure par libelle* (Paris, 1932).

[2] Until the sixteenth century the Novels were known from two sources, the *Epitome Iuliani* and the *Authenticum*, see *Lib. Pauperum of Vacarius*, ed. F. de Zulueta (Selden Soc. xliv, 1927), p. lii.

of the canon law.[1] To these sources, civilian as well as canonist, ecclesiastical judges turned when hearing cases.[2] The *Decretum* was introduced into England soon after its compilation, and manuscripts of the twelfth century survive in some quantities.[3] Little is known, however, about the transmission of the civil law books. The Roman lawyer Vacarius, who came to England probably in the mid 1140s, and who was teaching in England, presumably at Oxford, before the study of civil law was prohibited by King Stephen, made known the Code and the Digest through his *Liber Pauperum*[4] (and incidentally acted several times as a papal judge delegate);[5] but no complete English twelfth-century manuscripts of the *Corpus Iuris* appear to have survived.[6] Robert de Chesney, however, is known to have had a copy of the Digest which he requested Gilbert Foliot to have corrected and glossed for him;[7] Abbot Benedict of Peterborough (1177–94) left a set of the *Corpus Iuris Civilis* to his monastery; and a copy of the Institutes is recorded at Canterbury in the 1170s.[8] These cannot have been isolated instances, and the paucity of the references to civil law texts almost certainly does not indicate their absence from England.

Procedural difficulties, as distinct from legal, are strongly evident in the period immediately following the completion of Gratian's *Decretum*. There is little about canonical procedure

---

[1] See J. Rambaud-Buhot in *Histoire du droit et des institutions de l'Église en Occident*, vii, ed. G. Le Bras (Paris, 1965), 51–8, and 119–29.

[2] See, for example, Morey and Brooke, *Gilbert Foliot*, p. 59: ' His [Foliot's] letters show that he applied the authorities of Roman law to problems of procedure in canon law courts without hesitation.'

[3] See Kuttner, *Repertorium*. For a summary of the available legal literature, both canonist and civilian, and its transmission to England, see now R. C. van Caenegem, *Royal Writs in England from the Conquest to Glanville* (Selden Soc. lxxvii, 1959), pp. 360–73, esp. 365 ff.

[4] Ed. de Zulueta, pp. xiii–xxiii.

[5] See *A.N.C.*, p. 287 n. 18: to this list of Vacarius's occurrences as a judge delegate may be added *Early Yorkshire Charters*, ix, ed. C. T. Clay (Yorks. Archaeol. Soc. Rec. Ser., Extra Ser. vii, 1952), no. 159.

[6] See Morey and Brooke, *Gilbert Foliot*, p. 67; they cite W. Senior, 'Roman Law Manuscripts in England', *Law Quarterly Review*, xlvii (1931), 337–44. Senior, however, is more concerned with thirteenth- and fourteenth-century manuscripts; N. R. Ker's *Medieval Libraries* shows no surviving twelfth-century manuscripts of the *Corpus Iuris Civilis* and few civilian works altogether.

[7] Morey and Brooke, *Gilbert Foliot*, p. 66.

[8] Senior, 'Roman Law Manuscripts in England', p. 337.

in the *Decretum*,[1] compared with the plentiful chapters in the *Quinque Compilationes* and the sections 'De Rescriptis', 'De Appellationibus', 'De Officio et Potestate Judicis', 'De Excepcionibus', and 'De Dolo et Contumacia' of the *Decretales*. Allusions to procedural troubles in the Church courts, both ordinary and delegated, of the 1150s occur in John of Salisbury's letters, which show that the outline of the *ordo judiciarius* was not yet developed, uniform, or fully understood.[2] For instance, an appeal was made from the court of Walter, bishop of Coventry, to Theobald, archbishop of Canterbury, when the bishop who was acting as judge delegate was responsible only to the pope and was sitting in the superior court, as one of the parties realized.[3] If an answer could not be found when a difficulty arose, and if technical details were not provided in the rescript, reference was made to the pope, who as supreme judge over all the courts defined procedure.[4] Between 1140 and 1191 the development of decretal legislation took place. Decretal collections, the earliest of which date from about 1175, reflect procedural inquiries as well as legal, and procedural sections are found in the *Collectiones Cantabrigiensis* (the first part), *Cottoniana* (ff. 225ᵛ et seq.), and *Peterhusensis* (ff. 27ᵛ et seq.). The two latter are 'Worcester' collections of *c.* 1191 and 1194 at the earliest.[5] These collections were made by the judges or their clerks for their own personal use, and were frequently appended to copies of the *Decretum* and filed and bound up with other legal material.[6] Some of the decretals from these collections found their way via the Five Compilations

---

[1] *Decretum*, C. II qu. 1–6 and 8; C. III qu. 6–7, 9, and 11; and C. IV qu. 1–6.

[2] *J.S.L.*, nos. 53, 57, 70–1, 74, and 83—an exception is pleaded against the judge in the latter.

[3] See the letter of Theobald reporting this to the pope, *J.S.L.*, no. 54, of *c.* 1154–9.

[4] e.g. *Papal Decretals relating to Lincoln*, nos. iv, vi, xii, xiv–xv, xviii, and xxi.

[5] See Duggan, *Decretal Collections*, pp. 47–8 and 104–7. The '*Wigorniensis Altera*' is described by Duggan as an illustration of an English primitive collection devised on a basis of personal and local interest. It is very small, containing ten decretals sent by Alexander III to judges delegate (Duggan, p. 46).

[6] Important collections come from Worcester, Exeter, and Canterbury, and were presumably made for important judges delegate, Roger of Worcester, Bartholomew of Exeter, and Richard of Canterbury (ibid., pp. 94, 118, and 149). M. Cheney, 'Compromise of Avranches', p. 181, citing Kuttner, *Repertorium*, pp. 273–6.

to Gregory IX's compilation of the canons, and so became general law. To search through the textbooks of the Roman and canon law for a ruling on a particular procedural point was no easy task. Procedural information is scattered all through the *Corpus Iuris Civilis*, and therefore could not readily be consulted. For this reason procedural treatises were devised to help judges and litigants. Such works are comparable in their private origin to the collections of decretals. Among the first is the *Ordo Iudiciorum* of Bulgarus, which was dedicated to Aimericus, chancellor of the Roman Church, who held office from 1123–41; it is described by Kantorowicz as 'the oldest evidence of a scientific give-and-take connection between the glossators of the Civil law and the Curia'.[1] Gratian's *Decretum* and the legal renaissance of the twelfth century sparked off the composition of a host of such manuals of procedure.[2] Amongst the earliest are the anonymous commentary on Causa II question 1 of the *Decretum*, which begins with the words 'In principio de ordine iudiciario agitur', and which is much disputed as to date but was probably composed between 1160 and 1175,[3] and an anonymous treatise from France, *Incerti Auctoris Ordo Iudiciarius, pars summae legum, et tractatus de prescriptione*.[4] There are also the Anglo-Norman *Ulpianus de Edendo* or *Incerti Auctoris Ordo Iudiciorum of c.* 1140,[5] and two English treatises—the *Ordo Iudiciarius* of 1182–5,[6] probably by an English canonist attached to the court of the archbishop of Dublin, and the *Practica legum et decretorum* of *c.* 1183–9, which was written by William Longchamp, bishop of Ely, before his

---

[1] H. Kantorowicz and W. W. Buckland, *Studies in the Glossators of the Roman Law* (Cambridge, 1938), pp. 70–1. Acting as a judge delegate of the pope, Bulgarus delivered a judgement in his own lecture room on 8 July 1151 (p. 68), an instance of the close connection between the legal writers and the practitioners, and between the civilians and the canonists.

[2] See *Studies in the Glossators*, p. 72, where Kantorowicz lists them with their editors (his n. 8), and Stickler, cols. 1132–43, esp. 1135–8.

[3] Ed. F. Kunstmann in *Kritische Ueberschau der deutschen Gesetzgebung und Rechtswissenschaft*, ii, ed. L. Arndts, J. C. Bluntschli, and J. Potzl (Munich, 1855), 17–29. Stickler dates this 1171. [4] Ed. C. Gross (Innsbruck, 1870).

[5] Ed. G. Haenel (Leipzig, 1838). Dated by Stickler.

[6] Ed. J. F. von Schulte, 'Der *Ordo iudiciarius* des Codex Bambergensis P. I. 11.', *Sitzungsberichte der Kaiserlichen Akademie der Wissenschaften*, lxx (Vienna, 1872), 285–326.

chancellorship.[1] Two further treatises, from Christ Church, Canterbury, were discovered by Professor Kuttner and Miss Rathbone,[2] and an *Ordo Iudiciarius* of *c.* 1202–9 is in Baltimore, Walters Art Gallery MS. W 15.[3] Too much importance should not be attached to these treatises. Kantorowicz has said that in the twelfth century they were far ahead of practice.[4] What their circulation was, and whether they were regarded as authoritative by the judges, cannot be known. Much distortion has resulted from using them to explain the practices of a different period; they can only be expected to illuminate contemporary events. Professor Thorne, for instance, in asserting that the mechanism of appeals remained long unknown in England, used William of Drogheda's treatise, of 1239, to discuss all suits after 1172.[5] A more recent writer depended on Tancred, who completed his *Ordo Iudiciarius* in *c.* 1216, to introduce the background to a small collection of Alexandrian decretals.[6] But it may be noted that the *Summa de Ordine Iudiciario* of Ricardus Anglicus (de Mores) of *c.* 1196 and the *Summa Aurea* of William of Drogheda of 1239,[7] as well as the other more numerous works from the Continent which appeared owing to the impetus from the compilation of the *Decretales* in 1234, are not without forerunners. These, although not statutory works, deserve to be studied carefully with the suits of the time.

From the early thirteenth century there survive letter or precedent books giving the forms to be used by the judges and parties of the delegated courts when drawing up documents. Formularies of this kind are another consequence of

---

[1] See *A.N.C.*, p. 290. Longchamp's work is edited by E. Caillemer in 'Le Droit civil dans les provinces anglo-normandes au XIIᵉ siècle', *Mémoires de l'Académie Nationale des Sciences, Arts . . . de Caen* (1883), pp. 204–26.

[2] B.M. Royal MS. 10 B iv, f. 59ʳ⁻ᵛ, and ff. 33–41, cited in *A.N.C.*, p. 291 n. 7.

[3] *A.N.C.*, p. 291, and see below, pp. 47 ff., on a formulary in this MS.

[4] *Studies in the Glossators*, p. 72.

[5] S. E. Thorne, 'Le Droit canonique en Angleterre', *Rev. hist. de droit français et étranger*, 4ᵉ série xiii (1934), 508.

[6] *Papal Decretals relating to Lincoln*, pp. xx ff.

[7] On Richard see Stickler, col. 1137, and *A.N.C.*, pp. 291 and 338–9. On Drogheda see Stickler, col. 1136; F. de Zulueta, 'William of Drogheda', *Mélanges de droit romain dédiés à Georges Cornil*, ii (Paris, 1926), 641–57; and H. G. Richardson, 'Azo, Drogheda and Bracton', *E.H.R.* lix (1944), 22–47.

the revival of Roman law and procedure in the eleventh and twelfth centuries.[1] Although, as we have seen, procedural treatises survive from the twelfth century, no English examples of judge-delegate formularies appear, at least at first sight, to precede the pontificate of Innocent III, but it seems reasonable to suppose that there must have been such letter books, particularly from the judicially formative pontificate of Alexander III. In any case the distinction between a formulary and a procedural treatise is fine. The procedural writer, William of Drogheda, for example, sometimes gives a form in his treatise, and, as will be shown below, the basic letters in some of these formularies may be earlier than the dates of the pope who is mentioned.

A group of seven English formularies have been described by Professors Cheney[2] and Kuttner.[3] The English origin of London, B.M. Royal MS. 15 B IV, ff. 65ᵛ–6ʳ (L), Cambridge, Gonville and Caius MS. 150 (44), f. 119ʳ (C), Baltimore, Walters Art Gallery MS. W 15, ff. 79ᵛ–81ᵛ (B), and Vatican, MS. lat. 2343 (V) can be traced from the inclusion of a letter concerning 'the custom of the English Church'.[4] Montecassino MS. 136, pp. 223–4 and 231 (M), known only from the catalogue,[5] corresponds so closely with V (both have Italian appendices) and C in the forms, all of which are identical in subject and number (sixteen), as to suggest that it is also one of the group.[6] Lambeth MS. 105, f. 271ᵛ (A) has some relationship with Baltimore (B),[7] and in any case uses English names; while Bodleian MS. Laud

[1] H. G. Richardson, 'The Oxford Law School under John', *Law Quarterly Review*, lvii (1941), 324.

[2] C. R. Cheney, *English Bishops' Chanceries 1100–1250* (Manchester, 1950), pp. 124–30, discusses B, A, L, and O.

[3] S. Kuttner, '*Analecta Iuridica Vaticana* (Vat. lat. 2343)', *Studi e Testi*, ccxix (1962), 443–5, adds C, M, and V.

[4] Ibid., p. 444 and n. 6. F. Donald Logan has produced an edition based on C, L, and V, with three of the forms from B; see 'An Early Thirteenth-Century Papal Judge-Delegate Formulary of English Origin', *Studia Gratiana*, xiv (Collectanea Stephan Kuttner, iv, Bologna, 1967), 73–87.

[5] See *Bibliotheca Casinensis*, iii (Monte Cassino, 1877), 228–9. As Professor Kuttner notes, all the rubrics, incipits, and explicits are given.

[6] L has one less form, that concerning revocatory letters, and is therefore only fifteen in number, see Kuttner, *Analecta Iuridica*, p. 445 n. 2.

[7] The forms concerning the matrimonial 'petitio' and letters dimissory for a clerk moving from one diocese to another, which are found in both, are distinctly comparable.

lat. 17, ff. 223ᵛ–4ᵛ (O) makes mention of English places and English ecclesiastics. To these may be added a formulary of English origin in B.M. Cotton MS. Julius D II, ff. 150ʳ–4ʳ which uses the names of Canterbury clerics.[1]

The origin of B has been the subject of some dispute. Mr. Richardson has suggested that it is connected with the Oxford law school.[2] Professor Cheney, on the other hand, is convinced that there is 'absolutely no evidence for the repeated statements that the Baltimore MS. was written at Oxford' and that to assert that the forms were assembled there outsteps the evidence.[3] He has seen, however, a common core in B, L, A, and O (C, V, and M were unknown to him), and has associated it with the diocese of Lincoln and the bishop's chancery. But B is the most sophisticated formulary of the group, which contains also part of an *ordo judiciarius* and some secular forms.[4] In view of this and its use in the main of Oxford names—there are also some Northampton ones,[5] and these are crucial to Mr. Richardson's argument that it is a product of the early Oxford law school —an origin in the nascent university still seems the more tenable theory. The relationship between L and C is close, presenting the conclusion that both have been copied from a common source. Both are carelessly written. When collated, the more sensible readings of one correct the obvious corruptions of the other, indicating a common source, although perhaps not an immediate one. Because of the English letter, Kuttner has associated B with these two, and Cheney has seen definite connections between B and A. Two

---

[1] *C.F.*

[2] Richardson, 'Oxford Law School', pp. 319–38. This argument was accepted by Kuttner and Rathbone in *A.N.C.*, p. 291.

[3] Cheney, *Bishops' Chanceries*, pp. 125 n. 1 and 126–7.

[4] Eleven of the ecclesiastical forms, mainly concerning Oxford, were included in *Formularies which bear on the History of Oxford c. 1204–1420*, ii, ed. H. E. Salter, W. A. Pantin, and H. G. Richardson (Oxf. Hist. Soc. N.S. v, 1942) (cited as *Oxford Formularies*).

[5] The church of Crick (Northants.) is mentioned twice. An investigation of its patronage has not helped towards establishing the origin of the formulary. It passed from Roger de Camvill to the Estley or Astley family t. Henry II (J. Bridges, *History and Antiquities of Northamptonshire*, i, ed. P. Whalley, Oxford, 1791, pp. 557–62), in whose hands it remained at least until 1271 (*Rotuli Ricardi Gravesend Episcopi Lincolniensis*, ed. F. N. Davis, Linc. Rec. Soc. xx, 1925, p. 117).

later formularies in B.M. Add. MS. 8167,[1] mentioning the names of popes Gregory (IX) and Honorius (III), exhibit strains of B, A, L, and C, in format, and one mentions the church of St. Mary at Oxford.[2] A common origin for L, C, V, M, B, and A may therefore be suspected.

O, however, is not related in any obvious way to this group.[3] It is more closely comparable with the Canterbury formulary, which does not perpetuate the common core and which uses local names. To connect O with the diocese of Lincoln seems tenuous, although a connection with Oxford might be argued from the inclusion of some Oxford names.[4] But much more powerful arguments can be put forward for the compilation of the forms at Cirencester. The places which are mentioned are all within thirty miles of Cirencester: Winchcombe, Cerney (North or South), 'Leche' (Northleach, Eastleach, or Lechlade), and 'Culne' (Coln St. Dennis, St. Aldwyn, or Rogers) in Gloucestershire, Malmesbury and Bradenstoke (Wilts.), Blockley and Kempsey (Worcs.), and Oxford. Of the personnel who appear, R., abbot of Cirencester, is mentioned four times; R., abbot of Winchcombe, the prior of Bradenstoke, and Master R(obert) de Clipstone each occur three times; and R., dean of Cirencester, R., dean of Blockley, the prior of Cirencester, R., dean of 'Leche', and R., abbot of Malmesbury, twice. Master Alexander of St. Albans (Alexander Neckham), who entered the abbey at Cirencester between 1197 and 1201 and became abbot in 1213,[5] R., archdeacon of St. Albans, Master R(obert) de Bingham, Master J. de Pratis, J., archdeacon, and A. (? Adam), vice-archdeacon, of Oxford, J., dean of Langford (Oxon.), and G. de Bradewelle are all mentioned once. As meeting-places Cirencester occurs three times, and Winchester, Gloucester, and Salisbury each once.

---

[1] ff. 95ᵛ–7ʳ and 114ʳ–19ʳ.   [2] f. 114ʳ.

[3] Kuttner, *Analecta Iuridica*, p. 444, appears to see it as one of the group, as does Professor Cheney, but apart from the fact that it is a manual of the same type I can see no direct relationship between its letters and those of others in the group.

[4] Masters R(obert) de Clipstone, Alexander of St. Albans, R(obert) de Bingham, and J. archdeacon of Oxford, who is presumably Master John of Tynemouth, all have links with Oxford. See *P.J.D.*, pp. 105, 121, 126, 131; Emden, *Oxf. Reg.* and *A.N.C.*, pp. 317, 325.

[5] See Emden, *Oxf. Reg.* ii. 1342–3, and J. C. Dickinson, *The Origins of the Austin Canons and their Introduction into England* (1950), p. 188.

II

Furthermore, the formulary is built round two main cases, which give every appearance of being real. The first is a suit about tithes between the abbot of Séez (dioc. Séez, Orne, France), and J., clerk of Kempsey (Worcs.), who is also cited as Master J. de Kempsey, as Master J., rector of Cerney (Glos.) and as J., rector of 'Ebintone' (? Edington, Wilts.). The judges were R., abbot of Winchcombe (Ben. Glos.), and R. and R., deans of Cirencester and Blockley. The last two alternate with R., dean of 'Leche', and Master R(obert) de Clipstone. R. abbot of Winchcombe, is mentioned once as Ralph, and is presumably Ralph II, abbot from 1182 × 84 to (?) 1194.[1] The suit was heard in the parish church at Cirencester.[2] The second case recites a mandate of Pope Innocent III, which was dated at the Lateran on 20 February 1201[3] and appointed as judges the abbot of Cirencester, the prior of Bradenstoke, and the abbot of Malmesbury, who alternates with Master Alexander of St. Albans. The parties were Robert Pictor of Abingdon and J. knight, son of Robert de Rameseia (who is mentioned on one occasion as O. de Rameseia), and the case was about 100 shillings sterling and a pound of cumin which Robert Pictor was supposed to receive in return for some land. The cause must have been heard between 1201 and 1205, by which time Robert of Melun had ceased to be abbot of Malmesbury:[4] the vice-archdeacon of Oxford and J., dean of Langford, were asked to execute the sentence.[5] There seems little doubt that these are real cases, the details of which have been taken from actual documents. Since the first suit was heard in the parish church at Cirencester, it is possible that documents concerning it were deposited at the abbey there; and the inclusion of the abbot in the second commission could account for the presence also of those documents in Cirencester. Eight out of the thirteen forms in O concern these two suits. The prior of Cirencester occurs in two of the other five documents and the convent of Cirencester figures as a party in a third.

[1] *V.C.H. Glos.* ii. 72.   [2] O, f. 223^v, cols. i–ii.
[3] O, f. 224^r, cols. i–ii. The mandate comes from the third year of Innocent, for which the register is incomplete, and there is no trace of it.
[4] He died in 1205 (*Heads of Religious Houses*, ed. D. Knowles, C. Brooke, V. London, Cambridge 1972, 56). The final *actum* mentions the abbot of Malmesbury as R.
[5] O, f. 224^r, col. i–224^v, col. i.

The other two seem to be strays, the fourth mentioning St. Albans and the archdeacon of St. Albans, and the fifth Master R(obert) de Clipstone again. A plausible explanation of the origin of the formulary is that it was compiled in the Augustinian abbey at Cirencester, between 1182 and 1221,[1] by scribes working from original documents who added anything of use which came their way. During the thirteenth century the formulary was re-copied into the psalter in which it is now found, by which time some of the names had become corrupt.[2]

Another problem in the interpretation of these formulary books is the date of the composition of the forms. The connection between the date of the composition of B, A, L, and O, and the pontificate of Innocent III, was argued by Professor Cheney.[3] B, A, L, O, and C all give that pope's name. Cheney suggested that the hand of A 'cannot hardly be later than the first decade of the thirteenth century' and that H. bishop of Lincoln is Hugh of Avalon (1186–1200).[4] The date of B has been narrowed by Richardson to 1202–9, since the fourth year of King John (1202) is mentioned, and by an ingenious argument concerning the schools of Northampton the *terminus ante quem* is given as 1209. It also includes mention of popes Alexander (III) and Celestine (III). In fact B, like O, gives the impression of having been built up over the years, and some of the basic forms of the group appear to be earlier than Innocent III. Substitution of a contemporary name for an obsolete one is not unknown in letter forms,[5] and the primitive fount might date from as far back as the pontificate of Alexander III. There is the evidence of the additional letter of Pope Alexander III in L and of the use of his name in B,[6] but even if in origin the form of the group is earlier than has hitherto been thought,

---

[1] See above, p. 50 n. 1. The last letter or form (f. 224ᵛ, col. i) mentions J. archdeacon of Oxford, who must be Master John of Tynemouth archdeacon until 1221.

[2] Ker, *Medieval Libraries*, p. 52, attributes the psalter to Cirencester but on the grounds of the Cirencester names in the formulary.

[3] Cheney, *Bishops' Chanceries*, p. 124.

[4] Ibid., pp. 124, 127.

[5] H. G. Richardson, 'An Oxford Teacher of the Fifteenth Century', *Bulletin of the John Rylands Library*, xxiii (1939), 449, speaks of re-fashionings of a letter-writing tract indicated by the name of the pope, etc.

[6] L, f. 69ᵛ, and B, ff. 79ᵛ, col. i, 80ᵛ, col. ii.

the substitution of a later name shows that the form was still applicable when it was copied. If the major form is earlier than Innocent III's pontificate, the question of the date of the transcription arises. Impetus might have been provided by canon 38 of the Fourth Lateran Council (1215), which required judges to have clerks to draw up documents and make copies of the *acta* for each stage of the suit.[1] It may be that the stereotyped productions of L, C, V, and M, which mention only Innocent's name, date from the last year of the pontificate (1215–16) and were made in answer to a demand following the decree. But, on the other hand, such forms must have been needed and provided earlier, just as they were needed and provided afterwards. B.M. Add. MS. 8167 shows that the particular form of the group was copied until the 1240s at least;[2] and the Canterbury formulary, a more advanced type of manual, with an introduction and extended rubrics, and not one of the group, was composed after 1216 and probably soon after 1227,[3] as the forms were still required.

Questions as to the place and date of origin of the form which is common to B, A, C, L, V, and M will remain unanswered until a careful analysis of the manuscripts is made. When that has been done it may well be concluded that the form originated, as Richardson argued, at Oxford, perhaps in the law schools.[4] It is difficult to see otherwise why the writer should have used predominantly Oxford names and places, although his forms do not appear to be based on actual documents.[5] A reconstruction of the

---

[1] c. 11. *X*. II. 19, and see Drogheda, xiv, pp. 19–20, on how to compose *acta*.

[2] f. 96ʳ.

[3] *C.F.*, pp. 200–1.

[4] Richardson, 'Oxford Law School', pp. 319–38. See also 'The Schools of Northampton in the Twelfth Century', *E.H.R.* lvi (1941), 595–605.

[5] The judges mentioned are the prior of St. Frideswide's (3 times, once called D.), the abbot and prior of Oseney (both twice, and once called respectively A. and W.), the abbot of Thame (twice), the subprior of St. Frideswide's, the prior of Thame (called H.), the abbot of Bury St. Edmunds (W.), the abbot of Pipewell, the dean of Oxford, and possibly the prior of Bury and the prior of Pipewell (P. and W.), and several men who may have been attached to the Oxford schools, Master W. de Westal', W. de Branf', and W. of Lincoln diocese (all once). Cf. Cheney, *Bishops' Chanceries*, pp. 125–7, who also comments that the litigants were summoned to Oxford seven times, to the church of St. Peter in the East (5 times) and the church of St. Mary the Virgin (twice), and on the parties; but he connects them all with

transmission of the forms could be as follows. The original production, compiled by someone working in Oxford, served as an exemplar for B, although not directly, for B is very corrupt and must be at some distance from the parent manuscript. There is no hint of the manuscript's provenance. From B and other formularies, A with its extraordinary mixture of names—T., archdeacon of Wiltshire (not identified), H., bishop of Lincoln, the official of the archbishop of Canterbury, C. de Cantuar', a party, and the church of Wig' —may have been composed. The first part of the book containing A has been attributed to Bury St. Edmunds; the book also includes a collection of decretals of Innocent III,[1] but the relationship between A and these two sections is not clear, and therefore whether A belonged to Bury is not ascertainable. After A had been compiled, the basic form of B was then stripped of all proper names except that of the reigning pope, Innocent III, perhaps after his decretal on the making of court *acta*, and circulated in C, L, V, and M, for example. The only suggested medieval ownership for C is Gloucester, but this may not be tenable.[2] L is part of a grammar which belonged to Worcester cathedral, and the manuscript contains besides a collection of decretals.[3] V and M have Italian appendices and were presumably made for an Italian market. The two later formularies in B.M. Add. MS. 8167, which resemble these so closely, form part of a book which belonged to William Haseley, a monk of Westminster, who gave it to the abbey in *c.* 1250. Richardson describes this manuscript as 'an ordinary commercial production', and he notes a collection very similar to Haseley's

the diocese of Lincoln as the underlying link. The name of R. de Log occurs as a party. The Log family had land in the parish of St. Mary the Virgin, Oxford. A John Log is mentioned in *c.* 1210–20, and in 1238 Peter son of John Log gave lands and tenements to the canons of St. Frideswide's (*St. Frideswide's Cart.* i, nos. 431, 433, and 436). There are also four mentions of H. bishop of London (? Lincoln), a mention of the year in which H. bishop of Lincoln died; and London, St. Paul's, the dean of York, and the cathedral of St. Peter at York are also noted.

[1] M. R. James and C. Jenkins, *A Descriptive Catalogue of the Manuscripts in the Library of Lambeth Palace* (Cambridge, 1930), pp. 176–9, and Kuttner, *Repertorium*, pp. 305, 311 n. 1, and see also 335.

[2] See M. R. James, *A Descriptive Catalogue of the Manuscripts in the Library of Gonville and Caius College*, i (Cambridge, 1907), 36.

[3] See Duggan, *Decretal Collections*, pp. 81–4, who seems to favour an association with Exeter for the decretal collection (p. 84 n. 3).

book which was written at Thorney 'a generation or so later' by John Britton, precentor of the house.[1] The material is too sparse to bear the weight of an elaborate structure of argument, but the tracing of the common core in B, A, L, C, V, and M to one and not several founts would mean little more than that by stripping a particular fount of its names and places it was made a popular and useful form, and that these six manuscripts represent a chance survival. As a contrast to these general or 'commercial' productions, the evidence of the Canterbury formulary and of O suggests that at least some formularies were made primarily for domestic use, being the private collections of the clerks of bishops or abbots. The Canterbury formulary is distinctly traceable to the chancery of Christ Church from whence it was copied by a St. Augustine's scribe.[2] Similarly O has the appearance of originating at Cirencester in the Augustinian house there. Many problems about these formularies have not been solved, but it is sufficient to recognize for the present purpose that such collections must have been common in England between 1198 and 1254, and that these few remaining treatises are examples of the sort of manuals which would have been devised and used by most judges delegate and their clerks.

2. The Preliminaries of the Suit

(i) The Impetration or Application for the Mandate

Nothing is really known of how the machinery for the issue of papal rescripts worked before the pontificate of Innocent III, and even then the sources are surprisingly meagre.[3] But for a petitioner to open a suit before papal judges delegate it was necessary to procure a mandate from the pope. The petition which was presented was probably a written one. At any rate by the thirteenth century William of Drogheda instructs the applicant to put his case in writing,[4] and forms

---

[1] Richardson, 'Oxford Teacher', pp. 447–50. The Thorney book is now Cambridge, C.C.C. MS. 297.   [2] C.F., pp. 199–200.

[3] For the sources in general, see Barraclough's bibliography to his article 'Audientia Litterarum Contradictarum', cols. 1398–9; Herde, Beiträge, pp. 164–73, who deals mainly with Innocent IV and later when the sources become more numerous; and below.   [4] Drogheda, i, pp. 7–8.

of petition were made available to plaintiffs and their proc-tors.[1] The impetration, or application for the mandate, took place in the *Curia Romana*, at least this is the phrase used by the 1230s.[2] The term seems to be used loosely much as one might speak of taking a case to 'the Vatican' today.

There seems to be no evidence to support the supposition of Professor Barraclough that the *audientia litterarum contra-dictarum*, a court for the regulation of the proctors, existed in embryo, even if not as a separate office, before the time of Innocent III.[3] It may be, as he suggests, that its origins are connected with the development of the system of judicial delegation under Eugenius III and Alexander III; but this cannot be proved, and it was perfectly possible for the Chan-cery to issue a mandate without the *audientia litterarum con-tradictarum* playing a part in the process. The system of the *contradictio* is first mentioned in 1199,[4] and the *audientia publica* and the *audientia litterarum contradictarum* are not heard of until this period. Dr. Herde has assumed, indeed, that it was Innocent III who in his Chancery reforms created the institution of the *audientia publica*, and he implies that Innocent instituted the *audientia litterarum contradictarum* also, and with it the regular possibility of stopping the issue of a papal document or of changing its contents.[5] This was

---

[1] e.g. *Oxford Formularies*, p. 275 no. 5. A small book of forms of petition 'secundum cursum Romane curie' was written by the cardinal Guala Bichieri in 1226, ed. R. von Heckel in 'Das päpstliche und Sicilische Registerwesen', *Archiv für Urkundenforschung*, i (1908), 502–10. See also G. Barraclough, 'Formulare für Suppliken aus der ersten Hälfte des 13. Jahrhunderts', *Archiv für Katholisches Kirchenrecht*, cxv (1935), 435–56.

[2] See my article 'Canterbury Proctors', p. 313, and docs. nos. i–iv and vi.

[3] Barraclough, '*Audientia Litterarum Contradictarum*', cols. 1387, 1389. J. Teige, *Beiträge zur Geschichte der Audientia Litterarum Contradictarum*, i (Prague, 1897), esp. 14, argued without any real basis that there was a separate department of the *Curia* dealing with the expedition of writs as early as 'perhaps in the first half of the twelfth century'.

[4] *Quellen und Forschungen aus italienischen Archiven und Bibliotheken* (Königl. Preussisches Historisches Institut in Rom, x, 1907), 378, no. iii.

[5] Herde, *Beiträge*, pp. 164–8. Dr Herde has prepared a study of the *audientia litterarum contradictarum*, and an analysis of the whole group of formularies, to be published by the Bibliothek des Deutschen Historischen Instituts in Rome. The earliest, the Durrieu manuscript, dating from the middle years of the thirteenth century, which R. von Heckel had proposed to edit, is a most crucial source and has long awaited an editor (Barraclough, '*Audientia Litterarum Contradictarum*', col. 1394). On this MS. see also G. Tessier, 'Note sur un manuel à l'usage d'un officier de la Cour pontificale (XIIIe siècle)', *Études d'histoire du droit canonique dédiées à*

the *contradictio*. In the case of judicial business, the Chancery decided whether the suit should be delegated, and if so, what kind of mandate should be sent. The chosen form, detailing judges, etc., which followed the plaintiff's petition very closely, was then drawn up and at some later time read aloud in the *audientia publica*, a public sitting of the Chancery where general pronouncements were declared and comments made.[1] At this point an objection to the contents of the letter might be raised by the defendant's proctor. If no objection was made, the mandate was returned to the writing office for checking, sent for engrossing, and then sealed with the *bulla*. If, on the other hand, a protest was registered, the dispute was handed over to the *auditor litterarum contradictarum* for inquiry into the objection.

The operation of this procedure is described for the first time by Thomas of Marlborough, proctor of Evesham abbey, in 1205–6. He speaks of the reading in the *audientia publica*, where he made an objection, and of being called *ad audientiam contradictarum* on the next day, which might mean either going *for* the hearing of the contradiction in the Chancery or the *audientia publica*, or of going *to* the *audientia litterarum contradictarum*, a separate chamber.[2] The *Chronicon Montis Sereni* speaks of two letters being read in the *audientia* in 1223: one of these the proctor allowed to pass without comment, the other he contradicted. The next day the *magister contradictarum* caused the contradicted letter to be destroyed.[3] The existence of the process of the *contradictio* presupposes the system of reading the documents aloud, but it seems unlikely that the contradiction procedure operated

G. Le Bras, i (Paris, 1965), 357–71, esp. 369, and Herde, 'Der Zeugenzwang in den Päpstlichen Delegationsreskripten des Mittelalters', *Traditio*, xviii (1962), 265 ff. On the Trier MS., Stadtbibliothek Cod. 859/1097, which contains a formulary of the *audientia litterarum contradictarum*, see H. M. Schaller, 'Eine Kuriale Briefsammlung des 13. Jahrhunderts . . . ', *Deutsches Archiv für Erforschung des Mittelalters*, xviii (1962), esp. 174.   [1] Herde, *Beiträge*, pp. 166, 168.

   [2] *Chron. Abb. Evesham*, p. 199, and also p. 145 referring again to the contradiction process. On the whole case, see M. Spaethen, 'Giraldus Cambrensis und Thomas von Evesham über die von ihnen an der Kurie geführten Prozesse', *Neues Archiv der Gesellschaft für ältere deutsche Geschichtskunde*, xxxi (1906), 629–49.

   [3] 'Chronicon Montis Sereni', M.G.H., *Scriptorum*, xxiii (1874), 200. This is the first known mention of an officer, and the first to be noted by name is Master Otto who appears under Honorius III, see *Quinque Compilationes Antiquae*, p. 153, cited by Barraclough, '*Audientia Litterarum Contradictarum*', col. 1390.

in every case. It is as mistaken to think that proctors objected in all instances as it is to accept the old idea that all documents that were not seen by the pope went through the *audientia publica* and vice versa.[1] This is no longer acceptable. One method of issue did not necessarily preclude the other. According to Herde, the *audientia publica* acted to some extent as a public relations office where documents which the pope had seen could also be read if he thought it desirable.[2] Although there was a ruling for routine matters to follow a defined course and to be divided into either *litterae legendae* or *litterae dandae*, for important matters special rulings could be made.[3] This seems to point to the view that the pope may have played some part in the delegation of important cases. At least it should not be assumed that, because he was not necessary to delegation, he was never concerned with it or that he did not know of what was going on.

It may be that during Innocent III's pontificate the *audientia litterarum contradictarum* represents a stage in the process of the issue of a certain document, rather than a distinct office or court.[4] The *auditor litterarum contradictarum* worked in close conjunction with the vice-chancellor and on his behalf. He was present at the reading, and he heard the objection. In the investigation of its validity he merely took over some of the vice-chancellor's work, and it may have been some time before he got a separate chamber or office.[5]

Whether this procedure antedates 1198 or not, no documents from the *audientia litterarum contradictarum* appear to have survived from before the pontificate of Gregory IX.[6] The first known survival is a letter of Master Richard of Langdon, proctor of Richard le Grand, archbishop of Canterbury, recording his agreement not to bring the convent of Christ Church, Canterbury, before a Church court nor to

---

[1] Bresslau, pp. 282 ff.   [2] Herde, *Beiträge*, p. 168.
[3] Ibid., pp. 171–2.   [4] Ibid., pp. 165–6.
[5] There is an interesting instance in *Reg. Inn. IV* (no. 7295), of the *auditor litterarum contradictarum* being designated to act for the vice-chancellor, presumably in his absence. It illustrates the close relationship which was maintained between the two offices.
[6] On the documents and the procedure in general, see 'Canterbury Proctors'.

prejudice them in any way on account of a mandate which he had procured from Gregory IX, dated 10 September 1230.[1] The document resulted from the protest that Master Philip de Mortimer, proctor of Christ Church, had made in the *audientia publica*, and was a private or unofficial deed. The second is an official document, issued in the name of the *auditor litterarum contradictarum*, Master Robert of Somercotes, some time after 20 May 1238, and called a *cautio*.[2] It noted that the mandate that the archdeacon of Canterbury had obtained would not be valid against the prior and chapter of Christ Church. In other words, at the reading of the mandate in the *audientia publica* the proctor acting on behalf of Christ Church had objected to the issue of letters which might adversely affect his clients. The auditor had then after investigation accepted his protest.

It cannot be argued convincingly that an objection was made in every case.[3] Mandates, as we shall see, could be made out against a large number of people, and not all applicants would have been wealthy enough to employ standing proctors at Rome to look after their interests. No doubt in important cases they endeavoured to do so, but there must have been many documents which passed through the *audientia publica* without comment. The *contradictio* system also allowed for objections against the personnel of the judges and the place of hearing. Again this must have been extraordinary procedure. No documents recording decisions about these matters by the *auditor litterarum contradictarum* survive from before 22 April 1277,[4] but it seems likely that this variety of objection too came into being with the system of contradiction, and was thus in operation from the early years of Innocent III's pontificate.

---

[1] Canterbury, Cartae Antiquae, C 47, pd. 'Canterbury Proctors', App. doc. vi.

[2] Canterbury, Cartae Antiquae, A 206, pd. 'Canterbury Proctors', App. doc. vii.

[3] See 'Canterbury Proctors', pp. 321–3 and 324, and Herde, *Beiträge*, p. 167 and n. 334. Brentano, however, inclines to this view, *York Metropolitan Jurisdiction*, p. 157.

[4] Canterbury, Cartae Antiquae, C 284 and C 285, pd. 'Canterbury Proctors', App. docs. i, ii. See also forms of about the same date in *Die Formularsammlung des Marinus von Eboli*, ed. F. Schillmann (Bibliothek des Preussischen Historischen Instituts in Rom, xvi, 1929).

(ii) *The Place of the Hearing*

The question of the choice of the judges must be dealt with later,[1] but the question of where the delegated court was to sit concerns us now. No decision as to the place of meeting is ever recorded in the mandate, and it is probable that the place was only mentioned at Rome when the bench of judges was challenged. This lack of a specific instruction suggests that unless there was some additional document, as the *littere conventionales*, to make known the place on which the parties had agreed, the judges made their own decision.[2] In all cases, probably, the commissions sat in a church.[3] Also the location was supposed to be a safe one.[4] The place is by no means always specified in the *acta*, but an analysis of the places where the courts are known to have met between 1198 and 1254 suggests the following observations.

Generally speaking, the place of meeting was dictated by the composition of the group of judges. Cambridgeshire judges met at Barnwell or Cambridge; Suffolk judges at Bury St. Edmunds; Kentish judges at Canterbury; Sussex judges at Chichester; Bedfordshire judges at Dunstable; Herefordshire judges at Hereford; Lincolnshire judges at Lincoln; Norfolk judges at Norwich; Peterborough judges at Peterborough; and Stamford judges at Stamford.[5] There is also an indication that cases were heard in major towns, county towns, cathedral cities, towns situated on main routes, and towns where there were important religious houses, such as Oxford, Canterbury, Lincoln, London, Northampton, Cambridge, Dunstable, and St. Albans.[6] Boniface VIII was to

---

[1] See *P.J.D.*, pp. 109–18.

[2] 'Canterbury Proctors', pp. 318–21. Cf. Cooper, *Select Scottish Cases*, p. xxviii, who asserts that 'the judges delegate suited their own convenience as to the venue' without seeking to accommodate parties and witnesses, and see his nos. 17, 18, 22, 34, 40, and 44.

[3] In Anglo-Saxon churches special places were provided for the sitting of Church courts, *The Ecclesiastical Courts*, Report of the Commission set up . . . in 1951 (1954), p. 2.

[4] Bishop Mauger of Worcester, for instance, was granted the right to appeal if summoned to answer lawsuits in Wales, where he said it was dangerous for Englishmen to go (*Letters of Inn. III*, no. 406).

[5] See App. A (ii), below 284–96.

[6] See ibid., nos. 87–97 (Oxford, 11 examples), 15–23 (Canterbury, 9 examples), 60–7 (Lincoln, 8), 69–75 (London, 7), 78–83 (Northampton, 6), 9–14 (Cambridge, 6), 34–9 (Dunstable, 6), and 102–6 (St. Albans, 5).

declare in 'Statutum quod' that commissions of delegates were to sit in cities where there were generous supplies of experts available,[1] and Innocent IV foreshadowed this ruling in the second canon of the First Council of Lyons, 1245,[2] saying that the judges, who were to be dignitaries, should only summon the parties to cities and large places.

Sometimes the judges heard cases away from their home towns. A commission of Gloucester judges heard a case between two Buckinghamshire houses at Oxford;[3] and a commission of Cambridge judges made a settlement in Wallingford priory church in Berkshire, in a suit between Wallingford priory and Henry of Earley (Berks.) and his chaplain.[4] In these instances, when the judges made considerable journeys, it was probably for reasons of convenience. If, however, a plaintiff sought and obtained a commission to three judges at distance from one another, he ran the risk of objections from both the judges and the defendant. In a case between G(eoffrey de Burgh) archdeacon of Norwich and Master Robert of York about the bishopric of Ely, one of the members of the first commission was the archbishop of York, who was said to be too far from Ely to hear the cause without expense, and of the second commission, the abbot of Coverham (Yorks. N.R.), who was four days' journey from his colleagues, the abbot of Waltham (Essex) and the archdeacon of Huntingdon.[5]

Defendants were not supposed to be brought before judicial tribunals more than two days' journey from their own diocese,[6] but this seems often to have been ignored. William, son of Conan of Holbeach (Lincs.), was brought before a commission of Kentish judges by the prior and convent of Christ Church, Canterbury, and a settlement was made at Canterbury. The suit concerned an annual rent of four shillings from seven acres of land in Holbeach.[7] Beaulieu brought the prior and convent of St. Michael's Mount (Cornw.), in a suit about the tithes of St. Kaveran church,

---

[1] c. 11. 6. I. 3.
[2] *Sacrorum Conciliorum Collectio*, xxiii, ed. Mansi, p. 619.
[3] App. A (ii), no. 94.   [4] Ibid., no. 112.
[5] *Reg. Hon. III*, nos. 846, 1422 (*C.P.L.* i. 49, 55).
[6] c. 28. *X*. I. 3, and see, e.g., Peterborough, MS. 5, f. 135^{r-v}.
[7] App. A (ii), no. 19.

before the prior of Christchurch (or Twynham, Hants), and a settlement was made in the church there.[1] Sentence in a suit between Dunstable and Robert, rector of Bradbourne in the Peak (N. Derbys.), was given by St. Albans judges on 18 December 1214 in the abbey at St. Albans, and when Robert failed to pay the expenses, to which he had been condemned, he was brought south again in 1223, and this time heard sentence before the abbot and prior of Warden and the prior of Beadlow in Flitwick church (Beds.), which belonged to Dunstable priory.[2] In another Beaulieu case it was specifically stated in the mandate to the legate Otto, dated 15 October 1238, that Beaulieu, the defendants, might be brought beyond two days' journey but not beyond four or five.[3] The abbot of Lavendon was held to have acted 'maliciose' by the abbot of Prémontré when he impetrated letters from the general chapter to the abbots of Newhouse and Croxton who were six days' journey from his adversary, the abbot of St. Radegund's;[4] and papal examples show the defendants coming from as far away as 100 miles, which must have meant three to four days' travelling according to season and weather.

The plaintiff's choice of commission undoubtedly affected the decision about the place of hearing. In a suit between Lanthony and St. Julian's hospital, St. Albans, when the judges were obtained by Lanthony, they were Gloucester clerics, and the hospital of St. Julian at St. Albans had to come to Gloucester where sentence was given in the church of St. Mary by the abbey gate; and when the judges were obtained by St. Albans, they were Dunstable men, meeting at Dunstable.[5] The dean of Lincoln brought the prior and convent of Tutbury before Southwell judges, who met at

---

[1] App. A (ii), no. 28.

[2] App. A (ii), nos. 46, 102, and see *V.C.H. Beds.* i. 371.

[3] Beaulieu Cart., f. 130ᵛ. Cf. *Letters of Inn. III*, no. 125, where the Kentish defendants complained of being summoned more than four days' journey out of the diocese of Canterbury and into that of Lincoln, probably to Oxford. The impetrant was a canon of Dover; the judges were from Oxfordshire, namely the abbot of Thame, the prior of St. Frideswide's, and Master W. de Bram[feld ?], for whom see above, p. 52 n. 5.

[4] St. Radegund's (Bradsole) Cart., f. 42, pd. H. M. Colvin, *White Canons in England* (Oxford, 1951), pp. 339–40, and see p. 87.

[5] App. A (ii), nos. 37, 51.

Southwell; while the prior and convent brought the dean before Stafford judges, sitting at Stafford.[1] The prior of Newstead (Notts.) was summoned to answer the abbot of Chertsey (Surr.) by Oxford judges, who made a settlement in St. Mary's church, Oxford, a journey of about 100 miles from Newstead.[2] The abbot and convent of Westminster convened Andrew, vicar of Pershore (Worcs.), before the prior of St. Albans and the dean of Hertford, who gave a decision in the abbey of St. Albans (Herts.). Andrew was represented by a proctor.[3] Another case in which a decision was given at St. Albans, by the archdeacon, was between the convent of Holy Cross, Waltham (Essex), and the convent of Chepstow in Monmouthshire, who were contumacious, perhaps not surprisingly considering the length of the journey.[4] From Worcester to Bury St. Edmunds is again about 100 miles in distance, but it was at Bury that the case between the prior and convent of Eye and the archdeacon of Worcester concerning the church of Badingham (Suff.) was heard by the abbot and prior of Bury St. Edmunds and the prior of Great Bricett (also Suff.).[5]

Although there are instances of the plaintiff coming some distance—as the prior and convent of Lewes (Suss.) who appeared against W., rector of Weston Colville (Cambs.), at Carlton cum Willingham (one of the Lewes properties in Cambs.) before the prior of Merton (Surr.) and his co-judges, who are unspecified;[6] they also appeared against Nicholas parson of Sculthorpe (Norf.) before Huntingdon judges in the church of St. Mary at Huntingdon[7]—they are isolated and can possibly be explained by other factors, such as the likelihood of making a settlement. An analysis of the cases in which some of the religious houses were involved both as defendant and as plaintiff shows that, when they were acting as plaintiff, the suit was usually heard near home, when as defendant, they sometimes had a journey to make. In all the suits where the prior and convent of Christ Church, Canterbury, were acting as plaintiffs, and where the place of settlement is known, it was Canterbury.[8] In an instance

---

[1] *Reg. Antiq. Linc.* iii, no. 759.   [2] App. A (ii), no. 95.
[3] Ibid., no. 104.   [4] Ibid., no. 105.   [5] Ibid., no. 7.
[6] Ibid., no. 24.   [7] Ibid., no. 56.   [8] Ibid., nos. 15, 17–19, 21.

where they were defendants, they went to Boxley parish church in Kent, where the abbot and prior of Boxley and Master Th(omas) of Maidstone heard a case between them and Master Richard, rector of Cliffe-at-Hoo (Kent).[1] The prior and convent of Eye appeared as plaintiffs at Barnwell (Cambs.), Fornham All Saints (Suff.), Ipswich (Suff.), Norwich on two occasions, Bury on two occasions, and Westleton (Suff.),[2] and as defendants at Fressingfield (Suff.) and Lincoln.[3] The prior and convent of Lanthony by Gloucester as plaintiffs went to St. Mary's church Gloucester twice, and to Hereford cathedral and St. Mary's church Oxford,[4] and as defendants they went to Dunstable, Hereford, and St. Paul's, London.[5] St. Frideswide's occur only once as defendants, at Dunstable.[6] As plaintiffs they heard judgements at Flamstead (Herts.), in the churches of All Saints and St. Peter's by the castle at Northampton, in St. Mary's church, Oxford, in St. Andrew's chapel in St. Albans abbey, and at Westminster.[7] Acting by proctor the nuns of St. Michael's, Stamford (Northants.), were brought by the abbot and convent of Owston (Leics.) before the priors of Leicester, Belvoir (Lincs.), and Breedon (Leics.) in Breedon church, which belonged to Breedon priory;[8] but when they brought William Erl of North Luffenham (Rutland) before the deans of Stamford, Rutland, and Carlby (Lincs.), it was in the church of St. Mary at the bridge in Stamford.[9]

In a petition to Pope Innocent IV in 1248 to allow them not to be cited more than two days' journey from their monastery to answer lawsuits, the abbot and convent of Bardney alleged that they had either to expend much energy and money or lose the suit.[10] The archdeacon of the East Riding in seeking a similar indult stated that he had attended causes for eight days at a time. He was given an assurance that he should not be summoned to attend courts outside the diocese of York or more than two days' journey from his domicile.[11]

---

[1] App. A (ii), no. 4.   [2] Ibid., nos. 1, 6–7, 47, 58, 84–5, 116.
[3] Ibid., nos. 49, 63.   [4] Ibid., nos. 50–1, 54, 90.
[5] Ibid., nos. 37, 55, 74.   [6] Ibid., no. 35.
[7] Ibid., nos. 44, 78, 80–1, 91, 103, 118.   [8] *V.C.H. Leics.* ii. 8.
[9] App. A (ii), nos. 5, 110.
[10] Bardney Cart., f. 28 r–v, and *Reg. Inn. IV*, no. 3774.
[11] *Reg. Hon. III*, no. 6205 (*C.P.L.* i. 115).

These examples suggest that not only was the decree of the Fourth Lateran Council concerning impetration and summonses sometimes disregarded, but also that the advantage was with the plaintiff, who by his choice of judges usually indirectly determined the place where the court would sit. This seems to be supported by the above evidence; and the decree 'Statutum quod' of Boniface VIII showed an exact analysis of the state of affairs fifty years earlier by enacting that when the plaintiff and defendant were of the same city and diocese, the cause was not to be committed outside it, and that when the plaintiff and defendant were of different dioceses, the plaintiff should impetrate to delegates within the diocese of the defendant, or in another diocese not his own and not beyond one day distant.[1] The exact advantage gained by the plaintiff is impossible to assess, particularly in minor suits. It was the right of the defendant to object if he felt himself prejudiced. He could also petition for an indult if he was rich enough.

Indults were granted to the convents of Merton in 1231,[2] Oseney in 1232,[3] St. Augustine, Canterbury, in 1236 and 1253,[4] Spalding in 1238,[5] Sempringham, Nostell, and St. Mary, York, in 1245,[6] and St. Frideswide, Oxford, and Abingdon in 1250.[7] An indult granted to Cartmel priory (Lancs.) by Gregory IX conceded that they should not be summoned to courts of judges delegate more than two days' sail from their port, because of the danger from storms, the grave expenses, and the pressure to enter into unsuitable agreements.[8] Similar indults were also granted to seculars —the bishop and officials of Norwich in 1240,[9] the bishop elect of Winchester in 1253,[10] and the bishop of Llandaff in 1254, whose indult was to remain valid for three years.[11] The travelling distance beyond which these petitioners were not to be bound to go varied from one day, granted to Aymer de Valence bishop elect of Winchester by Innocent IV,[12]

[1] c. 11. 6. I. 3.   [2] Reg. Greg. IX, no. 728.   [3] Ibid., no. 985.
[4] Ibid., no. 3277; St. Augustine's Red Book, ff. 26ᵛ–27ʳ.
[5] Spalding Cart., f. 417ʳ.   [6] Reg. Inn. IV, nos. 1008, 1300, 1660.
[7] St. Frideswide's Cart. i, no. 55; Abingdon Cart., f. 24ʳ.
[8] Reg. Greg. IX, no. 1554.   [9] Ibid., no. 5269.
[10] Reg. Inn. IV, no. 6475.   [11] Ibid., no. 7967.
[12] Ibid., no. 6475.

to three days granted by Innocent III to St. Augustine's, Canterbury;[1] but the most usual period was two days, and some of the indults specified that they related to suits about goods and property only.[2]

(iii) *The Mandate*

The mandate, or rescript, which was drawn up in the Chancery, sealed with the leaden *bulla* on hemp cords, and issued in the pope's name, started the action, and was the authority by which the judges acted.[3] As such they quoted it when commanding officers to make a citation or execute a sentence on their behalf. When the abbot of Westminster, the prior of Merton, and Master William de Sancte Marie Ecclesia, judges delegate of Gregory IX, instructed the dean of Canterbury to cite the abbot and convent of St. Augustine, Canterbury, to appear at Southwark, they recited the papal mandate that they had received granting them this power.[4] Similarly, when judges delegate had passed sentence in a case between Master Baldwin, canon of Troyes, France, and Master W(illiam), archdeacon of Worcester and the convent of Lanthony, Gloucestershire, in 1235, they ordered the dean of Gloucester to carry it out, and sent him both a copy of their sentence and the papal mandate on whose authority they had proceeded.[5] Professor Le Bras has described the mandate and the appeal system as two of the most powerful means of papal centralization, both of which were provided by the Roman law.[6] Certainly to some extent papal power was disseminated by the mandate, which is comparable with the English royal writ.[7] Although its influence may have been

---

[1] St. Augustine's Cart., f. 66ʳ⁻ᵛ.

[2] *Reg. Greg. IX*, no. 985; Abingdon Cart., f. 24ʳ; *Reg. Greg. IX*, no. 3277; *Reg. Inn. IV*, no. 1660; *St. Frideswide's Cart.* i, no. 55; and *Reg. Greg. IX*, no. 728.

[3] Numerous original mandates survive: e.g. *The Priory of St. Radegund Cambridge*, ed. A. Gray (Cambridge Antiquarian Soc. xxxi, 1898), Ch. 6, p. 77; Lambeth Palace Library, Papal Documents, no. 30; and Windsor, Papal Bulls, no. 1.

[4] St. Augustine's Cart., f. 79ʳ.

[5] Lanthony Cart. A1, XVI, no. xvi. Another example of sending the papal mandate to the executive officer is in the Lewes Cart., f. 260ʳ, cal. *Lewes Cart. N.P.*, no. 135; but the original is not P.R.O. E 40/14071 as Bullock says.

[6] Le Bras, 'Droit romain', p. 391.

[7] William J. La Due wrote a thesis on this subject. An excerpt was published as *Papal Rescripts of Justice and English Royal Procedural Writs, 1150–1250. A Comparative Study* (Pontificia Universitas Lateranensis Institutum Utriusque Juris,

exaggerated, it was usually treated with respect by the judges, and scrutinized. When, for instance, a mandate arrived from which the *bulla* had been detached, the judges delegate, the abbots of Kirkstead, Bardney, and Barlings, declined to acknowledge it without a new order from Rome; and on another occasion the judges refused to act because the mandate lacked the 'o' in 'spoliarunt'.[1]

Broadly speaking, thirteenth-century mandates can be divided into two classes, the first inclusive, covering minor cases and cases of first instance, and the second particular, comprising major cases and cases of appeal. From the evidence of the Oseney cartulary the late Dr. H. E. Salter supposed that groups of cases were set aside for sending to Rome.[2] A wide mandate was then sought which could be used against a number of people on a variety of charges. This at least was the practice in minor cases. Salter's supposition is confirmed by the evidence. The prior and convent of St. Neots brought Robert, parson of Barnwell, Bartholomew, rector of Barton Bendish, and T., rector of Brampton, before judges delegate off one mandate.[3] By a mandate of 27 April 1233, the abbot and convent of Bec succeeded in bringing William Estormy and Elias, chaplain, the priory of St. Frideswide, Oxford, the abbey of Tewkesbury, and the nunnery of Godstow before Dunstable judges in suits about a chapel at Shalbourne (Berks. now Wilts.), tithes at Hidden and Eddington in Hungerford (Berks.), tithes at Lesser Ogbourne (Wilts.), and tithes in Wycombe (Bucks.).[4] The mandate also includes the name of the abbey of Abingdon among the defendants.[5] Thorney got one mandate against the rectors of Pertenhall (Beds.) and Tydd St. Giles (Cambs.) in 1224;[6] and similarly Christ Church, Canterbury, against the parson of Eythorne (Kent) and the brothers of

Theses ad Lauream, no. 155, Rome, 1960). Unfortunately the sections dealing with the English royal Chancery (chapters ii, iv) were omitted from the excerpt; but La Due draws attention in his conclusions to the expansion in the issue of papal mandates under Eugenius III (1145–53), and of royal writs under Henry II (1154–89).

[1] *Reg. Hon. III*, no. 2547 (*C.P.L.* i. 73); and *Letters of Inn. III*, no. 1052.
[2] *Oseney Cart.* vi, p. 339.
[3] See App. A (ii), nos. 12–14.
[4] Ibid., nos. 34–6, and Eton College, Bledlow Ch. C 5.
[5] Eton College, Bledlow Ch. C 5.
[6] Thorney Cart. ii, ff. 257ᵛ and 322ᵛ.

Notre Dame des Dunes in Sheppey;¹ Dover against certain chaplains in Dover;² Bardney against the Stixwould nuns and the archdeacon of Cleveland (Yorks. N.R.);³ and St. Frideswide's against the rectors of Souldern and Beckley (Oxon.).⁴

Besides the parties who were specified by name in the mandate, an unlimited number could be summoned by the clause 'et quidam alii'.⁵ The clause 'quidam alii' was not, however, to be taken to refer to more important persons than those actually named.⁶ A mandate of Gregory IX, issued from Perugia on 9 November 1229, and made out against the archdeacon of Essex, the rector of the church of East Lavant (Sussex), 'et quidam alii clerici et layci Londoniensis et Cicestrensis diocesum',⁷ was used also to bring to justice Robert de Dene, rector of St. Peter's, Lewes, and of the chapel of Smythwick; J., chaplain of the same; Richard, rector, and Gilbert, vicar, of Patcham; Walter, rector of Barcombe; and probably P., rector of Tarring (all Sussex).⁸ Philip, rector of East Hendred (Berks.), got a mandate against the convents of Bec, Abingdon, Reading, and Caen, and against William de Ferrieres, earl of Derby, and others ('quidam alii') of the Salisbury, Worcester, and Coventry dioceses.⁹ The abbot and convent of St. James, Northampton, summoned through one mandate of Honorius III, dated 4 February 1222, William, son of Richard Cav', Philip, John, and Reginald, clerk, and other parishioners of Hartwell (Northants.), 'auctoritate generalis clausule in

¹ App. A (ii), nos. 17–18. The Cistercian abbey of Dunes in Flanders was granted the church of Eastchurch in Sheppey by Richard I, *Calendar of Documents preserved in France*, i (918–1206), ed. J. H. Round (1899), p. 497, and see E. Hasted, *History and Topographical Survey of . . . Kent*, ii (Canterbury, 1782), 665. Presumably they had a cell at Eastchurch.

² App. A (ii), nos. 41–2.   ³ Ibid., nos. 60–1.   ⁴ Ibid., nos. 80–1.

⁵ See, e.g., Bradenstoke Cart., f. 119ᵛ; *Reg. Antiq. Linc.* iii, no. 647; Lanthony Cart. A I, III, no. lv, and A 2, ff. 221ᵛ and 223ʳ (two examples).

⁶ c. 15. *X*. I. 3 (Inn. III).

⁷ P.R.O. E 40/14190 (cf. E 40/14189), cal. *Lewes Cart. S.P.* ii. 101.

⁸ P.R.O. E 40/14157–9, cal. *Lewes Cart. S.P.* ii. 24–5, 34–5; P.R.O. E 40/14156, cal. *S.P.* ii. 26; Lewes Cart., ff. 116ᵛ–17ʳ, cal. ii. 39; P.R.O. E 40/14139, cal. ii. 56; and Lewes Cart., f. 103ʳ, cal. ii. 9–10.

⁹ Windsor Ch. xv. 41. 71 and Abingdon Cart., f. 53ʳ. Cf. P.R.O. E 135/21/33, which recites a mandate obtained by the rector of Odell (Beds.) against the prior and convent of Canons Ashby, the rector of Newington, Saer de Odell knight, 'et quidam alii Norwycens' Eliens' et Lincoln' civitatum et diocesum'.

literis domini pape contente scilicet quidam alii'.[1] In the Council of Lyons Innocent IV legislated that through the clause 'quidam alii' only three or four people were to be convened, and their names were to be expressed in the first citation.[2] When summoned by general letters 'in communi forma', which made no mention of the Cistercian order to which he belonged, the abbot of Beaulieu refused to obey the summons of the judges delegate, the abbot of Hyde, the prior of Breamore, and the dean of Winchester. An appeal was accordingly made to the pope by the plaintiffs, the prior and convent of Selborne.[3] The other defendants in this case, the abbot of Tiron and the prior of Andwell, also declared that they could not be summoned by the general clause 'quidam alii'.[4]

If all the defendants were not mentioned specifically by name in the mandate, it was difficult for the proctors at Rome to know when to make a contradiction on behalf of clients who might well be prejudiced. For this reason indults were sought granting exemption from summons unless mention of the order, rank, or church was made in the mandate. The Premonstratensians were allowed by Gregory IX, for example, to treat as invalid impetrated letters containing the clause 'quidam alii' that did not make a note of their order.[5] The archbishop of Canterbury was allowed not to answer a judicial summons unless his title was referred to in the papal letters.[6] The treasurer of York declared that neither his office nor the parson J. was mentioned in letters that the convent of Eye had procured, addressed to the abbot of Langley and his colleagues. After the judges had

---

[1] Northampton, St. James's Cart., f.109^{r-v}.

[2] c. 2. 6. I. 3, and also *Die Päpstlichen Kanzleiordnungen von 1200–1500*, ed. M. Tangl (Innsbruck, 1894), p. 56 n. 2.

[3] Magdalen College, Oxford, Selborne Ch. 373 (Macray, *Calendar* i. 24); and see c. 6. *X*. I. 3 (Alex. III).

[4] Magdalen College, Oxford, Selborne Ch. 373. Cf. O, f. 223^v, col. i, a formulary example: the prior of Séez appeals to the pope because he was not mentioned in the mandate which J. rector of 'Ebintone' (? Edington, Wilts.) had obtained about tithes belonging to the convent of Séez; and c. 21. *X*. I. 3.

[5] *Chartulary of Cockersand Abbey*, i, pt. i, ed. W. Farrer (Chetham Soc. xxxviii, 1898), p. 39.

[6] *Reg. Greg. IX*, no. 2989. Cf. the archbishop of York who was not bound to answer papal letters addressed to parsons and canons of York, *Reg. Hon. III*, no. 6231 (*C.P.L.* i. 116).

refused to admit this exception, he appealed to the pope, who ordered the dean, the master of the schools, and Master Robert de Gravele, canon of Lincoln, to hear the cause if it was as alleged or to return the case to the abbot of Langley and his commission.[1] When a mandate was sent to the abbot and prior of Warden and the prior of Dunstable in 1215, a special note was made in it that the abbot and convent of Westminster were to answer the charge.[2] Westminster held that they could not be summoned without special letters, and they had presumably received an indult to this effect. A similar indult was granted by Honorius III in 1220 to the prior and convent of Christ Church, Canterbury, conceding that they should not be held to pay attention to letters which did not mention the church of Canterbury.[3]

The charge of the mandate was also elastic enough to enable the plaintiff to summon such groups on a collection of charges, for instance 'super possessionibus, decimis, debitis et rebus aliis',[4] 'super possessionibus, legatis et rebus aliis',[5] and 'super subjectione, obediencia, professione, visitatione, procuratione et rerum ejusdem ecclesie dispositione'.[6] By the use of provisos, furthermore, recent decisions of the pope and *Curia* on points of law and new modes of procedure could be brought to the attention of the judges and the parties without drawing up specific forms for each case. The ruling of the Fourth Lateran Council (canon 32), that vicars' portions should be sufficient, was often called to the attention of the judges by a proviso included in the mandate in causes which concerned benefices, pensions, or apportionment of tithes.[7] Most of the mandates containing this proviso date from the pontificate of Honorius III, but a mandate of the legate Ottobon of 1266 also included it.[8] Other provisos about issuing sentences of excommunication or of interdict

---

[1] Eye Cart., f. 39ᵛ.
[2] Westminster Domesday, f. 228ʳ⁻ᵛ (f. 452ʳ⁻ᵛ ibid.).
[3] Canterbury, Reg. A, f. 33ʳ.   [4] *Montacute Cart.*, no. 171.
[5] Bodleian MS. Dodsworth 76, f. 1.
[6] St. Paul's, Press A, Box 23, Ch. 864.
[7] Hefele, *Conciles*, v, pt. ii. 1359–60; and, for examples, Binham Cart., f. 185ʳ; P.R.O. E 40/14953; P.R.O. E 40/14253, cal. *Lewes Cart. N.P.*, no. 73 (although Bullock has this as E 40/14298); Dover Cart., f. 226ᵛ; P.R.O. E 40/14955; Leeds Cart., f. 10ʳ; *Chertsey Cart.*, no. 92; P.R.O. E 40/14071; and Lanthony Cart. A 1, VIII, no. lxxviii.   [8] Binham Cart., f. 187ᵛ.

were sometimes added to the mandate without basic alteration to the stereotyped form.[1]

Specific mandates were issued more rarely, for dealing with cases of importance which might influence the law of the Church, for appeal cases where individual instructions were needed, and when influential persons were involved.[2] Innocent IV wrote on 18 April 1246 to the abbot of Bourne, the prior of St. John, Northampton, and the archdeacon of Buckingham, instructing them how to deal with a case that had been sent to him on appeal by the prior and convent of Spalding.[3] A mandate of Innocent III to the priors of Marton and Malton and H., dean of Ryedale (Yorks. N.R.), mentioned specifically that the church of Branxton (Northumb.), which belonged to Kirkham priory's church of Kirknewton in Glendale, had been seized by certain malefactors in the skirmishes in those parts. The judges were ordered to restore the church to the canons, if this appeared just when they had established the truth.[4] Often specific mandates commanded the judges to decide the cause within a certain time, 'mandamus quatinus, partibus convocatis, audiatis causam et eam infra v. mensium spatium post receptionem presentium studeatis judicio vel concordia terminare', or to remit it with full details to Rome.[5]

3. 'Jus' or the Commencement of the Suit

(i) Citation and Contumacy

On returning from Rome, the plaintiff or his proctor informed the judges of his impetration or appeal, presented his mandate to them, and asked them to summon the defendants. A form is provided in the Lambeth formulary:

A. B. C. judicibus D. clericus salutem. De sanctitatis vestre confidens equitate ad vos litteras summi pontificis inpetravi, ut de causa que

---

[1] Abingdon Cart., ff. 53ʳ–4ʳ, and Windsor Ch. xv. 41. 71: 'proviso ne in terram ipsius comitis [of Derby] excommunicationis vel interdicti sentenciam proferatis nisi super hoc a nobis mandatum receperitis speciale'.

[2] e.g. Westminster Domesday, ff. 228ʳ, 276ʳ, and 448ʳ.

[3] Spalding Cart., f. 418ᵛ. Cf. Magdalen College, Oxford, Selborne Ch. 373 (see above, p. 68).

[4] Kirkham Cart., f. 89ᵛ, and see P.R.O. DL 25/563.

[5] B.M. Harley Ch. 84 F 45, and see Bodleian MS. Chs. Bucks. a 3, Ch. 45.

vertitur inter me et C. super ecclesia illa diligenter congnoscatis (*sic*) et fine debito terminetis. Quapropter sanctitati vestre supplico ut nobis certum diem prefigatis et prefatum C. ut prefixa a vobis die coram presencia vestra juripariturus et sufficienter instructus in ecclesia illa appareat, auctoritate apostolica cogetis vel citetis.[1]

As the abbot of Humberston and the priors of Thornton and Grimsby reported: 'Hujus igitur auctoritate mandati ad instanciam predictorum abbatis et conventus de Neuhus [Newsham, Lincs.] citavimus pluries et legittime . . .'[2] When the plaintiff had presented the mandate to the delegates, he obtained from them a sealed *memorandum* acknowledging their receipt of it. Drogheda makes a note of it: 'Forma memorandi. Memorandum quod R. et J. iudices a domino papa delegati receperunt mandatum domini papae sub hac forma: Gregorius etc.'[3] This step seems to have been a precaution which the plaintiff would take if he were business-like.[4] The archdeacon of Northampton and the dean of Haseley (Oxon.) reported that they had received a mandate of Honorius III, dated 6 July 1222, in which Geoffrey, rector of Steeple Aston (Oxon.), challenged Bradenstoke priory and others to answer him about tithes and other matters.[5]

The procedure followed the formal course of the *ordo judiciarius*. Alongside this plenary procedure, which is outlined below, a second method of judicial procedure was gradually developed, termed summary,[6] to deal with affairs demanding immediate action, such as cases about the validity of an election, the possession of a benefice, or a marriage case. The summary procedure dispensed with the formal charge (the libel) and the formal declaration of disagreement (the *litis contestatio*), and it allowed, for example, no objections against the conduct of the action (dilatory exceptions).[7] But it was not an alternative mode of procedure until

---

[1] A, f. 271ᵛ, col. i, and cf. B.M. Add. MS. 8167, f. 116ᵛ.
[2] B.M. Harley Ch. 44 E 20.   [3] Drogheda, vii, p. 11.
[4] See Maitland, *Roman Canon Law*, p. 112.
[5] Bradenstoke Cart., f. 147ʳ.
[6] On the revival of the concept of summary procedure and its gradual extension, see C. Lefebvre, 'Les Origines romaines de la procédure sommaire au XIIᵉ et XIIIᵉ s.', *Ephemerides Iuris Canonici*, xii (1956), 149–97.
[7] Fournier, pp. 231–2.

Clement V's decretals,[1] although it had an effect on certain elements of the suit at an earlier date.

The judges now summoned the defendant. The first citation was expected to contain details about the suit and to include the papal mandate which outlined the charge or *editio*.[2] As Tancred writes:

> Attamen delegati iudices in prima citatione consueverunt tenorem commissionis sibi factae in literis citationis totum de verbo ad verbum inserere et reo, qui ad iudicium vocatur, transmittere, ut sciat, qui sunt, qui eum ad iudicium vocant, et cuius auctoritate. Et in literis citationis contineri debet, quod die tali, loco tali, tali actori, coram ipsis iudicibus responsurus accedat.[3]

The second and third citations, however, omitted both the mandate and the *editio*,[4] and sometimes the defendant may have been issued with a separate copy of the charge.[5] Almost certainly the plaintiff was summoned verbally at the time that he presented the mandate to the judges. At any rate no written examples summoning the plaintiff to court have survived.

A citation was either simple or peremptory. It was usual for simple citations to be made three times,[6] the third summons being peremptory. Tancred says that the parties ought to be summoned by three edicts, or by one peremptory order which substitutes for them all: 'debent vocari tribus edictis vel uno pro omnibus peremtorio'.[7] The judges in the Alvingham case ordered the dean of Walcot to cite the defendant by one peremptory edict: 'Mandamus quatinus uno pro tribus edicto peremptorie scietis Petrum dictum personam

---

[1] c. 2 *Clem*. ('*Clementis Papae V Constitutiones*' in *Corpus Juris Canonici*, ii, ed. E. Friedberg, Leipzig, 1881) V. 11, and c. 2 *Clem*. II. 1.

[2] *C.F.*, no. (1); C, f. 119ʳ, col. i; L, f. 65ᵛ, col. i; and B, ff. 79ᵛ, col. i; 80ᵛ, col. ii; and 81ᵛ, col ii (the first and last of these examples are printed in *Oxford Formularies* ii, nos. 4 and 11).

[3] Tancred, p. 133; cf., e.g., B.M. Wolley Ch. v. 27.

[4] See *C.F.*, nos. (3), (4), (5), and A, f. 271ᵛ, col. i.

[5] Damasus Hungarus, '*Summa de Ordine Iudiciario*', *Quellen zur Geschichte des Römisch-Kanonischen Processes im Mittelalter*, iv, pt. iv, ed. L. Wahrmund (Innsbruck, 1926), lxxxvii, p. 61. For Damasus Hungarus see Stickler, col. 1137, who dates his work as between 1210 and 1216. On making the *editio*, see *C*. ii. 1; *D*. ii 13; and *Lib. Pauperum*, ii, tit. 1.

[6] This is presumably what 'post legitimas citationes ei factas' means (B.M. Stowe Ch. 58).   [7] Tancred, p. 132.

duarum partium ecclesie de Staynton'.[1] When the first or second citation was peremptory, it was usually because speed was necessary; for instance in marriage suits when delay might spiritually endanger the parties, and in suits where the thing which was sought in the libel was perishable.[2] In some cases two peremptory citations might be made before punishment was threatened, as, for example, when an important person was summoned.[3] The most frequent practice in England, however, seems to have been to issue simple edicts and then a peremptory one.[4] In most cases when simple citations were issued, the defendants had to be summoned all three times before they came to court. The phrases 'sepe ac sepius et tandem peremptorie fecimus evocari', 'pluries et tandem peremptorie . . . citato', 'sepe et sepius fecimus evocari', are a common occurrence in final *acta*.[5]

Citations were made at definite intervals—'per legittima dierum spacia'.[6] According to the Roman law, ten days were allowed between each simple citation and thirty days for a peremptory one. In 1254 the defendants in a case were summoned 'trinis edictis per intervalla triginta dierum'.[7] A *memorandum* of a citation is dated 4 March 1252, and the party was summoned to appear on 16 March.[8] Presuming that the citation would reach its destination the following day, this would be a period of ten days before the court day. In all citations the charged party was ordered to

[1] Alvingham Cart., f. 5ʳ. On this suit see App. B (ii), pp. 315–16.

[2] See *C.F.*, no. (3); A, f. 271ᵛ, col. i—a peremptory citation apparently on the second edict; B, ff. 79ᵛ, col. i; 81ᵛ, col. ii; and B.M. Harley Ch. 84 F 44. Drogheda has examples of the second citation being peremptory and the third being a second peremptory citation (xvi and xvii, pp. 21–2).

[3] See *C.F.*, no. (6). C, f. 119ʳ, col. i, and L, f. 65ᵛ, cols. i and ii, give examples of three peremptory citations.

[4] A, f. 271ᵛ, col. i: 'Hujus igitur auctoritate mandati C. clericum primo ac secundo citavimus et tercio illi diem prefiximus peremptorium'; B.M. Add. MS. 8167, f. 116ʳ⁻ᵛ; B.M. Egerton Ch. 382: 'semel secundo et tercio edicto peremptorio citavimus'; Canterbury, Cartae Antiquae, L 135: 'Et quia jam tercio vocati estis pro eadem causa a nobis predictum diem vobis constituimus peremptorium'; and *C.F.*, no. (5).

[5] P.R.O. E 326/2268; E 40/14953-4; Thorney Cart. ii, ff. 257ᵛ, 383ʳ; and Bodleian MS. Dodsworth 76, f. 1. [6] Binham Cart., f. 185ʳ.

[7] Magdalen College, Oxford, Steyning Chs. 12, and 16, cal. L. F. Salzman, *Chartulary of the Priory of S. Peter at Sele* (Cambridge, 1923), no. 25.

[8] B.M. Harley Ch. 84 F 35.

desist or come to answer.[1] The defendant in the Canterbury formulary was ordered to make satisfaction within eight or fifteen days or to appear.[2] The fact that the citation had been made would be proved in front of the judges by witnesses or certified by the delegate.[3]

A peremptory summons contained the warning that the suit would be heard whether the defendant appeared before the court or not; and one formulary example orders the defendant to appear ready to put forward any dilatory exceptions so that the suit would not be delayed.[4] Furthermore, if the defendant failed to appear before the court after the legitimate citations, or refused to reply to the accusation, he was declared contumacious, and as such could be punished. He did not automatically lose the suit.

Suspension or inhibition from celebrating the sacraments was the usual penalty for a clerk, although excommunication could also be imposed.[5] In 1195, for example, the archbishop of York was suspended for contumacy.[6] The papal decretal 'Ex Concilio Africano' did not, however, approve of the deprivation of benefices.[7] In a document which was addressed to the judges, the dean of Cirencester reported that he had declared William, rector of Hampton Gay (Oxon.), suspended because of contumacy and that he had cited him again to appear before the court.[8] It was usual in declaring the punishment of suspension to cite the party again peremptorily, as the dean of Ewell reported that he had done in 1235 × 40;[9] for the longer the contumacy continued, the greater would be the penalty to be exacted.[10]

---

[1] *C.F.*, no. (1).   [2] Ibid., nos. (1), (2), and (4).
[3] Ibid., nos. (1), (2); and c. 4. *X.* II. 15 (Greg. IX).
[4] B.M. Add. MS. 8167, f. 114ᵛ.   [5] *C.F.*, no. (7).
[6] *Chronica Magistri Rogeri de Houedene*, iii, ed. W. Stubbs (R.S. li, 1870), 305, 309, and 315. Cf. Canterbury, Christ Church Letters, ii, no. 12, where the judges, the prior of Abingdon and the prior and subprior of St. Frideswide's, declined to suspend the bishop of Exeter for contumacy because it might endanger many souls.
[7] c. l. *X.* II. 1. 'De iudiciis—Contumax in non comparendo vel non respondendo excommunicari potest; beneficio autem privari non debet.'
[8] Bodleian MS. Chs. Oxon. a 5, Ch. 364. This document is unfortunately torn. It dates probably from *c.* 1260.
[9] *Oseney Cart.* ii, no. 1112.
[10] *C.F.*, no. (7); and, e.g., 'Charters and Muniments belonging to the Marquis of Anglesey', cal. I. H. Jeayes, *Collections for a History of Staffordshire*, ed. Staffs. Rec. Soc. (1937), no. 58 (hereafter cited as 'Burton Chs.'), where the rest of the

Excommunication was used mainly against contumacious laymen. The ordinance of William the Conqueror, probably of 1072, stipulated excommunication as the punishment for not answering a triple citation before the Church courts.[1] Excommunication, and possibly an order to pay costs, may have composed the 'tota poena' which was inflicted on Ivo Wint' (? of Winchester), a layman, for contumacy in a suit against the abbot and convent of Beaulieu about a tenement.[2] The person who remained for more than forty days under sentence of excommunication was liable to be arrested and imprisoned by a writ of 'de excommunicato capiendo' directed to the sheriff, but it is difficult to form any opinion of the actual effect of excommunication at this time.[3]

Following the Roman law practice, in lawsuits of real action over property, interim judgement could be passed against a contumacious party after a summary investigation.[4] Such decisions provided the plaintiff with possession of the thing sought for a year's duration, subject to the case being reopened within this time. If the suit was reopened, the defendant had to pay the costs which he had previously incurred; if the case was dropped, the plaintiff, after the lapse of a year and without further investigation, was declared to be the right and true possessor.[5] The obvious contumacy of Ingeram, a rector of Rousham (Oxon.), in a suit against Oseney resulted in a judgement of the tithes in dispute *causa rei servande* to the abbot and convent.[6] When the bishop and chapter of Le Mans (Sarthe, France) did not

defendants, who had been contumacious, are peremptorily cited to appear to put forth dilatory exceptions on the second court day.

[1] *Die Gesetze der Angelsachsen*, i, ed. F. Liebermann (Halle, 1903), 485.
[2] Beaulieu Cart., f. 136ʳ.
[3] R. Phillimore, *The Ecclesiastical Law of the Church of England*, ii, 2nd edn. (1895), 964. Cf. Curialis, '*Ordo*', *Quellen zur Geschichte*, i, pt. iii, ed. L. Wahrmund (Innsbruck, 1905), i, p. 29. On the whole subject, see F. D. Logan, *Excommunication and the Secular Arm in Mediaeval England* (Pontifical Institute of Mediaeval Studies, Studies and Texts, 15, Toronto, 1968).
[4] R. W. Lee, *Elements of Roman Law*, 3rd edn. (1952), p. 442; P. J. Schierse, 'Legislation on Sequestration in Roman Law and in the Decretals of Gregory IX', *The Jurist*, xxiii (1963), 291–313, esp. 306; X. II. 15: 'De eo qui mittitur in possessionem causa rei servande', and esp. c. 3. X. II. 6 (Inn. III): 'Si lite non contestata reus est contumax, si fieri potest, mittitur actor in possessionem causa custodiae; alias reus excommunicabitur.' For forms, see A, f. 271ᵛ, col. i; B, f. 79ᵛ, cols. i–ii; L, f. 65ᵛ, col. ii; C, f. 119ʳ, cols. i–ii; and *C.F.*, no. (8).
[5] Tancred, p. 137. [6] *Oseney Cart.* iv, nos. 156 A and B (cf. C and D).

come to the hearing of a suit, nor commission a proctor to act on their behalf, the judges, Stephen, prior of St. Swithun's, and Guy, prior of Southwick, declared in favour of the dean of Salisbury's possession of the lesser tithes of Deverill (Wilts.), *causa rei servande*. Three weeks before the statutory year, the proctor of the bishop and chapter of Le Mans, Wimund of Deverill, appeared and promised to stand in judgement. But against his oath he was again contumaciously absent on the day appointed for the parties to appear, and a final sentence was given in favour of the dean.[1] Some time before 1214, the archdeacon of Exeter and his fellow judges delegate were said by R(ichard de Hegham), archdeacon of Essex, one of the parties, to have proceeded illegally in giving R. Peverel a portion of the church of Ermington (Devon), *causa rei servande*, because their jurisdiction had at that time been revoked.[2] When the rector of Withersfield (Suff.) was contumacious, he was at first fined, and then suffered a judgement *causa rei servande* against him. If he would not pay the one mark fine for the expenses of the opposing party or resisted the *missio in possessionem*, he was to be suspended.[3] These interim judgements were frequent in England, and they must have contributed to a respect for the efficiency of the canon law. For Scotland Lord Cooper records two unusual instances concerning judgements *causa rei servande*. In one instance the defendant appeared before the judges, but refused to reply, and was therefore guilty of verbal contumacy. Interim possession was awarded to the plaintiff, which became *vera possessio*.[4] In the other the judges delegate, being advised that an order of *missio in possessionem* would be attended by risk of bloodshed, placed the defendant's lands under interdict instead.[5]

After Hugh de Bilney, a clerk, had waited in vain for three months at Rome for his adversary Thomas to appear

---

[1] *Vetus registrum Sarisberiense . . . Register of S. Osmund*, i, ed. W. H. Rich Jones (R.S. lxxviii, 1883), pp. 354–6, and for another instance of this practice in operation see Belvoir, Large Cart., f. 77ʳ and Small Cart., p. 29, where the priory of Belvoir was granted an interim *missio* and was then finally adjudged the tithes in question. [2] *Montacute Cart.*, no. 143.
[3] Windsor Ch. xi G 37 (3). On this suit see App. B (ii), p. 315. [4] Cooper, *Select Scottish Cases*, p. 36. [5] Ibid., pp. 9–10.

and answer about the church of Kimberley (Norf.), a mandate was sent to the abbot of Dereham ordering him to
condemn Thomas in costs as contumacious unless he could
show lawful impediment for his failure to appear.[1] In such
an instance the case may well have gone by default; for
contumacy could have an effect on the disposition of the
cause itself, although the judgement usually depended on
other supports as well. A sentence was passed on John,
chaplain of the church of Sedlescombe (Suss.), by W., abbot
of Combwell, and F., prior of Leeds; John had absented
himself throughout the case and had not sent a proctor to
make reply. It was decided that he ought not to take tithes
from the monks of Robertsbridge, and perpetual silence was
imposed on him about them. In this case the judges took
counsel of wise and discreet men, and they also examined
Robertsbridge's privileges about the tithes.[2] When the prior
and convent of Chepstow contumaciously did not appear to
hear sentence (nor probably previously), the archdeacon of
St. Albans, a subdelegate of the prior, did not hesitate to
promulgate sentence against them and in favour of the
abbot and convent of Holy Cross, Waltham, in the conventual church of St. Albans on 25 July 1251. The judge acted,
he said, after hearing the intention and proofs of Waltham
and having taken the advice of men who were learned in the
law.[3] These are cases where the defendant was contumacious. If the *actor*, on the other hand, having ignored the
first round of citations, still refused to come when cited a
year later, sentence would automatically be declared against
him.[4]

Forms of letters, which were used for absolving the
contumacious from the penalties that they had incurred, are
provided in the Canterbury formulary.[5] In these examples
the rural dean was ordered to absolve the penitent, when he

---

[1] *Reg. Greg. IX*, no. 4803, where the mandate is addressed to the archdeacon of
Dereham; but since there was no such archdeacon, this would seem to be a mistake
for the abbot of Dereham, or, possibly but less likely, for the archdeacon of Norfolk.

[2] B.M. Egerton Ch. 382.

[3] B.M. Egerton Ch. 409 (App. B (ii), no. 7). Cf. *Oseney Cart.* iv, no. 415c,
where Thomas de Boues, rector of Harwell (Berks.), was contumacious, and sentence was given against him on 7 Aug. 1217.

[4] Magdalen College, Oxford, Steyning Ch. 16, cal. *Sele Cart.*, no. 25.

[5] *C.F.*, no. (9), and cf. Curialis, '*Ordo*', xx, p. 10.

had offered security to attend the court. A form for restoring possession is also given.[1]

(ii) *The Libel, Exceptions, and Altercations*

Once in court, the defendant heard the libel or *editio*.[2] In some instances the papal letters were used as an *editio*, as in a suit between the convents of Bullington (Lincs.) and Garendon (Leics.) in 1251.[3] The libel was expected to contain the following information:

> Conventi nomen et nomen convenientis
> Iudicis et nomen scribes causamque petendi
> Et quascumque petas res, omnes scribere debes,[4]

and had to be in writing.[5] Libels are frequently quoted in full.[6] This, for instance, was the libel that the proctor of the abbot and convent of St. Valéry delivered to the rector of Hinton Waldrist (Berks.) in 1239–40:

> Ego procurator . . . propono quod ipse ecclesiam sancti Walerici decimis provenientiis de dominico quondam Walteri, Widonis et Reginaldi patronorum sancti Walerici contra justiciam spoliavit, unde peto dictas decimas prefatis abbati et monachis restitueri et prefatum rectorem ad restitutionem perceptorum, que decem marcas sterlingorum estimo, condempnari. Hoc dico salvo jure addendi et cetera.[7]

The written *intentio* of the plaintiff, James, rector of Charwelton (Northants.), against the abbot and convent of Biddlesden (Cist. Bucks.) is quoted in a document of 1253:

> . . . recitata partis attricis intentione sub forma subscripta concepta, 'Coram vobis domine precentor de Bernewell [Barnwell, Aug. Cambs.] judex a domino papa delegate, petit Petrus Fannel procurator domini Jacobi rectoris ecclesie de Charewolton quatinus compellatis dominos

---

[1] *C.F.*, no. (10).
[2] Windsor Ch. xi G 14.
[3] P.R.O. E 135/6/13 (App. B (ii), no. 2), and cf. Alvingham Cart., f. 5ʳ (App. B (ii), no. 1) and above, p. 72.
[4] Arnulphus, xii, p. 16. Cf. *Henrici de Segusio Cardinalis Hostiensis Summa Aurea* (Lyons, 1597), lib. ii, p. 91ᵛ.
[5] c. 1. *X*. II. 3. For forms see Arnulphus, pp. 15–20.
[6] e.g. Pershore Cart., ff. 111ᵛ, 113ʳ; West Dereham Cart., f. 60ᵛ; P.R.O. E 42/384; B.M. Stowe Ch. 58; and Thorney Cart. ii, f. 257ᵛ.
[7] New College, Oxford, Takeley Ch. 229. St. Valéry was a Benedictine abbey in the diocese of Amiens (Cottineau, ii, col. 2912).

abbatem et conventum de Bitlesdene et sentencialiter condempnetis eosdem ad solvend' decimas minutas provenientes de manerio . . .'[1]

He sought other things also in several articles.

The final phrase 'salvo sibi jure mutandi vel minuendi vel addendi' follows a set form that allowed the plaintiff to change the libel, to add to it, or to withdraw part of it, up to the moment of contesting the suit.[2] It concluded the series of articles of which the libel consisted. When William of Englefield (Berks.), knight, had delivered his libel, he declared that he would prove either or both of his accusations.[3] If a declaration of what was sought was omitted from the libel, the defendant could appeal;[4] and Innocent III also declared that precision should be aimed at, especially in real actions: 'Quum agitur reali, non sufficit rem generaliter peti, sed debet ita specificari, ut evitetur obscuritas et aequivocatio.'[5] It was usual to include an article seeking expenses, those already incurred and those yet to be incurred, and damages.[6] Roger, rector of Oddington (Oxon.), in his *editio*, sought three marks yearly as expenses,[7] but it was not wise to exaggerate the claim or to be too specific on this point early in the suit.[8]

The defendant did not have to give an answer immediately. He might ask for *inducie deliberatorie*, a term of twenty days, to decide whether he was answering the case or not, and, if he was replying, to decide on his defence.[9] The defendant Peter applied for this period of delay and was granted it by the judges, in his suit with the convent of Alvingham.[10] An entry in the St. Neots cartulary, 'Elapsis postea legitimis induciis deliberandi super eodem libello propositis', shows another instance where the requested delay was granted.[11] The writer of the Canterbury formulary says, however, that

[1] B.M. Harley Ch. 84 F 45. Cf. the *intentio* recited in Norwich Ch. 680, where the prior and convent sought two parts of all the tithes from the demesne of Hubert de Ria the first in Swanton (Norf.).

[2] See *C.F.*, no. (1); Windsor Chs. xi G 15, and xi G 37 (4) (App. B (ii), no. 6); and Warter Cart., f. 46ᵛ.

[3] B.M. Add. Ch. 20372 (App. B (iv), no. 7).

[4] c. 49. *X.* II. 28 (Inn. III).   [5] c. 2. *X.* II. 3, and cf. c. 3.

[6] Dover Cart., ff. 50ᵛ, 51ʳ; cf. Bodleian MS. Chs. Oxon. a 8, Ch. 29b.

[7] *Thame Cart.*, no. 37.   [8] c. 1. *X.* II. 11 (Greg. IX).

[9] B.M. Royal MS. 10 B iv, f. 59ʳ (see above, p. 46 n. 2).

[10] Alvingham Cart., f. 5ʳ (App. B (ii), no. 1).   [11] St. Neots Cart., f. 130ᵛ.

this term could be denied to the defendant if a full account of the charge had been included in the citatory letters.[1] This reflected the decision of Celestine III in 1193: 'Induciae deliberatoriae denegantur reo, si per literas citatorias plene potuit instrui, et deliberare super eo, de quo quaeritur.'[2] When the proctor of Bec added to his first charge the allegation that the rector of Withersfield had despoiled the convent over six years, the rector sought another period of *inducie deliberatorie*, but the judge ruled against the application.[3] If it was a minor change, a further delay could be refused, but if it was an important addition to the libel, the defendant was usually allowed a new period in which to decide whether to withdraw from or press on with the suit in its altered form.[4]

As soon as the defendant appeared in court he could put forward dilatory or peremptory exceptions.[5] A dilatory exception was directed not against the right on which the action was founded, but against the conduct of the action; while a peremptory exception could relieve the defendant from the duty of contesting the suit, and might be instrumental in deciding it. The loser in a dilatory or peremptory exception was ordinarily punished by being condemned to pay the consequent costs.[6]

Even if the greater number of dilatory exceptions were frivolous and disallowed, instances remain of bona fide objections, which to some extent seem to justify this procedure. Out of numerous dilatory exceptions that were put forward by the rector of Withersfield, the judge accepted three as worthy of discussion and quashed the rest.[7] The three accepted were that the acts in question were invalid, seeing that they contained conflicting evidence, that the papal letters were not valid, because at the time of impetration the cause was not imminent, and that furthermore the rector

[1] *C.F.*, no. (1).
[2] c. 2. *X*. II. 8.
[3] Windsor Ch. xi G 37(4) (App. B (ii), no. 6).
[4] c. 3. *X*. II. 8 (1220).
[5] See W. W. Buckland, *Textbook of Roman Law from Augustus to Justinian*, 3rd edn., revsd. P. Stein (Cambridge, 1963), p. 656; and Collinet, *Procédure par libelle*, pp. 304–15.
[6] cc. 5, 6. *X*. II. 14 (Inn. III). In the same way the loser of the principal cause or main issue was usually bound to pay the expenses, c. 17. *X*. I. 34 (Greg. IX).
[7] Windsor Ch. xi G 37(10).

had been summoned before several different judges over this negotiation. The triple exception of the abbot and convent of Bec, which was put forward by their proctors Peter of Swyncombe and John of Bledlow against the prior and convent of Dover in 1245, alleged that the letters of Dover's proctor could not be counted as valid, because they lacked the necessary clause *judicatum solvi*, because they did not express the name of the proctor, and because they were not sealed by the prior. This was accepted by the judges. Consequently the judges deemed that the prior and convent of Dover were unrepresented, and thus guilty of contumacy until then, and as such they ordered them to pay two marks sterling expenses within twenty days, otherwise they would be censured further. A mandate was sent by the judges to the dean of Dover ordering him to compel the prior and convent to pay or to suspend them, and to summon them to appear on 22 September to answer Bec in the continuation of the suit. The document reporting this is dated 26 July 1245 in the church of Pinner (Middx.).[1]

A decretal of Innocent III stated that all dilatory exceptions were to be put forward on or before a day to be arranged by the judges, and that none was to be admitted afterwards.[2] As soon as the libel had been read, this day was fixed. A document dated on the day after Palm Sunday in Norwich cathedral contains much information about dilatory exceptions. On this day Philip de Fleg, rector of Waxham (Norf.), appeared personally and proposed certain dilatory exceptions, seeking a day for proposing them all, whereupon he was granted the day after 'Quasimodo' Sunday.[3] The year in which this took place is not known, but the lapse of time would have been a fortnight. Compared with this, an *actum* dated at Lichfield in the cathedral church on the Wednesday

---

[1] Windsor Ch. xi G 27 (App. B(ii), no. 3).

[2] c. 4. *X*. II. 25. See also Tancred, p. 142; and, e.g., B.M. Harley Ch. 75 B 2: 'Facta est eis sufficiens editio de terris et rebus aliis super quibus eis injuriari dicebantur, et postea prefixus est eis dies ad omnes exceptiones dilatorias que sibi competerent proponendas'; Harley Ch. 84 F 43: 'Cum datus esset dies ad proponendum omnes exceptiones dilatorias . . .'; Harley Ch. 84 F 36; Windsor Ch. xi G 16; and 'Burton Chs.' 58.

[3] Bodleian MS. Chs. Norfolk a 6, Ch. 624. This was not the first day on which the suit was heard. The document refers to the names of the other defendants as being included 'in actis primi diei litis'.

before the feast of St. Leonard (4 November) 1248 stipulated that, with the consent of the parties, the Thursday after the feast of St. Nicholas (10 December) (thus about a month later) had been agreed upon for proposing all dilatory exceptions and proceeding as the law should dictate; meanwhile peace was to be preserved between the parties.[1] In the Alvingham suit, a delay of about two and a half months was granted. The parties appeared before the judges on 17 July 1245 in the chapel of St. Michael at Malton, and were told that 7 October was the final day for proposing all dilatory exceptions.[2] On the day appointed for proposing all dilatory exceptions, Marcellus, rector of Dalham (Suff.), the defendant in a case with the abbot and convent of Bec, was absent. The judge therefore declared that it would no longer be possible for him to propose them, and he ordered him to be cited again to contest the suit.[3]

When the exceptions had been put forward and admitted, they were argued over and discussed, presumably on the same day, until some decision was reached, but sometimes a separate day was appointed. The judges, the master of the schools at Malton, and the subprior of Kirkham and the dean of Buckrose, who were subdelegates, wishing to think more fully about the exceptions which had been proposed by Peter, parson of Stainton, appointed 5 November for discussing them. On 12 November 1245, again in the chapel at Malton, the judges after taking counsel refused to admit the exceptions, and declared that on 4 December the suit should be contested in front of the principal judges, the master of the schools at Malton and the priors of Bridlington and Kirkham, in the church of Winthorpe (Notts.).[4]

An exception against the claim of Richard, rector of Odell (Beds.), who asserted that half of the tithes near Woodend and of Allegho belonged to him, was proved by the defendants, the prior and convent of Canons Ashby. They produced an instrument of a former decision before judges delegate, in which it was shown that the tithes had been adjudged to them. Such a peremptory exception over the

[1] Bodleian MS. Chs. Oxon a 1, Ch. 11.   [2] Alvingham Cart., f. 5ᵛ.
[3] Windsor Ch. xi G 16 (App. B (ii), no. 4).
[4] Alvingham Cart., f. 5ᵛ (App. B (ii), no. 5).

thing in judgement, *res judicata*,[1] if sufficiently supported by evidence, could decide the case, as in this instance, when the judges, after satisfying themselves on the authenticity of the document, absolved the prior and convent from the petition of the *actor*.[2] Similarly after Walter, successor of Th', rector of Easton (Suffolk), had impetrated letters to the prior of St. Frideswide's and other judges, the abbot and convent of St. John, Colchester, placed an exception (*res judicata*), saying that the letters included no mention of a former sentence in their favour. This plea was not admitted by the judges, and so an appeal was made, Colchester obtaining letters to the prior of Holy Trinity, Ipswich, and others.[3] The final exception of four, put forward by Peter, parson of St. Andrew's, Stainton, against the convent of Alvingham, namely that having been properly presented to the church and instituted in it he was entitled to the fruits thereof, was held to be peremptory by Alvingham. And seeing that this statement was a direct contradiction of their assertion that they held the church, the prior and convent of Alvingham claimed that the suit was contested. It was not, however, accepted, at least at a later date, that through a peremptory exception the suit was automatically contested.[4]

Frequently altercations are recorded: 'post multas altercationes', 'diutius esset altercatum', 'per multum tempus inter ipsos esset in judicio altercatum super premissis', and altercations usually meant delays.[5] After many altercations the rector of Odell confessed that he had no right to the tithes of Stockinge, Woodend, and of the land which Walter the forester held.[6] Altercations could be over any point, and so might come before or after the contestation of the suit. Sometimes they concerned dilatory exceptions, as was recorded in the Christchurch (Twynham) cartulary.[7] The proctors of Bec and Tewkesbury engaged in long altercations over exceptions in 1233–4 in Dunstable priory

---

[1] *D.* xliv. 2; and *Lib. Pauperum*, viii, tit. 32.   [2] P.R.O. E 135/21/33.

[3] P.R.O. E 42/384. See also O, f. 224ʳ, cols. i–ii, where a peremptory exception was dimissed by the judges and sentence declared in favour of the plaintiff.

[4] c. 2. 6. II. 3 (Bon. VIII).

[5] e.g. Bradenstoke Cart., f. 105ʳ; P.R.O. E 40/14198; and *St. Frideswide's Cart.* ii, no. 980.

[6] Canons Ashby Cart., f. 110ᵛ.   [7] Christchurch Cart., f. 92ʳ.

church.[1] Prolonged altercations concerned the payment of arrears in a suit about tithes between Daventry priory and Thomas, rector of Lubbenham (Leics.).[2] Thomas agreed that he ought to pay six and a half marks yearly for tithes as had been decided before judges delegate of Innocent III,[3] but he insisted that he had only ceased payment because of war. The prior and convent of Daventry also sought four marks debt for non-payment. It was finally agreed that Thomas should pay the six and a half marks yearly in future and that the charge about arrears should be dropped.[4]

4. 'Litis Contestatio'

The contestation of the suit had now been reached. The name and concept of the *litis contestatio* were adopted from the sources of late Roman law.[5] The main purpose of citing the parties was to see if the suit was contested. The *litis contestatio* was an important stage in the procedure. It consisted of the narration or accusation by the plaintiff, and the definite, contradictory, and opposing reply to this, which was made by the defendant in court,[6] such as this example:

. . . facta est litis contestatio in hunc modum: videlicet quod predictus T. actor petiit capellam, decimas et obventiones omnes de Gatesbir' tanquam pertinentes ad ecclesiam suam de Westmeln' jure parrochiali, quas priorem et canonicos sancte Trinitatis London' injuste detinere dicebat occupatas, mere intendens petitorium. Procurator vero dictorum prioris et canonicorum sancte Trinitatis litem contestando respondit quod memorata capella, decime et obventiones de Gatesbir' jure parrochiali spectabant ad ecclesiam suam de Brakyng', eo quod villa de Gatesbir' tota sita esset infra limites parrochie sue de Braking', et etiam eadem ecclesia in possessione erat tam capelle quam decimarum

---

[1] Canterbury, Cartae Antiquae, L 381.

[2] Daventry Cart., f. 150ᵛ.

[3] Ibid., f. 151ʳ.

[4] In 1245 the same case came before the official of Lincoln, and there was a new settlement (f. 152ʳ). In 1289 Daventry conceded these tithes from the fee of Hugh Poherius to the then rector for a sum of money.

[5] C. iii. 9; Collinet, *Procédure par libelle*, chapter vi, section ii; Buckland, *Textbook of Roman Law*, pp. 632, 667, 695; and *D.D.C.* iv, cols. 475 ff.

[6] Tancred, pp. 196–201, and cf. P.R.O. E 40/14953: '. . . Intentione prioris et monachorum contra eundem W. et responsione ejusdem W. ad intentionem eorumdem prioris et conventus . . .'

et obventionum predictarum et ita ad ecclesiam de Westmeln' minime pertinebant.[1]

The formal contradiction signified legally the commencement of the process, and that there was bona fide contention between the parties. Without this there could be no case:

Non per positiones et responsiones, sed per petitionem in iure propositam et responsionem secutam fit litis contestatio, qua omissa nullus est processus.[2]

An agreement to come to a composition or to submit to an ordination would remove the necessity of contesting the suit;[3] and if there was no contested case, there could be no proof or sentence. As the *Decretales* stated, 'lite non contestata non procedatur ad testium receptionem vel ad sententiam diffinitivam'.[4] In a formulary example, when ordering delegates to hear witnesses if they are too infirm to come to court, the judges send a copy of the *litis contestatio* with their seals appended to it to prove that the suit had been contested.[5]

The oath of calumny, which was taken over from the Roman law, was sworn after the suit had been contested.[6] It was probably omitted unless specifically requested on the motion of one of the parties. Notices of it are rare. It was intended to prevent chicanery and vexatious litigation. The plaintiff promised that he had not brought the case in bad faith, and that he would not produce false instruments, corrupt the judges, or ask for unnecessary delays; the defendant, for his part, swore to conduct his defence in an equally honest manner.[7] In 1237 Otto, the legate in England, enacted that the oath should be taken, because after it the truth was more easily shown and cases were more quickly terminated.[8] On 16 April 1238 Gregory IX wrote to the prior

---

[1] P.R.O. E 212/28, and cf. Canterbury, Cartae Antiquae, L 351.
[2] c. l. *X*. II. 5 (Greg. IX). For this see, e.g., B.M. Harley Ch. 84 F 45; Warter Cart., f. 46ᵛ; and *Malmesbury Reg.* i. 388: 'Dictorum vero abbatis et conventus procurator *litem contestando* reddit quod . . .'
[3] e.g. Abingdon Cart., f. 90ᵛ; *Glos. Cart.* i, no. ccxxxvi.
[4] c. l. *X*. II. 6.   [5] *C.F.*, no. (22).
[6] See *C.* ii. 58(59); *Lib. Pauperum*, ii, tit. 40; 'De Iuramento Calumniae', title 7. *X*. II; Tancred, pp. 201–7; Fournier, p. 175; and St. Neots Cart., f. 130ᵛ: '. . . facta litis contestatione juramento etiam de calumpnia subsecuto . . .'
[7] Fournier, p. 175.   [8] *C.S.* ii, pt. i. 256, no. [24].

and convent of Christ Church, Canterbury, allowing them
to force their adversaries to take this oath and the oath *de
veritate dicenda*, provided that they were willing to take them
themselves.[1] Either the parties or their proctors, if it was
specified in the proctorial constitution, might take the oath.[2]
The prior and convent of Alvingham granted this power to
their proctors in 1245: 'concedentes eisdem plenam potestatem jurandi in animam nostram de calumpnia'.[3] The oath
de veritate dicenda, of speaking the truth, and not the oath
of calumny, was taken in the thirteenth century in spiritual
causes.[4] It enforced the oath-taker to say only what he knew
to be true.

The Proof

If the defendant denied the charge and contested the suit,
the plaintiff was given a probatory term in which to prove
his case.[5] Similarly if the defendant put forward exceptions
and they were accepted by the judges, it was his duty to
prove them within the term which was assigned to him.
Interrogatories, or positions, were devised to help towards
the proof. The plaintiff, on a day appointed by the judge
after the oath of calumny or *de veritate dicenda* had been
taken, set forth a series of separate allegations which he had
extracted from the libel. He then demanded from his adversary on oath the answer of 'Yes' or 'No' to each one of these.
The answers were the *responsiones*. The aim of positions was
to fix neatly the points on which the parties disagreed, and
to expose exactly what was to be proved.[6] The judges' duty
at this stage was to separate and elucidate the opposing
statements. The onus of proof was on the *actor*.[7] Negative
proof was not accepted, and the aim of the *actor* was to get
his adversary to make an admission, or several admissions,
that irrefutably proved his case.

---

[1] Lambeth Palace Library, Papal Documents, no. 33.
[2] cc. 3, 4. *X*. II. 7 (Eug. III), c. 3. 6. II. 4, and, e.g., *Reg. Antiq. Linc.* ii, no. 386.
[3] Alvingham Cart., f. 5ʳ.
[4] Fournier, p. 176; c. 2. *X* II. 7; and *C.S.* ii, pt. i. 256, no. [24].
[5] *Ecclesiastical Courts*, p. 15.
[6] Fournier, pp. 178–80. See also Collinet, *Procédure par libelle*, pp. 354–5.
[7] Fournier, pp. 176, 178. The canon law took over the Roman maxims: 'Actore
non probante reus absolvitur', and 'Onus probandi incumbit ei qui dicit'.

To commence the proof, each party collected evidence for its case. Evidence was of two kinds: oral, that is the attestations of the parties and of the witnesses, and written, consisting of the information provided by authentic charters. In most cases both varieties of evidence were used to build up the whole proof, and the judges reported:

> . . . propositis, auditis et intellectis attestationibus, instrumentis necnon et rationibus utriusque partis, cum, tam per depositiones testium quam per rationes necnon per inspectiones instrumentorum coram nobis in jure exibitorum, nobis constaret evidenter . . .[1]

Evidence was sent to the *Curia* for suits that were to be decided there. In 1251 a mandate was dispatched from Pope Innocent IV to the bishop of Ely, ordering him to have careful transcripts made and forwarded to the *Curia* of the evidence of the dean and chapter of Hereford in their dispute with Bishop Peter of Aigueblanche.[2]

The oral attestation of witnesses was placed as first rank evidence.[3] When the nuns of Godstow asserted that the croft whose tithes were claimed by Robert, parson of Wytham (Berks.), was not within the boundaries of his parish, and that in any case they had exemption by papal privilege because the croft was newly brought into cultivation, they went on to bring forward witnesses and to prove it, so that the sentence followed in their favour.[4] Because of the necessity of giving witnesses due warning to appear, the judges appointed a distinct and separate court day for their production. Letters were sent to them, ordering them to come and cautioning them to give true testimony.[5] A letter in the Lambeth formulary threatens a witness with punishment for contumacy if he should be absent.[6]

On arrival before the court, the witnesses were sworn in. Admission, as it was called, was followed by examination.

---

[1] P.R.O. E 40/14953.

[2] *Charters and Records of Hereford Cathedral*, ed. W. W. Capes (Hereford, 1908), p. 89.

[3] See *D.* xxii. 5; *C.* iv. 20; and *Lib. Pauperum*, iv, tit. 17. In some cases a jury might be used, see, e.g., New College, Oxford, Writtle Ch. 401.

[4] *Godstow Reg.* i, no. [31]. Cf. Exeter Cart., p. 54, where the proof of several witnesses on oath produced a sentence, and, e.g., Canterbury, Cartae Antiquae, L 351: 'cum nobis postmodum per testes idoneos de jure constaret Cant' ecclesie . . .'

[5] See Wells, Lib. Albus, i, f. 97ᵛ; and *C.F.*, no. (20).   [6] A, f. 271ᵛ, col. iii.

The witnesses were asked specific questions, sometimes framed so as to produce definite answers of 'yes' or 'no'. Witnesses of both sides might be interviewed, those of the plaintiff coming first. They were heard separately and in private,[1] either by the judge or by a commissioner deputed to act for him, who on occasion might take attestations on the spot in order to save the expense of bringing witnesses to court.[2] Meanwhile the clerk was busy noting their replies.[3] In a form in the Cirencester formulary showing how witnesses' attestations were to be recorded, Ralph the chaplain stated on oath that he was present in the church of Cerney when Robert de Rameseia promised to pay 100s. to Robert Pictor at certain times, and that he had watched Robert swear on the altar to keep to this arrangement. Asked about the day and the time, he said that he did not remember except that it was a good while before Easter. Samson the chaplain, on oath, agreed with this testimony, but he could not recall whether it happened before or after Easter.[4]

A singular feature of early attestations is the large number of witnesses who were called upon to give evidence. In a case heard at Rome between the archdeacon of Canterbury and the monks of St. Augustine's, the archdeacon's witnesses were more numerous than the monks', but the delegates were ordered to give judgement for the monks if the quality of their witnesses was better.[5] To remedy a state of affairs which was wasting the time of the courts, Innocent III legislated that not more than forty witnesses might be pro-

[1] Gratia of Arezzo, 'Summa de Iudiciario Ordine' in Pillii, Tancredi, Gratiae Libri de Iudiciorum Ordine, ed. F. Bergmann (Göttingen, 1842), p. 371; R. Burn, Ecclesiastical Law, iii, revsd. R. Phillimore, 9th edn. (1842), 310; and P.R.O. E 135/4/17. The hearing in private was contrary to the Roman law procedure of Justinian.

[2] c. 8. X. II. 20 (Eug. III), and c. 52 (Hon. III). See also St. Frideswide's Cart. ii, no. 820, where the abbot of Pipewell and the prior of St. Andrew's, Northampton, examined witnesses on behalf of Pandulf; and B.M. Add. MS. 8167, f. 119ʳ, a formulary example.

[3] Warter Cart., f. 46ᵛ: 'Unde judices testes quos utraque pars duxerat producendos admiserunt, et eosdem diligenter examinaverunt, et eorum dicta in scriptis redigerunt . . .'; and Ecclesiastical Courts, p. 15.

[4] O, f. 224ʳ, col. i. An example of the testimonies of ten men survives from a suit between Lewes priory and the parson of Burnham Thorpe, Norfolk: P.R.O. E 40/14099, cal. Lewes Cart. N.P., no. 72; and of some attestations before arbiters in Belvoir, Small Cart., pp. 36–7.

[5] Letters of Inn. III, no. 659.

duced in any one case.[1] In about 1244 the chapter of Wells appealed to the pope, saying that the subdelegates of the priors of Chacombe and Wroxton, R., prior of the hospital of St. John at Northampton, and Master Thomas de Skireford, summoned an excessive number of witnesses. They appear to have called on all the canons and vicars of Wells, who it was pleaded were 'numerous and in diverse parts'.[2]

The attestations, or depositions, of the witnesses were published and then disputed by the parties: ' . . . attestationibus publicatis, habita quo sufficienti disputatione in testes et eorum dicta . . .'[3] A separate day was usually chosen for discussing the attestations,[4] and when in 1255 a day was fixed for this purpose by the dean of Chichester, the defendant was cited by the dean of Storrington (Suss.) to appear in court so that the suit could proceed.[5] The published reports of witnesses' attestations were sometimes preserved in case of further dispute:

Et de consensu partium examinandi sunt testes quos utraque pars duxerit producendos per viros fidedignos a partibus eligendos, quorum dicta in scriptis fideliter redacta deponentur in ede sacra apud Stokes sub sigillis examinatorum, ita quod si post decessum dicti rectoris super hoc contingat questionem oriri per hoc possit veritas declarari.[6]

Each party was reponsible for paying the expenses of its own witnesses.[7] When a settlement was made in 1208 between the monks of Bardney and the nuns of Stixwould, it was agreed between the parties that if there should be a further controversy, the expenses of witnesses should be shared.[8]

The most desirable proof was the *confessio in jure*, which

---

[1] c. 37. *X*. II. 22. Cf. *Reg. Antiq. Linc.* iii, no. 759, where the judges speak of examining a 'multitude' of witnesses of both sides, as is the custom.

[2] Wells, Lib. Albus, i, f. 97ᵛ.

[3] Canterbury, *Sede Vacante*, bk. iii, no. 447, p. 156; P.R.O. E 40/14221: '. . . et ad publicationem attestationum perventum fuisset, illis publicatis predicta causa amicabili compositione conquievit . . .'; and Exeter Ch. 815: '. . . et habita sufficienti dispiccione super attestationibus . . .'

[4] Norwich Ch. 1686 (App. B (ii), no. 8), and see O, f. 224ʳ, col. ii, where the day for discussing the depositions was the same as the sentence day.

[5] Magdalen College, Oxford, Findon Ch. 49.

[6] P.R.O. E 40/14036.

[7] *C.F.*, no. (21); and Burn, *Ecclesiastical Law*, iii. 309.

[8] Bardney Cart., ff. 240ʳ-1ʳ.

the plaintiff endeavoured to extract from his adversary.[1] It had to be conceded voluntarily or it would be held invalid, and it had to be made before the judge in the adversary's presence.[2] Confessions were frequently given. On the day that was selected for the production of witnesses by the prior of Monkton Farleigh and the prior and dean of Malmesbury in 1227, the defendant, Osbert, vicar of Tew (Oxon.), confessed that he had no right to the tithes in question.[3] In a suit which was brought against them by the abbot and convent of Bec in 1225, Laurence and William, rectors of the church of Wimborne All Hallows (Dorset), made a confession, 'tam ex inspectione instrumentorum quam vicinie fama'.[4]

The *confessio in jure* could be made at any point in the procedure, a fact illustrative of its accepted importance. In 1237 in Chichester cathedral, Milo, vicar of West Greenwich, made a confession before contestation of the suit had taken place, admitting that the things which were sought by the abbot and convent of Bayham in their edition belonged to them:

Cum igitur coram nobis in dicta causa isset usque ad litem precise contestandam legittime processum, demum dictus vicarius dictorum abbatis et conventus in judicio plene confitebatur intentionem, dicens res petitas prout in editione continentur ad dictos abbatem et conventum de jure pertinere. Qua confessione coram nobis in judicio legittime facta, omnia in dicta editione contenta dictis abbati et conventui sentencialiter adjudicavimus, in omnibus ordine juris observato . . .[5]

Very often, as in a St. Neots case, a confession was linked with other proofs, and the judgement was made on a broad basis,[6] although a sentence could follow immediately on a confession without any other supporting evidence. When

---

[1] See *C.* vii. 59: *D.* xlii. 2; *Lib. Pauperum*, vii, tit. 55; and Burn, *Ecclesiastical Law*, iii. 324.

[2] c. 3. *X.* II. 18 (Greg. IX), and see, e.g., St. John's College, Oxford, Ch. xix. 2: '. . . partibus coram nobis [the judges] in judicio constitutis, prenominate capelle rector Philippus spontanea et mera voluntate sua recognovit . . .', and Bodleian MS. Dodsworth 76, f. 1.

[3] Bradenstoke Cart., f. 147ᵛ.   [4] Windsor Ch. xi G 12.

[5] Bayham Cart., f. 60ᵛ, and see Pipewell Cart. (A), f. 31ᵛ, for a charter of confession of Reginald, rector of Desborough (Northants.), in a case against Pipewell.

[6] St. Neots Cart., f. 111ᵛ (2 examples). See also Canterbury, Cartae Antiquae, C 1270, and *St. Frideswide's Cart.* ii, no. 732.

Richard, chaplain of 'Crucheston' (? Cruxton in Maiden Newton, Dorset), confessed that he had paid and ought to pay eight shillings yearly to the church of Bruton (Som.) for the chapel of Cruxton, sentence was declared against him at once.[1]

Literal proof in the form of instruments could be produced at any moment before the *conclusio in causa*, when the judges declared that no more evidence might be put forward.[2] Such documentary proof was frequently employed and was obviously important.[3] The abbot and convent of Cormeilles (Ben. dioc. Lisieux, France), whose documents had been burnt in a fire, pleaded with Gregory IX for a mandate to certain ecclesiastics ordering them to examine witnesses and take depositions about the convent's possessions, in order that they might have new documentary evidence compiled, because, as they said, they feared a lawsuit. The request was granted, and the abbots of Strata Florida and Valle Crucis and the prior of Valle Crucis were ordered to set about this task.[4] Many suits were conveniently brought to an end by the production and inspection of instruments.[5] In the Alvingham suit charters were produced of the patron of the church of Stainton, of the bishop of Lincoln, of the chapter of Lincoln, and of the archbishop of Canterbury.[6] Faced with this kind of proof, the party could only recognize the right of its adversary after inspecting the authenticity of the documents. Alexander, parson of Kerdiston (Norf.), on inspecting the original deeds and noting the other proofs of Lewes, declared publicly that he would not claim any right again to the said tithes from the demesne of William of Kerdiston on behalf of his church.[7] Roger de Lurdingdedale, rector of Lenham (Kent), was forced to resign the prebend of Guston when he saw the letters which he had made on receiving the farm and also the letters of a

[1] *Bruton Cart.*, no. 282.
[2] c. 9. *X.* II. 22 (Inn. III); *C.* iv. 21; *D.* xxii. 4; and *Lib. Pauperum*, iv, tit. 18.
[3] See, e.g., L, f. 66ʳ, col. 1; C, f. 119ʳ, col. ii; Norwich Ch. 1686 (App. B(ii), no. 8); *N.L.C.*, no. 9; and Eye Cart., f. 41ʳ⁻ᵛ.   [4] *Reg. Greg. IX*, no. 1155.
[5] e.g. Leeds Cart., f. 10ᵛ; Northampton, St. Andrew's Cart. (A), ff. 56ʳ–7ʳ; Pipewell Cart. (A), ff. 29ᵛ–31ᵛ; and Dover Cart., f. 226ᵛ: 'Et ad probationem juris sui protulerunt scriptum autenticum H. bone memorie quondam Cant' archiepiscopi . . .'   [6] Alvingham Cart., f. 5ᵛ.
[7] Lewes Cart., f. 255ᵛ, cal. *Lewes Cart. N.P.*, no. 122.

former abbot of St. Augustine's, Canterbury.[1] In 1229 the plaintiff, Master Richard of Wallingford, rector of Cliffe-at-Hoo, after he had inspected the privileges of the convent of Canterbury, renounced his petition about the tithes of two mills, one water mill, sheep folds, and certain lands.[2] In suits which had been before judges delegate and were reopened, the instrument of a former papal settlement sufficed for sentence to be declared immediately. In 1254 the abbot and convent of Westminster exhibited a fifty-five-year-old decision, which had been made by judges delegate appointed by Celestine III, about a pension of five marks owed to them yearly for the church of Bloxham (Oxon.) by the abbess and convent of Godstow.[3] Master Eustace de Normanvilla, rector of Kenardington (Kent), when he had been brought into court by the prior and convent of Dover, showed the document of a former composition. An arrangement was made on this basis, arbiters being appointed to arrange who should possess the tithes not mentioned in the composition.[4]

5. 'Judicium'

When all the evidence had been put before the court, it was time for the judges to appoint a day on which they would give sentence, and to summon the parties to appear before them then.[5] A final or definitive sentence, which decided the cause itself, entailed a condemnation or an absolution.[6] Whereas in one case the parson of Eythorne (Kent) was condemned to pay five shillings yearly,[7] in another the judges pronounced that the abbot and convent of Bardney were absolved from the charge of Richard, clerk of Bassingham (Lincs.) and parson of Burton by Lincoln.[8] Likewise, either the plaintiff was declared to have succeeded in his proof or to have failed in it, 'pronunciamus R. actorem intentionem

---

[1] St. Augustine's Red Book, f. 274ʳ.

[2] Canterbury, Cartae Antiquae, C 280.

[3] Westminster Domesday, f. 379ᵛ, and see f. 378ᵛ also. Cf. P.R.O. E 135/21/33 (see above, pp. 82–3).   [4] Dover Cart., f. 229ᵛ.

[5] See the *Ordo Judiciarius* in B, f. 81ᵛ, col. i, for comments on the citation to the sentence.

[6] *C.* vii. 45; *Lib. Pauperum*, vii, tit. 41; and Fournier, p. 208.

[7] Canterbury, Cartae Antiquae, L 351.   [8] Bardney Cart., f. 203ʳ⁻ᵛ.

suam sufficienter probasse',[1] or 'pronunciamus R. actorem in probatione intentionis sue defecisse'.[2] The prior and convent of Norwich were declared to have proved their intention by the deposition of witnesses on oath and the production of charters, whereas Robert Buttamund, rector of Thornham (Norf.), was said to have failed in his proof and was condemned to pay the wheat, barley, beans, and peas in question, and six marks to cover arrears and expenses.[3] If the charge of the *actor* was proved, silence was imposed on the defendant about the case and vice versa.[4]

The sentence had to be written,[5] and the papal mandate was to be quoted in full.[6] The form of the sentence, which the judges delivered sitting,[7] began with an invocation.[8] Sentence could not be pronounced on a feast day, nor when the sun had gone down.[9] Egerton Charter 409 in the British Museum provides a fine example of a clerk's draft up to and including the sentence.[10] There are a number of deletions of words which had been written twice, of omission marks, and of rephrasing attempts. The document is unsealed. It is obvious that most final *acta*, owing to their importance, must have been prepared in rough and then checked and scrutinized. Several introductory paragraphs intimate the necessity of the sentence being in writing. As one document commences:

Universis sancte matris ecclesie filiis ad quos presens scriptum pervenerit . . . prior Christi ecclesie de Thwinham Winton' diocesis salutem in domino. Rerum gestarum series idcirco litteris commendatur ne lapsu temporis humana prolabente memoria ex jam sopite litis materia litem suscitandi posteris occasio preparetur, ne quod provisum est ad concordiam tendat ad noxam et ne innocencie malicia vel ignorancia prejudicium pariat et jacturam sane cum causa que vertebatur . . .,

and although this is the usual kind of 'harangue' it does suggest a basic realization of the threats to which the

---

[1] *C.F.*, no. (23); P.R.O. E 40/14953; and B.M. Cotton MS. Nero C iii, f. 199.

[2] *C.F.*, no. (24); and P.R.O. E 212/28.

[3] Norwich Ch. 1686 (App. B (ii), no. 8).

[4] B.M. Egerton Ch. 382; Bayham Cart., f. 60ᵛ; *Godstow Reg.* i, no. [31]; and A, f. 271ᵛ, col. iii.   [5] *C.F.*, no. (24). See also Arnulphus, i, p. 46.

[6] *C.F.*, no. (23).   [7] Tancred, p. 270.

[8] e.g. Magdalen College, Oxford, Steyning Ch. 16; Alvingham Cart., f. 5ᵛ; and B.M. Harley Ch. 84 F 45.   [9] Tancred, p. 271.   [10] App. B (ii), no. 7.

sentence might be subjected if no authentic record was made.[1] But by no means all suits were terminated by sentences. Many ended with compositions,[2] and some were discontinued. At any point the suit might be discontinued, if the *actor* voluntarily renounced his petition or the *reus* withdrew his defence. Hugh, the abbot, and the convent of Oseney withdrew their suit against the canons of St. Frideswide's, and promised not to renew the controversy.[3] In most cases such withdrawals followed a confession or realization that the opposite party was in the right, as when Hugh de Lunde, rector of Brocklesby (Lincs.), withdrew from his suit against the Cistercian nuns of Nun Cotham in 1238/9.[4] In 1288 Stephen de Tawelle, rector of Westmill (Herts.), renounced his suit on seeing a document of a previous settlement made by judges delegate;[5] and in the same way in about 1221 Master William of Purleigh, rector of Purleigh (Essex), inspected instruments of the nuns of Wix, recognized their right, and renounced his action.[6] These were renunciations by the *actor* as was that of Master Simon of London, rector of Launton, in 1214,[7] that of the prior and convent of Shelford (Aug. Notts.),[8] and that of the prioress and nuns of Stamford, which was made by their proctor, A., chaplain, in about 1217.[9]

If the defendant renounced the continuation of his defence, he might be rewarded or placated by the judges or by the *actor*, and vice versa. For instance, when the proctor of Newton Longville ceded all right on behalf of the convent, the tithes were declared to be Notley's, but Notley were

---

[1] Beaulieu Cart., f. 132^{r–v}. See also St. Neots Cart., f. 130^v; B.M. Cotton MS. Nero C iii f. 199; and *C.F.*, no. (26).

[2] Formularies give examples: A, f. 271^v, col. iii; L, f. 66^r, col. i; C, f. 119^r, col. ii; and B.M. Add. MS. 8167, ff. 96^v–7^r. See also the very careful composition which Richard, prior of Dunstable, arranged between the abbot and convent of Bec and the rector of Withersfield in 1241, after a prolonged and complicated case lasting some six years, Windsor Ch. xi G 22, and Chapter V for some further comments on compositions.

[3] *St. Frideswide's Cart.* ii, no. 703 (dated by Wigram *c.* 1200).

[4] Nun Cotham Cart., f. 38^v.   [5] P.R.O. E 42/232.

[6] P.R.O. E 40/14044(2).   [7] Westminster Ch. 15684.

[8] Castle Acre Cart., f. 47^r (no date).

[9] Canons Ashby Cart., f. 50^r. Cf. Torre Cart., f. 60^v, where M., the prioress, and the convent of Kington St. Michael (Ben. Wilts.) renounced their suit against the abbot and convent of Torre.

ordered to pay twelve and a half marks yearly to Newton.[1] Similarly, when William, clerk of Lewes, renounced his quarrel against Robert of Little Canfield (Essex) about the church of Canfield, Robert gave William three marks.[2] In a suit between the abbot and convent of St. Augustine, Canterbury, and Henry, archdeacon of Canterbury, about the churches of Milton and Faversham (Kent), the archdeacon remitted all actions against St. Augustine's about the church of Milton, and resigned the papal letters that he had impetrated about it. The abbot and convent, for their part, remitted to the archdeacon the fruits of Faversham, and those in store-houses.[3] Such arrangements were common,[4] and seem to be part of the prevalent desire to make compositions that would last rather than let the cause drag on to a sentence, and perhaps an appeal and the reopening of the suit.

Sometimes suits were reciprocally withdrawn. In 1236 Abbot Luke and the convent of Abingdon, and Andrew, vicar of Marcham (Berks.), renounced all quarrels and suits which were between them before ordinary and delegated judges.[5] In the church of Ware the prior and convent of Lewes and Master E(dmund), rector of Ovingdean, renounced suits reciprocally, and the rector remitted another suit which he was conducting against the monks before judges delegate at Salisbury.[6] In a similar arrangement, the abbot and convent of Thorney abandoned their suit about the church of Twywell (Northants.) against H. de Leckeburn, rector of Whittlesey (Cambs.), while he renounced his plea against Thorney about the lesser tithes of the demesne of Twywell, which he was pressing before the archdeacon of Northampton.[7] Furthermore a mutual agreement might be made between the parties to place the cause before arbiters, or to come to an out-of-court arrangement.

---

[1] *N.L.C.*, no. 62.

[2] Lewes Cart., f. 307ᵛ, cal. *Lewes Cart. S.P.*, ii. 119 (the date is not given—t.N., R., and R., abbots of Buildwas, Haughmond, and Lilleshall, therefore probably *c.* 1220–40, see R. W. Eyton, *Antiquities of Shropshire*, vi. 333, vii. 300, and viii. 225). [3] St. Augustine's Red Book, f. 257ʳ.

[4] e.g. Exeter Cart., p. 14; and B.M. Harley Ch. 44 I 25.

[5] Abingdon Cart., ff. 69ᵛ–70ʳ.   [6] P.R.O. E 40/14227.

[7] Thorney Cart. ii, f. 384ʳ. See also *Reg. Antiq. Linc.* iii, no. 759.

Appeal

The discontinuation of the suit might also be caused by an appeal to Rome. The system of appeal was taken over from the Roman law; but whereas in Roman law appeal could only be made after the sentence was given, canon law recognized that appeal could be made at any moment during the course of the suit, although an appeal against a final judgement had to be made within ten days of the sentence.[1] The effect of the appeal to Rome was immediate. As soon as it had been lodged, it was illegal for the judges to proceed further in the suit's conduct, pending instruction. Letters known as *apostoli* were sent by the judges to Rome, in which the grounds of the appeal were stated, as well as the matter of the suit and the point at which the appeal had been made —whether at the beginning of the suit, after contestation, or after the sentence.[2] The judges also usually fixed a date before which the appeal was to be followed up.[3] An appeal which was made by William de Walda, rector of Lamport and Faxton (Northants.), from the sentence of the judges delegate, Elias, prior of Westminster, and Master William of Purleigh, was later renounced by him and he swore not to molest the prior and convent of Lewes again in any way, and consented to submit to compulsion by the official of the archbishop of Canterbury if necessary.[4]

When making an appeal to Rome, the appellant might also appeal to the archbishop of his province, whose right it was, acting as vice-gerent of the pope, to maintain the *status quo* of the plaintiff pending litigation, and to protect his person and property. This right seems to have been granted to provincials remote from Rome; and Canterbury and York had it.[5] As early as 1146, when Bernard, abbot of Cerne, appealed to Eugenius III, Gilbert Foliot, abbot of Gloucester, asked Archbishop Theobald for the protection of

---

[1] *X.* II. 28; and see also A. Amanieu, 'Appel', *D.D.C.* i, cols. 764–807.

[2] *D.* xlix. 6; *Lib. Pauperum*, vii, tit. 62; A, f. 271ᵛ, col. i; and B, f. 79ᵛ, col. i, f. 80ᵛ, col. ii.

[3] Windsor Ch. xi G 37 (4) (App. B (ii), no. 6).

[4] P.R.O. E 40/7896.

[5] For details of the operation of the system, see now P. J. Wood, 'Tuitorial Appeal to the Archbishops of Canterbury and York in the Thirteenth Century' (Edinburgh M. Litt. thesis, 1970).

Bernard's church during his absence.[1] By the time of the archiepiscopate of Hubert Walter (1193–1205) the practice of seeking the tuition of the see of Canterbury while lodging an appeal to Rome was well established. Documents of this period refer to: '. . . ad apostolicam sedem et ad vestram cujus interest appellationes rite factas tueri appellavit . . .',[2] and '. . . post appellationem ad dominum papam pro tuitione juris sui quod in eadem habet ecclesia rite interpositam, et etiam ad nos ne status appellationis ipsius in aliquo turbaretur . . .'[3]

The archbishop on receiving the appeal or *provocatio* was bound to establish whether tuition should be granted. If it was granted, arrangements had to be made for its retention and observance, and an *inhibitio* was sent to prohibit the judges from proceeding any further. In the early years of the tuitorial appeal system it is unlikely that there were any courts to deal with this type of business.[4] Archbishop Hubert Walter invoked the help of local ecclesiastics, issuing mandates to delegates instructing them to establish whether the appeal had taken place legally and to revoke anything which had been done after it.[5] The procedure was still the same under Archbishop Edmund. On 4 April 1236 he ordered the priors of Monks Kirby and Combe to inquire into the appeal that had been made by Hugh, rector of Kenilworth. The priors were told to establish whether the appeal was legal, and if they saw fit, to revoke anything which had taken place after it, and to fix a time within which the appeal was to be prosecuted.[6] Most of the material concerning tuitorial appeals dates from the vacancy in the see of Canterbury between 1240 and 1245, when the prior and convent of Christ

---

[1] *Letters and Charters of Gilbert Foliot*, ed. Morey and Brooke, no. 56.

[2] Canterbury, Christ Church Letters, ii, no. 245.

[3] Canterbury, S(*ede*) *V*(*acante*), bk. i, p. 133 (*a*). See also Christ Church Letters, ii, nos. 232 and 242, for further appeals 'ad tuitionem' during Hubert Walter's archiepiscopate.

[4] M. M. Morgan, 'Early Canterbury Jurisdiction', *E.H.R.* lx (1945), 394.

[5] Canterbury, *S.V.*, bk. i, p. 133(*a*), and see Cheney, 'Harrold Priory', no. 9.

[6] B.M. Add. Ch. 21289. Cf. Churchill, *Canterbury Administration*, i. 463, and B. L. Woodcock, *Medieval Ecclesiastical Courts in the Diocese of Canterbury* (Oxford, 1952), p. 65, who state that protection once granted lasted for a year and a day.

II

THE PROCEDURE OF THE COURTS

Church asserted their right to this jurisdiction.[1] Normal practice in the method of dealing with appeals therefore cannot necessarily be inferred from this period, but their methods seem to be a continuation of earlier practice; and it is noteworthy that the prior and convent dealt at least with some of the business by delegation.[2] An official, however, sometimes made an appearance on their behalf.[3]

The terminology of the appeal indicates the changes which were to take place. The most regular form, which is recorded among the *sede vacante* material of 1240–5, was 'ad ecclesiam Cant' pro tuitione' or 'ad tuitionem sedis Cantuar' '.[4] This gave way to 'ad sedem apostolicam et pro tuitione curie Cantuariensis',[5] and it has been suggested that it is to the archiepiscopate of Boniface of Savoy, who was elected in 1243 and consecrated in 1245, that we must look for the beginnings of an organized court.[6]

The competence of provincial tuition does not seem to have been limited to certain types of cases. Cases among the *sede vacante* material concern tithes, churches, election, the establishment of vicarages, and marriage.[7] Archbishop Pecham, however, declared against tuitorial appeal in matrimonial cases.[8] It is likely that tuitorial appeal was made most frequently in suits about property and possession. The majority of suits going to Rome concerned possessions and property, and this may reflect that predominance. It is impossible to estimate the number of appeals to Rome in which the tuition of Canterbury was also sought, but it would seem valid to conclude that the system must have stopped some frivolous appeals by withholding the grant of protection after examination had been made. This would have been a

---

[1] It is found mainly in M 364, a magnificent roll of suits, and *S.V.*, bks. ii and iii. The prior and convent of Christ Church asserted their right especially against the bishop of London, who claimed this jurisdiction, see *S.V.*, bk. ii, p. 199.
[2] Morgan, 'Early Canterbury Jurisdiction', p. 394, and *S.V.*, bk. ii, pp. 200(*b*), 202(*a*) and (*b*).
[3] M 364, nos. 12 and 16, and *S.V.*, bk. ii, p. 200(*a*).
[4] e.g. *S.V.*, bk. iii, p. 161(*b*), and Cartae Antiquae, M 364, no. 2.
[5] See Churchill, *Canterbury Administration*, i. 428.
[6] Morgan, 'Early Canterbury Jurisdiction', p. 398.
[7] *S.V.*, bk. ii, pp. 196(*b*), 200(*b*), and M 364, nos. 10 and 11.
[8] Churchill, *Canterbury Administration*, i. 462.

valuable contribution to the efficient working of the machinery of the courts.

Although the Romano-canonical procedure was open to abuse, it had the makings of a system of average efficiency, thoroughness, and fairness. It might be said that the procedural techniques showed too great a concern to be fair by catering for appeal at any point in the suit, which the procedure of the Roman law had not allowed. The central machinery, necessary for the initial stages of the suit, worked in favour of the plaintiff, on the assumption that the defendant could object, at least at a later date. Because the defendant was not safeguarded in the early stages at Rome, he had to be allowed the right of appeal before judgement.[1] Basically this was a weakness, but it was a machinery which in many cases seems to have worked and, what is more, to have worked without serious delays.[2] Legal delays, which were an integral part of the procedure by libel, were an essential device to protect all concerned, plaintiffs, defendants, and judges. In the English southern province, the judges delegate and their entourages demanded increasing procedural definition from the popes, collected instructions and forms, and seem to have made every effort to develop uniformity. If the procedure erred on the side of rigidity, at least it led to uniformity and to a system which was easily administered even by men not specifically trained in the law. A study of the court documents has shown the way in which the procedure before the courts usually corresponded closely to the papal enactments, the procedural treatises, and the formularies.

[1] For a contemporary comment on the abuse of this practice, and other malpractices, see the poem 'Bulla fulminante' of Philip the chancellor of Paris and a satirical poet, F. J. E. Raby, *History of Christian Latin Poetry*, 2nd edn. (Oxford, 1953), p. 397. Philip was born at the end of the twelfth century and died in 1236 or 1237 (p. 395).

[2] See *P.J.D.*, pp. 216–17, and App. A (iv).

APPENDIX. A LIST OF SOME OF THE MEETING-PLACES OF THE COURTS

Place	Judges	Parties	Date of settlement unless otherwise stated	Reference
1. Barnwell ch. (Cambs.)	Bp. and archd. of Ely	Pr. of Eye v. parson of Dennington (both Suff.)	1202–3	Eye Cart., f. 35ʳ⁻ᵛ
2. Barnwell (Cambs.)	Prs. of Barnwell, Anglesey (Cambs.), and d. of Cambridge	Walden v. r. of Pleshey (both Essex)	1223	Walden Cart., ff. 43ᵛ–4ʳ
3. Barnwell priory ch. (Cambs.)	Pr. of Barnwell	Leeds v. r. of Harbledown (both Kent)	1250	Leeds Cart., f. 8ᵛ
4. Boxley parish ch. (Kent)	Abb., pr. of Boxley, and m. Thomas of Maidstone	R. of Cliffe-at-Hoo (Kent) v. Christ Church, Canterbury	1229	Canterbury, Cartae Antiquae, C 280
5. Breedon ch. (Leics.)	Prs. of Leicester, Belvoir (Lincs.), and Breedon (Leics.)	Owston (Leics.) v. Stamford, St. Michael's (Northants.)	1236/7	Bodleian MS. Dodsworth 76, f. 1
6. Bury St. Edmunds (Suff.)	Prs. of Bury St. Edmunds, Ixworth, and Great Bricett (all Suff.)	Eye v. r. of Tattingstone and Bures (all Suff.)	1213	Eye Cart., ff. 42ᵛ–3ʳ
7. Bury St. Edmunds, chapel of St. Denis (Suff.)	Abb., pr. of Bury St. Edmunds, and pr. of Great Bricett (Suff.)	Eye (Suff.) v. archd. of Worcester	1218	Ibid., ff. 35ᵛ–6ʳ
8. Bury St. Edmunds (Suff.)	Abb. and pr. of Bury St. Edmunds	Binham v. r. of Bacton (both Norf.)	1222	Binham Cart., f. 185ʳ
9. Cambridge	Ds. of Cambridge, Wilbraham, and Chesterton (all Cambs.)	R. of Radwinter (Essex) v. Holy Trinity, Aldgate	1233	P.R.O. E 40/13828 (c); E 40/14302

	D. of Cambridge	R. of Charwelton (Northants.) v. Biddlesden (Bucks.)	1253	B.M. Harley Ch. 84 F 45
10. Cambridge, All Saints ch. nr. the hosp.	D. of Cambridge	R. of Charwelton (Northants.) v. Biddlesden (Bucks.)	1253	B.M. Harley Ch. 84 F 45
11. Cambridge, St. Mary's ch.	Prec. of Barnwell (Cambs.), chanc. and d. of Cambridge	Anglesey (Cambs.) v. Newton Longville (Bucks.)	1227	N.L.C., no. 86
12. " "	Prec. of Barnwell (Cambs.) and d. of Cambridge	St. Neots (Hunts.) v. r. of Brampton (Northants.)	1232	St. Neots Cart., f. 112^{r-v}
13. " "	Prec. of Barnwell (Cambs.) and d. of Cambridge	St. Neots (Hunts.) v. r. of Barton Bendish (Norf.)	1232	St. Neots Cart., f. 111^v
14. " "	" "	St. Neots (Hunts.) v. parson of Barnwell (Northants.)	1232	St. Neots Cart., ff. 111^v–12^r
15. Canterbury, Christ Church	Pr. of St. Gregory's, Canterbury, archd. and pen. of Canterbury	Christ Church, Canterbury v. Guines (dioc. Thérouanne, W. Flanders)	1218	Canterbury, Cartae Antiquae, F 31
16. " "	Abb. of Faversham (Kent), prs. of St. Gregory's, Canterbury, and St. Augustine's, Canterbury	Dover v. Langdon (both Kent)	1219	Langdon Cart., ff. 102^r–3^r
17. " "	Prs. of St. Augustine's Canterbury, Monks Horton, and Faversham (all Kent)	Christ Church, Canterbury v. parson of Eythorne (Kent)	1220	Canterbury, Cartae Antiquae, L 351
18. " "	" "	Christ Church, Canterbury v. Dunes in Sheppey (dioc. Thérouanne, W. Flanders)	1220	Canterbury, MS. Scrapbook A, p. 13, Ch. 25
19. Canterbury	Prs. of St. Augustine's, Canterbury, St. Gregory's, Canterbury, and Faversham (Kent)	Christ Church, Canterbury v. William, son of Conan of Holbeach (Lincs.)	1222	Canterbury, Cartae Antiquae, H 120

Place	Judges	Parties	Date of settlement unless otherwise stated	Reference
20. Canterbury, Christ Church	Abb. of Langdon (Kent) and pr. of St. Gregory's, Canterbury	Dover v. r. of Brookland (both Kent)	1224/5	Dover Cart., f. 226^v
21. ,, ,,	Pr. of St. Gregory's, Canterbury, off. and pen. of Canterbury	Christ Church, Canterbury v. William of Cheriton, knt.	1230	Canterbury, Cartae Antiquae, F 8
22. ,, ,,	Abbs. of Langdon, St. Radegund's, and pr. of Monks Horton (all Kent)	R. of Meopham (Kent) v. Christ Church, Canterbury	1234	Canterbury, Cartae Antiquae, M 123
23. ,, ,,	Abb. of St. Augustine's, Canterbury, pr. of St. Gregory's, Canterbury, and d. of Canterbury	Faversham (Kent) v. Holy Trinity, Aldgate	1234	P.R.O. E 40/13828(f)
24. Carlton cum Willingham (Cambs.)	Pr. of Merton (Surr.) and co-judges (unspecified)	Lewes (Suss.) v. r. of Weston Colville (Cambs.)	1236	P.R.O. E 40/9649, cal. *Lewes Cart. Camb. Portion*, ed. Bullock and Palmer, nos. 23, 73
25. Chertsey (Surr.)	Abb., pr. of Chertsey, and pr. of Reading (Berks.)	Westminster v. r. of St. James, London	1231	Westminster Domesday, f. 476^v
26. Chichester, St. Faith's ch.	Bp., prec., and archd. of Chichester	St. Augustine's, Canterbury v. r. of Iwade (Kent)	1202	Canterbury, Cartae Antiquae, C 1270 and pd. *Reg. of St. Augustine's Canterbury*, p. 546
27. Chichester cath.	Prs. of Boxgrove, Arundel, and Tortington (all Suss.)	Bayham (Suss.) v. v. of West Greenwich (Kent)	1237	Bayham Cart., ff. 60^v–61^r

28. Christchurch (alias Twynham) ch. (Hants)	Pr. of Christchurch	Beaulieu (Hants) v. St. Michael's Mount (Cornw.)	1238	Beaulieu Cart., ff. 132v-4r
29. Cirencester abbey ch. (Glos.)	Pr. of Cirencester (ordainer)	Malmesbury v. r. of Somerford (both Wilts.)	1251	*Malmesbury Reg.* ii. 218
30. Colchester, St. Botolph's ch. (Essex)	Prs. of Thoby and Tiptree (both Essex)	Colchester, St. John's v. r. of Easton (Suff.)	1240	P.R.O. E 42/384
31. Christian Malford (Wilts.)	Pr. of Bradenstoke (Wilts.), archd. of Bath, and d. of Cirencester (Glos.)	R. of Crudwell v. Malmesbury (both Wilts.)	1231	*Malmesbury Reg.* i. 386, and ii. 60
32. Dersingham (Norf.)	Pr. of Rudham and d. of Walsingham (both Norf.)	Binham v. Shouldham (both Norf.)	1232	Binham Cart., ff. 146v-7r
33. Dover, St. Peter's ch. (Kent)	Prs. of Dover and Folkestone (both Kent)	Bayham v. v. of Hellingly (both Sussex)	1240	Bayham Cart., f. 60v
34. Dunstable (Beds.)	Prs. of Dunstable, Caldwell, and prec. of Dunstable (both Beds.)	Bec (dioc. Rouen, France) v. William Estormy and Elias, chapl.	1234	Windsor, Arundel White Book, p. 174
35. Dunstable priory ch. (Beds.)	„	Bec (dioc. Rouen, France) v. St. Frideswide's, Oxford	1234	Windsor Ch. xi G 75 and pd. *St. Frideswide's Cart.* ii, no. 1135
36. „	„	Bec (dioc. Rouen, France) v. Tewkesbury (Glos.)	1234	Canterbury, Cartae Antiquae, L 381
37. „	Pr. and subpr. of Dunstable	St. Julian's hosp., St. Albans (Herts.) v. Lanthony (Glos.)	1239	Lanthony Cart. A 1, X, no. cviii
38. „	Pr. of Dunstable	Bec (dioc. Rouen, France) v. rs. of Withersfield and Dalham (both Suff.)	1241	Windsor Chs. xi G 14-16 and 37

Place	Judges	Parties	Date of settlement unless otherwise stated	Reference
39. Dunstable, St. Peter's ch. (Beds.)	Off. of archd. of Bedford	Dunstable v. r. of Cublington (Bucks.)	1239	Dunstable Cart., f. 55^v, cal. *Dunstable Cart.*, no. 67
40. Exeter cath.	Not named	Prec. of Salisbury v. a can., the bp. and c. of Exeter	1236	Exeter Cart., p. 79
41. Faversham abbey ch. (Kent)	Sacr. of Faversham	Dover (Kent) v. chapl. of St. Mary's chapel and r. of St. John's chapel, Dover	1246	Dover Cart., f. 51^r
42. " "	" "	Dover (Kent) v. chapl. of St. James's chapel, Dover	1246	Dover Cart., f. 50^v
43. Flamstead (Herts.)	Abb. of Warden, pr. of Dunstable (both Beds.), and d. of Berkhamsted (Herts.)	R. of Covenham (Lincs.), and d. of Salisbury v. Chertsey (Surr.)	1218	*Chertsey Cart.*, no. 91
44. " "	Prs. of Dunstable (Beds.), St. Albans (Herts.), and archd. of St. Albans	St. Frideswide's, Oxford v. r. of Shipton-on-Cherwell (Oxon.)	1227	*St. Frideswide's Cart.* ii, no. 1021
45. Flitton (Beds.)	Prs. of Beadlow, Chicksands, and d. of Weston (all Beds.)	Dunstable (Beds.) v. Merton (Surr.) and r. of chapel of Whipsnade (Beds.)	1231 (mandate)	Dunstable Cart., f. 53^r, cal. *Dunstable Cart.*, no. 501
46. Flitwick ch. (Beds.)	Abb., pr. of Warden, and pr. of Beadlow (both Beds.)	Dunstable (Beds.) v. clerk of Bradbourne (Derbys.)	1223	Dunstable Cart., f. 77^r, cal. *Dunstable Cart.*, no. 937
47. Fornham All Saints ch. (Suff.)	Abb. and pr. of Bury St. Edmunds (Suff.)	Eye v. parson and v. of Stradbroke (both Suff.)	1221	Eye Cart., ff. 36^v–7^v
48. Frating (Essex)	Abbs. of Colchester and St. Osyth's (both Essex)	Binham v. r. of Bacton (both Norf.)	1218	Binham Cart., f. 185^{r-v}

49. Fressingfield, St. Peter's ch. (Suff.)	Prs. of Rumburgh, Mendham, and d. of Hoxne (all Suff.)	R. of Occold v. Eye (both Suff.)	1221	Eye Cart., f. 36r
50. Gloucester, St. Mary's ch. in the south	Pr. of St. Oswald's, Gloucester, and ds. of Dymock (Glos.) and Gloucester	Lanthony (Glos.) v. r. of Alvescot (Oxon.)	1231	Lanthony Cart. A I, III, no. lv
51. Gloucester, St. Mary's ch. by the abbey gate	Subpr. of St. Oswald's, Gloucester, and d. of Gloucester	Lanthony (Glos.) v. St. Julian's hosp., St. Albans (Herts.)	1238	Lanthony Cart. A I, X, no. lxxiiii
52. Grimsby (Lincs.)	Abb. of Humberston, prs. of Thornton and Grimsby (all Lincs.)	Newsham v. Nun Cotham (both Lincs.)	1228	B.M. Harley Ch. 44 E 20
53. Hereford, St. Ethelbert's ch.	Bp., d., and prec. of Hereford	Bp. of Llandaff (Glam.) v. Gloucester	1204	Glos. Cart. ii, nos. dxix, dxx
54. Hereford cath.	Abbs. of Abbey Dore (Heref.), Flaxley (Glos.), and d. of Hereford	Lanthony (Glos.) v. chapl. of Chirton (Wilts.)	1214	Lanthony Cart. A I, VIII, no. lxxx
55. Hereford	D. and chanc. of Hereford	R. of Alvington v. Lanthony (both Glos.)	1243/4	Lanthony Cart. A I, III, no. cviii
56. Huntingdon, St. Mary's ch.	Pr., archd., and d. of Huntingdon	Lewes (Suss.) v. r. of Sculthorpe (Norf.)	1219 and 1225	P.R.O. E 40/14067 and Lewes Cart., ff. 260v-1r, cal. N.P., nos. 112, 138
57. Hyde abbey ch. (Hants)	Pr. of Hyde, archd. of Surrey and d. of Winchester	R. of Ringwood (Hants) v. Christchurch (or Twynham, Hants)	1239	Christchurch (Twynham) Cart., f. 62v
58. Ipswich, St. Matthew's ch. (Suff.)	Prs. of Holy Trinity, St. Peter's, Ipswich, and d. of Ipswich	Eye v. rs. of St. Martin's, Dunwich (both Suff.)	1226	Eye Cart., ff. 34v-5r

Place	Judges	Parties	Date of settlement unless otherwise stated	Reference
59. King's Lynn, St. Margaret's ch. (Norf.)	Abb. of Dereham and pr. of Castle Acre (both Norf.)	Waltham (Essex) v. Kirkstead (Lincs.)	1237/8	Waltham Cart., f. 142ᵛ, and Kirkstead Cart., f. 189ʳ
60. Lincoln chapter	Chanc. and two cans. of Lincoln	Bardney v. Stixwould (both Lincs.)	1208	Bardney Cart., ff. 240ʳ–1ʳ
61. " "	" "	Bardney (Lincs.) v. archd. of Cleveland (Yorks. N.R.)	1209	Bardney Cart., f. 92ʳ–ᵛ
62. Lincoln cath.	M. William de Novo Castro and Peter de Mixebyrii	Bolton v. r. of Ilkley (both Yorks. W.R.)	1215/16	Bodleian MS. Dodsworth 76, f. 44
63. Lincoln chapter	D., m. of the schools, and a can. of Lincoln	Treas. of York v. Eye (Suff.)	[1224]	Eye Cart., ff. 39ᵛ–4cʳ
64. Lincoln	Prec., subd., and m. of the schools of Lincoln	Bridlington (Yorks. E.R.) v. Westminster	1238	Westminster Domesday, f. 470ʳ
65. Lincoln cath.	D., m. William de Novo Castro, and a can. of Lincoln	Bullington (Lincs.) v. Garendon (Leics.)	1250/1 (intermediate acta)	P.R.O. E 135/6/13
66. " "	D., prec., and chanc. of Lincoln	Bullington (Lincs.) v. Garendon (Leics.)	1251	B.M. Harley Ch. 53 A 23
67. Lincoln	Can. of Lincoln	Bardney v. r. of Willoughby (both Lincs.)	c. 1251	Bardney Cart., ff. 105ʳ–6ʳ
68. Llandaff cath. (Glam.)	Pr. of Carmarthen (Carmarth.)	Clifford v. Abbey Dore (both Heref.)	c. 1252 (intermediate acta)	P.R.O. E 135/24/4
69. London	D. of Arches	R. of Stewkley v. Newton Longville (both Bucks.)	1238	N.L.C., no. 54

70. London, St. Magnus the martyr's ch.	Pr. of Tandridge and d. of Southwark (both Surr.)	Westminster v. Godstow (Oxon.)	1254	Westminster Domesday, f. 379v
71. London, St. Paul's cath.	D. and prec. of London	St. Evroult (dioc. Lisieux, France) v. R., knt., of Coventry dioc.	[1206] (intermediate acta)	B.M. Wolley Ch. v 27
72. "	D. of London, archd. of Middlesex, and m. R. de Arcubus	Bp. of Norwich v. prs. of Binham and Wymondham (all Norf.)	1228	Binham Cart., ff. 47v–8r
73. "	Prs. of Waltham (Essex) and Westminster	St. Augustine's, Canterbury v. v. of Chislet (both Kent)	1233	St. Augustine's Cart., f. 75r
74. "	Can. of St. Davids and a can. of St. Angelus, Ferentino (staying in England)	Master B., can. of Troyes (France) and r. of Painswick (Glos.) v. archd. of Worcester, and Lanthony (Glos.)	1235	Lanthony Cart. A I, XVI, no. xvi
75. "	Archd. and chanc. of London	St. Valéry (dioc. Amiens, France) v. r. of Hinton Waldrist (Berks.)	1240	New College, Oxford, Takeley Ch. 229
76. Luton, St. Mary's ch. (Beds.)	Abb. of Woburn (Beds.), prs. of St. Albans (Herts.) and Dunstable (Beds.)	R. of Launton (Oxon.) v. v. of Launton	1214	Westminster Ch. 15684
77. Malmesbury, St. Paul's ch. (Wilts.)	Prs. of Monkton Farleigh (Wilts.), Malmesbury, and d. of Malmesbury	Bradenstoke (Wilts.) v. v. of Canford (Dors.)	1227	Bradenstoke Cart., ff. 112v–13r
78. Northampton, All Saints ch.	Prs. of St. John's, St. James's, and d. of Northampton	St. Frideswide's, Oxford v. r. of Souldern (Oxon.)	1236/7	St. Frideswide's Cart. ii, no. 980

Place	Judges	Parties	Date of settlement unless otherwise stated	Reference
79. Northampton, All Saints ch.	Pr. of Canons Ashby (Northants.) and m. of the hosp. of St. John, Northampton	St. Andrew's, Northampton v. Thomas de Esseby, clerk	1246	Northampton, St. Andrew's Cart. (A), ff. 208r-9r
80. Northampton, St. Peter's ch. by the castle	Prs. of St. John's, St. James's, and d. of Northampton	St. Frideswide's, Oxford v. r. of Souldern (Oxon.)	1233	St. Frideswide's Cart. ii, no. 978
81. ,, ,,	,,	St. Frideswide's, Oxford v. r. of Beckley (Oxon.)	1233/4	St. Frideswide's Cart. ii, no. 732
82. Northampton, St. Peter's ch.	Archd. of Northampton (ordainer)	St. Andrew's, Northampton v. r. of Yardley Gobion (Northants.)	1233	Northampton, St. Andrew's Cart. (A), f. 94r-v
83. ,, ,,	Pr. of St. James's, Northampton	Parson of Wytham (Berks.) v. Godstow (Oxon.)	1244/5	Godstow Reg. i, no. [31]
84. Norwich	Pr. of Norwich, m. Walter of Suffield and Thomas of Fakenham (arbiters)	Eye (Suff.) v. Horsham St. Faith (Norf.)	1240	Eye Cart, ff. 45v-6r
85. Norwich cath.	Abb. and pr. of Langley (Norf.)	Eye v. parson, v., and H., knt., of Rickinghall (both Suff.)	1220	Ibid., ff. 46v-7r
86. Nottingham, St. Mary's ch.	Subpr. of Lenton (Notts.)	Biddlesden (Bucks.) v. v. of Thornborough (Bucks.) and d. of Buckingham, and Luffield (Northants.)	1251/2 (intermediate acta)	Bodleian MS. Chs. Bucks. a 4, Ch. 91, and B.M. Harley Ch. 84 F 36
87. Oxford, All Saints ch.	D. of Oxford and m. Elias de Daneis	R. of Yatton (Som.) v. Malmesbury (Wilts.)	1230	Malmesbury Reg. ii. 30, 59

No.	Judges delegate	Case	Date	Reference
88. Oxford, St. Frideswide's priory ch.	Prs. of St. Albans (Herts.), Dunstable (Beds.), and chanc. of Oxford	Warden (Beds.) v. r. of Great Paxton (Hunts.)	c. 1233	*Reg. Antiq. Linc.* iii, no. 829
89. Oxford, St. Mary's ch.	Pr. of Oseney (Oxon.) and d. of Oxford	Abingdon (Berks.) v. r. of Chesterton (Warw.)	1210	Abingdon Cart., f. 144^v
90. "	Pr. of Eynsham (Oxon.), chanc. and d. of Oxford	Lanthony v. r. of Painswick (both Glos.)	1229	Lanthony Cart. A 1, III, no. liv
91. "	Roger de Cantilupe and m. Philip de Hanneya	St. Frideswide's, Oxford v. certain burgesses of Oxford	1221 (mandate)	*St. Frideswide's Cart.* ii, no. 721
92. "	Chapls. of St. Peter's in the East, and of St. John the Baptist's, Oxford	Burton (Staffs.) v. Gresley (Derbys.)	early 13th cent.	*Burton Chs.* 58
93. "	Master J. de Poppleton, R. de Thetford, and S. de Dyham	R. of Charwelton (Northants.) v. Biddlesden (Bucks.)	c. 1230 (intermediate acta)	B.M. Harley Ch. 84 F 43
94. "	Pr. of St. Oswald's, Gloucester, archd. and d. of Gloucester	Notley v. Newton Longville (both Bucks.)	1235	*N.L.C.*, no. 62
95. "	Archd. and d. of Oxford	Abb. of Chertsey (Surr.) v. pr. of Newstead (Notts.)	1237	*Chertsey Cart.*, no. 92
96. "	D. and chanc. of Oxford	St. Martin's, London v. Walden (Essex)	1237	Walden Cart., f. 43^{r-v}
97. Oxford, St. Peter's ch. in the east	M. Ralph of Sempringham	R. of Withcote v. r. of Pickwell (both Leics.)	1241	B.M. Cotton MS. Nero C iii, f. 199^r
98. Peterborough, St. Thomas's chapel (Northants.)	Abb., pr. of Thorney (Cambs.), and pr. of Peterborough	Dereham (Norf.) v. Philip de Burnham, knt.	1210	West Dereham Cart., ff. 260^v-1^r

Place	Judges	Parties	Date of settlement unless otherwise stated	Reference
99. Peterborough (Northants.)	Pr. of Peterborough	Thorney (Cambs.) v. r. of Thurleigh (Beds.)	1251	Thorney Cart. ii, ff. 323ʳ, 325ʳ
100. Pinner ch. (Middx.)	D. of Middlesex and Baldric chapl.	Bec (dioc. Rouen, France) v. r. of Great Wratting (Suff.), and Dover (Kent)	1245 (intermediate acta)	Windsor Ch. xi G 27
101. Reading (Berks.)	D., prec., and chanc of Salisbury	R. of Brightwalton (Berks.) v. Battle (Suss.)	1224	P.R.O. E 327/51
102. St. Albans abbey ch. (Herts.)	Pr., archd. of St. Albans, and pr. of Redbourn (both Herts.)	Dunstable (Beds.) v. r. of Bradbourne (Derbys.)	1214	Dunstable Cart., f. 45ʳ, cal. Dunstable Cart., no. 391 (where it is wrongly dated 1215)
103. St. Albans, St. Andrew's chapel (Herts.)	Prs. of Dunstable (Beds.), St. Albans, and archd. of St. Albans	St. Frideswide's, Oxford v. r. of Noke (Oxon.)	1229	St. Frideswide's Cart. ii, no. 976
104. St. Albans abbey ch. (Herts.)	Pr. of St. Albans and d. of Hertford	Westminster v. v. of Pershore and the chapl. of Wick nr. Pershore (both Worcs.)	1234	Westminster Domesday, f. 576ʳ
105. ,,	Archd. of St. Albans	Waltham (Essex) v. Chepstow (Mon.)	1251	B.M. Egerton Ch. 409
106. ,,	Pr., archd., and prec. of St. Albans	R. of Great Paxton (Hunts.) v. warden and ministers of St. Hugh's altar in Lincoln cath.	1253	Reg. Antiq. Linc. ii, no. 386
107. St. Neots (Hunts.)	Pr. of Bushmead (Beds.)	St. Neots v. r. of Wimbish (Essex)	1247	St. Neots Cart., ff. 130ᵛ-1ᵛ

108. Salisbury cath.	Pr. of Ivychurch, d. of Wilton (both Wilts.), and succ. of Salisbury	R. of East Hendred (Berks.) v. Bec (dioc. Rouen, France)	1230	Windsor Ch. xv. 41. 71
109. " "	"	R. of East Hendred v. Abingdon (both Berks.)	1231	Abingdon Cart., f. 53r
110. Stamford, St. Mary's ch. at the bridge (Lincs.)	Ds. of Stamford (Lincs.), Rutland, and Carlby (Lincs.)	Stamford, St. Michael's v. William Erl of North Luffenham (Rutland)	1237	P.R.O. E 326/2268
111. Steppingley ch. (Beds.)	Abb., pr. of Warden, and pr. of Beadlow (both Beds.)	Pr. of Dunstable (Beds.) v. R. Pudifet of Berkhamsted (Herts.)	1222	Dunstable Cart., f. 46v, cal. Dunstable Cart., no. 405
112. Wallingford priory ch. (Berks.)	Pr. of Barnwell (Cambs.) and chanc. of Cambridge	Wallingford v. Henry of Earley and his chapl. of Earley (Berks.)	1236	Bodleian MS. Chs. Berks. a 1, Ch. 17
113. Ware ch. (Herts.)	Pr. of Waltham (Essex) and colleagues (unspecified)	Lewes v. r. of Ovingdean (both Suss.)	1236	P.R.O. E 40/14227
114. Wells	Abb. of Muchelney, pr. and prec. of Taunton (both Som.)	R. of 'Cumton' v. St. Valéry (dioc. Amiens, France), and r. of Hinton Waldrist (Berks.)	1220	New College, Oxford, Takeley Ch. 139
115. Wells cath.	Two cans. of Wells	D. and c. of Exeter v. Roger d'Olly, knt.	1247	Exeter Ch. 640
116. Westleton (Suff.)	Abb. of Leiston, pr. of Blythburgh, and pr. of Wangford (all Suff.)	Eye (Suff.) v. clerk of 'Wltorp' (? Woolsthorpe, Lincs.)	1218	Eye Cart., ff. 43r-4r
117. Westminster	Bp. of Lincoln, abbs. of St. Albans (Herts.) and Stratford (Essex)	Westminster v. Godstow (Oxon.)	1197	Westminster Domesday, f. 378v, and Godstow Reg. i, no. [308]

Place	Judges	Parties	Date of settlement unless otherwise stated	Reference
118. Westminster	Abp. and archd. of Canterbury	St. Frideswide's, Oxford v. Fulk, knt., and others	1224	Bodleian MS. Chs. Oxon. a 10, Ch. 79
119. Wilton, St. Nicholas's ch. (Wilts.)	D. and m. of the schools of St. Edward, Shaftesbury (Wilts.)	R. of 'Cumton' (? Compton, Berks.) v. Reading (Berks.)	1234	Reading Cart., ff. 114^{v}–15^{r}
120. Winchester cath.	Abb. and pr. of Waverley (Surr.), pr. of Sherborne (Dorset)	Reading (Berks.) v. Préaux (dioc. Lisieux, France) and G., clerk of Newbury (Berks.)	1216–27 (mandate)	Reading Cart., f. 112^{v}
121. Worcester cath.	Bp. and prec. of Hereford	Malvern (Worcs.) and v. of Pershore v. Pershore (both Worcs.)	1204	Westminster Domesday, f. 574^{v}

III

CANTERBURY PROCTORS AT THE COURT OF 'AUDIENTIA LITTERARUM CONTRADICTARUM'

Little is known of the early history of the court of *audientia litterarum contradictarum*. Professor Barraclough has suggested that its origins must be sought in the 1150's and 1160's, when under the popes Eugenius III and Alexander III there was considerable development of judicial procedure by rescript.[1] To begin a suit before papal judges, the plaintiff or his proctor produced a letter to the pope announcing the petition, stating the 'libellus' or charge, and beseeching him for the cause to be heard at Rome, or, more frequently, for a mandate to judges delegate.[2] It is likely that the plaintiff would have informed the charged party of his action, and that by this time the defendant's proctor, too, would have been instructed in the matter and would be ready to appear at the papal court.

The court of *audientia litterarum contradictarum* controlled the activities of the proctors and, as its name implies, dealt with disputed mandates when the defendant's proctor objected to the issue of a particular rescript, The proctor's powers depended on his commission or proxy. There were two classes of proctor, firstly proctors who were appointed to deal with causes 'agendo et defendendo' in the courts of justice, and then proctors appointed 'ad impetrandum' at Rome, or wherever the papal court was.[3] The constitution of Master Richard of Langdon (Languedona) as proctor 'in curia Romana' of Richard Wethershed, archbishop of Canterbury, in 1230, granted him powers 'ad impetrandum et contradicendum et conveniendum in judices.'[4]

---

[1] See G. Barraclough, 'Audientia Litterarum Contradictarum,' DDC 1 (1935) 1387, and R. von Heckel, 'Das Aufkommen der ständigen Prokuratoren an der päpstlichen Kurie,' *Miscellanea Fr. Ehrle* II (Studi e Testi 38; Rome 1924) 291-4. — I wish to thank Professor Kuttner for generous help in the preparation of this article.

[2] See e. g. Historical Manuscripts Commission [= HMC] *Report on the MSS. of Wells Cathedral* (London 1885) 1, 59 (Liber Albus I, fols. 2^v, 95^r and 96^r). The dean and chapter wanted their case to be heard, if possible, by the pope. In the event of this being refused, they mention judges in England and France who would be acceptable to them.

[3] H. M. Chew, ed., *Hemingby's Register* (Wilts. Arch. and Nat. Hist. Soc. Records Branch 18; Devizes 1962) 99 no. 132 (dated 19 Sept. 1333).

[4] Canterbury, Dean and Chapter Archives, Cartae Antiquae C 47 (see p. 324 *infra*). (Appendix, document VI).

Master Simon de Boys, who was constituted proctor of the prior and convent of Barnwell at the court of Rome, was given powers [5]

> ad impetrandas litteras simplices et legendas graciam seu justiciam continentes, et ad contradicendum nec non ad consentiendum in judices et loca et ad judices recusandos et etiam ad substituend' procurator' loco sui et ad omnia premissa facienda.

Forms of procuration 'ad impetrandum' in John of Bologna's formulary, which was dedicated to Archbishop Pecham, and in which supposed Christ Church, Canterbury, examples are given, with dates from 1281 to 1284,[6] grant powers of impetrating in the Roman *curia*, of contradicting both straightforward and important letters, and of suggesting, consenting on, and refusing, the place where the court should meet and the composition of the bench of judges.[7] In the event of a disputed mandate, the auditor or master of the court began his duties by checking the proctors' credentials. Bonaguida of Arezzo, in his *Consuetudines cancellarie*, outlines the auditor's authority over the proctors:[8]

> Consuetudo cancellarie est, quod non valet procuratio, si fiat in curia, nisi sit facta sub sigillo auditoris contradictarum.
> Item consuetudo cancellarie est, quod debeant habere speciale mandatum ad impetrandum litteras, alias per generale eas impetrare non potest.

The petition which was made by the applicant is dissected by William of Drogheda, a thirteenth-century procedural writer and legist, 'Incipit ars componendi litteras secundum stilum Romanae curiae.' He speaks of the general clause 'et quidam alii,' and the clauses 'alias graves et iniuriosi sibi existentes quam plurimum et molesti,' the 'testes,' 'quod si non omnes,' and finally the 'datum.'[9] Then he gives an example:[10]

> Forma petitionis apud papam pro litteris dimmissoriis.
> Significat sanctitati vestre W. perpetuus vicarius de Asseleia (?Ashley),

---

[5] Barnwell Register, B. M. Harley MS 3601, fol. 78ʳ (1266-97), printed in J. Willis Clark, ed., *Liber Memorandorum Ecclesie de Bernewelle* (Cambridge 1907) 205-6.

[6] In one form, Thomas, prior of Christ Church (also called P. and H. elsewhere), appoints and authorizes Master P. de Bononia.

[7] John of Bologna in Ludwig Rockinger, ed., 'Briefsteller und Formelbücher des eilften bis vierzehnten jahrhunderts,' *Quellen und Erörterungen zur Bayerischen und Deutschen Geschichte* 9 (Munich 1863) 606-10.

[8] J. Teige, 'Beiträge zum päpstlichen Kanzleiwesen des XIII. und XIV. Jahrhunderts,' *Mitteilungen des Instituts für Österreichische Geschichtsforschung* [= MIOG] 17 (1896) 414. Barraclough, *art. cit.* 1390, cites this as from L. Wahrmund, ed., 'Die consuetudines Curiae romanae,' *Archiv für Katholisches Kirchenrecht* 79 (1899) 3-19, and in particular 18, but in fact this is not the same text.

[9] William of Drogheda, 'Summa Aurea' in L. Wahrmund, ed., *Quellen zur Geschichte des Römisch-kanonischen Processes im Mittelalter* 2 (Innsbruck 1914) 7-8.

[10] *Ibid.* 8.

quod W. de Pokevelt rector eiusdem ecclesiae, et quidam alii clerici et laici Lincolnensis, Londinensis, Hecfordiensis (*sic*) dyocesis et civitatis super decimis, debitis, conventionibus et rebus aliis iniuriantur eidem, alias graves et iniuriosi ei existentes quam plurimum et molesti. Petit iudices decanum, praecentorem, archidiaconum Hecfordiae, Hecfordiensis dyocesis. Quod si non omnes etc. Testes etc. Datum etc.

Another example is provided in an Oxford formulary.[11] It is headed 'Petitio,' and continues:

> Significat sanctitati vestre A. de Crec miles quod cum ecclesia de Crec sit de eius advocatione B. clericus de Crec Lincolniensis diocesis (Crick, Northants.) citra eius assensum et voluntatem eam iniuste occupavit. Petit ergo a sanctitate vestra quatinus scribatis abbati de Oseneia et priori de Osen' et suppriori sancte Fretheswithe quod si ita res se habeat, remota appellatione, eum non differant amovere vel quod canonicum fuerit statuatis ; nullis liceat[12] etc ; quod si non omnes etc.

The impetration or seeking of letters took place in the *curia Romana* — 'in Romana curia impetrans' and 'impetraret litteras apostolicas' — where it was decided whether the case should be delegated, and if so what kind of mandate should be sent and to whom. As early as the pontificate of Alexander III, one of the parties in a case is found suggesting a judge,[13] and the examples given above suggest that it was normal, at least by the early thirteenth century, for the plaintiff to propose the names of judges. In his formulary of *c.* 1312, Bernold, a Cistercian monk of Kaisersheim (Swabia, Bavaria), records the instance of an abbot writing to another at the *curia* asking him to get judges for him, '. . . quos idem lator presencium nominabit.'[14] The mandate was drawn up to concur closely with the plaintiff's proctor's account of the case, and in line with the available forms. In most, stereotyped wording prevails in the composition, following the form of petition which

---

[11] H. E. Salter, W. A. Pantin and H. G. Richardson, ed., *Oxford Formularies* (Oxford Historical Society New Series 5; Oxford 1942) 275 no. 5. The editor, H. E. Salter, calls this 'An appeal to the Pope.' It is a 'petitio,' as it says, not an appeal (cf. Drogheda II 8: 'Forma petitionis'). The procedure was probably identical for a case on appeal, but the grounds of the appeal would be mentioned in the impetration. Further examples in this formulary (Baltimore, Walters MS W 15) are: sections 5 ('De Petitionibus': *Oxf. Form.* 274 no. 1), 14, 34 and 41 (all unedited). Section 5 commences 'Si quis summo pontifici aliquod negotium intimare voluerit, sic agere debet.' I am much indebted to Father Donald Logan who lent me his complete transcription of this formulary, which is on folios 79ᵛ-81ᵛ of the manuscript.

[12] Among differences in transcription, most of them minor ones, Father Logan transcribes this, I think rightly, as 'litteris.'

[13] *Comp. I.* 2.11.2, ed. Ae. Friedberg, *Quinque Compilationes Antiquae* (Leipzig 1882) 15; Dom A. Morey, *Bartholomew of Exeter* (Cambridge 1937) 48, thinks that the choice of a judge by an interested party was the exception rather than the rule in the twelfth century.

[14] Bernold in Rockinger, *ed. cit.* 874 no. xiv.

Drogheda quotes.[15] At this point the mandate, which was more in the shape of a draft than a final copy, and thus not sealed,[16] was read out aloud. Professor Barraclough, in his article on the court of *audientia litterarum contradictarum*, written in 1935, maintained that the reading took place in that court, a new offshoot of the Chancery, before the auditor.[17] More recently Dr. Peter Herde, following the late Dr. R. von Heckel who wrote on the subject, has challenged this view. He holds that the reading took place in the *audientia publica* (a public sitting of the Chancery), in the presence of the vice-chancellor, the *auditor litterarum contradictarum*, the papal notaries and correctors, and the proctors. If no objection was raised, the minute was returned to the Chancery for checking, sent to the engrosser's office for the making of a clean copy if necessary, then affixed with the *bulla*, and finally handed over to the plaintiff or his proctor on the payment of a fee. If, on the other hand, an objection or contradiction was raised against the contents of the letter, the vice-chancellor handed the problem over to the *auditor litterarum contradictarum* to be settled in his court.[18]

The first mention of the *audientia publica* and of the *audientia litterarum contradictarum* occurs under Innocent III, and it seems likely that these institutions as such arose at the same time as Innocent's more precisely regulated Chancery reforms dealing with the process of the contradiction. There seems no doubt that at a later date (i.e. after 1331),[19] the two names had come to denote the same office. Yet Dr. Herde considers that it is difficult to see why such evidence as survives should carefully discriminate between *audientia publica* and *audientia litterarum contradictarum* if the offices were identical from the start.[20] As he points out, Thomas of Evesham,* who brought a case to the *curia* in 1205-6, reports that he protested against the letters of

* Read: Thomas of Marlborough

[15] See above at note 10.

[16] Peter Herde, *Beiträge zum päpstlichen Kanzlei- und Urkundenwesen im 13. Jahrhundert* (Münchener Historische Studien 1; Kallmünz 1961) 166.

[17] Barraclough, *art. cit.* 1389.

[18] Herde, *op. cit.* 166. The basis for his view is Bonaguida of Arezzo, an advocate at the Roman *curia* under Innocent IV, whose work was edited by Josef Teige, *art. cit.* in MIOG 17 (1896). The particularly important passage (on p. 409) runs, '. . . si littere contradicuntur in audientia coram vicecancellario, deveniunt postea incontinenti ad manus illius, qui est dominus et ipse querit ab eo, qui contradixit in audientia, quare contradixit . . .'. See also the poem of Master Henry the Poet of Wurzburg, who writes of the chancery under Urban IV (1261-4), and speaks in general terms of the duties of the *arbiter contradictarum*, quoted by R. L. Poole, *Lectures on the History of the Papal Chancery* (Cambridge 1915) 164. A comprehensive study by Dr. Herde on the *audientia litterarum contradictarum* from the thirteenth to the sixteenth century is in preparation.

[19] See the constitution of John XXII in M. Tangl, *Die päpstlichen Kanzleiordnungen von 1200-1500* (Innsbruck 1894) 111.

[20] Barraclough, *art. cit.* 1387, and G. Mollat, *Les Papes d'Avignon 1305-78* (9th ed. Paris 1949) 471, treat them as the same; Barraclough, it seems, for the earlier period also.

his opponent in the *audientia publica*, and that on the following day he argued about the matter with his opponent in the *audientia contradictarum*.[21] All the other sources, including those discussed beyond, speak of the first step of the *contradictio* as taking place in the *audientia publica* whereas the final decision was issued by the *audientia litterarum contradictarum*, fortified with its seal.

The *auditor litterarum contradictarum* was both a Chancery official and a judge. In the event of a contradiction, it was his duty to decide whether it was a reasonable one. In considering the disputed documents, he could act in several ways.[22] Firstly, he could turn down the objection as unfounded, or for lack of empowerments of the protesting proctor, and could then release the document for sealing. Secondly, he could agree with the objection and annul the letter, whereupon the process would start again from the beginning. A number of instances survive of cancelled mandates. In neither of these eventualities did the auditor draw up further documents.

He might, however, after negotiation with the proctors, draw up a new document if the objection was against the details of the delegation, for instance the persons included in the commission of judges or the place of hearing. It was the auditor's duty in this event to act as arbitrator, appointing the third judge if the parties could not agree without his assistance, and suggesting the meeting place.[23] On his instructions the Chancery would issue a new mandate, and when this happened, the auditor himself reported the agreement over the delegation process in a document composed after the issue of the new mandate, and sealed with the seal of the court of *audientia litterarum contradictarum* and not with the *bulla*.[24]

Finally, the mandate could be sent for sealing and dispatch in its original form, although the two parties had agreed on certain conditions which would

---

[21] Herde, *op. cit.* 165 and n. 326.

[22] Herde, *op. cit.* 167. The source for this is the formulary which goes under the name of Innocent IV's vice-chancellor, Marinus of Eboli: F. Schillmann, ed., *Die Formularsammlung des Marinus von Eboli* (Bibliothek des Preussischen Historischen Instituts in Rom 16; Rome 1929). Numbers 3366-3425 concern the *audientia litterarum contradictarum* and date from 1276-7, mentioning Gerard of Parma as auditor in some of the examples. The information contained in the formulary was used by Barraclough in his article (1391). Dr. Robert Brentano, *York Metropolitical Jurisdiction and Papal Judges Delegate (1279-1296)* (University of California Publications in History 58 ; Berkeley and Los Angeles 1959), also used it. On the life and works of Marinus, see now P. Herde, 'Marinus von Eboli "Super revocatoriis" and "De confirmationibus",' *Quellen und Forschungen aus italienischen Archiven und Bibliotheken* 42/43 (1964) 119-264, at pp. 120-48.

[23] See Barraclough, *art. cit.* 1392.

[24] See Appendix, documents nos. II, IV, VIII, XIII, XIV and photographs, and J. Teige, *Beiträge zur Geschichte der Audientia litterarum contradictarum* (Prague 1897) 65, for a description of the seal.

have to be taken into consideration in applying the legal effectiveness of the document. This the auditor certified in an additional document, called a *cautio*, which he drew up himself. These accepted forms of procedure can be found in Marinus' formulary.

Few of the documents, which were issued by the *auditor litterarum contradictarum*, have hitherto been discovered, and very few of these are originals. Durham DCA Loc XIV 4 j appears to be the only known *littere conventionales*. It is not however, an original document, but a contemporary transcript. This was found by Dr. Robert Brentano:[25] it is also registered in British Museum Cotton MS Julius D IV on folio 139r-v. A *cautio* was discovered amongst the State Archives in Vienna and published by Diekamp in 1883,[26] and two more from Munich have now been published by Dr. Herde.[27] Besides these, there are a few examples in formularies and registers.[28]

Two remarkable and sizeable groups of original *littere conventionales* and *cautiones* have survived among the extremely rich collection of charters at Christ Church, Canterbury. Both groups were brought, or were sent back from Rome and Avignon, by the proctors of the house, and have remained in the Christ Church muniments ever since. That they have escaped destruction is fortunate, since they throw some further light on the activities of the *audientia litterarum contradictarum*. There are five *littere conventionales* (two concern the same case) coming from 1277 to 1279,[29] and nine *cautiones* ranging in date from 1230 to 1328.[30]

The first two *littere conventionales* are documents of Gerard, master of the schools of Parma, *auditor litterarum contradictarum* under John XXI,

---

[25] It is printed by him: Brentano, *op. cit.* Appendix VII.

[26] W. Diekamp, 'Zum päpstlichen Urkundenwesen von Alexander IV bis Johann XXII (1254-1334),' MIOG 4 (1883) 536-8 Doc. no. II: dated 1274.

[27] Herde, *Beiträge* Anhang II nos. 1 and 2. Two further documents from the court, which are neither *littere conventionales* nor *cautiones*, are P.R.O. DL 4/10/21, and Westminster Abbey Muniments 32644; the latter cited by Brentano (218).

[28] They are: Gerard of Parma in *Die Formularsammlung des Marinus von Eboli* nos. 3366-3382 (with examples of both documents); Stadtbibliothek Trier no. 859/1097 fols. 37v, 43v-44r, 45r (the MS contains a formulary of the *audientia*), and T. Smičiklas, ed., *Codex Diplomaticus Regni Croatiae* IV (Zagreb 1906) 493 no. 429 (a *cautio* of 1252), all of which are cited by Herde. To these may be added a *cautio* of 1249 which'is registered in the Easby Cartulary, B. M. Egerton MS 2827 fols. 319v, 320r.

[29] Canterbury, Dean and Chapter Archives, Cartae Antiquae C 285, C 284, Sede Vacante Scrapbook [= S. V.] ii. 205, Cart. Antiq. A 106, and Christ Church Letters ii. 316 (Appendix, documents I-V).

[30] Cartae Antiquae C 47, A 206, D 75, A 218, C 1291, S. V. ii.102, and Cart. Antiq. L 403, C 1297 and C 1299 (Appendix, documents VI-XIV). In the course of writing this article I discovered, unexpectedly, a tenth document of this kind, also from Christ Church. It is now in Lambeth Palace Library (Papal documents no. 128a), and was forming the cover of MS 795, a Hollingbourne rental of the Dean and Chapter of Canterbury.

dated 22 April 1277 at Viterbo.[31] They are the earliest yet known. The other three are in the name of James, canon of Bologna, *auditor litterarum contradictarum* under Nicholas III.[32] The format of the documents, both 'super convenientia judicum'[33] and 'super convenientia loci et judicum,'[34] is distinctly comparable with the examples of *littere conventionales* of 1276 which are contained in the Marinus formulary,[35] and also with the transcript of the Durham document discovered by Brentano and dated 1281. The first example 'super convenientia loci et judicum' corresponds with the Canterbury documents of the same genre, C 284, S.V. Book ii. 205 and A 106. It shows the parties agreeing on the third judge without the help of the auditor:[36]

> tandem prefati procuratores J. pro parte sua prepositum ecclesie Mutinensis et C. pro parte sua archidiaconum Cremonensem iudices elegerunt et in venerabilem patrem Reginensem episcopum tanquam in medium et communem iudicem communiter et concorditer convenerunt,

as in A 106:

> tandem prefati procuratores Egidius pro parte sua venerabiles patres . . Episcopum Norwicen' et Philippus pro sua . . Archiepiscopum Cantuarien' judices elegerunt et in . . Archidiaconum Londonien' tamquam in medium et communem judicem communiter et concorditer convenerunt.

The formulary also gives an example of the auditor assigning the third judge if the parties cannot agree,[37]

> Et si non possent convenire de tertio iudice (et de loco), auditor daret hoc modo : Nos vero ex officio nostro iudicem (vel locum) eisdem partibus medium et communem iudicem (vel locum) duximus deputandum,

as in our C 285 (and S.V. Book ii. 205):

> Nos vero ex officio nostro venerabilem patrem . . Episcopum Roffen' eisdem partibus tamquam medium et communem judicem duximus deputandum.

As with the procedure for finding the third judge, the parties themselves

---

[31] C 284, C 285 (Appendix, documents I and II).

[32] S.V. ii.205, A 106, Ch. Ch. Letts. ii.316 (Appendix, documents III-V).

[33] C 285, Ch. Ch. Letts. ii.316.

[34] C 284, S.V. ii.205, A 106. It does not seem possible to argue anything about the diplomatic of the documents from the sealing method. Two of the letters have seals, one on a tag (C 284), and the other on a tongue (A 106), but they are both 'super convenientia loci et judicum.' C 285 'super convenientia judicum' has a tongue, so probably does S.V. ii. 205 'super convenientia loci et judicum.'

[35] Numbers 3383-4 of the Marinus formulary (on p. 389 of the Schillmann edition), are printed in full in J. Teige, *Beiträge* (n. 24 *supra*) 50 nos. (I) and (II).

[36] No. 3383; Teige (I).

[37] *Ibid.*

might decide on a place, or, be assigned one by the auditor. The judges deputed the place in C 284:

> hoc acto de communi consensu inter procuratores prefatos quod dicti judices apud civitatem Roffen' quam eis pro loco deputavimus conveniant tractaturi de causa et negotio infrascriptis . . . .

In the other two documents it is recorded that the place was agreed upon without the auditor's intervention:[38]

> hoc acto de communi concordia inter procuratores prefatos quod iidem judices apud London' conveniant tractaturi ibidem de causa et negotio infrascriptis . . .,

and,[39]

> hoc acto de communi concordia inter procuratores prefatos quod iidem judices apud civitatem Londonien' conveniant tractaturi ibidem de causa et negotio infrascriptis . . .

Comparable with the latter forms are Marinus numbers 3383 and 3387. Number 3387 reads:[40]

> . . . Hoc acto de communi concordia inter procuratores prefatos quod iidem iudices in civitate Aquensi, quam pro loco elegerunt, conveniant tractaturi ibidem de causis et negociis infrascriptis . . .

It is noted in the formulary that if there is no disagreement over the place the 'hoc acto de communi' clause shall be omitted.

No information about the parties' choice of judges, or their assignment by the auditor, or about the decision over the place of hearing, is contained in the mandate. From the following evidence it appears that, without exception, regulars chose regulars as judges, and seculars appointed seculars, assuming that in Christ Church Letters ii. 316, where both the parties 'agreed' on all the judges, the abbot of Chertsey was in fact included on the Christ Church proctor's suggestion, and the dean of the Arches, or the archdeacon of Lewes, at the vicar of Lympne's request.

The first two *littere conventionales*, dated 22 April 1277, concern the same case. The arrangements 'super convenientia judicum' were as follows:[41]

(1) Master Mathias Teatinus (of Chieti, Italy), proctor of Richard (de Strat-

---

[38] S. V. ii.205 (Appendix, document III).

[39] A 106 (Appendix, document IV).

[40] Teige, *op. cit.*, 51 (III). Cf. Marinus no. 3383 (Teige, *op. cit.* 50 (I): 'hoc acto de communi consensu inter procuratores prefatos, quod utraque pars iudicem suum Regium adducat ibidem de causa et negotio infrascriptis iuxta rescriptum apostolicum tractaturi . . .'.

[41] C 285 (Appendix, document I).

ford?),[42] rector of Cliff near Rochester (Kent), the plaintiff, chose the *archdeacon of Rochester* (John de Sancto Dionysio),[43]

(2) Master Philip de Pomonte, proctor of Christ Church, Canterbury, chose the *prior of Rochester,* and

(3) the auditor chose the *bishop of Rochester* (Walter of Merton).[44]

The other document, 'super convenientia loci et judicum,' written by a different scribe on the same day and reciting the same mandate, recorded the arrangements about the judges, but it was also added that *Rochester* had been decided on, with the consent of both the proctors, as the place of hearing.[45]

The next *littere conventionales* of James, canon of Bologna, detailed both the agreement about the judges and about the place in the one document:[46]

(1) John Bacun, rector of Eastry (Kent),[47] chaplain of the bishop of Porto (Robert Kilwardby, archbishop of Canterbury),[48] chose the *archdeacon of London* (Geoffrey de Mortimer),[49]

(2) Philip de Pomonte, proctor of Christ Church, Canterbury, chose the *prior of St. Mary's Southwark,*[50] and

(3) the auditor chose the *abbot of Westminster* (Richard de Ware).[51]

The place for meeting, with the assent of the proctors of both the parties, was declared to be *London.* In the two further documents of James, canon of Bologna, the arrangements were as follows. In the first:[52]

(1) Giles de Adria, clerk, proctor of Richard de Aulanby, rector of Adisham (Kent), chose the *bishop of Norwich* (William Middleton),[53]

---

[42] E. Hasted, *The History and Topographical Survey of Kent* III (Canterbury 1797) 514, says that Richard de Stratford was rector in 1277.

[43] T. Duffus Hardy, ed., John Le Neve, *Fasti Ecclesiae Anglicanae* II (Oxford 1854) 580.

[44] F. M. Powicke and E. B. Fryde, ed., *Handbook of British Chronology* (2nd ed. London 1961) [= HBC] 248: he died 27.x.1277.

[45] C 284 (Appendix, document II).

[46] S.V. II.205 (Appendix, document III).

[47] John Bacun is recorded as rector of Eastry on 2 December 1283 (Lambeth Palace Library, Reg. Pecham fol. 203ᵛ). The rectory was in the patronage of the archbishop (Hasted, *op. cit.* X 118), but nothing further is known of John.

[48] Kilwardby was promoted to the cardinal bishopric of Porto in 1278. C. Eubel, *Hierarchia Catholica Medii Aevi* I (Münster 1913) 36, says on 4 April, and HBC 211, on 12 March, the date according to Eubel (p. 9) of his creation as a cardinal. He died on 12 September 1279.

[49] J. Le Neve, *op. cit.* II 319.

[50] Possibly Stephen (no date), or Alan, died 1283. In 1283-4 a prior of St. Mary's (this Alan?) was dean of the Arches, and therefore a likely choice (*Victoria County History* [= V.C.H.], *Surrey* II [London 1905] 111).

[51] V.C.H. *London* I (London 1909) 455.

[52] A 106.   [53] HBC 242.

(2) Philip de Pomonte, proctor of Christ Church, Canterbury, chose the *archbishop of Canterbury* (John Pecham),[54] and

(3) general consent was given to the *archdeacon of London* (Geoffrey de Mortimer).[55]

They agreed that *London* should be the place of hearing. In the other:[56] Peter, perpetual vicar of Lympne (Kent), and Philip de Pomonte, proctor of Robert of Selsey (Seleseye, Selescia), monk of Christ Church, Canterbury, agreed upon the abbot of Chertsey, the dean of the Arches and the archdeacon of Lewes. Only the last document makes no arrangement about the place where the judges were to sit. The circumstances in which C 285, which does not record the place, and C 284 which does, were written — this being the only difference between the two documents — can only be conjectured. It is feasible that an omission about the place was made by mistake in the first document, to be discovered and rectified immediately by the composition of the second.[57] The places, which were selected in the other cases, Rochester and London, seem to be the obvious choices in view of the personnel of the commissions. When the place was not stipulated, as in Christ Church Letters ii. 316, the judges presumably suited themselves as to the place of meeting, within the framework of decreed canonical procedure. The first stipulation which was made by the pope as to the place where the courts were to meet, was that they should be held in a safe or neutral locality.[58] In the Fourth Lateran Council it was declared that no one was to be summoned more than two days' journey from his own diocese to answer before a church tribunal, unless both the parties agreed to this.[59] A continuous series of indults, which were granted to certain people, conceded that they should not be summoned more than two days' journey in suits before church courts. An investigation into the places where the courts actually met in thirteenth-century English suits shows that on occasion the meeting place was in the church of one of the parties, and that the judges had to travel some distance. Generally speaking, however, the place of the tribunal seems to have been one which was accessible to both parties and judges.[60] An interesting *me-*

---

[54] *Ibid.* 211.   [55] J. Le Neve, *Fasti* II 319.

[56] Christ Church Letters ii.316 (Appendix, document V).

[57] See Appendix, documents I and II.

[58] X.2.28.47: Innocent III to the Bishop of Worcester, 'Appellari potest, si locus non tutus partibus assignatur, etiamsi sit scriptum appellatione remota.'

[59] X 1.3.28; C. J. Hefele, *Histoire des conciles*, tr. and rev. by H. Leclercq, V (Paris 1913) 1363 (can. 37), and e. g. Lord Cooper, *Select Scottish Cases of the Thirteenth Century* (Edinburgh 1944) no. 17.

[60] As shown in the Appendix — 'A List of Some of the Meeting Places of the Courts' — of my unpublished Oxford thesis, *The Jurisdiction of the Papacy in Cases of Appeal and of First Instance in England from 1198 to 1254, with particular reference to the Southern Province* (Oxford 1960). [See now Study II above, 284-96.]

morandum, in a Spalding cartulary, records that on Friday 18 October 1247, the making of peace was considered at Whaplode (Lincs.) between the prior of Castle Acre and the prior of Spalding in a suit before judges delegate at Stamford. It was decided that a more efficacious agreement would be reached in the church of Spalding on 6 July coming (1248) and if peace was not made then, the suit should proceed at Stamford in the church of St. Michael in Cornstall on 11 July. Meanwhile the suit should remain in the same state as on the aforesaid Friday (18 October).[61] Even if the place of hearing was decided on at Rome, or by the judges, there could be much movement before the court finally settled down. The complete absence of evidence in the mandate as to where the court was to meet seems to suggest that this fact was not held to be important by the delegators, unless the parties made a point of getting it settled at Rome. To the parties, however, it could be more than a matter of passing interest.

There arise here several questions concerning the interpretation of the *littere conventionales*. From the formulary evidence it can hardly be held that an objection was made in every case. It would have been a costly and slow process if the selection of judges was always made by the bargaining method of the parties choosing a judge each, and the auditor the third. Furthermore, it would not entirely explain how one and two judges were sometimes appointed. It seems extremely likely that a large proportion of mandates, or drafts,[62] went through the stage of reading in the *audientia publica* without any objection being made. To begin with, a certain number of suits would probably have been undefended. The initial advantage in a suit was with the plaintiff, and, in line with canonical procedure, it was left to the defendant to object. Then in some instances commissions must have been accepted as fair and neutral by the defendants' proctors. The proposal of a biased and hostile commission by the plaintiff's proctor would have been a chancy and hazardous step, and one which would be known to lead to opposition, delays and expense. Dr. Brentano says that 'casual indirect references to this sort of procedure' (i.e. the selection of judges by the parties and auditor), suggest 'that it was common enough,' and he inclines towards thinking that it was the norm.[63] Dr. Herde, however, on the other hand, considers it to have been abnormal procedure, and thinks that contradiction, which meant revision, was an unusual event.

---

[61] Spalding Cartulary, B. M. Add. MS 35,296 fol. 418v. The judges delegate were the abbot of Bourne, the prior of St. John, Northampton, and the archdeacon of Buckingham. At the end, it is noted that this document was sealed by the prior of Castle Acre.

[62] Mandates were, at the best of times, rough and small documents, written on the worst cuts of parchment, and a good deal of revision might take place without recopying.

[63] Brentano, *op. cit.* 157. Also Barraclough, *art. cit.* seems to suggest that this process took place in every case.

It seems probable that the process of contradiction was only brought into play when influential persons were involved, or when the contents of the suit were deemed sufficiently important by the defending proctor to warrant an effort being made to get at least one satisfactory judge. All our cases were contested on behalf of the prior and convent of Christ Church, Canterbury, an important religious house with several standing proctors at Rome. The 1277 case, which is outlined in C 284 and C 285, concerned the tithes of Cliff near Rochester in Kent. The marshland in the parish afforded valuable pasturage, and throughout the thirteenth century the tithes of them were in continual dispute between the prior and convent of Christ Church, who owned considerable lands there, and the rectors. They came to a composition in 1229, and there must have been a further quarrel after the suit of 1277, for there is record of another instrument of 1290.[64] The second suit, in which the Christ Church proctor made an objection, concerned the rights of John, rector of Eastry (Kent).[65] It is known that at the end of the thirteenth century there were endless suits between the convent of Christ Church and the rectors, about the partition of the tithes.[66] In the final mandate in the case the judges were exhorted to revoke whatever had been done to John's prejudice since he had set out for Rome, both it seems on a pilgrimage and to present his case. The last two suits[67] were about the jurisdiction of Robert of Selsey, monk of Christ Church, who was appointed official of Canterbury by the prior and chapter during a vacancy in the archbishopric, either after the promotion of archbishop Robert Kilwardby to the cardinal bishopric of Porto on 12 March 1278 and before the appointment of Robert Burnell sometime between 14 June and 10 July 1278, or after the quashing of Burnell's election, which took place before 25 January 1279, and the provision of John Pecham, who was consecrated on 19 February 1279, and received the temporalities on 30 May 1279.[68] Richard de Aulanby, rector of Adisham (Kent),[69] refused to show obedience to Robert of Selsey, alleging that he had no jurisdiction and that he would prove it. The jurisdiction, he said, belonged in the city and diocese of Canterbury to the archdeacon, and so that Robert should not proceed against him he appealed to Rome, whereupon Robert excommunicated him. He, therefore, appealed again to Rome, but Robert ignored this, and had the sheriff imprison Richard. In the other suit, Peter, perpetual vicar of Lympne,[70] the plaintiff, alleged that Robert, without authority, had

---

[64] Hasted, *op. cit.* III 513.   [65] S. V. ii.205.

[66] HMC *8th Rep.* 326, citing Canterbury, Dean and Chapter Archives, Register C.

[67] A 106 and Christ Church Letters ii.316.   [68] HBC 211.

[69] The church was in the patronage of Christ Church and exempt from the jurisdiction of the archdeacon, according to Hasted (*op. cit.* IX 183-4).

[70] The church was in the patronage of the archdeacon of Canterbury (Hasted, *op. cit.* VIII 301).

promulgated sentences of excommunication and interdict against him. In none of these important suits is it surprising that the defendants' proctor made an objection.

The subsequent career of Robert of Selsey, on whose behalf master Philip de Pomonte made an objection, demands some attention, and gives further information as to why he retained a proctor at Rome.[71] Between 1280 and 1286, as a proctor of Christ Church, he was borrowing money at Rome.[72] From 1281-2 he carried out several commissions on behalf of the archbishop, and on 13 May 1283, he received instructions as Pecham's proctor at Rome.[73] Ten years later in 1293, he acted as a proctor of the prior and chapter of Christ Church at Rome in a suit about their jurisdiction *sede vacante*.[74] He is a typical professional monk proctor at the Roman *curia*, appearing sometimes on behalf of the archbishop and sometimes on behalf of the prior and convent. He was still alive in 1337 when his name occurs in the Christ Church Library borrowers' list.[75]

Another problem concerns the place of the *littere conventionales* in the procedure. Dr. Brentano seems to consider that the process, which is described in the *littere conventionales*, preceded the first mandate.[76] Dr. Herde, on the other hand, considers that the *littere conventionales* of the *auditor litterarum contradictarum* followed a preceding delegation rescript, which had been read out and contradicted, so that the auditor had to settle the matter.[77] Neither of them has attempted to explain why the letters are dated after the mandate which is quoted, be it the first or the final one, although the procedure they record preceded it. Obviously the document cannot have been drawn up for curial reasons, and the reason for its composition must lie in the fact that it was important for the proctor to take home authentication of proceedings, which were not detailed in the mandate, but which nevertheless depended on the mandate for their validity.

A further point of difficulty is the long gap which sometimes took place between the issue of the mandate and the issue of the *littere conventionales*. The Canterbury examples show intervals varying from five days to as long

---

[71] For Robert of Selsey, see W. G. Searle, *The Chronicle of John Stone . . . Lists of Deans, Priors and Monks of Christ Church Monastery* (Cambridge Antiquarian Society 34; Cambridge 1902) 169, 176, and the references he gives there, especially C. T. Martin, ed., *Registrum Epistolarum . . . Peckham* I (Rolls Series 77; London 1882) 51, referring in a letter dated 18 August 1279 to his appointment during the vacancy.

[72] HMC *5th Rep.* 451, citing Canterbury, Cartae Antiquae P 56, 57, 58 and C 1286.

[73] *Reg. Epist. Peck.* I 188, 300, and II (1884) 551.

[74] I. J. Churchill, *Canterbury Administration* I (London 1933) 561, citing Cambridge University Library MS Ee v 31, fol. 65ᵛ.

[75] J. B. Sheppard, ed., *Literae Cantuarienses* II (Rolls Series 85; London 1888) 150.

[76] Brentano, *op. cit.* 156-8.

[77] Herde, *op. cit.* 166 n. 334.

as a month and a half.[78] It is possible that the new mandates in disputed cases were read out again in the *audientia publica* before despatch, and had to wait their turn, and that the complementary documents of the auditor were then drawn up on the day of re-reading or shortly after.

Since the mandate could be made out both generally and inclusively, that is to say, it could cover a variety of charges, and it could be issued against more than one person,[79] it was the duty of standing proctors at the *curia* to protest against any issue of letters which might bring before the courts, or prejudice, their masters or clients. Procuratorial letters of appointment usually granted the power of seeking and agreeing to *cauciones*.[80] If the protest was accepted by the *auditor litterarum contradictarum*, he drew up a *cautio* which attested that the mandate was not valid against certain persons. The practice of issuing an official *cautio* in the name of the auditor seems to have become the norm.[81] Like the procedure for choosing the judges and the place of hearing, this action finds no place in the mandate.

Original *cautiones*, which have been discovered previously, date from 1253 (two documents) and 1274.[82] The Canterbury collection includes documents of seven auditors, Robert of Somercotes (Sumercota, Sumercote), Gerard, master of the schools of Parma, James, canon of Bologna, Guy de Novavilla, canon of Limoges, Bernard Roiardi, archdeacon of Xanten, Peter Després, archbishop of Aix, and Bertrand, archbishop of Embrun. The first of the Canterbury sequence, although not issued by the auditor, is undoubtedly a document of this kind, closely connected with the official *cautio*.[83] It bears the early date of 1230, and is a letter of master Richard of Langdon,[84] proctor of Richard Wethershed, archbishop of Canterbury, promising not to convene the convent of Christ Church nor to do anything to their prejudice, by virtue of a mandate of Gregory IX, which had been granted to him on 10 September of the same year; his seal was added to it. Master Philip

---

[78] Mandates	Auditor's documents	Delay	Reference
17 April 1277	22 April 1277	5 days	C 284, 285
25 Nov. 1278	11 Jan. 1279	1 ½ months	S.V. II.205
13 Feb. 1279	15 March 1279	1 month	A 106
23 March 1279	31 March 1279	8 days	Ch. Ch. Letts. II.316

[79] See J. Teige, *art. cit.* (n. 8 *supra*) 412, forms of petitions: 'Attende insuper, quod de tribus diocesibus et de tribus civitatibus, ut patet exemplum in premissa petitione, possunt per illam clausulam "quidam alii" conveniri, de pluribus minime; et istud Romana curia diligenter observat.'

[80] See John of Bologna's formulary in Ludwig Rockinger, *op. cit.* 608-9.

[81] J. Teige, *Beiträge* 56 (II) gives a plain form.

[82] See notes 26 and 27 *supra*. [83] C 47 (Appendix, document VI).

[84] Master Richard of Langdon became the official of archbishop Edmund Rich, see W. Stubbs, ed., *The Historical Works of Gervase of Canterbury* II (Rolls Series 73; London 1880) 165, 170-1).

de Mortimer, proctor of Christ Church, had protested in the *audientia publica*. The document was witnessed by master Simon Langton, archdeacon of Canterbury,[85] Walter, at one time archbishop-elect of Canterbury,[86] and master Robert of Somercotes.

No original documents of the *audientia litterarum contradictarum* seem to have survived from before 1238, during the auditorship of master Robert of Somercotes,[87] who witnessed the previous charter. In that year, the archdeacon of Canterbury, complaining that the possessions of the archdeaconry had been illegally seized, got letters from Gregory IX to Otto, cardinal deacon of St. Nicholas in Carcere and papal legate in England, to which Thomas, monk and proctor of the prior and chapter of Christ Church, objected, fearing

---

[85] Langton became archdeacon in 1227, see K. Major, ed., *Acta Stephani Langton* (Canterbury and York Series 50; Oxford 1940) xix.

[86] Walter de Eynesham (or Hempsham), monk of Canterbury (J. Le Neve, *Fasti* I 11). He was a clerk of archbishop Langton (*Acta Stephani Langton* 18, 37, 42, 47, 52-3, 55, 59, 61), and official (xlviii n. 1).

[87] Master Robert of Somercotes, an Englishman, was *auditor litterarum contradictarum* from at least 1 March to 20 May 1238 (Lucien Auvray, ed., *Les Registres de Grégoire IX* [Bibliothèque des Écoles Françaises d'Athènes et de Rome, série 2, 9 ; Paris 1896-1955, hereafter cited as *Reg. Greg. IX*] no. 4123 : A 206). He is not included in Bresslau's list (H. Bresslau, *Handbuch der Urkundenlehre für Deutschland und Italien* I [2nd ed. Leipzig 1912] 284 n. 1). His career illustrates how a man with legal training might rise to a powerful position within the *curia*. He was possibly a relative of master Laurence of Somercotes, the author of an election tract, who is thought to have come from the Lincolnshire town of Somercotes (J. C. Russell, *A Dictionary of Thirteenth Century Writers* [Bulletin of the Institute of Historical Research, Supplement no. 3; London 1936] 81). He had been educated at Paris and at Bologna (P. Bruno Griesser, 'Registrum Epistolarum Stephani de Lexinton,' *Analecta Sacri Ordinis Cisterciensis* 8 [Rome 1952] 315 n. 101). From 1235 until 1237 he was in the service of the Crown, expediting the royal business at Rome (W. W. Shirley, ed., *Royal . . . Letters . . . of the Reign of Henry III* I [Rolls Series 27; London 1862] 463: *Calendar of the Patent Rolls 1232-47* [H.M.S.O. London 1906] 95, 134-5, 156, 173, 176 : *Close Rolls 1234-7* [H.M.S.O. London 1908] 130, 300: *Calendar of the Liberate Rolls 1226-40* [H.M.S.O. London 1916] 243). By 23 May 1236 he had become a papal subdeacon (*Reg. Greg. IX* nos. 3155, 3171). In 1239 he was created cardinal deacon of St. Eustace by Gregory IX (Eubel, *op. cit.* 6). From 1239 to 1241 he acted as an auditor from time to time (e. g. *Reg. Greg. IX* nos. 4709, 6091: L. Cardella, *Memorie Storiche de' Cardinali* I [Rome 1792] 256). It is intimated by Matthew Paris that he would have been elected pope as successor to Gregory IX, had he not died in 1241 in the course of the conclave which finally elected Celestine IV (Sir F. Madden, ed., *Matthaei Parisiensis . . . Historia Anglorum* II [Rolls Series 44; London 1866] 457). He had been provided with the churches of Croydon and Castor (Northants.), which it was later endeavoured to obtain for his relative, probably nephew, John of Somercotes, who was chaplain to the Roman, Richard de Annibaldis, cardinal deacon of St. Angelo, and in the employ of the King of England (*Reg. Greg. IX* nos. 946, 3171, 5981-2: P. R. O. Llanthony Cart., Chancery Masters Exhibits C 115/A 1 fol. 125r, 125v: *Close Rolls 1242-7* [H.M.S.O. London 1916] 146). He is buried in the church of St. Chrysogonus in Trastevere (L. Cardella, *op. cit.* I 257).

that his party might be brought before the courts. The letter of master Robert of Somercote, a *cautio*, confirmed that this would not be so. No seal remains, but two holes for cords are visible and the final sentence of the document attests that it was sealed with 'our seal,' presumably the seal of the *audientia litterarum contradictarum*.[88]

The *cautiones* of 1276 and 1278, issued respectively by Gerard master of the schools of Parma, and James, canon of Bologna, are strikingly similar to the formulary examples of 1276-7. [89] The first recorded that master Mathias, *canonicus Theatin'* (Chieti, Italy), proctor of Dover priory, had got letters from Innocent V to the archdeacon of Middlesex, concerning the alienated possessions of the priory, to which master Philip de Pomonte objected, lest Christ Church should be convened:[90] the second that master Luke of Guarcino, proctor of Leeds, had obtained letters from Nicholas III, firstly to the prior of Rochester, and then to the prior of Southwark, about the alienated possessions of the priory, against which master Philip de Pomonte, proctor of Christ Church, protested.[91] Both these documents come in the category of *cautiones* 'ea que de bonis,' for which a major and a minor form are given in the formulary,[92] as do A 206, Sede Vacante Scrapbook ii.102, and C 1299, *cautiones* of 1238, 1287 and 1328. These also concerned alienated tithes and possessions. Walter de Meldona, rector of Chart by Sutton (Kent), got letters from Honorius IV in 1287, and master Thomas de Boynthon, proctor of St. Alban's, impetrated from John XXII in 1328. The mandates included the order:[93]

> mandamus quatinus ea que de bonis ipsius ecclesie (monasterii) per concessiones hujusmodi alienata inveneris illicite vel distracta non obstantibus litteris renunciationibus penis juramentis (litteris instrumentis juramentis renunciationibus penis) et confirmationibus supradictis ad jus et proprietatem ejusdem ecclesie (monasterii) legitime revocare procures.

The formulary also gives examples for the drawing up of *cautiones* when the subject matter of the case concerned indults and liberties, or prebends.[94] The subject matter of the remaining Canterbury *cautiones* include presentation to a church, tithes, and prejudicial acts in the course of an appeal in a case about possessions.[95]

---

[88] A 206 (Appendix, document VII).

[89] Marinus nos. 3366-9 and 3376 (Schillmann edition, *Formularsammlung*, 387-8).

[90] D 75 (Appendix, document VIII).   [91] A 218 (Appendix, document IX).

[92] Marinus nos. 3366, 3369; 'Cautio super hiis "ea que de bonis" in maiori forma' and ' "Ea que de bonis" in minori forma.'

[93] S. V. ii.102 and C 1299 (Appendix, documents XI, XIV). Bracketed readings are those of the second document.

[94] Marinus nos. 3367, 3368.

[95] C 47, C 1291, L 403 and C 1297.

With the exception of one document, which is almost certainly wrongly dated,[96] the dating shows that the auditor's document, recording the procedure before him, was drawn up after the mandate, as one would expect. The intervals of time between the composition of the mandate and the publication of the *cautio* vary from five days to one month and four days.[97] Herde reports that he knows of no example where the document quoted in the *cautio* (i.e. the mandate), is of a later date.[98] This implies that the mandate was already dated when it was read out, and that the date of the auditor's document represents near enough the date of the acceptance of the objection by the impetrant's proctor and the *auditor litterarum contradictarum*. The document recording the *cautio* was then sent back to the client of the proctor who had made the objection, to be used in conjunction with the mandate to the judges if the plaintiff sought to summon him before a delegated court. The Canterbury *cautiones* all record objections, which were made by different proctors of the house — master Philip de Mortimer, Thomas, monk and proctor, master Philip de Pomonte, Nicholas de Sancto Victore, master Ralph de Lacu, master Brice of Sharsted and master John of Malling (Mallinge).[99]

Of the Canterbury proctors, nothing more can be found out about master Philip de Mortimer or Thomas, monk and proctor, and they may have acted more in a temporary than in a permanent capacity; but master Philip de Pomonte, who appears in both kinds of document, *littere conventionales* and *cautiones*, was a highly skilled and professional pleader, in all probability an Italian.[100] All the *littere conventionales*, and two of the *cautiones*, were acquired and brought or sent back by him. His name is written, in various forms, on the tongues of D 75, C 285 and A 106, a place where the contra-

---

[96] C 1291 (Appendix, document X). The date of the mandate, a mandate of protection, would seem to be correct since it corresponds with the date of the mandate to the judges to hear the case, a not uncommon procedure in the same suit. It seems probable, therefore, that the scribe wrote 'xv Kal. Jan' incorrectly for 'xv kal. Feb' in dating the auditor's document. It is odd, however, that the mistake was not noticed and rectified.

[97]
Mandates	Auditors' documents	Reference
11 May 1276	21 May 1276	D 75
5 Sept. 1278	22 Sept. 1278	A 218
8 Jan. 1287	18 Dec. 1286 (18 Jan. 1287)	C 1291
8 Jan. 1287	13 Jan. 1287	S.V. ii.102
13 Dec. 1316	20 Dec. 1316	L 403
20 Dec. 1319	23 Jan. 1320	C 1297
15 Feb. 1328	6 March 1328	C 1299

[98] Herde, *op. cit.* 166-7 and n. 330.

[99] C 47, A 206, D 75 and A 218, C 1291 and S. V. ii.102, L 403, C 1297, C 1299.

[100] On the professionalism of the proctors and the rise of procuratorial families (e.g. Peter and Philip of Assisi 1289-96, and Peter of Anagni), see R. von Heckel, *op. cit.* (n. 1 *supra*) 320.

dictor's name is frequently written.[101] He appeared at the *curia* on behalf of Christ Church between 1276 and 1279, and in the latter year on behalf of Robert of Selsey.[102] On 1 May 1282, in a deed dated at Mortlake, he was appointed Archbishop Pecham's proctor at Rome in company with James de Trebys, an appointment which was prolonged on 20 September at Aldington.[103] In 1289 he was receiving a salary as proctor of the prior and convent, for which he gave a receipt.[104] By 1291 he had ceased to be the convent's proctor, when a letter to the prior from Nicholas de Sancto Victore announced his death.[105]

Nicholas de Sancto Victore was also employed by Christ Church at Rome, between 1286 and 1287, and again in 1289 and 1291.[106] Herde identifies him as acting on behalf of the convent of St. Agnes, Wurzburg, in 1284, and the friars minor at Regensburg in 1286.[107] Like master Philip de Pomonte, he appears to have been an Italian (perhaps from San Vittore del Lazio, Frosinone). This is not so with the three fourteenth-century Canterbury proctors, who were Englishmen and Oxford masters. Master Ralph de Lacu (de la Lee) was proctor in a case at the Roman *curia* concerning disputed claims to the church of Finningham (Suffolk) in 1302-3, and represented the university against the Dominicans at Rome in 1312. He was in receipt of a pension from Worcester cathedral priory in 1313-14, for legal services, and acted on behalf of Christ Church in 1316.[108] By 1309 he had been made a canon and prebendary of St. Chad's, Shrewsbury, and in 1323 was dean of Westbury-on-Trym (Glos.).[109] Master Brice of Sharsted was a proctor of the court of Canterbury in 1316 and 1319, and in receipt of an annual pension of £2, and then proctor of Christ Church at Rome in 1319-1320.[110] He represented Bishop Hethe of Rochester at Rome in 1321,[111] and was his clerk from 1321-5. In 1326 and

---

[101] See MIOG 4 (1883) 536-8 'J. de Ancora'; P.R.O. DL 41/10/21 'J. Bhont' (for J. Bohun?); L 403 'R de lacu', and Westminster Abbey Muniments 32644 'P. de asisio'.

[102] See above p. 322f.

[103] *Reg. Epist. Peck.* III (London 1885) 1023, 1058 (fols. 65ᵛ and 151ʳ: see also 20ᵛ, 22ʳ, 24ᵛ, 27ᵛ, 28ʳ, 28ᵛ, 142ᵛ, 143ʳ, 143ᵛ, 150ᵛ).

[104] Canterbury, Dean and Chapter Archives, Cartae Antiquae C 224.

[105] HMC *Var. Coll.* I (London 1901) 259: (Eastry Letters III 119).

[106] C 1291, S. V. ɪɪ.102 (Appendix, documents X, XI) C 224 and *Var. Coll.* I 259 (Eastry Letters III 119).

[107] Herde, *op. cit.* 95, 100.

[108] A. B. Emden, *A Biographical Register of the University of Oxford* I (Oxford 1958) 560 (hereafter cited as *Oxf. Reg.*), additions in *Bodleian Library Quarterly* 7 (1964) 152, and L 403.

[109] *Oxf. Reg.* I 560.

[110] R. A. L. Smith, *Canterbury Cathedral Priory* (Cambridge 1943) 75, and C 1297 (Appendix, document XIII).

[111] E. Göller, *Die Einnahmen der Apostolischen Kammer unter Johann XXII* (Paderborn 1910) 139.

1327 he is found advising the prior of Christ Church on questions of church patronage.[112] In 1327 he was an advocate in the court of Arches. A Mertonian, he is said to have maintained friendly relations with Christ Church, Canterbury, bequeathing them his books on canon law in his will.[113] Master John of Malling, proctor of Christ Church in 1328, although not listed among the Oxford and Cambridge masters, may surely be presumed to have come from the Kentish town of that name.[114] He was the prior's agent in the *curia* in 1327 when a letter was sent to him warning him to be on his guard against the proceedings of Thomas of Sandwich, a fugitive monk, who it is thought will probably appear at the *curia* to impetrate. He was also asked to tell their friends in the *curia* about Thomas, and to return information by the messenger, or another one to be sent soon, about other causes and negotiations.[115]

The proctors of the other parties, for the most part, present a similar front of professionalism and legal learning. Master Mathias of Chieti appeared on behalf of Dover priory in 1276,[116] and on behalf of Richard, rector of Cliff (Kent) in 1277.[117] He was engaged by Bishop Pontissara at Rome in 1283, and by Archbishop Winchelsey in 1299.[118] He also had commissions from the master general and the convent of the Humiliati and from Hermina, abbess-elect of St. Mary's Troyes in 1280 and 1286.[119] Master Luke of Guarcino (diocese of Alatri) represented Leeds priory twice in 1278, and the bishop of Down (Ireland) in 1279.[120] Giles de Adria, clerk, who appeared as proctor of Richard de Aulanby, rector of Adisham in Kent, in 1279, possibly came from Atri in the province of Teramo, and may have been a kind of poor man's Italian lawyer.[121] With the fourteenth century, the tendency for the proctors to be English, and probably mostly English educated, is again noticeable. Master Nicholas de Lodelawe, in company with master Ralph de Lacu, represented Oxford University in the quarrel with the Dominicans over the

---

[112] *Lit. Cant.* I (1887) 186-9, 237.

[113] *Oxf. Reg.* III (1959) 1681.

[114] *Ibid.* II (1958) 1209, has a master Ralph de Malling, who was rector of Stourmouth (Kent) from 1323 to 1354, but no John.

[115] *Lit. Cant.* I 230.

[116] D 75 (Appendix, document VIII): this document mentions him as canon of Chieti.

[117] C 284 (Appendix, document II).

[118] C. Deedes, ed., *Registrum Johannis de Pontissara* (Canterbury and York Series 19; London 1915) 271-2: Lambeth Palace Library, Reg. Rob. Winchelsey fol. 313, and see R. Graham, 'The Administration of the Diocese of Ely during the vacancies of the See, 1298-9 and 1302-3,' *Transactions of the Royal Historical Society* 4th series 12 (1929) 58.

[119] Jules Gay and Suzanne Vitte, ed., *Les Registres de Nicolas III* (Bibliothèque des Écoles Françaises d'Athènes et de Rome, série 2, 14; Paris 1898-1938) no. 634, and Maurice Prou, ed., *Les Registres d'Honorius IV* (Bibliothèque . . . série 2, 7; Paris 1888) no. 671.

[120] A 218 (Appendix, document IX), MS Lambeth 795, and *Reg. Nic. III* no. 589.

[121] A 106 (Appendix, document IV).

curriculum in 1312. By 1316 he was rector of Monks Risborough (Bucks.), and represented Ralph de Drayton, rector of Lowick (Northants.) as proctor at Avignon, and in the same year he was given licence to study at an English university for three years.[122] He seems to have been resident at Avignon at least by the 1330's and tried to influence the pope against the appointment of Robert de Wyville as bishop of Salisbury in 1330. As a non-resident pluralist (he held canonries at York, Salisbury and Dublin),[123] he died some two days' journey from Avignon in 1334.[124] He had represented the archbishop of York in 1332.[125] The purchase of his books, including some on canon and civil law, is recorded in Hemingby's register in 1342.[126] Master Ralph of Horncastle, who was a proctor of the convent of St. Augustine's, Canterbury, in 1319-20 and 1321, and of the abbot in 1323 and 1327, was proctor of the bishop of Llandaff at Rome in 1324 and 1325, and of John, bishop of Carlisle, in 1327.[127] He was provided to several benefices and the canonries of St. John's Howden, Hereford and Southwell.[128] He has been confused with Master Alan de Horncastle by Dr. Emden and does not appear among his list of Oxford masters.[129] A similar difficulty arises with master Thomas de Boynthon, proctor of St. Alban's in 1328, who does not appear either amongst the Oxford or Cambridge masters,[130] but who in 1331 and 1332 represented Simon Meopham, archbishop of Canterbury, as proctor, and in 1330 and 1331 the bishop of Meath (Ireland).[131]

In conclusion, we come to the importance of the mandate in the judge delegate procedure. The *littere conventionales* and the *cautiones* were devised to be used in conjunction with the mandate, to curb its powers against acting too heavily in favour of the plaintiff, but in no way to replace it. The mandate or rescript, was drawn up in the Chancery, sealed with the leaden bulla on hemp cords and issued in the pope's name. It set the machinery of the courts into

---

[122] *Oxf. Reg.* II 1155, L 403 (Appendix, document XII).

[123] Göller, *op. cit.* 168.

[124] *Oxf. Reg.* II 1155, and W. H. Bliss, ed., *Calendar of Entries in the Papal Registers relating to Great Britain: Papal Letters* II (H.M.S.O. London 1895) 399, 406. It is noteworthy that he himself was bishop-elect of Salisbury by 1333 (*Calendar of Papal Letters* II 410).

[125] Göller, *op. cit.* 98.

[126] *Hemingby's Register* (note 3 *supra*) 110 no. 166.

[127] C 1297 (Appendix, document XIII), Göller, *op. cit.* 51-2, 60, 78, 173, 182, 197, 200.

[128] *Calendar of Papal Letters* II 172, 300, 354, 366, 374.

[129] *Oxf. Reg.* II 965, and see Göller, *op. cit.* 60, 78, 173 and LXXXV, also C. L. Shadwell and H. E. Salter, *Oriel College Records* (Oxford Historical Society 85; Oxford 1926) 261 n. 303.

[130] C 1299 (Appendix, document XIV). In 1331 as rector of St. Mary's, Gateshead, he received a canonry and became prebendary of Beverley on the petition of Queen Isabella (*Calendar of Papal Letters* II 359). Göller (*op. cit.* 215) gives him as appearing on behalf of St. Alban's also in 1328.

[131] Göller, *op. cit.* 93, 96, 241, 248.

action. All judicial authority was derived from it, and it was impossible to proceed without it. It was quoted at most stages of the suit, for example at citation and sentence, and was not superseded until the judges' final *actum* was completed. Even then, it was not always destroyed. In 1220, the judges delegate produced letters of the lord pope (i. e. the mandate) when summoned to answer before the king for a decision in a case about advowson.[132] The power of the mandate, which was distinctly comparable with the royal writ, was at the heart of the whole judge delegate system.

Numerous original mandates survive. The common form, in which so many are written, became inevitable owing to the immense amount of litigation which was sent to Rome. Dr. Salter supposed that groups of cases were designated for Rome;[133] in the same way general mandates were returned for dealing with a collection of cases against several different people. It was impossible for all these people to retain proctors or to get a chance to protest at Rome. The Dover cartulary records the priory appearing against two different parties before the same judge on the same day,[134] and the St. Neot's cartulary includes three settlements all made at the beginning of April 1232 before the precentor of Barnwell and the dean of Cambridge.[135] These are instances of inclusive mandates.

The papal Chancery was in no way concerned with checking the rights and wrongs of the plaintiff's case, at least at the stage when the rescript was drawn up, nor with commenting on the commission which had been sought. All this was the responsibility of the proctor, and the Chancery was prepared to allow for objections by the provision of the *audientia litterarum contradictarum*. The *auditor litterarum contradictarum* did not issue even corrected mandates, but merely authenticated documents for the proctors' use, just as he controlled their activities. The essence of the *audientia litterarum contradictarum* lies in the fact that it was a court for the proctors, and in this light it must be admitted that those, like the convent of Christ Church, Canterbury, who were wealthy enough to employ proctors at Rome to safeguard and press their rights, had an advantage over the poor and undefended.

London.

---

[132] *Curia Regis Rolls* IX (H.M.S.O. London 1952) 52.

[133] H. E. Salter, ed., *Cartulary of Oseney Abbey* VI (Oxford Historical Society 101; Oxford 1936) 339.

[134] Dover Cartulary, Lambeth Palace Library, MS 241 fols. 50ᵛ, 51ʳ.

[135] St. Neot's Cartulary, B. M. Cotton MS Faustina A IV, fol. 111ᵛ (2 cases) and fol. 112ʳ. St. Neot's presented three beneficed clerks, Robert parson of Barnwell, Bartholomew, rector of Barton Bendish, and T. rector of Brampton.

332

APPENDIX

I

Littere super convenientia judicum of Gerard, Master of the schools of Parma, papal chaplain and *auditor litterarum contradictarum*, dated 22 April 1277 at Viterbo.

Omnibus presentes litteras inspecturis Gerardus magister scolarum ecclesie Parmen' domini pape capellanus et ipsius litterarum contradictarum auditor salutem in domino. Noveritis quod cum inter magistrum Mathiam Teatin' procuratorem magistri Riccardi rectoris ecclesie de Clive pro ipso in Romana Curia impetrantem ex parte una, et magistrum Philippum de Pomonte procuratorem . . Prioris et conventus ecclesie Christi Cantuarien' pro ipsis contradicentem ex altera, aliquamdiu super convenientia judicum foret in nostra presencia litigatum, tandem prefati procuratores Mathias pro parte sua . . Archidiaconum et Philippus pro sua . . Priorem Roffen' judices elegerunt. Nos vero ex officio nostro [1] venerabilem patrem . . Episcopum Roffen' eisdem partibus tamquam medium et communem judicem duximus deputandum. Ad quos diriguntur littere apostolice sub hac forma: Johannes episcopus etc. venerabili fratri . . Episcopo et dilectis filiis . . Priori et . . Archidiacono Roffen' salutem etc. Conquestus est nobis magister Riccardus rector ecclesie de Clive quod . . Prior et conventus ecclesie Christi Cantuarien' super decimis et rebus aliis injuriantur eidem. Ideoque discretioni vestre per apostolica scripta mandamus quatinus partibus convocatis audiatis causam et appellatione remota fine debito decidatis. Facientes etc. Testes autem etc. Quod si non omnes etc. duo vestrum etc. Dat' Viterbii xv kalendas Maii pontificatus nostri anno primo.[2] In cujus conventionis testimonium presentes litteras fieri fecimus et audiencie contradictarum sigillo muniri. Dat' Viterbii x kalendas Maii pontificatus domini Johannis pape xxi^{mi} anno primo.ˈ

Jo - lo.

Tongue for seal ('pomont' is written on the end of the tongue): no trace of the wax.

Reference: Canterbury, Dean and Chapter Archives, Cartae Antiquae C 285.

Measurements : $7^3/_4{}''$ × $3^3/_4{}''$.

Medieval endorsement (hand *x*, 14th century): Assensus procuratoris nostri et procuratoris Ricardi rectoris de Clive in judices in Anglia pro decimis de Clive. tempore J. pape. xxi^{mi}.

II

Littere super convenientia loci et judicum of Gerard, Master of the schools of Parma, papal chaplain and *auditor litterarum contradictarum*, dated 22 April 1277 at Viterbo.

Omnibus presentes litteras inspecturis Gerardus magister scolarum ecclesie Parmen' domini pape capellanus et ipsius litterarum contradictarum auditor

---

[1] Text 'nostrum'. [2] 17 April 1277.

C 285 = Appendix, Document I

*Reproduced by kind permission of the
Dean and Chapter of Canterbury.*

C 284 = Appendix, Document II

*Reproduced by kind permission of the
Dean and Chapter of Canterbury.*

III

salutem in domino. Noveritis quod cum inter magistrum Mathiam Theatin' procuratorem magistri Riccardi rectoris ecclesie de Clive pro ipso in Romana Curia impetrantem ex parte una, et magistrum Phylippum de Pomonte procuratorem . . Prioris et conventus ecclesie Christi Cantuarien' pro ipsis contradicentem ex altera, aliquamdiu foret super convenientia loci et judicum in nostra presencia litigatum, tandem prefati procuratores Mathias pro parte sua . . Archidiaconum et Phylippus pro sua . . Priorem Roffen' judices elegerunt. Nos vero ex officio nostro venerabilem patrem . . Episcopum Roffen' eisdem partibus tanquam medium et communem judicem duximus deputandum. Hoc acto de communi consensu inter procuratores prefatos quod dicti judices apud civitatem Roffen' quam eis pro loco deputavimus conveniant, tractaturi de causa et negotio infrascriptis juxta rescriptum apostolicum quod ad eos dirigitur sub hac forma: — Johannes episcopus etc. venerabili fratri . . Episcopo et dilectis filiis . . Priori et . . Archidiacono Roffen' salutem etc. Conquestus est nobis magister Riccardus rector ecclesie de Clive quod . . Prior et conventus ecclesie Christi Cantuarien' super decimis et rebus aliis injuriantur eidem. Ideoque discretioni vestre per apostolica scripta mandamus quatinus partibus convocatis audiatis causam et appellatione remota fine debito decidatis. Facientes etc. Testes autem etc. Quod si non omnes etc. duo vestrum etc. Dat' Viterbii xv kalendas Maii pontificatus nostri anno primo.[1] In cujus conventionis testimonium presentes litteras fieri fecimus et audiencie contradictarum sigillo muniri. Dat' Viterbii x kalendas Maii pontificatus domini Johannis pape xxmi primi anno primo.

Vesica shaped red wax seal of the *audientia litterarum contradictarum* on a tag. Size $1^1/_{16}'' \times 4^3/_{16}''$.
Reference: Canterbury, Dean and Chapter Archives, Cartae Antiquae C 284.
Measurements : $8^1/_4'' \times 4^1/_4''$.
Medieval endorsement (hand *x*, 14th century): Convenientia loci et judicum in Anglia inter nos et Ricardi Rectorem de Clive tempore J. pape xxi.

III

Littere super convenientia loci et judicum of James, Canon of Bologna, *doctor decretorum*, papal chaplain and *auditor litterarum contradictarum*, dated 11 January 1279 at St. Peter's, Rome.

Omnibus presentes litteras inspecturis Jacobus canonicus Bononien' decretorum doctor domini pape capellanus et ipsius litterarum contradictarum auditor salutem in domino. Noveritis quod cum inter Johannem capellanum venerabilis patris . . Episcopi Portuen' rectorem ecclesie de Estrya Cantuarien' diocesis pro se in Romana Curia impetrantem ex parte una, et Philippum de Pomonte clericum procuratorem . . Prioris et conventus ecclesie Christi Cantuarien' pro ipsis contradicentem ex altera, aliquandiu super convenientia loci et judicum foret in nostra presencia litigatum, tandem prefati Johannes pro parte sua . . Archidiaconum Londonien' et Philippus pro sua . . Priorem beate marie de Suwerk' Wintonien' diocesis judices elegerunt. Nos vero ex officio nostro . . Abbatem Westimon' ejusdem diocesis tamquam medium et

---

[1] 17 April 1277.

334

communem judicem eisdem partibus duximus deputandum. Hoc acto de communi concordia inter procuratores prefatos quo iidem judices apud London' conveniant, tractaturi ibidem de causa et negotio infrascriptis secundum rescriptum apostolicum quod ad eos dirigitur sub hac forma: — Nicolaus episcopus etc. dilectis filiis . . Abbati Westimon' et . . Archidiacono Londonien' ac . . Priori beate marie de Suwerk' Wintonien' diocesis salutem etc. Inclinati precibus dilecti filii Johannis capellani venerabilis fratris nostri Portuen' . . Episcopi rectoris ecclesie de Estrya Cantuarien' diocesis apud sedem apostolicam constituti presentium vobis auctoritate mandamus quatinus quicquid in prejudicium ipsius rectoris postquam ipse causa peregrinationis et pro quibusdam suis et ecclesie predicte de Estrya negotiis promovendis iter arripuit ad sedem veniendi predictam inveneris temere attemptatum in statum debitum legitime revocare curetis. Contra' etc. Dat' Rom' apud Sanctum Petrum vii kalendas Decembris pontificatus nostri anno primo.[1] In cujus conventionis testimonium presentes litteras fieri fecimus et audiencie contradictarum sigillo muniri. Dat' Rome apud Sanctum Petrum iii idus Januarii pontificatus domini Nicolai pape iii anno secundo.
Jo

All signs of sealing method removed: the document has been cut.

Reference: Canterbury, Dean and Chapter Archives, Sede Vacante Scrapbook II, p. 205.

Measurements: $7^3/_4''$ × $4^3/_4''$.

Medieval endorsements (13th century): Copia littere que inpetrat' de attemptat' post arreptum versus cur' Joh' bacu' et convenient' judicum in eadem
custus littere ii d' qua

(hand *x*, 14th century): tempore N. papa iii.

IV

Littere super convenientia loci et judicum of James, Canon of Bologna, *doctor decretorum*, papal chaplain and *auditor litterarum contradictarum*, dated 15 March 1279 at St. Peter's, Rome.

Omnibus presentes litteras inspecturis Jacobus canonicus Bononien' decretorum doctor domini pape capellanus et ipsius litterarum contradictarum auditor salutem in domino. Noveritis quod cum inter Egidium de Adria clericum procuratorem Riccardi de Aulanby rectoris ecclesie de Adesham pro ipso in Romana Curia impetrantem ex parte una, et Philippum de Pomonte clericum procuratorem . . Prioris et conventus ecclesie Christi Cantuarien' ordinis sancti Benedicti pro ipsis contradicentem ex altera, aliquandiu super convenientia loci et judicum foret in nostra presencia litigatum, tandem prefati procuratores Egidius pro parte sua venerabiles patres . . Episcopum Norwicen' et Philippus pro sua . . Archiepiscopum Cantuarien' judices elegerunt et in . . Archidiaconum Londonien' tamquam in medium et communem judicem communiter et concorditer convenerunt. Hoc acto de communi concordia inter procuratores prefatos quod iidem judices apud civitatem Londonien' conveniant, tractaturi ibidem de causa et negotio infrascriptis juxta rescriptum apostolicum quod ad eos dirigitur sub hac forma: — Nicolaus episcopus etc. venerabilibus fratribus . . Archiepiscopo Cantuarien' et . . Episcopo Norwicen' ac dilecto

---

[1] 25 November 1278.

filio . . Archidiacono Londonien' salutem etc. Sua nobis magister Riccardus
de Aulanby rector ecclesie de Adesham Cantuarien' diocesis petitione monstravit quod licet omnimoda jurisdictio spiritualis vacante sede Cantuarien' in
civitate et diocesi Cantuarien' ad . . Archidiaconum Cantuarien' et non ad
alium de antiqua et approbata et hactenus pacifice observata consuetudine
pertinere noscatur, tamen Robertus de Selescia monachus ecclesie Cantuarien'
ordinis sancti Benedicti predicta sede vacante predicto rectori pro sua voluntate mandavit ut ratione dicte ecclesie sibi nomine . . Prioris et conventus
ejusdem ecclesie Cantuarien' predicti ordinis manualem obedienciam exhiberet.
Ex parte vero predicti rectoris fuit coram eodem Roberto excipiendo propo-
situm quod, cum super hiis et omnibus aliis jurisdictio spiritualis ad predictum
Archidiaconum et non ad alium vacante sede memorata de consuetudine premissa spectaret, prout superius est expressum et dictus rector erat legitime
probare paratus, idem exhibere hujusmodi obedienciam que jurisdictionem
predictam spectabat eidem Roberto, cum sedes vacaret eadem et dictus monachus ab eodem Archidiacono penes quem propter hujusmodi vacacionem dicte
sedis dicta jurisdictio residebat super hoc nullam potestatem haberet, minime
tenebatur. Et ne dictus Robertus contra prefatum rectorem hujusmodi occasione procederet, pro parte predicti rectoris ad sedem apostolicam extitit
appellatum, at idem Robertus hujusmodi appellatione contempta in ipsum
excommunicationis sentenciam promulgavit. Propter quod dictus rector iterato ad sedem appellavit eandem, sed predictus Robertus appellationibus hujusmodi vilipensis ipsum magistrum Riccardum per vicecomitem secularem
Cancie dicte diocesis capi fecit et carcerali custodie mancipari. Quocirca discretioni vestre per apostolica scripta mandamus quatinus vocatis qui fuerint
evocandi et auditis hinc inde propositis quod justum fuerit appellatione post-
posita decernatis, facientes etc., proviso ne in universitatem de Cancie excommunicationis vel interdicti sentenciam proferatis nisi a nobis super hoc mandatum receperitis speciale. Quod si non omnes etc. duo vestrum etc. Dat'
Rome apud Sanctum Petrum idibus Februarii pontificatus nostri anno secundo.[1] In cujus conventionis testimonium presentes litteras fieri fecimus et
audiencie contradictarum sigillo muniri. Dat' Rome apud Sanctum Petrum
idibus Martii pontificatus domini Nicolai pape iii anno secundo.

Vesica shaped red wax seal of the *audientia litterarum contradictarum* on a tongue (' P. de
    P.' 'd ii' is written on the end of the tongue). Size $1^{1}/_{8}{''} \times 1^{1}/_{4}{''}$.
Reference: Canterbury, Dean and Chapter Archives, Cartae Antiquae A 106.
Measurements: $10^{1}/_{2}{''} \times 5^{1}/_{2}{''}$.
Medieval endorsements (?15th century): Littere conventionales contra litteram rectoris
    ecclesie de Adesham Canc' dioc' constat (? a later misreading of 'custus') ij de
    (hand *x*, 14th century): tempore N pape iii.

V

Littere super convenientia judicum of James, Canon of Bologna, *doctor decretorum*, papal chaplain and *auditor litterarum contradictarum*, dated
31 March 1279 at St. Peter's, Rome.

Omnibus presentes litteras inspecturis Jacobus canonicus Bononien' decretorum doctor domini pape capellanus et ipsius litterarum contradictarum au-

---

[1] 13 February 1279.

336

ditor salutem in domino. Noveritis quod cum inter Petrum perpetuum vicarium ecclesie de Limene Cantuarien′ diocesis pro se impetrantem ex parte una, et Philippum de Pomonte clericum procuratorem Roberti de Seleseye monachi [1] ecclesie Christi Cantuarien′ ordinis sancti Benedicti pro ipso contradicentem ex altera, aliquamdiu super convenientia judicum foret in nostra presencia litigatum tandem prefati Petrus et Philippus procuratores in . . Abbatem de Certeseye Wintonien′ diocesis . . Decanum ecclesie beate Marie de Arcubus Londonien′ et . . Archidiaconum de Lewes in ecclesia Cicestren′ judices communiter et concorditer convenerunt ad quos diriguntur littere apostolice sub hac forma: — Nicolaus episcopus etc. dilectis filiis . . Abbati de Certeseye Wintonien′ diocesis . . Decano ecclesie beate Marie de Arcubus Londonien′ et . . Archidiacono de Lewes in ecclesia Cicestren′ salutem etc. Conquestus est nobis Petrus perpetuus vicarius ecclesie de Limene Cantuarien′ diocesis quod Robertus de Seleseye monachus ecclesie Christi Cantuarien′ ordinis sancti Benedicti in eum in quem nullam habebat jurisdictionem ordinariam seu etiam delegatam temeritate propria excommunicationis et interdicti sentencias promulgavit. Ideoque discretioni vestre de utriusque partis procuratorum assensu per apostolica scripta mandamus quatinus partibus convocatis audiatis causam et appellatione remota fine debito decidatis. Facientes etc. Testes autem etc. Quod si non omnes etc. duo vestrum etc. Dat′ Rome apud Sanctum Petrum x kalendas Aprilis pontificatus nostri anno secundo.[2] In cujus conventionis testimonium presentes litteras fieri fecimus et audiencie contradictarum sigillo muniri. Dat′ Rom′ apud Sanctum Petrum ii kalendas Aprilis pontificatus domini Nicolai pape iii anno secundo.

All signs of sealing method removed: the document has been cut.
Reference: Canterbury, Dean and Chapter Archives, Christ Church Letters ii no. 316.[3]
Measurements: $7^1/_2{}''$ × $4^1/_4{}''$.
The document has been pasted down: the endorsements are therefore obscured.

VI

Cautio of Master Richard of Langdon, proctor *in curia Romana* of R[ichard Wethershed], Archbishop of Canterbury, *post* 10 September 1230.

Universis sancte matris ecclesie filiis ad quos presens scriptum pervenerit magister Ricardus de Languedona procurator venerabilis [4] patris R. Archiepiscopi Cantuarien′ salutem in domino. Noverit universitas vestra quod constitutus a prenominato domino meo procurator in curia Romana ad impetrandum et contradicendum et conveniendum in judices pro eodem quasdam litteras impetravi sub hac forma: — Gregorius episcopus servus servorum dei venerabili fratri R. Archiepiscopo Cantuarien′ totius Anglie primati salutem et apostolicam benedictionem. Ex parte tua fuit expositum coram nobis quod quam plures tam religiosi quam seculares tue diocesis, asserentes se de indulgencia sedis apostolice obtinere ut tam ecclesias quam alia ecclesiastica beneficia auctoritate propria possint intrare, ea te vel aliquo predecessorum tuorum

---

[1] Text 'monachum'.
[2] 23 March 1279.
[3] Mentioned in HMC *Var. Coll.* I 243.
[4] Text 'dn̄srabilis'.

C 47 = APPENDIX, DOCUMENT VI

Reproduced by kind permission of the
Dean and Chapter of Canterbury.

III

III

penitus inconsulto ingressi vel agressi pocius ac imponentes de novo pensiones in eis vel veteres adaugentes[1] detinent minus juste, denegando indulgencias ex[h]ibere.[2] Licet cogi possessorem dicere titulum super possessionibus incivile[3] dicatur, quia tamen taliter arripi ecclesiastica beneficia sacris est canonibus interdictum, fraternitati tue per apostolica scripta mandamus quatinus contra tales nisi indulgencias quas se habere proponunt ex[h]ibeant vel alia munimenta, cum de jure communi sis tutus, libere officii tui debitum exequaris. Dat' Anagnie iiii idus Septembris pontificatus nostri anno quarto.[4] Quibus magister Philipus de Mortuo Mari procurator Prioris et conventus ecclesie Christi Cantuarie in publica audiencia contradixit timens ne auctoritate dictarum litterarum aliquid in prejudicium juris predictorum prioris et conventus fieri posset vel quocumque modo possent per easdem conveniri. Ad elidendam vero timoris hujus suspicionem eidem bona fide procuratorio nomine promisi quod auctoritate predictarum litterarum neque prior neque conventus convenirentur nec aliquid in prejudicium juris ipsorum fieret per easdem. Et in hujus rei testimonium presentibus litteris sigillum meum apposui. Hiis testibus magistro S. Archidiachono Cantuarien' Wualtero quondam electo Cantuarien' et magistro Roberto de Sumercota et multis aliis.

Slit for seal on tag.

Reference: Canterbury, Dean and Chapter Archives, Cartae Antiquae C 47.

Measurements: 6″ × 9¹/₂″.

Medieval endorsement (hand *x*, 14th century): Cautio Ricardi de Langdon' procuratoris R. Archiepiscopi Cant' quod litere subscripte ad nostrum prejudicium se non extendant. G. papa.

VII

Report of a *cautio*, by Master Robert of Somercotes, papal subdeacon and *auditor litterarum contradictarum*, *post* 20 May 1238.

Omnibus presentes litteras inspecturis magister Robertus de Sumercote domini pape subdiaconus et ejusdem litterarum contradictarum auditor salutem in domino. Noverit universitas vestra quod cum . . Archidiaconus Cantuar' in hunc modum litteras apostolicas impetrasset: — Gregorius episcopus etc. dilecto filio O. sancti Nicolai in Carcere Tullian' diacono cardinali apostolice sedis legato salutem etc. Dilecti filii Archidiaconi Cantuar' devotis precibus inclinati presentium tibi auctoritate mandamus quatinus ea que de bonis ad ipsum ratione archidiaconatus sui Cantuar' spectantibus alienata inveneris illicite vel distracta ad jus et proprietatem ipsius legitime studeas revocare. Contra' etc. Testes autem etc. Dat' Lat' xiii kalendas Junii pontificatus nostri anno xii.[5] Ipsis litteris frater Thomas monachus et procurator . . prioris et capituli ecclesie Christi Cantuar' in audiencia publica contradixit timens ipsos conveniri per eas quas demum ea conditione absolvit ut per eas dicti prior et capitulum non valeant conveniri, quod pars altera promisit firmiter coram

---

[1] Text 'adugentes'.
[2] The scribe has left a space after 'exibere.'
[3] Text 'possessionis in civile'.
[4] 10 September 1230.
[5] 20 May 1238.

338

nobis. In cujus rei testimonium presentes litteras nostro sigillo fecimus communiri.

Holes for cords.

Reference: Canterbury, Dean and Chapter Archives, Cartae Antiquae A 206.

Measurements: $5^1/_2'' \times 4''$.

Medieval endorsement (hand x, 14th century): Cautio [. . . .] archidiaconi quod non extendat ad nostrum prejudicium. G. papa.

VIII

Report of a *cautio*, by Gerard, Master of the schools of Parma, papal chaplain and *auditor litterarum contradictarum*, dated 21 May 1276 at the Lateran.

Omnibus presentes litteras inspecturis Gerardus magister scolarum ecclesie Parmen' domini pape capellanus ejusque litterarum contradictarum auditor salutem in domino. Noveritis quod cum magister Mathias canonicus Theatin' procurator . . Prioris et conventus prioratus Dovorie Cantuarien' diocesis pro ipsis super hiis que de bonis ipsius alienata invenirentur illicite vel distracta ad jus et proprietatem ejusdem prioratus legitime revocandis ad Archidiaconum Middelsexie in ecclesia Londonien' sub dato Lateran' v idus Maii pontificatus nostri anno primo.[1] Eisdem litteris Philippus de Pomonte clericus procurator . . Prioris et conventus ecclesie Christi Cantuarien' ordinis sancti Benedicti pro ipsis in audiencia publica contradixit quas tandem ea conditione absolvit quod dicti Prior et conventus non conveniantur per litteras supradictas quod pars altera promisit firmiter coram nobis. In cujus rei testimonium presentes litteras fieri fecimus et audiencie contradictarum sigillo muniri. Dat' Lateran' xii kalendas Junii pontificatus domini Innocentii pape v anno primo.

Vesica shaped brown wax seal of the *audientia litterarum contradictarum* on a tongue, ('P. d' pomonte' is written on the end of the tongue). Size $1^1/_6'' \times 1^5/_{16}''$.

Reference: Canterbury, Dean and Chapter Archives, Cartae Antiquae D 75.

Measurements: $8'' \times 3''$.

Medieval endorsement (hand x, 14th century): Cautio procuratoris Prioris et conventus Dovor' quod per literas suas perquisitas non conveniamur.

Innocentius papa quintus.

IX

Report of a *cautio*, by James, Canon of Bologna, *doctor decretorum*, papal chaplain and *auditor litterarum contradictarum*, dated 22 September 1278 at Viterbo.

Omnibus presentes litteras inspecturis Jacobus canonicus Bononien' decretorum doctor domini pape capellanus ac ipsius litterarum contradictarum auditor salutem in domino. Noveritis quod cum magister Lucas de Guartino clericus procurator . . Prioris et conventus monasterii de Ledes per Priorem

---

[1] 11 May 1276.

soliti gubernari ordinis sancti Augustini Cantuar' diocesis pro ipsis impetraret litteras apostolicas sub hiis formis: — Nicolaus episcopus etc. dilecto filio . . Priori ecclesie Roffen' salutem etc. Pervenit ad audienciam nostram quod tam dilecti filii . . Prior et conventus monasterii de Ledes per Priorem soliti gubernari ordinis sancti Augustini Cantuarien' diocesis quam predecessores eorum qui fuerunt pro tempore, decimas terras domos prata pascua [1] silvas molendina piscarias possessiones redditus jura jurisdictiones et quedam alia bona ipsius monasterii, datis super hoc litteris juramentis interpositis factis renunciationibus et penis adjectis, in gravem ejusdem monasterii lesionem nonnullis clericis et laicis, aliquibus eorum ad vitam, quibusdam vero ad non modicum tempus et aliis perpetuo, ad firmam vel sub censu annuo concesserunt, quorum aliqui super hiis litteras confirmationis in forma communi a sede apostolica impetrasse dicuntur. Quia vero nostra interest super hoc de oportuno remedio providere, discretioni tue per apostolica scripta mandamus quatinus ea que de bonis ipsius monasterii per concessiones hujusmodi alienata inveneris illicite vel distracta, non obstantibus litteris juramentis renunciationibus penis et confirmationibus supradictis ad jus et proprietatem ejusdem monasterii legitime revocare procures. Contradictores etc. Testes autem etc. Dat' Viterbii nonis Septembris pontificatus nostri anno primo.[2] Item Nicolaus episcopus etc. dilecto filio . . Priori de Suwyk' Wintonien' diocesis salutem etc. Querelam dilectorum filiorum . . Prioris et conventus monasterii de Ledes per Priorem soliti gubernari ordinis Sancti Augustini recepimus continentem quod nonnulli clerici tam religiosi quam seculares etiam in dignitatibus seu personatibus constituti necnon comites barones milites et alii laici Cantuarien' et Roffen' civitatum et diocesum qui castra villas terras possessiones domos prata pascua molendina et nonnulla alia bona immobilia sub annuo censu seu redditu a monasterio ipso tenent, huiusmodi censum seu redditum eidem Priori et conventui exhibere non curant, quamquam clerici comites barones et alii supradicti castrorum villarum et aliorum premissorum bonorum possessionem pacificam habeant ac fructus cum integritate percipiant eorundem, propter quod prefatis Priori et conventui grave imminet prejudicium et eidem monasterio non modicum detrimentum. Cum autem pro parte dictorum Prioris et conventus ad nostram providenciam super hoc habitus sit recursus, discretioni tue per apostolica scripta mandamus quatinus si est ita, clericos comites barones et alios supradictos ad exhibendum prefatum censum seu redditum Priori et conventui memoratis integre, ut tenentur, monitione premissa per censuram ecclesiasticam appellatione remota previa ratione compellas, proviso ne in terras dictorum comitum et baronum excommunicationis vel interdicti sentenciam proferas etc. Testes autem etc. Dat' Viterbii vii idus Septembris pontificatus nostri anno primo.[3] Eisdem litteris magister Philippus de Pomonte clericus procurator . . Prioris et conventus ecclesie Christi Cantuarien' pro ipsis prepositis balivis et officialibus ipsorum in audiencia publica contradixit, quas tandem ea conditione absolvit quod dicti Prior et conventus prepositi balivi et officiales ratione officiorum que a Priore et conventu tenent eisdem non conveniantur nullumque ipsis super jure et jurisdictione ipsorum per predictas litteras prejudicium g[e]neretur nec ad ipsos eedem littere aliquatenus extendantur, quod pars altera promisit firmiter coram nobis. In

---

[1] Text 'pascia'.   [2] 5 September 1278.   [3] 7 September 1278.

cujus rei testimonium presentes litteras fieri fecimus et audiencie contradictarum sigillo muniri. Dat' Viterbii x kalendas Octobris pontificatus domini Nicolai pape iii anno primo.

Slit for tag.

Reference: Canterbury, Dean and Chapter Archives, Cartae Antiquae A 218.

Measurements: $10^1/_4'' \times 7''$.

Medieval endorsement (hand *x*, 14th century): testimonium Jacobi canonici baion' (*sic*) quod Phil' de Pomonte contradixi [. . . . .] litteris coram ipso ad[1] in audiencia in qua[2] contra nos et nostros fuerunt.

tempore N. papa.

X

Report of a *cautio*, by Guy de Novavilla, Canon of Limoges and *auditor litterarum contradictarum*, dated 18 December 1286[3] at St. Sabina's, Rome.

Omnibus presentes litteras inspecturis Guido de Novavilla canonicus Lemovicen' litterarum domini pape contradictarum auditor salutem in domino. Noveritis quod cum Walterus de Meldon' rector ecclesie de Chert juxta Sutton' Cantuarien' diocesis pro se impetraret litteras apostolicas sub hac forma: — Honorius episcopus etc. dilectis filiis . . maiori ac . . de Middelsexia Archidiaconis et magistro Johanni de Luco canonico Londonien' salutem etc. Dilecti filii Walteri de Meldon' rectoris ecclesie de Chert juxta Sutton Cantuarien' diocesis apud sedem apostolicam constituti precibus annuentes, presentium tibi auctoritate mandamus quatinus quicquid inveneris in ejus prejudicium temere attemptatum postquam idem rector causa peregrinationis et pro quibusdam suis et dicte ecclesie negotiis promovendis iter arripuit ad sedem veniendi predictam in statum debitum legitime revocare procures. Contra' etc. Dat' Rom' apud Sanctam Sabinam vi idus Januarii pontificatus nostri anno secundo.[4] Eisdem litteris Nicolaus de Sancto Victor' procurator . . Prioris et capituli ecclesie Christi Cantuarien' pro ipsis ac prepositis balivis et aliis officialibus suis in audiencia publica contradixit, quas tandem ea conditione absolvit quod dicti Prior et capitulum ac prepositi balivi et alii officiales ratione officiorum que a Priore et capitulo tenent eisdem non conveniantur per litteras supradictas nec ad ipsos eedem littere aliquatenus extendantur quod pars altera promisit firmiter coram nobis. In cujus rei testimonium presentes litteras fieri fecimus et audiencie contradictarum sigillo muniri. Dat' Rom' apud Sanctam Sabinam xv kalendas Januarii pontificatus domini Honorii pape iiii[u] anno secundo.

P

Probably a tongue: cut.

Reference: Canterbury, Dean and Chapter Archives, Cartae Antiquae C 1291 (cf. Sede Vacante Scrapbook II, p. 102).

Measurements: $8'' \times 3^1/_2''$.

---

[1] 'ad' deleted. [2] Text 'quam'.
[3] This is presumably a mistake, see p. 327 at n. 96 *supra*.
[4] 8 January 1287.

Medieval endorsement (hand *x*, 14th century): Cautio Walteri rectoris de Chert quod per-
quisitum infra scriptum non extendatur ad nos et nostros.
Honorii pape nostri quarti.

XI

Report of a *cautio*, by Guy de Novavilla, Canon of Limoges and *auditor
litterarum contradictarum*, dated 13 January 1287 at St. Sabina's, Rome.

Omnibus presentes litteras inspecturis Guido de Novavilla canonicus Lemovicen' litterarum domini pape contradictarum auditor salutem in domino.
Noveritis quod cum Walterus de Meldon' rector ecclesie de Chert juxta Suttonam Cantuarien' diocesis pro se impetraret litteras apostolicas sub hac forma:
— Honorius episcopus etc. dilecto filio . . Archidiacono Colestrie in ecclesia
Londonien' salutem etc. Ad audienciam nostram pervenit quod tam dilectus
filius Walterus de Meldona rector ecclesie de Chert juxta Suttonam Cantuarien'
diocesis quam predecessores sui ejusdem ecclesie rectores qui fuerunt pro tempore, decimas redditus terras vineas possessiones domos prata pascua nemora
molendina jura jurisdictiones et quedam alia bona ad ecclesiam ipsam spec-
tantia, datis super hoc litteris interpositis juramentis factis renunciationibus et
penis adjectis, per gravem ipsius ecclesie lesionem nonnullis clericis[1] et laicis,
aliquibus eorum ad vitam, quibusdam vero ad non modicum tempus et aliis
perpetuo, ad firmam vel sub censu annuo concesserunt, quorum aliqui dicuntur super hiis confirmationis litteras in forma communi a sede apostolica
impetrasse. Quia vero nostra interest lesis ecclesiis subvenire, discretioni tue
per apostolica scripta mandamus quatinus ea que de bonis ipsius ecclesie per
concessiones hujusmodi alienata inveneris illicite vel distracta, non obstantibus
litteris renunciationibus penis juramentis et confirmationibus supradictis ad
jus et proprietatem ejusdem ecclesie legitime revocare procures. Contra' etc.
Testes autem etc. Dat' Rom' apud Sanctam Sabinam vi idus Januarii pontificatus nostri anno secundo.[2] Eisdem litteris magister Nicolaus de Sancto
Victore procurator . . Prioris et capituli ecclesie Christi Cantuarien' pro ipsis
ac prepositis balivis et aliis officialibus suis in audiencia publica contradixit,
quas tandem ea conditione absolvit quod dicti Prior et capitulum ac prepositi
balivi et officiales ratione officiorum que a Priore et capitulo tenent eisdem non
conveniantur per litteras supradictas nec ad ipsos eedem littere aliquatenus
extendantur, quod pars altera promisit firmiter coram nobis. In cujus rei
testimonium presentes litteras fieri fecimus et audiencie contradictarum sigillo
muniri. Dat' Rom' apud Sanctam Sabinam idibus Januarii pontificatus domini
Honorii pape iiii[ti] anno secundo.
P

Probably a tongue: cut.
Reference: Canterbury, Dean and Chapter Archives, Sede Vacante Scrapbook II, p. 102
(cf. Cartae Antiquae C 1291).
Measurements: $10^1/_2{''} \times 3^3/_4{''}$.
Medieval endorsement (hand *x*, 14th century): Cautio ne per istas literas perquisitas nobis et[3]
nec nostris fiat prejudicium.
Tempore Honorii iiij.

---

[1] Written twice.   [2] 8 January 1287.   [3] 'et' ? deleted.

XII

Report of a *cautio*, by Bernard Roiardi, Archdeacon of Xanten, papal chaplain and *auditor litterarum contradictarum*, dated 20 December 1316 at Avignon.

Omnibus presentes litteras inspecturis Bernardus Roiardi archidiaconus Xanctonen' domini pape capellanus ac ipsius litterarum contradictarum auditor salutem in domino. Noveritis quod cum Nicolaus de Lodelawe procurator Radulfi dicti de Drayton' rectoris ecclesie de Luffewyk Lincolnien' diocesis pro ipso impetraret litteras apostolicas sub hac forma: — Johannes episcopus etc. dilecto filio . . Priori monasterii de Novo loco juxta Staunford' per Priorem soliti gubernari Lincolnien' diocesis salutem etc. Sua nobis Radulfus dictus de Drayton' rector ecclesie de Luffewyk Lincolnien' diocesis petitione monstravit quod licet ipse dictam ecclesiam nulli alii de jure debitam fuisset canonice assecutus eamque aliquamdiu pacifice possedisset et tunc etiam possideret, tamen Adam de Narehamton' clericus dicte diocesis falso asserens ecclesiam ipsam vacare licet nec de jure nec de facto vacaret, se ad eam tanquam ad vacantem a vero ipsius ecclesie patrono venerabili fratri nostro . . Lincolnien' Episcopo presentari temere procuravit. Et quia dictus episcopus presentationem hujusmodi prout debuit non admisit, dictus Adam ad Cantuarien' curiam loci metropoliticam in vocem frivole appellationis prorupit dictumque rectorem fecit pretextu appellationis hujusmodi, primo coram . . Decano ecclesie Beate Marie de Arcubus Londoniarum generali auditore causarum curie bone memorie Roberti archiepiscopi Cantuarien' tunc viventis, et eo postmodum viam universe carnis ingressi[1] coram . . Officiali capituli ecclesie Cantuarien' tunc per ipsius archiepiscopi obitum pastore carentis, ad judicium evocari. Idem namque officialis omisso dicte appellationis articulo in principali causa de facto procedens diffinitivam[2] contra dictum rectorem sentenciam promulgavit, a qua ipso ad sedem apostolicam appellavit sed dictus rector justo ut asserit impedimento detemptus non est appellationem hujusmodi infra tempus legitimus prosecutus quare dictus rector nobis humiliter supplicavit ut hujusmodi lapsu temporis non obstante providere sibi super hoc paterna diligencia dignaremur. Quocirca discretioni tue per apostolica scripta mandamus quatinus vocatis etc. Testes autem etc. Dat' Avinion' idibus[3] Decembris pontificatus nostri anno primo.[4] Eisdem literis magister Radulfus de Lacu procurator . . Prioris et capituli ecclesie Christi Cantuarien' pro ipsis in audiencia publica contradixit, quas tandem ea conditione absolvit quod Prior et capitulum predicti non conveniantur per literas apostolicas supradictas nec ad ipsos eedem litere aliquatenus extendantur, quod pars altera promisit firmiter coram nobis. In cujus rei testimonium presentes litteras fieri fecimus et audiencie contradictarum sigillo muniri. Dat' Avinion' xiii kalendas Januarii pontificatus domini Johannis pape xxii anno primo.

Signs of red wax of seal on a tongue, ['R. de lacu ii c'' is written on the tongue].
Reference: Canterbury, Dean and Chapter Archives, Cartae Antiquae L 403.

---

[1] Text 'ingresse'.
[2] Text 'diffininitivam'.
[3] Text 'idus'.
[4] 13 December 1316.

C 1297 = APPENDIX, DOCUMENT XIII
*Reproduced by kind permission of the
Dean and Chapter of Canterbury.*

C 1299 = Appendix, Document XIV

*Reproduced by kind permission of the
Dean and Chapter of Canterbury.*

III

Measurements: $9^3/_4'' \times 6^3/_4''$.
No medieval endorsements.

XIII

Report of a *cautio*, by Peter [Després], Archbishop of Aix and *auditor litterarum contradictarum*, dated 23 January 1320 at Avignon.

Omnibus presentes litteras inspecturis Petrus permissione divina Aquen' archiepiscopus ac audiencie litterarum contradictarum domini pape officium gerens salutem in domino. Noveritis quod cum magister Radulphus de Horncastr' procurator venerabilium virorum et religiosorum Abbatis et conventus monasterii Sancti Augustini Cantuar' pro ipsis inpetraret litteras appostolicas sub hac forma: — Johannes episcopus etc. dilecto filio . . Priori Sancti Gregorii extra Cantuariam salutem etc. Ex parte dilectorum filiorum . . Abbatis et conventus monasterii Sancti Augustini Cantuarien' ad Romanam ecclesiam nullo medio pertinentis ordinis Sancti Benedicti nobis est oblata querela quod nonnulli parochiani ecclesie de Faveresham Cantuar' dyocesis, quam idem Abbas et conventus in usus proprios canonice obtinent et in qua per proprium vicarium curam gerentem parochianorum ipsius ecclesie faciunt deserviri, de proventibus terrarum vinearum ortorum nemorum pratorum et aliorum que infra limites parochie ipsius ecclesie obtinent decimas eidem ecclesie debitas eisdem Abbati et conventui solvere indebite contradicunt, ad excusandas excusaciones in peccatis quandam pravam consuetudinem que corruptela dicenda est potius pretendentes, videlicet quod de talibus nulli ad huc decimas persolverunt. Cum igitur tanto graviora sint crimina quanto diutius infelicem animam detinent alligatam, et in signum universalis dominii[1] quasi quodam titulo speciali sibi decimas dominus reservavit, discretioni tue per appostolica scripta mandamus quatinus si est ita prefatos parochianos ut consuetudine hujusmodi non obstante decimas de predictis eidem ecclesie debitas dictis Abbati et conventui integre ut tenentur exsolvant, monitione premissa per censuram ecclesiasticam appellatione remota previa ratione compellas. Testes autem etc. Dat' Avinion' xiii kalendas Januarii pontificatus nostri anno quarto.[2] Eisdem litteris magister Bricius de Sharsted procurator venerabilium virorum Prioris et capituli ecclesie Cantuarien'[3] pro ipsis in audiencia publica contradixit, quas tandem ea conditione absolvit quod dicti Prior et capitulum ac eorum officiales et ministri ut parochiani ecclesie de Faverisham Cantuar' dyocesis non conveniantur per litteras appostolicas supradictas nec ad ipsos eedem littere aliquatenus se extendant, quod dictus magister Radulphus procurator promisit firmiter coram nobis. In cujus cautionis testimonium presentes litteras fieri fecimus et audiencie contradictarum sigillo muniri. Datum Avinion' x kalendas Februarii pontificatus domini Johannis pape xxii anno quarto vero domini millesimo ccc vicesimo.
.G.

Vesica shaped red wax seal of the *audientia litterarum contradictarum* on a tongue looped through like a tag. Size $1^1/_{16}'' \times 1^5/_{16}''$.

---

[1] Text 'domini'.   [2] 20 December 1319.
[3] Something scratched out with a knife here, and the scribe has drawn a line to prevent forgery.

344

Reference: Canterbury, Dean and Chapter Archives, Cartae Antiquae C 1297.
Measurements: $10^1/_4'' \times 5^1/_2''$.
No medieval endorsements.

XIV

Report of a *cautio*, by Bertrand [de Deux], Archbishop of Embrun and *auditor litterarum contradictarum*, dated 6 March 1328 at Avignon.

Omnibus presentes litteras inspecturis Bertrandus miseratione divina archiepiscopus Ebredunen′ et audiencie litterarum contradictarum domini pape auditor salutem in domino. Noveritis quod cum magister Thomas de Boynthon′ in Romana curia procurator nomine procuratorio venerabilium et religiosorum virorum dominorum . . Abbatis et conventus monasterii Sancti Albani ad Romanam ecclesiam nullo medio pertinentis ordinis Sancti Benedicti Lincolnien′ diocesis pro ipsis impetraret litteras apostolicas sub hiis formis: — Johannes episcopus etc. dilecto filio . . Abbati monasterii de Rameseya Lincolnien′ diocesis salutem etc. Ad audienciam nostram pervenit quod tam dilecti filii abbas et conventus monasterii Sancti Albani ad Romanam ecclesiam nullo medio pertinentis ordinis Sancti Benedicti Lincolnien′ diocesis quam predecessores eorum decimas terras domos possessiones vineas prata pascua nemora molendina jura jurisdictiones et quedam alia bona ipsius monasterii, datis super hoc litteris confectis exinde publicis instrumentis interpositis juramentis factis renuntiationibus et penis adjectis, in gravem ipsius monasterii lesionem nonnullis clericis et laicis aliquibus eorum ad vitam, quibusdam vero ad non modicum tempus et aliis perpetuo ad firmam vel sub censu annuo concesserunt, quorum aliqui[1] super hiis confirmationis litteras in forma comuni a sede apostolica impetrasse dicuntur. Quia vero nostra interest super hoc de oportuno remedio providere, discretioni tue per apostolica scripta mandamus quatinus ea que de bonis ipsius monasterii per concessiones hujusmodi[2] alienata inveneris illicite vel distracta, non obstantibus litteris instrumentis juramentis renunciationibus penis et confirmationibus supradictis ad jus et proprietatem ejusdem monasterii legitime revocare procures. Contradictores etc. Testes autem etc. Dat′ Avinion′ xv kalendas Marcii pontificatus nostri anno duodecimo.[3] Item Johannes episcopus etc. dilecto filio . . Abbati monasterii de Rameseya Lincolnien′ diocesis salutem etc. Dilectorum filiorum Abbatis et conventus monasterii Sancti Albani ad Romanam ecclesiam nullo medio pertinentis ordinis Sancti Benedicti Lincolnien′ diocesis precibus inclinati presentium tibi auctoritate mandamus quatinus ea que de bonis ipsius monasterii alienata inveneris illicite vel distracta ad jus et proprietatem ejusdem monasterii legitime revocare procures. Contradictores etc. Testes autem etc. Dat′ Avinion′ xv kalendas Marcii pontificatus nostri anno duodecimo.[4] Eisdem literis magister Johannes de Mallinge procurator venerabilium et discretorum virorum dominorum . . Prioris et capituli ecclesie Cantuarien′ pro ipsis et eorum officialibus commissariis et ministris in audiencia publica contradixit, quas tandem ea conditione absolvit quod prefati Prior et capitulum domini sui et eorum offi-

---

[1] Text adds 'dicuntur' here.
[3] 15 February 1328.

[2] Text 'hujus'.
[4] Same date.

III

ciales commissarii et ministri non valeant per ipsas litteras quolibet conveniri nec eedem littere ad eos aut eorum alterum aliqualiter se extendant, quod prefatus Thomas procurator nomine procuratorio supradicto promisit firmiter coram nobis. In cujus cautionis testimonium presentes litteras fieri fecimus et audiencie contradictarum sigillo muniri. Dat' Avinion' ii nonas Marcii pontificatus domini Johannis pape xxii anno duodecimo anno vero domini millesimo ccc xxviii.

Vesica shaped red wax seal of the *audientia litterarum contradictarum* on a tongue. Size $1^1/_{16}{}'' \times 1^5/_{16}{}''$.

Reference : Canterbury, Dean and Chapter Archives, Cartae Antiquae C 1299.

Measurements: $12^1/_4{}'' \times 5^1/_4{}''$.

Medieval endorsement (hand *x*, 14th century) : Cautio procuratoris Abbatis et conventus monasterii sancti Albani Lincoln' diocesis quod Prior et capitulum ecclesie Christi Cant' nec eorum officiales vel ministri trahantur in causam per literas apostolicas. Ea que de bonis.

ADDENDA

To Appendix

VIIIa   Report of a *cautio*, by James, Canon of Bologna, *auditor litterarum contradictarum*, dated 11 July 1278 at Viterbo. Letters obtained by Master Raynald de Aquila, proctor of the master and brothers of St John of Jerusalem, not to be used to the prejudice of the abbot and convent of Westminster (WAM 9181).

IXa   Report of a *cautio*, by James, Canon of Bologna, *auditor litterarum contradictarum*, dated April probably 1279, of the objection of Master Guido Novarien', proctor of the dean and chapter of Lincoln, against Philip de Pomonte, proctor of the prior and chapter of Canterbury (Lincoln D & C. A/4/9 no. 1).

XIVa   Letters patent of Bertrand, Archbishop of Embrun, *auditor litterarum contradictarum*, dated 7 May 1324 at Avignon, reporting a *cautio*. Peter de Luffenham, clerk, had objected that he could not litigate in England on account of the power of Robert, archdeacon of Westminster. The proctor of Robert promised no harm to Peter (WAM 5999).

*

*   *

Since 1965, when this article was written, much important work has been done on the *audientia litterarum contradictarum*. Of particular significance is the publication of Professor Herde's two volume edition of the formularies (Bibliothek des Deutschen Historischen Instituts in Rom xxxi & xxxvi) in 1970, and 'Ein Formelbuch Gerhards von Parma mit Urkunden des Auditor litterarum contradictarum aus dem Jahre 1277' (*Archiv für Diplomatik* 13) and the second

III

edition of his *Beiträge* in 1967. Also in 1970 came Professor Winfried Stelzer's 'Über Vermerke der beiden Audientiae auf Papsturkunden in der zweiten Hälfte des 13. Jahrhunderts' (MIOG 78 [1970]) and further articles by him on the *audientia litterarum contradictarum* and the proctors, published between 1969 and 1970, should also be consulted. They are in MIOG 77 (1969) 291-313; *Römische historische Mitteilungen* 11 (1969) 210-21; and *Archivum Historiae Pontificiae* 8 (1970) 113-38. I fully retract my statement (on pp. 314, 321) that the mandates were more in the shape of drafts when read in the *audientia publica*; worse, I incorrectly attributed this opinion to Professor Herde.

To p. 316 n.29: *Add* Ch. Ch. Letts. II. 11 of 1278 provides one more example.

To p. 327 n.100: *Add* Pomonte appears also for Percival de Lavania against the dean and chapter of Lincoln, 2-23 March 1274 (Lincoln D. & C. Dij/66/2/11).

To p. 328 n.102: *Add* and for the prior and chapter, April prob. 1279 (Linc. D. & C. A/4/9 no.1).

IV

PROCTORS REPRESENTING BRITISH INTERESTS AT THE PAPAL COURT, 1198-1415

In view of the very small amount of material on proctors in the papal registers between Innocent III's pontificate and that of Martin V, an investigation of the endorsements on bulls surviving in England from this period may have some value. For this purpose the bulls issued between those dates and now at the Public Record Office, the British Museum, the Bodleian Library, the Lambeth Palace Library, and the Dean and Chapter Library and Archives at Canterbury, have been examined.[1]

From Innocent III's pontificate at least, endorsements begin to appear in the top centre on the back of certain papal documents.[2] These endorsements can be connected in some instances with the proctor who sought the issue of the document. In this position his symbol, initial letter, or name, was written. The use of initial letters and symbols suggests that the proctors at the papal court were still a comparatively small and minor group. The refinements introduced, however, into the machinery of issue of papal documents during the thirteenth century brought an increasing number of proctors to the papal court, and it became necessary to write the names in full.

Proctors came to the papal court for two purposes, to seek letters of grace granting confirmations, favours, and indults, and to impetrate the necessary documents in a lawsuit and perhaps follow such a suit to a conclusion before the Rota. In short their duties were to get and receive bulls. Gradually there arose a group of standing proctors, whose livelihood centred round the

---

[1] No attempt has been made to examine collections in Ireland and Scotland, but material relating to these countries which has been found in English deposits has been used. The only other sizeable collection of bulls in England is at Durham. This has not been examined for the present purpose. Robert Brentano's *Two Churches: England and Italy* (Princeton 1968) appeared after this article was written. The chapter 'The Connection' contains some material on Durham proctors from Durham endorsements, plus some general observations. Bulls addressed to Bavarian petitioners between 1198 and 1303 have been studied closely by Peter Herde, *Beiträge zum päpstlichen Kanzlei- und Urkundenwesen im dreizehnten Jahrhundert* (Münchener Histor. Studien, Abt. Geschichtliche Hilfswissenschaften 1; 2nd ed. Kallmünz 1967), who provides a list of their proctors on pp. 136-48. Similarly A. Largiadèr, *Die Papsturkunden des Staatsarchivs Zürich* (Zürich 1963), has compiled a list of proctors between 1198 and 1415 (73-5) from the endorsements on the bulls at Zurich.

[2] See R. von Heckel, 'Das Aufkommen der ständigen Prokuratoren an der päpstlichen Kurie', *Miscellanea Fr. Ehrle* II (Studi e Testi 38; Rome 1924) 290ff.

papal court and who moved with it from Rome to Orvieto, Anagni, or Perugia. But there were also occasional proctors who represented a fellow national, a religious corporation, or a relative perhaps, and who carried out this office as a matter of convenience in an isolated instance.

In assessing these endorsements, therefore, it may be possible to answer the following questions: how many of the proctors were standing proctors; what proportion of them were English and what proportion Italian; what sort of documents were endorsed; and finally why proctors' names appear on some documents and not on others.

*
* *

English kings, queens and princes employed proctors at the papal court throughout the period. The first clear endorsement appears on a bull for King John, dated 15 April 1214 at St. Peter's Rome, and was made by a proctor called Thomas.[3] Thomas is followed by a list of unidentifiable persons until Richard de Neville who endorsed bulls of 1239 and 1240.[4] In 1243 he is referred to as being a king's proctor of longstanding at Rome, and in that year he was appointed firstly as a proctor to obtain letters and contradict them in the court of Rome and to select judges and consent to them, and secondly to serve with Master Henricus de Secusia (of Susa; later cardinal bishop of Ostia) and the abbot of Hautecombe (Cistercian, diocese of Geneva, France) in the affair of the confirmation of Boniface of Savoy as archbishop of Canterbury.[5] Master Henricus de Secusia, the canonist Hostiensis, was doubtless the most eminent of Henry III's proctors and served between 1240 and 1244, appearing before the legate Otto's court in cases concerning clerks, and before the pope as the king's proctor in the case against William Raleigh, bishop of Winchester.[6] He seems comparable with another royal proctor Guido de Rosilione (Rossillon), archdeacon of Lyons, an influential person involved in the king's dealings and amply rewarded.[7] In contrast to these professional legal advisers and important men the king employed a series of royal clerks at the papal court between 1245 and 1262: Master Peter de Tayo (signs Tayo) between 7 April and 21 July 1245, appearing on the Liberate rolls of 1245

---

[3] Public Record Office [= PRO] SC7/19/22.

[4] PRO SC7/15/12, 18; and possibly 35/23 as 'R.'

[5] *Calendar of the Patent Rolls 1232-47* [= CPR] (H.M.S.O. London 1906) 373, 375.

[6] *Ibid.* 241, 409, 411, and PRO SC7/20/3. Geoffrey Barraclough, 'The English Royal Chancery and the Papal Chancery in the reign of Henry III', MIÖG 62 (1954) 365-78, esp. 368ff.

[7] SC7/53/8, and CPR 1247-58, 325.

and 1255,[8] Reginald in 1246-9,[9] Master John de Chishull proctor at Rome between 1250 and 1255,[10] Master Robert Anketil between 1241 and 1252,[11] Master Roger Lovel (? two clerks of this name) between 1250 and 1256 and between 1261 and 1262,[12] Finatus of Savoy between 1256 and 1260,[13] and Master John de Hemmingford between 1261 and 1262.[14] The well-known proctor Petrus of Assisi was employed by the king or the queen in 1267.[15] After Master Th[omas] de Wymbis (1272-4)[16] the royal proctors seem to be without exception Italian, Leonardus de Venafro (1285),[17] Bonifacius de Vercellis (1289),[18] Gentilis de Castrobono (1290),[19] Guillelmus de Sancto Geminiano (1291),[20] and N. de Vico (1298-1302).[21] At Avignon the king employed Master Andreas Sapiti from 1313 to 1334,[22] and Bernardus de Barrio (Bari) in 1317.[23] The royal proctors were not precluded from accepting other sporadic appointments, but all the evidence suggests that on the whole the king of England had his own proctors at Rome and Avignon, who were primarily responsible to him, but who might accept other work if their royal commitments allowed.

---

[8] SC7/20/13, 17-19, 21/3,7,11,15,18, and 22/33; CLibR 1245-51, 15; 1251-60, 195, 219.

[9] SC7/21/1,13, and 53/5.

[10] Bodleian Library, MS Chs.Staffs. 54; PRO SC7/22/30, 35/2, and CPR 1247-58, 441.

[11] CPR 1232-47, 244, and PRO SC7/20/21-25,27-30,32-8,41, and 22/31-2.

[12] PRO SC7/20/6,10-11,20,40,43, 21/17,23,29, 3/34,45, 33/4-6, 9,11; CPR 1247-58, 68-9, and CPR 1258-66, 150,155,192, 197. Master Roger Lovel served also as a proctor of Tewkesbury abbey (Ben. Glos.), and, at the instance of the Tewkesbury monks, he represented Richard de Clare, earl of Gloucester and Hereford, in 1251 (H. R. Luard, ed., *Annales Monastici* I [Rolls Series 36; London 1864] 129).

[13] PRO SC7/2/22-3, 3/10, and CPR 1258-66, 113. See also Largiadèr, *op. cit.* 73, who has a proctor, Finatus, in 1244.

[14] CPR 1258-66, 192,197,213-14, and SC7/33/17.   [15] SC7/10/5.

[16] SC7/16/3, and CPR 1272-81, 47.   [17] SC7/19/3.

[18] SC7/32/1,6-8, and 12. In 1297 he appeared for the hospice of Altopascio (see R. Fawtier, ed., *Les Registres de Boniface VIII* [Bibliothèque des Écoles Françaises d'Athènes et de Rome, série 2, 4; Paris 1939, hereafter cited as *Reg. Bon. VIII*] xxxiv, citing Archives Nationales L 252 no. 2²).

[19] SC7/30/21.

[20] SC7/30/13-14,17, and 31/2,4,6-8,10-13,15,17,18, and 20-21. G. de Sancto Geminiano is usually mentioned in the endorsements as *pro domino . . Ostien'* (Latinus Frangipani [Malabranca] O.P. promoted cardinal bishop of Ostia on 12 March 1278, died on 10 August 1294), so it may in fact have been the cardinal who was in the king's pay. He appeared for Fürstenzell (Cist. dioc. Passau) in 1300 (Herde, *op. cit.* 140).

[21] PRO SC7/6/1-2,4-5,8,12-13, 7/5-6,8-9,15,17,19, and 8/5. N. de Vico (? Nicolaus Novellus de Vico of Alatri diocese, in the *familia* of the pope and a papal notary) acted between 1296 and 1303 for the Holy See and the kings of France and England (*Reg. Bon. VIII*, xxxvi).

[22] CPR 1313-17, 45; CPR 1330-4, 558; British Museum [= BM] Cotton Ch. vi 6; and PRO SC7/24/5, 25/7,13, and 56/17B,21,25.

[23] SC7/24/3-4,6,9-10, 25/15-16,22-23, and 30.

The religious orders had their own standing proctors at Rome, or before the papal court, to protect their general interests. Cluniac standing proctors include Bartholomeus (1247), and Giso (1278-82). Bartholomeus obtained bulls for the Cluniac houses of Montierneuf and Longpont, which came to rest in England.[24] In 1279 Giso obtained six general bulls for the order, dated between 23 January and 22 April at St. Peter's, which were despatched to England, and on 6 July 1278 at Viterbo he obtained a bull for the prior and convent of Lewes, and on 9 February 1282 at Orvieto for the prior of Lewes, John.[25] This illustrates that individual houses of the order might use the general proctor. Paulus, who signs from the Lateran on 21 January 1256, was probably a general proctor of the order, although he might be identified with a Paulus who occurs in 1250 and 1253,[26] but Bonaspes de Assisio, whose name appears on a mandate of 1277 ordering the abbot of St. Corneille, Compiègne, to recover goods of the Cluniac order which had been illicitly alienated, also appears for the Poor Clares and the Cistercians and so cannot be regarded as exclusive to the Cluniacs.[27] Cistercian endorsements were mainly by general proctors of the order: Sy[mon] in 1244, and in 1243-4 for Rufford, and also in 1244 Frater E. and Frater H., and in 1255-6 Frater F.[28] Petrus of Assisi got a bull for Clairvaux at Anagni on 28 April 1259 and two general Cistercian bulls at Lyons in 1274, which led von Heckel to suggest that perhaps he was a Cistercian.[29] The Templars' bulls between 9 September 1255 and 12 February 1256 were endorsed (in this case at the bottom centre) by Frater R. and Ph.[30] On 25 January 1262 W. de Mere impetrated for them,[31] in 1265 Frater Eustachius *capellanus*,[32] in 1272 Petrus Fortialis,[33] and in 1295 Thomas de Aqua-

---

[24] BM Add. Chs. 1543-4.

[25] Add. Chs. 1549-59 (one of which is in quintuplicate and one in duplicate), SC7/35/11, and 28/18.

[26] Add. Ch. 1546, and SC7/19/21, 30.

[27] BM Add. Chs. 1547-8 and 67079. See also Herde, *op. cit.* 137 and 146, where he appears in 1267 as proctor for Altötting collegiate church (dioc. Salzburg) and for the monastery of Seeon (Ben. dioc. Salzburg).

[28] BM Harley Ch. 111 A 13-15, Add. Chs. 17852-4, 17856-8; Add. Chs. 17849-51 and 17855; and Harley Ch. 75 A 2 and Add. Ch. 12778. Frater Wilielmus who endorsed for Quarr (Savigny) in 1237 was perhaps a Cistercian general proctor (BM Stowe Ch. 571). A *Willelmus cist' ord'* endorses a Cistercian document of 1249 (Lambeth Palace Library, PD no. 46).

[29] Harley Chs. 111 A 23-5, and von Heckel, *art. cit.* (n. 2 *supra*) 319. This is also argued by Herde (and that he was a Cistercian abbot), *op. cit.* 133-4, but challenged by Brentano in *Speculum* 39 (1964) 154-5.

[30] Lambeth PD no. 55 and PRO SC7/2/19, 3/11,33-5,37-8, 46.

[31] SC7/33/10.

[32] SC7/10/10.

[33] SC7/16/8.

munda.[34] Thomas de Aquamunda endorsed bulls for the French Templars in 1296 and 1297.[35] B. de Guarcino appeared for the Templars in 1286, but also acted for the prior of Lenton (Augustinian) in 1289, for William de Lamberton elected bishop of St. Andrews, in 1298, and for the bishop of Glasgow and the bishop of Sodor in 1299.[36] As a contrast to the Cistercians and Templars, whose English bulls were always distinctively marked with 'Cist. ord' and 'T', the Hospitallers' bulls are few in number and do not have distinguishing marks or show any instances of proctors of the order.[37] For Sempringham the endorsements between 1248 and 1250 are Por. . .us (1248-9), Electus Parmen' (1249) and ? P. Ferrariis (1250).[38] Whether these were proctors of the order or men engaged for specific purposes from the ordinary supply of proctors, it is impossible to say.

An investigation of individual religious houses as employers of proctors has produced lists for Bury St. Edmunds (Benedictine, Suffolk), Rufford (Cist. Notts.), and Holy Trinity Aldgate (Aug. London). The Bury endorsements reveal Rad. pon. in 1248, Rolandus in 1251 and 1254, R. d'Albo monasterio in 1256, P. of Orvieto in 1262, and John de Ely in 1345.[39] R. d'Albo monasterio worked also for Holy Trinity Aldgate. P. of Orvieto was a proctor from 1260 to 1282 numbering among his clients the house of lepers at Verona, Kenilworth priory (Aug. Warwicks.), Selby abbey (Ben. Yorks. W.R.), Roger de Nortone, newly elected abbot of St. Albans, and the notorious pluralist Bogo de Clare, besides Bury.[40] John de Ely represented John (de Cumba), abbot of Combe, at Avignon, when he was provided to the bishopric of Cloyne in 1333. He was thus presumably a standing proctor at Avignon for at least twelve years, and one of English birth.[41]

---

[34] PRO SC7/6/14. See also Herde, *op. cit.* 145 and 147, where he appears for the German Templars in 1297, for St. Andrew's Worms (Ben.) in 1298, and with Nicholas de Aquamunda for St. Zeno Würzburg (Austin canons) in 1300.

[35] See Fawtier in *Reg. Bon. VIII*, xxxviii, citing A[rchives] N[ationales] L. 280 no. 40 and L. 281 nos. 66, 69.

[36] Lambeth PD no. 78, SC7/31/5, 8/4 and 6/10. Fawtier in *Reg. Bon. VIII*, xxxiv, identifies him with Benedictus Johannis Atracesii de Guarcino, the well-known notary who worked for the Caetani.

[37] PD no. 58 (specific bull for Buckland), SC7/6/16 (G. de Sancto P. — endorsement), and BM Add. Ch. 70819 (specific bull for Châlons-sur-Marne hospital). Jacobinus de Parma, however, represented French and German hospitallers (Herde, *op. cit.* 141, and Fawtier in *Reg. Bon. VIII*, xxxv).

[38] PD no. 43, BM Stowe Chs. 572-3.

[39] Lambeth PD nos. 44,48,51-2,59,65 and 88.

[40] BM Add. Ch. 37633; Harley Ch. 43 A 45; Lambeth PD no. 70; and PRO SC7/33/1, 58/2.

[41] SC7/56/24.

Rufford employed Rad. Rog. in 1229, D. de Sparco in 1235 (possibly acting for Sawtry), Symon (a general Cistercian proctor) in 1243-4, Frater R. Camereari in 1255, P. of Assisi (for Th' de Brampton) in 1283, Johannes de Reynbach in 1360, Jo. de Stratford in 1364, N. Leudacale in 1375, B. de Monasterio in 1380, and Johannes de Scribanis in 1409.[42] Frater R. Camereari was presumably a Cistercian, the endorsement including a note to the effect that the document was to be obtained or collected for Rufford before or after the general council.[43] No further details are known of Johannes de Reynbach, Jo. de Stratford, N. Leudacale, B. de Monasterio, and Johannes de Scribanis, but P. of Assisi was a professional proctor who represented a number of English houses: Kenilworth (Aug. Warws.), Durham (Ben.), Dale (Premonstratensian, Derbyshire), and Westminster (Ben.).[44]

Holy Trinity Aldgate provides a much fuller list which allows more general conclusions to be drawn. With the exception of Haymo, who endorses in 1229, the proctors between 1226 and 1250 are specified only by initials, N., S., M. and B.[45] Haymo might be identified with the Haymo endorsing for Gateshead hospital in 1228.[46] From 1251 the proctors are more clearly identifiable. Eunufrius occurs as a standing proctor following the papal court between 1251 and 1261 from Lyons to Naples, to the Lateran, to Viterbo. Besides Holy Trinity he acted for the archbishop of Armagh on four occasions, and the dean and chapter of St. Paul's, London, on one occasion.[47] Paulus, too, occurring in 1253 might be a standing proctor.[48] On 6 May 1254 at Assisi Frater (...) Sancto Helya endorsed a document for the prior of Holy Trinity.[49] It is possible that this is the same person as Roger de Sancto Helia, proctor of Christ Church Canterbury in 1241, but his description there as a clerk and

---

[42] BM Harley Chs. 111 A 9, 12, 20, 26, 29-31, 36 and 33.

[43] Harley Ch. 111 A 20. The document is dated 19 August 1255, and it is possible that *concilium generale* might be taken to mean the Cistercian general chapter which met on 14 September.

[44] BM Harley Ch. 43 A 42; R. Brentano, *York Metropolitan Jurisdiction and Papal Judges Delegate (1279-1296)* (Berkeley and Los Angeles 1959) 116 and 127; BM Wolley Ch. xi 23; and Westminster Abbey Muniments 32644. For Petrus of Assisi see now Herde, *op. cit.* 133-4, and the references given between 137-46.

[45] PRO SC7/15/25, 35/17, 15/28, 19/20,24, and 21/19. S., who endorses a Holy Trinity bull of 15 December 1233, might be the same as the S. who endorsed a bull for Poughley (Aug.), dated 20 February 1238 (SC7/15/36).

[46] SC7/64/45.

[47] SC7/1/37, 3/3, 2/31, 19/28, 61/4, and Lambeth PD no. 63. See also Herde, *op. cit.* 137 (as Eunufridus) where his name occurs on a document of 1255 for the monastery of Attel (Ben. dioc. Freising).

[48] SC7/19/30, and see above n. 26.

[49] SC7/20/42.

his position as a substitute proctor make this unlikely.[50] In 1255 Holy Trinity were represented at the papal court by one of their canons named Ralph, and between 13 April 1282 and 3 February 1286 by J. de Burton.[51] Both these two would appear to be Englishmen, the latter possibly a standing proctor although no evidence survives of his acting for other parties. R. d'Albo monasterio, proctor twice for Holy Trinity in 1257, had acted for Bury in 1256.[52] He was not, however, the only proctor retained by Holy Trinity between 13 July and 21 November 1257, the name of T. Wold appearing on a document of 10 October in that year.[53] Similarly J. de Burton's name occurs on documents for Holy Trinity of 13 and 27 April 1282, but that of Petrus de Campello on one of 26 April 1282.[54] Roffredus appears in instances as separated as 28 March 1264 and 12 March 1274.[55] He might well be identifiable with Roffredus de Ferentino, a clerk of the English cardinal John of Toledo in 1254,[56] who also had the king's proctor Master Roger Lovel in his household.[57] A Roffredus de Ferentino, clerk, is mentioned as a proctor in a formulary example of c. 1277,[58] and an R. de Ferentino represented Hulme abbey in Norfolk in 1257.[59] P. de Sancto Andrea's name is on documents for Holy Trinity of 26 and 27 October 1267, and Francus de Podiobonizi's on one of 1 August 1290.[60] Francus de Podiobonizi was a standing proctor between 1282 and 1295 and got documents for Quarr abbey (Savigny, Isle of Wight), Waterbeach nunnery (Franciscan, Cambs.), Newent priory (Ben. alien, Glos.), and John de Berkhamstede, monk of St. Albans newly elected abbot of St. Albans.[61] The final occurrence of a Holy Trinity proctor's name

---

[50] Dean and Chapter Archives, Canterbury, Scrapbook B no. 91.

[51] B. de La Roncière et al. ed., Les Registres d'Alexandre IV (Bibliothèque des Écoles Françaises d'Athènes et de Rome, série 2, 15; Paris 1895-1959) no. 80; and SC7/18/30, 19/8, 28/13, 19,20, and 29/1.

[52] SC7/2/49, 3/49, and Lambeth PD no. 59.

[53] SC7/3/50.

[54] SC7/28/7.

[55] SC7/33/8,12,15 and 23, and 16/16.

[56] E. Berger, ed., Les Registres d'Innocent IV (Bibl. des Écoles Françaises d'Athènes et de Rome, série 2, 1; Paris 1884-1921) no. 7243.

[57] W. H. Bliss, ed., Calendar of Entries in the Papal Registers relating to Great Britain: Papal Letters [= CPL] I (H.M.S.O. London 1893) 277.

[58] See Herde, op. cit. 85, and idem, 'Ein Formelbuch Gerhards von Parma . . .', Archiv für Diplomatik 13 (1967) no. 5.

[59] BM Add. Ch. 14711.

[60] PRO SC7/11/9, 10/1A, 13/4, and 32/17. A P. de Sancto Andrea was a proctor acting for German interests between 1259 and 1261 (Herde, op. cit. 140, 142, and 145-6).

[61] BM Add. Ch. 15775; Cott. Ch. xi 19 (Fawtier in Reg. Bon. VIII, xxxiv, has him wrongly from this document as G.); Lambeth PD no. 77; and PRO SC7/30/10. See also Herde, op. cit. 136, an occurrence in 1290 for the monastery of Aldersbach (Cist. dioc. Passau).

is that of W. Cook, who acquired licences in 1395 for Walter Braytofte, canon of Holy Trinity, to choose a confessor and to have a portable altar.[62] A Walter Cook had appeared for Burscough priory (Lancs.), another Augustinian house, in 1387.[63]

An examination of the evidence does not suggest that the proctors confined their duties to working for specific religious orders. Brentano pointed out that Petrus of Assisi was employed by two major Benedictine houses, but it can also be shown that he represented an English Cistercian, Premonstratensian, and Augustinian house. For the Benedictines there is evidence of a considerable number of proctors acting only once for whom no other occurrences can be found: Asaltas Eberienge (Cherienge) for Elstow (Ben. nuns, Beds.) in 1235,[64] Brefond for Wix (Ben. nuns, Essex) in 1237,[65] Adam Rom' for St. Mary's York in 1246,[66] Matheus for Crowland (Ben. Lincs.) in 1249,[67] Thomas de Sancto Egidio for Whitby (Yorks. N.R.) in 1253,[68] Robert de Londoniis for St. Swithun's Winchester in 1254,[69] Pentaculum Salomon for Hatfield Regis in 1256,[70] and Master Th' for Faversham in 1274.[71] Similarly with the Augustinians we have Guardia representing Haliwell (Aug. canonesses, London) in 1238,[72] A. representing Drax (Yorks. W.R.) in 1251,[73] and Johannes for Poughley in 1256.[74] Where we have one or two occurrences they were usually for houses of different orders. R. Salsarius' name occurs on documents for Wix (Aug.) and Bath (Ben.) in 1283.[75] Master John de Malling (Mallengg) represented Ravenstone (Aug. Bucks.) in 1317 and the prior of Christ Church Canterbury in 1328.[76] H. de Hemesby's name is on a document for Keynsham (Aug. Somerset) of 1224 and one for Spalding (Ben. alien, Lincs.) of 1240.[77] N[icholas] de Sancto Victore, in the pay of Christ Church Canterbury in 1289/90, had acquired a document at Rieti in 1288 for Alfonso, son of Velasco Gometii

---

[62] SC7/8/13-14.
[63] BM Harley Ch. 43 A 41. A Walter Cook was prebendary of Milton Ecclesia in the cathedral of Lincoln between 1395 and 1424. He was provided archdeacon of Buckingham in 1399 but despoiled by royal clerks in the same year (J. Le Neve, *Fasti Ecclesiae Anglicanae 1300-1541*, I: Lincoln Diocese, comp. H. P. F. King [Athlone Press 1962] 15, 92).
[64] BM Harley Ch. 43 A 36.   [65] SC7/15/26.
[66] SC7/19/25.   [67] Lambeth PD no. 47.
[68] *Ibid.* no. 50.   [69] *Ibid.* no. 53.
[70] SC7/64/61.
[71] Lambeth PD no. 69.
[72] BM Harley Ch. 43 A 37.
[73] BM Add. Ch. 21095.
[74] SC7/3/18,23.
[75] SC7/28/12, 29/4, and Lambeth PD no. 76.
[76] Bodleian Library MS Chs. Bucks. 22 and Canterbury, Cartae Antiquae C 1299.
[77] Lambeth PD nos. 23, 35.

of Portugal, a friar minor.[78] In the mid 1280's he had German clients, and in between 1295 and 1297 he was working for French interests.[79] Proctors accepted cases from wherever they came, religious, seculars, or laymen. Thomas de Pontecurvo (Frosinone) represented the hospital of St. Mary Magdalene at King's Lynn in 1300: according to Fawtier he obtained documents probably at the request of the king of France in 1297 and 1298.[80] A. de Silvestro (de Silvestris) got a document for the bishop of St. Davids in 1252 and one for Roche (Cist. Yorks.) in 1256.[81] Lucas de Guarcino represented the two Augustinian houses of Leeds (Kent) and Chetwode (Bucks.) but he had also worked for the bishop of Down (Ireland) in 1279.[82]

Individual religious and laymen, and groups of laymen, brought the proctors much work. Petrus de Anagnia represented the merchants of Siena in 1254 and the archbishop of Dublin and his suffragans in 1261.[83] Johannes de Serron (Suenon') acted for the dean of Cashel and the king of Scotland in 1260.[84] Simon Boerii got a document for William de Bohun, earl of Northampton, and his wife in 1343, and for Gregory, provost of Killala, provided to the bishopric of Elphin in 1357.[85] Johannes Lemosini (Lemosan) got documents for John de Karlil B.C.L. of Carlisle diocese, Howel ap Grono bishop of Bangor, and for the incumbent of a chapel in Chichester diocese or for the bishop.[86] H. de Newerk got documents at Beaucaire for Antony Bek, and John, son of Henry de Hastings, and Isabel, daughter of William de Valence, in 1275.[87]

---

[78] Canterbury, Cartae Antiquae C 224, and PRO SC7/30/3. See also Herde, op. cit. 142 and 147, for the friars minor at Regensburg (1286) and for St. Agnes Würzburg (1284). Another important Canterbury proctor at this time was M. George de Interampnis (see Canterbury, Cart. Antiq. A 46, Cambridge University Library MS. Ee. v. 31 (Eastry Reg.) fol. 65r, and von Heckel, art. cit. 320 n. 2 for Angelus de Interampnis).

[79] Fawtier in Reg. Bon. VIII, xxxvi (citing AN L. 270 no. 20, J. 700 no. 101, and J. 701 no. 109).

[80] Lambeth PD no. 81; Fawtier in Reg. Bon. VIII (citing AN J. 702 no. 122 and 122 bis, and Herde, op. cit. 140 and 143, for Benedictines in 1289 and 1300. A J. de Pontecurvo appears in 1295 acting for the king of France (SC7/6/18) and for ?Edward I (SC7/40/7). He was a papal scriptor and chaplain to Cardinal Matheus Orsini (Fawtier in Reg. Bon. VIII, xx and xxxv).

[81] SC7/22/36 and Lambeth PD no. 56.

[82] Lambeth PD nos. 74, 128a, and Jules Gay and Suzanne Vitte, ed., Les Registres de Nicolas III (Bibl. des Écoles Françaises d'Athènes et de Rome, série 2, 14; Paris 1898-1938) no. 589.

[83] SC7/19/27 and 33/3. For his German occurrences between 1253 and 1274, see Herde, op. cit. 142-5.

[84] SC7/3/21-2.

[85] SC7/54/3 and 64/12.

[86] Lambeth PD no. 92, and SC7/17/15, and 64/4.

[87] SC7/16/15,21 and 27. He is probably to be identified with Master Henry de Newark, canon of St. Paul's in 1294, dean of York (1290) and later archbishop of York until his

152

Philippus Forzoli acted for Roland Jorze, newly provided to the archbishopric of Armagh, in 1311, and for Walter Reynolds, translated to Canterbury in 1313.[88] Petrus de Ascibilis represented an Irish abbot and a bishop in 1317-18,[89] and Nicholas de Lascy, a canon of Bangor and a canon of St. Asaph, in 1343.[90] William de Neuton appeared similarly for an English priest, William de Saxeby, in 1343, and an English layman, Thomas de Hollande knight, in 1354.[91]

*
* *

The names of the three proctors, H. de Newerk (1275), Nicholas de Lascy (Lacy: 1343), and William de Neuton (1343 and 1354), suggest that they were of English origin, which raises the question of nationality. With a few exceptions the connection of English proctors with English suits comes from the period of the Avignonese papacy. Obviously there had always been some nationals involved in suits from their own countries, particularly during the thirteenth century when proctors were not infrequently canons or monks representing their own houses.[92] Nor were Englishmen excluded from following careers in the papal *curia* and becoming standing proctors. H. de Hemesby, who represented Keynsham in 1224 and Spalding in 1240, appears to be one such.[93] Simon de Peling, who represented Clothall hospital in Hertfordshire at Lyons in 1245,[94] John de Gelham, who got a document dated 29 September 1289 at Rieti for Robert de Elenton, elected abbot of Holy Cross Waltham,[95] Philip de Barton, who represented M(atheus Orsini) cardinal deacon of St. Mary in Porticu, at Orvieto in 1290,[96] and W. de Donnebroke, whose name appears on the bull confirming Robert Winchelsey as archbishop dated at Aquila on 24 September 1294,[97] were probably also men of this kind, embarked on proctorial careers. But the evidence for English proctors is scarce until

death in 1299; see J. Le Neve, *Fasti Ecclesiae Anglicanae 1066-1300*, I: St. Paul's London, comp. Diana E. Greenway (Athlone Press 1968) 31, and C. T. Clay, ed. *York Minster Fasti* I (Yorks. Archaeol. Soc. Rec. Ser. 123, 1957 for 1958) 10.

[88] SC7/44/11 and 15.
[89] SC7/56/9-10.
[90] SC7/12/2,8, and 13/13.
[91] SC7/12/1,7, and 22/16.
[92] See above pp. 149-50, and e.g. Canterbury, Cartae Antiquae A 206 and P 53, for Thomas monk and proctor of Christ Church Canterbury in 1236 and 1238.
[93] Lambeth PD nos. 23 and 35.
[94] BM Harley Ch. 111 A 16.
[95] SC7/60/2.
[96] SC7/31/3. For his later preferment, see J. Le Neve, *Fasti Ecclesiae Anglicanae 1300-1541*: I (1962) 83, IV (1963) 48, V (1963) 33, and X (1964) 49.
[97] SC7/9/7.

the fourteenth century.[98] From the period of the Avignon popes come Master John de Malling (1317), Roland de Stamfeld (1327), William de Nassington (1327), John de Ely (1333 and 1345), John de Couplandia (1335), William de Cotton (1335), William de Beggeworthe (1342), David Martyn (1349), Richard de Wysebeche (1352), Thomas Deuworth (1357), Jo. de Stratford (1364), W. Dany (or Davy; 1364).[99] They equal the number of Italians and other nationals,[100] and outnumber the Italians as a group. There may have been more Englishmen than Italians concerned with English cases, although the two English royal proctors of the period were Italian, Bernardus de Barrio (Bari) and Master Andreas Sapiti, a Florentine.[101] After the papacy left Avignon Englishmen continued to seek careers as proctors, men such as Reginald Walpole and Walter Cook.[102]

There is enough evidence to show that if there were Englishmen available they were not necessarily chosen by their compatriots. How far then do national connections play a part in proctorial appointments? Probably where the influence was needed was in the higher realms, for a cardinal, for instance, who would recommend a suitable proctor. When W. de Lexinton, chaplain of the English cardinal John of Toledo, wanted an indult to hold more than one benefice, the proctor whose name appears on the resultant bull of 16 March 1247 was Johannes de Asisio.[103] Probably this proctor was engaged at the instance of Cardinal John of Toledo. In 1255 Master Roger Lovel the king's proctor, who had also held the office of chaplain to Cardinal John of Toledo, was dispensed to hold a plurality of benefices at the Cardinal's

---

[98] Herde has come to similar conclusions concerning the proctors of Bavarian petitioners, who in the thirteenth century were mainly Italians (op. cit. 129 and 136).

[99] Bodley MS. Chs. Bucks. 22; PRO SC7/64/11,14; SC7/56/20; SC7/56/24 and Lambeth PD no. 88; SC7/35/20; SC7/42/3; SC7/64/13; SC7/12/6; SC7/45/2; Lambeth PD no. 90; BM Harley Ch. 111 A 30; and SC7/34/2.

[100] ?11 Italian, 1 German, 1 Flemish. Taveruinus Novarien' (1310 - SC7/11/22), Johannes de Lupico (1313 - SC7/44/9), Leo de Sena (1317 - SC7/56/5), Guido de Lesployedern (1317 - SC7/25/26), R. de Sancto Merveo (1317 - SC7/24/8,11), Petrus Ascibilis (1317-18 - SC7/56/9-10), Jacobinus Frassus (1320 - SC7/24/14,18), Cione de Ficull' (1320 - SC7/56/11), Matheus de Prato (1328 - SC7/56/19), Simon Boerii (1343 and 1357 - SC7/54/3 and 64/12), Galfridus Burgeys* (1345 - SC7/13/11), Alexander de Sancto Cassian (1348 - SC7/44/7), Johannes de Reynbach (1360 - Harl. Ch. 111 A 29), Johannes Lemosini (1367,71,73 - PD no. 92; SC7/ 17/15, 64/4), Willelmus de Amersford* (1371 - SC7/48/1), N. Leudacale (1375 - Harl. Ch. 111 A 31).   * Dr Zutshi has pointed out that these two were English.

[101] See above p. 145.

[102] Lambeth PD no. 94; BM Harley Ch. 43 A 41, SC 7/8/13-14, and see above p. 150.

[103] BM Harley Ch. 111 A 7. Cf. PRO SC7/31/3, a document issued at the instance of Matheus, cardinal deacon of St. Mary in Porticu, in 1290: the proctor was Philip de Barton. And cf. also SC7/30/15, on which the Cardinal's name appears and not the proctor's.

request.[104] When Master Johannes, canon of Veroli, cousin and chaplain of Gaufridus de Alatro, cardinal deacon of St. George *ad velum aureum*, was appointed bishop of Clonfert in 1266, a document connected with his appointment bore the name of Roffridus de Ceperano, *consanguineus* of the Cardinal, as proctor.[105] Not only do we find cardinals recommending the issue of documents and presumably choosing the proctors, but also their names appear on documents to suggest that they were directly associated with the issue. A document for Clairvaux issued in 1256 bears the name of John of Toledo, who had been a monk there, and also of Ambrose (?his clerk).[106] A document issued in 1255 for the Cistercians in England, and in places subject to the king of England, also bears the name of the same Cardinal John of Toledo.[107] Documents making grants to cardinals and papal officials sometimes have the name of the beneficiary in the place where the proctor's name usually occurs, perhaps in instances where the beneficiary appeared in person to ask for the grant in question. For example, two documents for Stephen Langton, cardinal deacon of St. Adrian, were endorsed *Card'*,[108] the document confirming the provision of Bartholomeus, chaplain of P. de Colonna, to the rectory of St. Nicholas, Middleton (Hants), bears his name in the place where that of the proctor would usually be found,[109] and there are many more instances of this practice.[110]

Frequently the endorsements link up with the names of the recipients, for instance Hugh de Neville,[111] and in two instances with the fathers of the recipients. The name of Odo Brancaleone occurs on the dorse of a document of 1237 restoring Theodinus, clerk, his son, to the church of St. Margaret,

---

[104] CPL (n. 57) I 324, and see also 277.

[105] SC7/44/17.

[106] Harley Ch. 111 A 22.

[107] SC7/2/30. See also J.-M. Canivez, ed., *Statuta Capitulorum Generalium Ordinis Cisterciensis* II (Bibl. de la Revue d'Histoire Ecclésiastique, fasc. 10; Louvain 1934) 419, for another approach to him. Cf. perhaps the name of the cardinal bishop of Sabina which appears on a document for the convent of St. Michael at Bamberg (Ben.) in 1249 (Herde, *op. cit.* 138), and of ?R. cardinal whose name endorses a document for William marquis of Montferrat in 1291 (SC7/30/11).

[108] SC7/18/23 and 50/9.

[109] SC7/8/1. Fawtier in *Reg. Bon. VIII*, xxxiv, has him in this instance (I think wrongly) as the proctor.

[110] See the documents for Master Johannes Aston papal chaplain (SC7/19/29 and 20/44), Master Gervase de Londoniis papal chaplain (SC7/3/36), M. Stephanus Anibaldi (SC7/2/18), the archbishop of Messina (SC7/3/12), Blasius chaplain and nephew of Pope Alexander IV (SC7/38/1), Ubaldinus nephew of O. cardinal of St. Mary in Via Lata (SC7/2/24-26), Matheus cardinal deacon of St. Mary in Porticu (SC7/30/15), Adomarus cardinal priest of St. Anastasia (SC7/11/3), and Master Martinus clerk of the papal *camera* (SC7/15/24).

[111] SC7/64/7.

South Elmham,[112] and that of Jacobus de Ponte, citizen of Rome, on a document of 1253 ordering provision for his son Stephanus de Ponte, canon of the basilica of the Prince of the Apostles, to a benefice or benefices worth forty marks in the province of Canterbury.[113] These must be instances where it was important to keep the recipient's name in mind either to facilitate the issue of the document or to safeguard its delivery. It is not unknown for orders to have the name of the officers instructed to carry them out in the place usually reserved for the proctors,[114] and it is possible that the name appearing in that position is sometimes that of a messenger (e.g. ?Ardena) and not that of a proctor.[115] The problem of who endorsed leads us to the question of which documents were endorsed with proctorial names and which were not, and at what point these endorsements were made.

*
* *

The main varieties of documents for which proctors were used were as follows: documents concerning the appointment of bishops and archbishops, frequently asking the king for their good receipt following papal confirmation of election, translation, or papal provision — Philippus Forzoli got a document of this kind for Walter Reynolds in 1313 and Matheus de Prato for Simon Meopham in 1328[116] — documents requesting the restoration of temporalities,[117] and documents concerning clerical conduct.[118] These were obviously profitable and rapidly expanding fields of business for the proctors by the late thirteenth century. In 1282 Guido Novarien' (de Novaria) obtained a document for John de Pontissara, archdeacon of Exeter, now provided to the bishopric of Winchester, asking the king to take him into his favour, and in 1286 he obtained a similar document for John le Romeyn, precentor of Lincoln and canon of York, whose election to the archbishopric of York

---

[112] SC7/15/7.

[113] SC7/19/26.

[114] E.g. PRO SC7/22/29, an order to Master Albertus, papal notary and legate, in 1254, commanding him to induce the king of England to pursue the Sicilian business vigorously, endorsed *Magistro Alberto not' domini pape*.

[115] See SC7/46/6 (date 1227), and ? 35/12 (date 1289). Perhaps Philip de Ardena, king's envoy, and proctor within England — the differentiation between the two is often difficult (see CPR 1232-47, 4,47,84-5, 90). Mary C. Hill, *The King's Messengers 1199-1377* (London 1961) 32, 82-4, has a courier called Robert of Arden but he occurs in 1343.

[116] SC7/44/11 and 56/19, and e.g. 56/5,20.

[117] SC7/9/7, and 2/28,35 — the last documents in favour of the archbishop of Armagh obtained by Michael, proctor, cf. perhaps Herde, *op. cit.* 40, 138.

[118] SC7/6/22.

the pope had confirmed.[119] Similarly newly appointed abbots found it wise to engage proctors to impetrate documents from the pope to the king soliciting the royal favour, as did William de Bernham, elected abbot of Bury St. Edmunds, who engaged William de Cotton for this purpose in 1335,[120] and Roger de Nortone, elected abbot of St. Albans in 1263, who employed P. of Orvieto.[121] Petrus Ascibilis obtained this variety of document for both a newly translated archbishop in 1317 and a newly appointed abbot in 1318.[122]

Documents assigning prebends and canonries are frequently endorsed by the impetrant's proctor.[123] An order, issued in 1257 to provide Stephanus de Ponte with benefices to the value of forty marks, was endorsed with the name of Jacobus de Famos (?Samos), presumably the proctor.[124] Documents of this kind dealt not only with the assignation of prebends, but also frequently with the recovery of possessions abstracted from them. In 1274 Antony Bek, prebendary of the chapel of St. Clement in Pontefract castle, got R. de Urbe- (veteri?) to procure for him a mandate ordering the restoration of the goods belonging to it.[125] In 1275 the same Antony Bek secured collation to the archdeaconry of Dorset and the promise of a prebend in Salisbury cathedral if or when one came vacant. His proctor in this instance was H. de Newerk.[126]

With the development of the provision of papal clerks and officials to the more lucrative benefices, it became necessary for religious houses wielding considerable patronage to maintain proctors at the papal court to prevent provisions which were not acceptable to them. Such rights of appointment had to be carefully guarded. In 1236 or before Gregory IX sent letters to Christ Church Canterbury asking them to provide Gregorius of Anagni, in the household of his nephew Matheus, to the benefice which Willelmus once messenger of pope Innocent III had occupied. The proctor of Christ Church, the monk Thomas, protested against the provision in the papal court. There, an agreement was made between Gregorius and Thomas, whereby Gregorius renounced the provision and Christ Church agreed to pay him ten marks in lieu of it.[127]

Laymen also had need of papal letters of different kinds. Proctors gained documents for different merchants in England. In 1296 the merchants of

---

[119] PRO SC7/28/14, and 51/3. In 1295 Franciscus de Atin' acted for John de Pontissara who was seeking a licence from the king to go to Rome (SC7/6/3: Fawtier in *Reg. Bon. VIII*, xxxiv, reads this as *de Acm'*).

[120] SC7/42/3.   [121] SC7/33/1.

[122] SC7/56/9-10.   [123] E.g. SC7/13/19.

[124] SC7/2/32.

[125] PRO SC7/16/7, and cf. 35/5 and 64/65 — the restoration of goods to churches.

[126] SC7/16/15 and 21.

[127] Canterbury, Cartae Antiquae P 53.

the Riccardi of Lucca living in England got letters endorsed with the name of Nicholaus Claus de Aricia to Edward I asking him to show favour to them,[128] and similar letters were obtained by Symon on behalf of the company of the Spini of Florence in 1299.[129] When some members of the same company were arrested in 1301 and their goods seized, they obtained a papal document to Edward I requesting him to release them and restore their goods. This document bears the endorsement S. de Spinis.[130] Individual laymen sought varied indults — for which they needed proctors — licences to have a portable altar,[131] to build chapels and have their own chaplains,[132] to choose their own confessors,[133] to contract marriage although within the forbidden degrees of relationship,[134] to allow their clerks to enjoy the fruits of their benefices for three years without residing,[135] and numerous other privileges of this kind.[136]

All these documents concerned grants, and proctors were frequently used to impetrate them. The other main class of document was concerned with judicial disputes, consisting of mandates and confirmations of settlements etc. A suit brought by Nicholas, rector of **Aythorpe Roding** (Ess.), against the abbot and convent of Tilty and others, resulted in the appointment of judges delegate. The mandate bore the proctor's name Nazarenus.[137] Similarly in 1306 when an appeal was made to the pope in a case about tithes, where the archbishop's commissary had pronounced sentence, a proctor was used (Nicholas de Campo Basso) to obtain a new mandate to judges delegate.[138] Sometimes, too, confirmations of sentences which had been passed by judges delegate were required, and proctors were used to impetrate these. There seems in fact to be no possible distinction connected with the type of document as to whether proctors were used or not. They were used for grants; they were used also for mandates. Within these two major documentary classifications there are instances of their being used for every variety of document, if we are to go by the endorsements, but not in every instance.

The fine collection of bulls for Holy Trinity priory, Aldgate, London, now preserved in the Public Record Office, offers ample scope for investigating exactly which of their documents bear the names of their proctors and exactly which do not. During Innocent III's pontificate they obtained three bulls

---

[1²8] SC7/7/4. According to Fawtier in *Reg. Bon. VIII*, xxxvi, Nicolaus Clar.(enti) de Luca.
[129] PRO SC7/8/3.   [130] SC7/6/9.
[131] SC7/32/9.   [132] SC7/2/12-13.
[133] SC7/24/11.   [134] SC7/16/27.
[135] SC7/64/11.
[136] E.g. absolution from a vow to go on a pilgrimage to Santiago (SC7/24/8), and licence to a layman and his wife for religious to eat meat at their table except on days when it is generally forbidden (SC7/64/12).
[137] SC7/15/27.
[138] SC7/10/31.

which survive. Two granted protection to them for their church and possessions; the third confirmed to Holy Trinity the churches of Braughing (Herts.), Broomfield (Essex), Black Notley (Essex), and Alswick (Herts.).[139] None of these documents were endorsed with the names of proctors. From Honorius III the convent obtained five bulls: one gave protection to the house for its possessions and for persons connected with the convent, the second confirmed leave to appropriate the church of Braughing, the third was a mandate obtained to judges delegate, the fourth a confirmation of a sentence passed by judges delegate, and the fifth an indult to the prior allowing him exemption from hearing delegated cases.[140] Only the confirmation of the sentence passed by judges delegate bears the name of a proctor, N.[141] Under Gregory IX two out of five of the bulls were endorsed: a bull of protection for the house, its possessions, and personnel, which bears the name Haymo, and a bull issued in connection with an appeal, which is endorsed S.[142] The three not endorsed were another bull of protection, a mandate, and a confirmation.[143] The content of the document does not, therefore, seem to have any effect on whether the proctor's name appears on the back or not. With the pontificate of Innocent IV all the bulls (six in number) bear endorsements,[144] and the name of the proctor, Roffredus, appears on all four bulls of Pope Urban IV for Holy Trinity. They are a mandate, ordering that the hospital of St. Katherine next the Tower should be restored to Holy Trinity by the bishop of London, an indult that they might bear witness in cases concerning their church, a grant that they should enjoy their privileges and indults, and the confirmation of a grant by Walter de Mandeville of the advowson of Broomfield church.[145] Similarly the proctors of Holy Trinity appear to have endorsed all the documents of the late thirteenth century in instances where one would expect to find endorsements, that is, where documents were requested, but by the end of the period the practice is sporadic again. A mandate of Urban VI, ordering that goods unjustly detained were to be restored to Holy Trinity, and an indult of John XXIII, for instance, are not backed with the names of proctors, and for Boniface IX's pontificate two indults for an individual canon record the name of the proctor while a third does not.[146] An explanation as to why J. de Burton, whose name appears on documents for Holy Trinity of 13 and 27 April and 3 and 4 June 1282, was not connected with an indult issued on 26 April in their favour, which bears the name Petrus

---

[139] SC7/35/3, 19/19, 35/1.   [140] SC7/18/24, 35/19, 18/5, 35/17, 18/27.
[141] SC7/35/17.   [142] SC7/15/25, 28.
[143] SC7/64/70, 15/23, 35/28.
[144] SC7/19/20,24, 21/19, 19/28,30, 20/42.
[145] SC7/33/12,8,15, 23.
[146] SC7/34/23, 24/17, 8/13,14, and 9.

de Campello, is perhaps to be sought out of a multitude of personal reasons.[147] This particular group of papal bulls might suggest that endorsement was the practice after the beginning of Innocent IV's pontificate but that it tailed off at the end of the fourteenth century.

*
* *

Professor Herde has argued that, when a proctorial endorsement was made, the proctor put his name on the unsealed document shortly before or shortly after the scribe wrote the fair copy. He asserts this on the grounds that the colour of the ink used by the proctor is the same as that in which the document was written.[148] Obviously the point when the name was written on the document might be expected to give a lead as to its purpose. It is most improbable that the proctor put his name on a blank document and in any case the parchment was provided by the chancery official at the necessary stage. The matter of the actual time of endorsement seems to be clinched, at least in one instance, by the endorsement of B. de Sugio. On 8 March 1302 he wrote a document confirming the sale of a tenement in Paris to his master Cardinal Johannes Monachus, signing his name on the right of the *plica*. He also endorsed it in the proctorial location. The endorsement and the signature on the *plica* are identical and there can be no doubt that in this instance the ink is the same.[149]

For the proctor to have put his name on the document after sealing would seem to have served no purpose unless perhaps a financial one. At first sight it might be supposed that proctorial endorsements were in some way connected with the payment of proctors. Royal proctors were paid salaries mainly by the provision of benefices. In 1243 the king instructed the archbishop of York to provide the royal proctor, Richard de Neville, with an ecclesiastical

---

[147] SC7/29/1, 28/13,20,19, and 7.

[148] Herde, *op. cit.* 133. Von Heckel, *art. cit.* 317, had established that the signatures were mostly autograph. They were not, however, always so; see for example Frater H. whose name appears on documents of 5 and 21 February 1244 (BM Add. Chs. 17849 and 17851), but a different hand has put his name on a document of 16 February 1244 (Add. Ch. 17850). The signature of Bonaspes of Assisi whose name appears on Add. Chs. 1547-8 and 67079 is autograph and possibly in the same ink as each document. But one document endorsed by P. of Assisi is certainly in a different ink from that in which his signature is written (Harley Ch. 111 A 26).

[149] BM Egerton Ch. 60. B. de Sugio appeared for the cardinal between 1299 and 1302. Fawtier in *Reg. Bon. VIII*, xxi and xxxiv, however, suggests that he cannot be considered as a proctor, but rather as an all purpose chaplain sent to collect the bull. Yet *pro* which is used in this instance indicates on behalf of, and it does not seem possible to accept his argument.

benefice worth forty marks a year.[150] A similar order went out in the same year for Master Robert Anketil to be given a benefice of eighty marks *per annum*, but immediate effect was not given to it as in 1245 the king promised to provide him with the first benefice of eighty marks *per annum* which came vacant. As late as 1253 he was still receiving forty marks a year until better provision was made for him.[151] During vacancies in the sees of Canterbury and Winchester, Master Henricus de Secusia was presented to the church of Monkton in Kent and to the wardenship of the hospital of St. Cross, Winchester.[152] Master John de Chishull was rector of Isleham (Cambs.), Upwell (Cambs.), Rotherfield (Suss.), Holton by Beckering (Lincs.), Haversham (Bucks.), and Buckminster (Leics.), before becoming provost of Beverley, archdeacon of London, dean of St. Paul's, chancellor and keeper of the seal, and finally bishop of London.[153] He had begun his career as a clerk of Peter Chaceporc.[154] Guido de Rosilione was presented to the livings of Rothwell (Yorks.), Preston in Amounderness (Lancs.), Wrotham (Kent), Meresye (?Marske near Richmond, Yorks.), and Ribchester (Lancs.) between 1241 and 1244.[155] In 1243 he was ordered to have ecclesiastical benefices bringing in 400 marks' rent and the first prebend which became vacant in Lichfield cathedral, and in 1244 he became a prebendary of Wells and of Chichester, and dean of St. Martin le Grand.[156] Master Roger Lovel, a kinsman of Philip Lovel the king's treasurer, became rector of St. John's Ipswich, South Tawton (Devon), and Gisburn (Yorks.).[157] On 1 September 1256 when a new appointment to South Tawton was directed, he is referred to as being dead.[158] If this is correct a second royal proctor called Roger Lovel followed in his footsteps and received the benefices of Wotton (?Northants.) and Ebbesbourne Wake (Wilts.).[159] The grant of fifty marks sterling as a pension to one of the sons of Master Andreas Sapiti, a clerk, was in all likelihood made to the Gualterus described as clerk of Master Andreas, whose name often appears on bulls gained by M. Andreas at Avignon.[160] This grant was to continue until proper provision of a benefice valued at fifty marks was made.[161] No other record of the payment of M. Andreas survives, but he was supposed to have taken the revenues of the archbishopric of Armagh during two vacancies, to which the king naturally objected.[162]

---

[150] CPR 1232-47, 373.   [151] CPR 1232-47, 364, 455, and CPR 1247-58, 210.
[152] CPR 1232-47, 240, 249, 252.
[153] CPR 1247-58, 205, 581; CPR 1258-66, 63, 147, 239, 251; and F. N. Davis, ed., *Rotuli Ricardi Gravesend episcopi Lincolniensis* (Lincoln Record Society 20; Lincoln 1925) 4.
[154] CPL I 273, and CPR 1247-58, 359.   [155] CPR 1232-47, 258, 387-8, 420.
[156] *Ibid.* 384, 388, 417, 421, 423.   [157] CPL I 289, and CPR 1247-58, 111, 121.
[158] CPR 1247-58, 496.   [159] *Ibid.* 583, and CPR 1266-72, 730.
[160] Cf. the sons of Peter Saracen; see Barraclough, *art. cit.* (n. 6 *supra*) 369 n. 31.
[161] CPR 1313-17, 117.   [162] CPR 1321-4, 346.

Proctors who were paid by monasteries received fixed salaries also. When William, monk and proctor of Christ Church Canterbury, appointed a substitute proctor, Roger de Sancto Helia clerk, to act for him in 1241, he agreed to pay him two marks a year presumably out of his own salary, which sum was to increase if the work increased.[163] This arrangement was to be valid for a year. Two Italian proctors of Christ Church, Philippus de Pomonte and Nicholaus de Sancto Victore, received a salary of sixteen marks for their work *in audientia domini pape* in March 1289/90, and Philippus is recorded as receiving a little douceur from Prior Ringmer in the shape of twenty shillings and a gold necklace.[164] Proctorial documents recording the payment of salaries were drawn up in the presence of other proctors. Master Ricardus de Spina and Robertus *dictus* Salsarius witnessed the payment of Philippus de Pomonte and Nicholaus de Sancto Victore in 1289/90. The document was dated from S. Maria Maggiore, in the vicinity of which the pope Nicholas IV had built a papal palace, presumably the scene of the proctors' activities in Rome.[165] Similarly Masters Ricardus de Spina and Reginald of St. Albans witnessed a document of Robert of Selsey, a proctor of Christ Church Canterbury, in 1285.[166]

Proctors were also granted expenses. Master Henricus de Secusia (Hostiensis) was given a letter of credit up to 400 marks on one occasion and two letters of credit up to 1000 marks on another.[167] Master Robert Anketil was granted twenty marks for his expenses at Rome in 1242, and in 1254 Guido de Rosilione was authorised to borrow 300 marks at the papal court.[168] Likewise Robert of Selsey was empowered to borrow up to fifty marks by his employers in 1280.[169] He seems to have run up considerable debts, owing 15s. 9d. and twenty florins to a butcher, and 17s. 4d. to a poulterer. Bonds to this effect were drawn up in the presence of witnesses.[170] In 1277 John of Battle, proctor of Christ Church Canterbury, who was retiring from the post, left debts for his successor Robert Poucyn to pay.[171] It might be, therefore, that endorsements were made to indicate to a person or house employing several standing proctors which one had actually undertaken the impetration,

---

[163] Canterbury Scrapbook B no. 91.

[164] Canterbury Cart. Antiq. C 224, and Scrapbook B no. 205.

[165] Canterbury Cart. Antiq. C 224. Cf. Herde, *op. cit.* 130 n. 26, who shows some of the proctors living in a joint establishment at Perugia in 1265.

[166] Canterbury Cart. Antiq. P 57.

[167] CPR 1232-47, 276, 417.

[168] CPR 1232-47, 270, and CPR 1247-58, 269.

[169] Canterbury Cart. Antiq. C 1286.

[170] Canterbury Cart. Antiq. P 58-9.

[171] Canterbury MS. Scrapbook C no. 9. There were two Poucyns, Robert, a monk of Christ Church, and Alexander, both of whom were active in c.1275 (Scrapbook C no. 8a).

or that they were connected with expense claims to show that the work had been carried out. But neither of these explanations is entirely satisfactory, for if financial considerations of any kind were involved it seems certain that an endorsement would occur on every document which was sought by a proctor from the Chancery.

It is more likely that the endorsement has something to do with the collection of documents and their ultimate direction or destination. Guillemain has suggested that by the fourteenth century many of the proctors at Avignon may have been notaries. Master Andreas Sapiti, for example, had been an apostolic notary in 1304, and doubtless the work of the two officers was closely connected.[172] A proctor's job was concerned with documents: it was his duty to get them drawn up and to collect them. Although the proctor did not necessarily deliver the documents himself he remained responsible for their collection and for this part of the process.[173] The endorsements which occur at the top on the reverse of papal documents appear to be either (1) proctorial signatures, or (2) the names of the recipients,[174] or (3) to concern their direction, for example 'Tradatur Nicholao de Lascy vel magistro Guillelmo Kervassal'.[175] Now Nicholas de Lascy had endorsed two other bulls on the same day as this note was written on a bull for John Toppau, rector of Llanfyllin (Montgomeryshire, Wales).[176] Similarly a bull, which was obtained by N. de Vico for Edward I, was endorsed by him, but an English hand has added 'Istam bullam portavit magister Petrus Aymerici apud Cobaham R.R.E. XXVII'.[177] Another papal letter which was procured for the Hospitallers by G. de Sancto P., who signed it, was collected by the master of the English Hospitallers according to the endorsement.[178] This seems to me to suggest that normally the proctor received the documents when they were drawn up, and made arrangements for their delivery, and this would also explain such endorsements as *P. de Ass' pro Warmacien'* and *P. de Ass' pro Th' de Brampton* (Rufford's petitioner or messenger).[179]

When the document left the scribe it was not put into the hands of the proctor again until after the sealing with the *bulla*. This would explain why the proctor seized the moment just before or just after the making of the fair copy to endorse it. It then proceeded to the corrector, who checked the fair

---

[172] B. Guillemain, *La Cour Pontificale d'Avignon 1309-1376* (Paris 1962) 569, 613.
[173] Cf. Fawtier in *Reg. Bon. VIII*, lxxi-lxxiii.
[174] A. Largiadèr, *op. cit. (supra* n. 1) 71-2: on recipients' names, proctors, and messengers.
[175] PRO SC7/12/8.   [176] PRO SC7/13/3, and 12/2.
[177] SC7/7/5: Fawtier in *Reg. Bon. VIII*, lxxi-lxxii, and Herde, *op. cit.* 77 n. 23, draw attention to this.
[178] SC7/6/16.
[179] BM Add. Ch. 6306 and Harley Ch. 111 A 26.

copy with the minute, and then through several further possible stages until it reached the bullator. The document's exact course was marked by various dorsal signs which were a provision against fraud. Whether the endorsement was the proctor's own provision against fraud, which enabled him to collect the document speedily without re-checking before he paid the sealing tax, or whether it was a mark put there for advertisement and prestige value, is uncertain. But if we accept the point of time at which the endorsement was made as being in any way indicative of its purpose (and that this was the point when the endorsement was made in a majority of cases) then I think that the former explanation is the more likely.

It is noticeable that the practice of endorsement became usual during the mid-thirteenth century, when the issue of documents had become more sophisticated and controlled, and that by this time the changeover from symbols to names had taken place. By the 1260's proctorial dynasties had arisen and professionalism had triumphed. The early existence of a group of English proctors perhaps reflects the English aptitude for, and interest in, administration.[180] For English petitioners, however, national considerations were not overwhelming when choosing proctors, especially during the mid-thirteenth century when it was considered that Italians knew more about curial practice. By the beginning of the fourteenth century Englishmen practising as proctors were relatively numerous at Avignon, and they managed the major part of their compatriots' business, but they were not employed by the English kings who in this respect were distinctly conservative. The growth of national groups of proctors during the period of the Avignonese popes reflected the rise of national separatism in the Church and the decline of the Italian hegemony.

---

[180] Herde, *op. cit.* 224-6, thinks that the oldest surviving manuscript of the earliest known formulary of the *audientia litterarum contradictarum* was probably copied by an English scribe — some time about the middle of the thirteenth century — from a manuscript of the papal chancery which was brought to England, and that a second formulary in the manuscript was also copied in England at a later date (i.e. at the end of the thirteenth century).

[*See over for Corrigenda.*]

IV

CORRIGENDA

To pp. 144-5: I originally identified Tayo as William de Tayden, also in the royal service, see C.R. Cheney, 'Some features of surviving original papal letters in England', *Annali della Scuola Speciale per Archivisti e Bibliotecarii dell' Università di Roma* (Atti del III Congresso internazionale di diplomatica: Relazioni e communicazioni Anno XII 1-2) (May 1973) p. 17: now more accessibly in *The Papacy and England 12th-14th Centuries* (Variorum, London 1982).

To p. 153 n.100: P.N.R. Zutshi, 'Proctors acting for English petitioners in the chancery of the Avignon popes (1305-1378)', *J.E.H.* 35 (1984) 22 n.33.

To p. 160: Dr Zutshi, *op. cit.* 24 n.19, has queried my statement that Gualterus was the son of Andreas Sapiti, citing J.R. Wright *(The Church and the English Crown, 1305-1334* [Toronto, 1980] 112-13, 118) who names five of the sons. He finds two instances of Sapiti acting with other proctors, one of them Philippus Forzoli, and considers Gualterus to have been only Sapiti's clerk. The question of a relationship between the two remains open.

V

The Judicial Activities of the General Chapters: I

Within the papacy's jurisdiction of Western Christendom, the general chapter of each religious order replaced the *Curia Romana* as the central legislative and judicial assembly. The text of the *Promulgatio Chartae Charitatis* elaborates this right of self-government and compares the hierarchy of the Cistercian order with that of the Roman Church:

'... sicut Christus Ecclesiam suam condidit sub Romano Pontifice, per quatuor Patriarchas, Archiepiscopos multos, sed plures ad huc Episcopos regendam; sic Cisterciensis ordo sub abbate Cistercii supremo capite, pro Episcopis abbates filios habeat, pro Archiepiscopis abbates quos patres vocant, pro Patriarchis primos illos quatuor, per quos in charitate radicatus, ac mutuis inter se officiis devinctus, sine alius interventu regeretur ...'.[1]

The general chapter had its origins, as a governing body, in the *Carta Caritatis*. The foundation of the legislative, judicial and executive activities of the general chapter rests in a section of the *CC.* The *Carta Caritatis* or Constitution of Cîteaux was the most fundamental redaction of monastic law of the twelfth century.[2] The question of the earliest text of the *CC.* has been raised recently. In 1945 Professor Joseph Turk published a new text of the *CC.* which he found in a MS. at Laibach.[3] He called it the *CC. Prior*, to distinguish it from the usual text, now called *CC. Posterior*. He considered it to be the primitive text of the Cistercian constitution, composed in about 1118–1119 and approved by Calixtus II on 23 December 1119.[4]

---

[1] *Statuta Capitulorum Generalium Ordinis Cisterciensis*, ed. J.-M. Canivez, Bibliothèque de la Revue d'Histoire Ecclésiastique, fasc. 9 (1933), i. 2; (hereafter cited as *Statuta*). The text of the *CC.*, which Canivez used, is the one now called *CC. Posterior* and attributed to the end of the twelfth century.

[2] Cf. J. Turk, 'Charta Caritatis Prior', *Analecta Sacri Ordinis Cisterciensis* (hereafter referred to as *A.S.O.C.*), Annus I (1945), 11, and J.-A. Lefèvre, 'A propos d'un nouveau texte de la "Carta Caritatis Prior" dans le MS. Metz 1247', *Revue Bénédictine* (hereafter referred to as *R.B.*), lxv (1955), 90.

[3] 'Charta Caritatis Prior', op. cit., 53–6: the whole MS. has been edited by Canisius Noschitzka, 'Codex manuscriptus 31 Bibliothecae Universitatis Labacensis', *A.S.O.C,*. Annus VI (1950), 1–124.

[4] 'Charta Caritatis Prior', op. cit., 11–61. These views are summarised by J.-A. Lefèvre in *R.B.*, lxv, 90.

V

THE JUDICIAL ACTIVITIES OF THE GENERAL CHAPTERS

The portion of the *CC. Prior* which concerns the holding of a general chapter proceeds as follows:

'*De generali capitulo abbatum apud cistercium.*

Harum ecclesiarum abbates omnes per annum semel illa die, quam inter se constituent, ad nouum monasterium ueniant, ibique de salute animarum suarum tractent; in obseruatione sancte regule uel ordinis si quid emendandum est uel augendum, ordinent; bonum pacis et caritatis inter se reforment'.[1]

The *CC. Posterior* is decidedly more explicit about the activities and powers of the assembly, and it specifies how lawsuits shall be dealt with:

'Si forte aliqua controversia inter quoslibet abbates emerserit vel de aliquo illorum tam gravis culpa propalata fuerit, ut suspensionem aut depositionem etiam mereatur, quicquid inde a capitulo fuerit definitum, sine retractione observetur.

Si vero pro diversitate sententiarum in discordiam causa devenerit, illud inde irrefragabiliter teneatur, quod abbas cisterciensis et hi, qui sanioris consilii et magis idonei apparuerint, iudicabunt, hoc observato, ut nemo eorum, ad quos specialiter causa respexerit, definitioni debeat interesse'.[2]

Professor Turk has argued that the text of the *CC.* was changed after the composition of the *Instituta* (assigned in date to 1134), with which the *CC. Posterior* has much in common, and that the *CC. Posterior* is the text which Eugenius III confirmed on 1 August 1152. The cause of the change in the constitution is to be found in the evolution of the order and in the new conditions with which it was confronted.[3]

The Belgian scholar J.-A. Lefèvre, on the other hand, is convinced that the *CC. Prior* of the *Codex Labacensis* is part of the text of the second codification of Cistercian law of 1151.[4] According to him the first codification of Cistercian law is composed of the *Exordium Cistercii*, the *Summa CC.* and the *Capitula.*[5] The fourth section of the *Summa CC.* concerns the general chapter. It opens 'De annuo abbatum capitulo', and continues:

'Sane hoc sibi praecipuum omnium mater ecclesia cisterciensis specialiter retinuit ut semel in anno sese (p. 86) visitandi, ordinis reparandi, confirmande pacis, conservande gratia caritatis abbates ad eam omnes pariter conveniant ubi in sinistris corrigendis domino cisterciensi sanctoque illi conventui reverenter singuli humiliterque obediant . . .'.[6]

---

[1] 'Charta Caritatis Prior', op. cit., 54, and 'Codex manuscriptus 31 Bibliothecae Universitatis Labacensis', *A.S.O.C.*, VI, 18–19 (vii).
[2] 'Charta Caritatis Prior', op. cit., 59, nos. 15 and 16; also printed in *Statuta*, i. pp. xxviii–xxix, XVIII and XIX.
[3] 'Charta Caritatis Prior', op. cit., 31, 34, 50.
[4] J.-A. Lefèvre, op. cit., 93.   [5] Ibid., 91.
[6] J.-A. Lefèvre, 'La véritable constitution cistercienne de 1119', *Collectanea Ordinis Cisterciensium Reformatorum* (hereafter referred to as *Coll. O.C.R.*), Annus XVI (1954), 85–6.

19

Thus the *Summa CC.* discusses the general chapter only in the widest of terms. This 'dossier' of *Exordium Cistercii, Summa CC.* and *Capitula* was presented to Calixtus II for approval in 1119.

The bull 'Ad hoc apostolicae sedis regimen', which was issued on 23 December 1119, unfortunately gives no hint as to which group of texts it is confirming:

'Siquidem consensu et deliberatione communi abbatum et fratrum monasteriorum vestrorum, et episcoporum, in quorum parochiis eadem monasteria continentur, quaedam de observatione Regulae B. Benedicti, et de aliis nonnullis quae ordini vestro et loco necessaria videbantur, capitula statuistis: quae nimirum ad majorem monasterii quietem, et religionis observantiam, auctoritate sedis apostolicae petitis confirmari. Nos ergo vestro in Domino profectui congaudentes, capitula illa et constitutiones auctoritate apostolica confirmamus. . .'.[1]

Between 1114 and 1119 Cistercian law was gradually evolved. The *Summa CC.* represents a codification of the law which had grown during these years, and is a '*pseudo-résumé*'. It was, doubtless, preceded by a *Carta Caritatis Primitive*, produced by Stephen Harding in 1114,[2] just as it was superseded later by a new compilation. The Constitution of 1119 disappeared to make way for another official text, as Cistercian law developed. The second 'dossier', which was approved by Eugenius III on 1 August 1152, consisted of the *Exordium Parvum*, the *CC. Prior* and the *Instituta*, and became the second official codification of Cistercian law.[3]

M. Lefèvre asserts that the date 1134 for the *Instituta* has no historical foundation.[4] The *Instituta* must be attributed to the period between 1119 and 1152. Like the *Capitula* or *Statuta*, they are composed of the decisions of the abbots at the annual general assemblies. After 1119 the general chapter continued to legislate, but not all the decisions were written down. The *Instituta* was the work of the general chapter of 1151, which kept only the sections of previous Cistercian law that warranted preservation.[5] Two sections of the *Instituta* concern the judicial operations of the general chapter, 'Quomodo cause in generali capitulo exorte diffiniantur' and 'Quomodo terminari debeat si qua forte controuersia inter abbates orta fuerit'. They have been dated by J.-B. van Damme as probably of 1125 and 1140 respectively.[6] Although the texts are easily available, it seems necessary to quote them in full:

[1] P.L. clxiii, col. 1147 BC; *Regesta Pontificum Romanorum*, ed. P. Jaffé revised by S. Loewenfeld, 2nd ed., i, Leipzig 1885, no. 6795.

[2] J.-A. Lefèvre, 'La véritable CC. Primitive et son évolution', *Coll. O.C.R.*, Annus XVI (1954), 19, 29, and 'La véritable constitution, ibid., 93.

[3] J.-A. Lefèvre, 'Le vrai récit primitif des origines de Cîteaux est-il l'Exordium Parvum?', *Le Moyen Age*, lxi (1955), 79–120.

[4] J.-A. Lefèvre, 'A propos de la composition des *Instituta Generalis Capituli apud Cistercium*', *Coll. O.C.R.*, Annus XVI (1954), 157–82, especially 157–8, 164.

[5] J.-A. Lefèvre, 'Pour une datation nouvelle des *Instituta Generalis Capituli*', *Coll. O.C.R.*, Annus XVI (1954), 241–66.

[6] J.-B. van Damme, 'La constitution cistercienne de 1165', *A.S.O.C.*, Annus XIX (1963), 84.

V

THE JUDICIAL ACTIVITIES OF THE GENERAL CHAPTERS

'Si quelibet causa sponte confessa uel clamore exorta in generali capitulo Cistercii nascatur, communi assensu omnium abbatum, si possit concorditer fieri, diffiniatur.

Si autem pro capacitate sensus uniuscuiusque, quod sepe accidit, inter se dissenserint, pater Cirterciensis (sic) monasterii quatuor abbatibus ad hoc idoneis hanc diffinire precipiat et quod illi utilius iudicauerint, omnis sancte multitudinis conuentus sine retractione teneat',[1]

and

'Si forte aliqua controuersia inter aliquos abbates nostri ordinis orta fuerit, conuocent uicinos abbates ordinis nostri et eorum consilio pacem ineant. Si uero nec sic sedari poterunt, reseruetur causa eorum ad annuum capitulum Cistercii et ibi ad arbitrium et ad nutum Cisterciensis capituli terminetur neque inde ad aliam audientiam liceat appellare'.[2]

The confirmation of Eugenius approved 'omnia quae continentur in charta vestra, quae appellatur, caritatis, et quaecumque inter vos religionis intuitu regulariter statuistis'. That the confirmation of Eugenius III is closely connected with the *CC. Posterior*, as Turk argued, is suggested by the sentence which is contained in the bull and proceeds as follows:

'Praeterea si aliqua controversia inter quoslibet abbates de ordine vestro emerserit vel de aliquo illorum tam gravis culpa fuerit propalata, ut suspensionem aut depositionem etiam mereatur, quidquid inde a capitulo fuerit canonice definitum, sine retractatione aliqua observetur.

Si vero pro diversitate sententiarum in discordiam causa devenerit, illud inde irrefragabiliter teneatur, quod abbas Cisterciensis, qui pro tempore fuerit, cum his, qui sanioris consilii et magis idonei apparuerint, iudicaverit observandum'.[3]

This is almost word for word the same as the section on lawsuits in *CC. Posterior*.[4] But for Lefèvre the *CC. Posterior*, which he assigns in date to between 1190 and 1200, forms part of the third codification.[5] From the beginning of the thirteenth century, the *CC. Posterior* was substituted in MSS. of Cistercian law for the *Summa CC.*, which had disappeared.[6] The interpretations of J.-A. Lefèvre concerning these early redactions of Cistercian law have been accepted only with reservation by J. Winandy

---

[1] 'Cistercii Statuta Antiquissima', ed. J. Turk, *A.S.O.C.*, Annus IV (1948), 21; 'Codex manuscriptus 31 Bibliothecae Universitatis Labacensis', *A.S.O.C.*, VI, 28; *Statuta* 1134, 30. There are slight variations between the texts.
[2] 'Cistercii Statuta Antiquissima', ed. J. Turk, 26; 'Codex manuscriptus 31 Bibliothecae Universitatis Labacensis', op. cit., 36; *Statuta* 1134, 70.
[3] Edited in *A.S.O.C.*, Annus IV (1948), 122–8, especially 123, 126, and in P.L., clxxx, col. 1542 CD, where the text is slightly different.
[4] See above p. 19.
[5] J.-A. Lefèvre and B. Lucet, 'Les codifications cisterciennes aux XIIᵉ et XIIIᵉ siècles d'après les traditions manuscrites', *A.S.O.C.*, Annus XV (1959), 13, 22.
[6] J.-A. Lefèvre, 'La véritable constitution', *Coll. O.C.R.*, XVI, 88.

and by Jean-Baptiste van Damme. Winandy has questioned whether the *Exordium Cistercii* and the *Exordium Parvum* constitute the prologues to the two codifications of Cistercian law, and he has decided that the *Exordium Cistercii* is later than 23 December 1119 and that the *Exordium Parvum* is earlier than 1152,[1] while Father van Damme has asserted that the text which was approved by Calixtus II did not include the *Summa CC.*, either partially or in entirety, and that the *CC. Prior* was compiled before the *Summa CC.*, which he assigns to 1123–30, probably 1123 or 1124.[2] G. de Beaufort appears to be in agreement with van Damme, querying whether the 1119 confirmation ratified not the *CC. Prior* but the *Summa CC.*, preceded by the *Exordium Cistercii* and followed by the *Capitula*.[3] Whether the arguments of J.-A. Lefèvre are accepted entirely or only in part, it is indisputable that the *CC. Posterior* and the *Instituta* represent an advance on the *CC. Prior* and the *Summa CC.* In all the texts the general chapter is shown as the supreme governing body of the order, with powers to expand, adapt and interpret. But, whereas in the *Summa CC.* and the *CC. Prior*, no specific stipulations were provided for composing controversies between abbots of the order, the *Instituta* and the *CC. Posterior* describe a more precisely regulated conduct for judicial affairs. The development which had taken place between the two issues of Cistercian law in the provisions for the hearing of lawsuits within the general chapter represents the work of the legislative body over a period of thirty years. By 1152 the foundations of Cistercian law were firmly established, and the way in which future Cistercian law would be made had been shown and accepted. The general chapter had been tried and found worthy. Future changes in the government of the order and in its administration were to be effected under its authority. The time was now ripe for new developments in the judicial organisation of Cîteaux and for the adoption of the institution of the general chapter by other monastic orders.[4]

Many of the monastic orders which originated at the same time as Cîteaux adopted the general chapter and made it an indispensable part of their government. At Tiron general chapters were held before 1120, but they were not an annual institution. A triennial chapter is recorded as taking place at Whitsuntide.[5] With Savigny annual general chapters appear very early, possibly due to Geoffrey the successor to Vitalis, who

---

[1] J. Winandy, 'Les origines de Cîteaux et les travaux de M. Lefèvre', *R.B.*, lxvii (1957), 49–76.

[2] Jean-Baptiste van Damme, 'Autour des origines cisterciennes', *Coll. O.C.R.*, Annus XX (1958), 37–60, 153–68, and continued in Annus XXI (1959), 70–86, 137–56.

[3] G. de Beaufort, 'La Charte de Charité cistercienne et son évolution', *Revue d'Histoire Ecclésiastique*, xlix (1954), 433 n.1. G. de Beaufort is the pseudonym of P. J. Bouton, a Trappist monk.

[4] Cf. Jacques Hourlier, *Le Chapitre Général jusqu'au moment du Grand Schisme*, Paris 1936, 48.

[5] *Calendar of Documents preserved in France*, ed. J. H. Round, i, London 1899, 353–4, cited by D. Knowles, *The Monastic Order in England*, Cambridge 1950, 202 n.2.

died in 1122. They were celebrated on the feast of the Trinity.[1] The white canons imitated their capitular organisation from Cîteaux. The *Carta Caritatis* served as a model for the Premonstratensians and their traditional organiser Hugh de Fosses.[2] The oldest Premonstratensian statutes have been thought to be those contained in the twelfth-century Premonstratensian customary from the abbey of Schäftlarn, Bavaria (MS.Clm17,174).[3] R. van Waefelghem has dated them as being before 1143 and perhaps before 1135:[4] Father van Dyck has argued that the redaction took place in 1130 to 1131.[5] The *Summa CC.* is undoubtedly one of its sources. The similarity of chapters 26, 27 and 28 of the Premonstratensian text with the *Summa CC.* is indisputable. Chapter 26 concerns the general chapter and is closely modelled on c. iv—'De annuo abbatum capitulo'—of the *Summa CC.* Both texts have been printed together by van Dyck. *PW.* reads as follows:

'De annuo colloquio.

Iterum statutum est quod semel in anno gratia sese visitandi, ordinis reparandi, confirmande pacis, conservande Karitatis, abbates omnes ad colloquium pariter conveniant in loco competenti quem communi consilio providerint, ubi in sinistris corrigendis domno abbati Praemonstratae ecclesiae quae mater est aliarum, sanctoque illi conventui reverenter singuli humiliterque obediant, et clamati veniam petant; quam clamationem non nisi abbates faciant'.[6]

Father van Dyck considers that the compiler of *PW.* also drew upon the *Instituta.*[7] J.-A. Lefèvre has come across two MSS. (Bibl. Ste. Geneviève Paris MS. 1207, and Bibl. Communale Trente MS. 1711), in which the *Instituta* are transcribed immediately after the text of the *Summa CC.*; he therefore suspects a MS. of this family as the source.[8] Although the foundation charter of St. Martin at Laon (1124) provides that disorders were to be remedied by a chapter of abbots at Prémontré,[9] and a bull of Innocent II of 3 May 1134, the 'Sacer Ordo vester', speaks of a general

---

[1] D. Knowles, op. cit., 202; C. Auvry, *Histoire de la Congrégation de Savigny*, i, Rouen 1896, 179, 201.

[2] C. Dereine, 'Le premier Ordo de Prémontré', *R.B.*, lviii (1948), 90, 92 n.1. The close connexion between the Premonstratensian statutes and the Cistercian legislative texts has been shown by J.-B. Mahn in *L'Ordre Cistercien*, Paris 1951.

[3] See 'Les premiers statuts de l'ordre de Prémontré', ed. R. van Waefelghem, *Analectes de l'Ordre de Prémontré*, ix (1913), 1–74. This text is referred to as *PW.*

[4] Ibid., 14, and J.-A. Lefèvre, 'La véritable constitution', *Coll. O.C.R.*, Annus XVI (1954), 92.

[5] Leo van Dyck, 'Essai sur les sources du droit Prémontré primitif concernant les pouvoirs du *Dominus Praemonstratensis*', *Analecta Praemonstratensia*, xxviii (1952), 87, and J.-A. Lefèvre, 'La véritable constitution', op. cit., 92.

[6] L. van Dyck, op. cit., 134–5.

[7] L. van Dyck, ibid., and J.-A. Lefèvre, 'A propos des sources de la législation primitive de Prémontré', *Analecta Praemonstratensia*, xxx (1954), 13.

[8] J.-A. Lefèvre, ibid., 12–19.

[9] J. C. Dickinson, *The Origins of the Austin Canons and their Introduction into England*, London 1950, 84. This document does not seem to have been noticed by van Dyck or Lefèvre.

chapter,[1] van Dyck has argued that the organisation of the Premonstratensian order which is outlined in the MS. of *PW.* was not put into practice at once. He suggests that the Roman pontiffs, at the request of the
abbots of Prémontré, and especially of Hugh de Fosses, introduced step
by step the organisation which had been envisaged in *PW.*, including the
general chapter.[2] In the edition of the statutes said to be of c. 1174 it was
stipulated that the congregation of abbots should take place at Prémontré
on the feast of St. Dionysius (9 October), and Alexander III in the bull
'In Apostolice Sedis' of 1177 confirmed the constitution of the order of
Prémontré in terms similar to those in which Eugenius III had approved
the organisation of Cîteaux.[3] Even if a general chapter which possessed
full powers was not functioning at Prémontré from the 1130s, it seems
to have been established by 1177 and it was obviously an imitation of the
Cistercian assembly.[4]

An important minority of the Augustinian order were members of the
small independent congregations, and these adopted the general chapter.[5]
The royal foundation of St. Victor at Paris (1113) was confirmed by
Pascal II in December 1114. Under the first abbot, Gilduin, St. Victor's
became the head of an order with its own general chapter. The date of
this development is not known, but it was certainly before 1139.[6] In that
year prior Gausbert and the chapter of St. Vincent of Senlis, on the death
of the third abbot, Baldwin, sent a letter to Gilduin of St. Victor asking
for a new abbot. The letter reveals the structure of the Victorine order and
shows the existence of general chapters.[7] They say:

'Abbas etiam noster, quicumque scilicet de cetero nobis prefuerit, ad
Capitulum vestrum generale per singulos annos veniet ut ibi de statu et pro-
fectu ordinis ipse pariter cum ceteris tractet'.[8]

According to J. C. Dickinson, the Victorine general chapters do not seem
to have flourished for much more than a century.[9]

The abbey of St. Nicholas Arrouaise in Picardy originated in about
1090, and became the mother house of an Augustinian congregation as

[1] P.L. clxxix, cols. 204C–206B, and L. van Dyck, op. cit., 119–20. Another bull
however, issued on the same day (the 'Proprium est ecclesiasticae'), makes no allusion
to the general chapter. Upon this apparent contradiction much of van Dyck's argument is based: he thinks that the 'Sacer Ordo vester' is a forgery.

[2] L. van Dyck, op. cit., 130–1.

[3] H. M. Colvin, *The White Canons in England*, Oxford 1951, 14, and L. van Dyck,
op. cit., 127.

[4] Much of the controversy about the date of the establishment of a general chapter
with the Premonstratensians centres round the use of the words 'colloquium' and
'capitulum generale': see H. M. Colvin, op. cit., 13–15.

[5] J. C. Dickinson, op. cit., 82, 88.

[6] Ibid., 85; R. Graham, *English Ecclesiastical Studies*, London 1929, 16, and J. Hourlier,
Le Chapitre Général jusqu'au moment du Grand Schisme, 118–20.

[7] F. Bonnard, *Histoire de l'Abbaye royale et de l'Ordre des Chanoines Réguliers de St.-Victor
de Paris*, i, Paris 1904, 147.

[8] Ibid., 148 n.4 (contd). The whole letter is printed in 147–8 n.4.

[9] J. C. Dickinson, op. cit., 86.

V

other communities submitted themselves to her authority. 'The order spread fast, and to maintain unity and correct any faults in the order the superiors "agreed to come once a year to a general chapter at their mother church of Arrouaise" ':[1]

'Itaque infra breve tempus excepta vicina flandria ipsa quoque anglia, scotia, burgundia et apud exteras gentes polonia de fratribus nostris novellas plantationes sponte suscipiunt et prelati earum ob unitatem servandum et corrigendam si quid in ordine excesserint ad generale capitulum semel in anno apud arroasiensem ecclesiam matrem suam venire consentiunt'.[2]

It was in the time of abbot Gervase (1121–1147) that these general chapters were instituted.[3] They began on St. Matthew's day.[4] P. Gosse, in his *Histoire de l'Abbaye d'Arrouaise*, is of the opinion that a general chapter was held as early as 1121, when the Cistercian customs were adopted, but the authority for this is not clear.[5] A deed of the bishop of Carlisle allowing the prior and convent of Carlisle to join the order of Arrouaise in 1140, which was evidently drawn up when the bishop was on the continent, was attested by Alvisus, bishop of Arras (1131–1148), and Milo, bishop of Terouanne (1131–1158). It stipulated:

'Adicimus quoque precipientes ut idem prior *ad capitulum beati Nicholai* sequenti anno, nisi canonica excusatione premissa, profisci non negligat, ubi que ad ordinem pertinent a pluribus auditis, et que corrigenda sunt diligenter correctis, in ordinis sui tenore fervescat'.[6]

A general chapter must, therefore, have been functioning before 1140.

In 1142 Anthelme, prior of the Grande Chartreuse, and his fellow Carthusian priors instituted and held the first general chapter for their order—'in eadem domo Carthusiae commune capitulum eis liceret habere, obtentu correctionis et emendationis totius propositi'.[7] Only two general chapters were held under Anthelme's presidency, and it was not until 1155 that Carthusian general chapters met annually on the feast of

---

[1] Ibid., and J. Hourlier, op. cit., 120.
[2] J. C. Dickinson, op. cit., 86–7 n.6 (Cartulary of St. Nicholas Arrouaise, Bibliothèque Municipale of Amiens MS. 1077, fol. 5ᵛ).
[3] J. C. Dickinson, op. cit., 86.
[4] J. Hourlier, op. cit., 167.
[5] Published at Lille in 1786. This is a very rare book and I have not been able to consult it. See J. C. Dickinson, op. cit., 87, and 77, and J.-A. Lefèvre, 'La véritable constitution cistercienne de 1119', *Coll. O.C.R.*, Annus XVI (1954), 79, 81–2, 89, 90–2, and P. Vermeer, 'De invloed van de CC. van Citeaux op de statuten van Arrouaise', *Studia Catholica*, xxviii (1953), 105–14. Vermeer favours the date 1130 for the Arrouaisian statutes.
[6] *Chapters of the Augustinian Canons*, ed. H. E. Salter, London 1922, xliv–xlv: this is printed on p. xlv. The italics are mine. See also D. Knowles and R. Neville Hadcock, *Medieval Religious Houses*, London 1953, 132.
[7] P.L. cliii, col. 1125: Acta Primi Capituli Ordinis Carthusiensis: Statuta Antiqua; and *Annales Ordinis Cartusiensis*, ed. C. Le Couteulx, ii, Monstrolii 1888, 5–6.

St. Luke (18 October).[1] The sixth enactment of the first general chapter declared that if any trouble occurred in any house, which required an immediate settlement, the prior of the Grande Chartreuse, if he could not deal with the question alone, was to summon as many of the Carthusian priors as seemed sufficient for a decision.[2] The Carthusian rule consists of the Customs of Guigo, the fifth prior (1110–1136), and of such statutes as were made permanent by the general chapters. The *Statuta Antiqua*, or compilation of 1259, consisted of three parts. The second part dealt with the general government of the monastery, the constitution of the general chapter, and the powers of the chapter and of the prior of the Grande Chartreuse.[3] The prior of the Grande Chartreuse was perpetual president of the general chapter, to which each prior promised obedience.[4]

On the death of St. Stephen de Muret (1124), the monks, whom he had directed, established themselves at Grandmont.[5] About the middle of the twelfth century Grandmont and its cells were organised as an order: the first general chapter was held in about 1154 or 1156.[6] Every year, on the feast of St. John the Baptist, 24 June, the head of each cell, who was called the 'corrector', and the chief lay brother, the 'curiosus', were expected to attend a general chapter at Grandmont.[7]

At Molesme an annual general chapter was also instituted.[8] It was of undoubted Cistercian origin, and was probably in existence in the last third of the twelfth century.[9] The first mention of a general chapter comes from 1212.[10] The date of the celebration of the general chapter varied: by the thirteenth century it was held regularly on 8 September.[11] The ruler of the women secured the right of attending either in person or by proxy.[12] There is no indication that the double order of Fontevrault ever adopted an annual general chapter: the order was organised on Cluniac rather than Cistercian lines.[13]

[1] E. Margaret Thompson, *The Carthusian Order in England*, London 1930, 86, 88: Dom Longin Ray, 'Chartreux', *Dictionnaire de Droit Canonique*, iii, col. 635: J. Hourlier, op. cit., 107—he says that the second general chapter was held in 1143.
[2] E. M. Thompson, op. cit., 88.
[3] Ibid., 109–10. The customs of prior Guigo were confirmed by Innocent II (p. 93).
[4] Ibid., 87.
[5] J. Hourlier, *Le Chapitre Général jusqu'au moment du Grande Schisme*, 112.
[6] Ibid.
[7] R. Graham, *English Ecclesiastical Studies*, 215, citing J. Levesque, *Annales Ordinis Grandimontis*, Trecis 1662, 118–21; cf. P.L., cciv, cols. 1037, 1160. Miss Graham says (op. cit., 230) that the correctors were bound to attend the general chapters frequently, if not every year. In 1182 Henry II was at Grandmont at the time of the convocation of the general chapter: R. Graham, op. cit., 217.
[8] *Cartulaires de l'Abbaye de Molesme*, ed. J. Laurent, i, Paris 1907, 171, and R. Graham, op. cit., 21.
[9] *Cartulaires de l'Abbaye de Molesme*, ed. J. Laurent, i. 267.
[10] Ibid., i. 268, and ii (1911), no. 658.
[11] Ibid., i. 268.
[12] R. Graham, *English Ecclesiastical Studies*, 21. No Cistercian abbess had the right to attend the general chapter, but there is evidence to show that in France and in Spain the Cistercian nunneries sent women representatives to attend a general chapter at the head nunnery of the province (ibid., 21–2).
[13] D. Knowles, *The Monastic Order in England*, 204.

V

The orders which were founded after Cîteaux established a general chapter as the supreme governing body. On the English order of Sempringham Cistercian influence was well established. Gilbert set out for Cîteaux in 1147 to ask the Cistercians to take charge of his monasteries. He was disappointed, because the abbots decided that they might not rule over another order, especially one which included women. However, both St. Bernard and Eugenius III were present at this chapter. St. Bernard helped Gilbert to draw up the *Institutes* of the order of Sempringham, while Eugenius III conferred on Gilbert the care of his order and in the following year confirmed its rule.[1] St. Gilbert instituted an annual general chapter at Sempringham on the three Rogation days, in imitation of the Cistercian chapter. As he said in the *Institutiones*, 'Volumus Cisterciensis capitula vestigia sequi',[2] and, he continued, 'There they may diligently discuss the observation of the holy rule and the order of its whole life, and the keeping of unbroken peace among themselves, that their way of life may not easily grow cold but continue through the space of many years'.[3]

Val-des-Choux was founded at the end of the twelfth century by Guy de Viard, a lay brother of the Carthusian priory of Loubigny in the diocese of Langres. It became the centre of an order which submitted to the rule of St. Benedict and to constitutions which were borrowed mainly from the Cistercians.[4] The general chapter held an important place and was assembled every year at Val-des-Choux on the day of the invention of the Holy Cross, to keep the indissoluble peace between them.[5] The other new Benedictine congregations adopted the general chapter system also. The congregation of the Sylvestrines, which was founded by St. Sylvester Gozzolini on Monte Fano near Fabiano in 1231, was approved by Innocent IV in 1247, and they held a general chapter every four years.[6] The Celestines originated shortly before 1264, when the order was approved by Urban IV, and they celebrated a general chapter from 1274 onwards.[7] The Olivetans were erected canonically in 1318, and the order summoned its first general chapter for the following year at Monte Oliveto.[8]

The mendicant orders found in the institution of a general chapter the means of maintaining unity and discipline. The Dominican friars copied and elaborated both systems of general and provincial chapters.

---

[1] R. Graham, *S. Gilbert of Sempringham and the Gilbertines*, London 1901, 12–13, 96, and Sir William Dugdale, *Monasticon Anglicanum*, ed. Caley, Ellis and Bandinel, vi. 2, London 1846, viii–xxii, (p. xi—'Quod commissum est ei a Domino Papa Regimen Ordinis sui'). See also J. C. Dickinson, op. cit., 78, and Watkin Williams, *S. Bernard of Clairvaux*, Manchester 1935, 240–1.

[2] R. Graham, op. cit., 49

[3] R. Graham, op. cit., 50, and *Monasticon*, vi. 2, lvii.

[4] Pascalis Vermeer, 'Cîteaux—Val-des-Choux', *Coll. O.C.R.*, Annus XVI (1954), 35–44.

[5] J. Hourlier, op. cit., 111.

[6] Ibid., 82.

[7] Ibid.

[8] Ibid., 83.

At the first general chapter of 1220 it was arranged that such meetings should be held annually in future, at Whitsuntide, alternately at Bologna and Paris, and it is said that it was in the 1220 chapter that the second part of the *Constitutiones* dealing with the governmental machinery of the order was formally adopted.[1] At the second general chapter, which was held in 1221, the order was divided into eight provinces.[2] The general chapter acted as a disciplinary body. Disputes between friars and doubtful questions were delegated to a small committee of judges for settlement: other matters came before the whole chapter for decision.[3] St. Dominic provided in the section 'de questionibus' that if any disputes ('which Heaven forbid') should arise between friars, they should not be brought before the whole chapter but should be submitted to friars who had been chosen as judges because they were specially suited for the task. These judges, together with the chief prelate, dealt with the settlement and ending of disputes. The ordinances were meant primarily for the general chapter, but at the end there is a statement to the effect that they may be applied also to the provincial chapter.[4] At the provincial chapter, also, a committee of judges was appointed to settle all disputes which had arisen between friars in the province. Whatever the judges decided the chapter was to accept and approve—'capitulum universaliter et unanimiter et devote suscipiat'.[5]

With the Franciscans, the general chapter became one of the principal elements of their organisation, but it was not instituted at the foundation of the order. Its adoption took place in 1239, after the dispute between some of the provinces and brother Elias, the General, when the provincials of France, England and Germany appealed to the pope. From 1239 the general chapter was the supreme authority in the order, possessing the fullness of legislative power and judging in the last resort.[6] The general chapter also became a fundamental element in the organisation of the lesser mendicant orders. The order of the Hermits of St. Augustine held their first general chapter in 1253;[7] the Servites had a general chapter in 1249.[8] For the order of the Blessed Virgin Mary of Mount Carmel, a general chapter was held in the East as early as 1188, at Tyre or Tripoli. In the West the first general chapter was celebrated in 1247: henceforth it met every three years at Whitsun.[9]

The older Benedictine congregations which had been created before Cîteaux, assimilated the general chapter into their organisation. A bull

---

[1] G. R. Galbraith, *The Constitution of the Dominican Order 1216–1360*, Manchester 1925, 36, 85.

[2] G. R. Galbraith, op. cit., 36.

[3] Ibid., 104.

[4] Ibid., 74–5; 'Die Constitutionen des Prediger-Ordens vom Jahre 1228', ed. P. H. Denifle, *Archiv für Litteratur- und Kirchengeschichte des Mittelalters*, i, Berlin 1885, 220.

[5] G. R. Galbraith, op. cit., 69 n.3.

[6] J. Hourlier, *Le Chapitre Général jusqu'au moment du Grande Schisme*, 144–8.

[7] Ibid., 149.

[8] Ibid., 154.

[9] Ibid., 151–2.

V

of Alexander III of 20 April 1176 proves the existence of a general chapter of the order of Vallombrosa.[1] According to the annals of the order of Camaldoli, the first general chapter was celebrated at Padua in 1239. There is no indication as to whether this was on the instruction of Gregory IX.[2] The general chapter was to be held on the Sunday after the Ascension of Our Lord, to counsel, correct and exhort, but the *Annales* mention no further chapter until 1271.[3] Cluny also adopted a regular annual general chapter from the Cistercian example. For the Cluniac branch of the Benedictines, Peter the Venerable called a general chapter in 1132.[4] Ordericus Vitalis took part in this re-union and described it in his *Historia Ecclesiastica*.[5] The occasion was conducted with true Cluniac splendour, but there seems to have been no provision for the establishment of annual convocations. A reference to a general chapter at Cluny in 1182 survives, and in 1189 Lucius III ordered bishops to protect monks going to the Cluniac chapter.[6] It is not, however, until the Statutes of abbot Hugh V of 1200 that the celebration of an annual general chapter, where the faults of superiors and religious were to be punished, is known to have been officially ordered.[7] There is a description of the working of the Cluniac general chapter in 1212,[8] but, on 15 March 1213, Innocent III addressed a letter to the abbots and priors of the Cluniac order convening them to a general chapter.[9] Again, on 13 January 1233, Gregory IX ordered the holding of a general chapter with three Carthusian abbots to guide the Cluniacs, which suggests that all cannot have gone well in these early general chapters.[10] Gradually, however, a general chapter was established on the model of Cîteaux, and, from the middle of the thirteenth century, it became a body exercising authority in the order. The Cluniac general chapter was held on the Sunday 'qua cantatur Jubilate', the third after Easter. The English priors were only obliged to come every two years.[11]

As part of the religious revival of the twelfth century isolated and voluntary attempts were made to establish local chapters for mutual aid

---

[1] Ibid., 81.

[2] Ibid., 79; J. B. Mittarelli and A. Costadoni, *Annales Camaldulenses Ordinis Sancti Benedicti*, iv, Venice 1759, 344.

[3] J. Hourlier, op. cit., 79.

[4] J.-M. Besse, 'L'Ordre de Cluny et son gouvernement', *Revue Mabillon*, i (1905), 98.

[5] P.L., clxxxviii, col. 935.

[6] J.-M. Besse, op. cit., 98, and *Recueil des Chartes de Cluny*, ed. A. Bernard and A. Bruel, v, Paris 1894, 656; J. Hourlier, op. cit., 73.

[7] J.-M. Besse, op. cit., 98 n.4. R. Graham, *English Ecclesiastical Studies*, 23, and P.L. ccix, cols. 882–96. Hourlier says that the general chapter was established in 1202 (op. cit., 73), but he gives no authority for this.

[8] R. Graham, op. cit., 24, citing *Recueil des Chartes de Cluny*, vi, Paris 1903, 5–13.

[9] P.L., ccxvi, col. 791, and U. Berlière, 'Innocent III et la réorganisation des monastères bénédictins', *R.B.*, xxxii (1920), 146.

[10] J. Hourlier, op. cit., 74; A. Bruel, 'Les chapitres généraux de l'ordre de Cluny depuis le XIIIe jusqu'au XVIIe siècle', *Bibliothèque de l'École des Chartes*, xxxiv (1873), 544, 549, 556; *Regesta Pontificum Romanorum 1198 ad 1304*, ed. A. Potthast, i, Berlin 1874, no. 9072. Hourlier gives 12 January, which seems to be a mistake.

[11] J. Hourlier, op. cit., 75–6; A. Bruel, op. cit., 549.

and correction among the unaffiliated houses of the older orders. A successful attempt was made in about 1130–1131 to introduce the Cistercian custom of holding annual general chapters among the abbots of monasteries of black monks in the diocese of Rheims. The first of these was held at Soissons in the abbey of St. Medard, a Cluniac house.[1] But this was no widespread movement, and in 1159 the monk Herbord, of the abbey of St. Michael at Bamberg, regretted that the Benedictine order had not taken over the institution of a general chapter at the example of the Augustinians, Cistercians and Premonstratensians:

'Sed mirum quod nostro ordini contigerit quod generale capitulum non admittit; cum Augustiniani, Cistercienses et Norbertini hoc polleant honore.'[2]

It is to the credit of the popes that they encouraged these instances of initiative and endeavoured to spread the adoption of general chapters among the Benedictines and Augustinians.[3] According to Horst and Mabillon, Innocent II prescribed that general chapters of black monks should be held annually.[4] On 17 November 1135 Innocent II encouraged abbots, congratulated them and promised to ratify what they agreed upon for the conservation of their monasteries and the correction of brothers.[5] In 1155 the general chapter of black monks of the archbishopric of Rheims wrote to Adrian IV on the subject of the deposition of the abbot of Latigny, asking him to approve their union, which Innocent II had confirmed by privilege.[6] For the regular canons, the bishop of Halberstadt established an annual reunion, which was approved by Innocent II in 1138.[7] Eugenius III, in a bull of 1145 which was addressed to the regular canons of Germany, provided that problems arising within the order should be settled where possible by the superiors meeting in council. He presented in some detail provisions for annual general chapters to remedy faults.[8]

General chapters were established in many provinces before the decree of Innocent III in 1215. On 27 February 1203 Innocent III ordered the abbeys which were immediately subject to the Holy See in Tuscany, the March of Ancona and the Duchy of Spoleto, to come to Perugia for a chapter.[9] Soon after 1203, the pope authorised the regular

---

[1] R. Graham, *English Ecclesiastical Studies*, 22; Watkin Williams, op. cit., 227; W. A. Pantin, 'The General and Provincial Chapters of the English Black Monks, 1215–1540', *T.R.H.S.* 4th series, x (1927), 204; and see P.L., clxxxii, col. 222.

[2] Quoted by U. Berlière, 'Les chapitres généraux de l'ordre de S. Benoît', *R.B.*, xviii (1901), 369 n.3.

[3] J.-M. Besse, op. cit., *Revue Mabillon*, i (1905), 97.

[4] Watkin Williams, op. cit., 228.

[5] J. Hourlier, op. cit., 71.

[6] Ibid., and P.L., clxxxii, cols. 713–14.

[7] J. Hourlier, op. cit., 117.

[8] J. C. Dickinson, op. cit., 81–2.

[9] U. Berlière, 'Innocent III et la réorganisation des monastères bénédictins', *R.B.*, xxxii (1920), 157; *Reg. Pont. Rom.*, ed. A. Potthast, i, no. 1843.

THE JUDICIAL ACTIVITIES OF THE GENERAL CHAPTERS

canons of the diocese of York to hold annual reunions.[1] In 1206 he recognised the usefulness of reunions which were projected by the Benedictine abbots of Denmark, with the abbot of Lund as superior, and he reserved the right to approve their decisions every four years.[2] On 20 July 1210, Innocent III congratulated the abbots of the province of Rouen on establishing a general chapter under the presidency of one of their number. He approved their decision and their plan to send a report of their deliberations and decrees every four years to Rome.[3]

By the decree 'In singulis regnis', canon 12 of the Fourth Lateran Council (1215), all orders of religious which were not already holding general chapters were commanded to hold them every three years in each kingdom or province. Two Cistercian abbots were to be invited to attend at first to show them how to proceed, since they were well acquainted with the method from long experience—'cum sint in hujusmodi capitulis celebrandis ex longa consuetudine plenius informati'.[4] This decree was met with vigorous action in England, but on the continent the 'Lateran' system of general chapters was not a great success.[5] With the Benedictines the general chapter never became a strong and indispensable part of the government of the order. Chapters were only celebrated triennially.[6] The presidents' powers and authority were limited in extent and time.[7] The extension of their jurisdiction was narrow, that is to say, they could deal only with cases between Benedictines of the province, and they were elected solely for one session and the interim period between chapters. All these factors contributed to severely checking the powers of the general chapter, but there is evidence that causes were heard there.[8]

The great majority of the houses of Austin canons never belonged to an independent congregation.[9] These were, therefore, subject to the new decree. On 29 February 1216, pope Innocent III issued a letter to the heads of the monasteries of the Augustinian order in the provinces of

---

[1] U. Berlière, op. cit., *R.B.*, xxxii (1920), 158; *Reg. Pont. Rom.*, ed. A. Potthast, i, no. 3045.

[2] J. Hourlier, op. cit., 87.

[3] U. Berlière, op. cit., *R.B.*, xxxii (1920), 158; P.L., ccxvi, col. 312; J. Hourlier, op. cit., 88.

[4] *Corpus jur. can.* III tit. xxxv—De statu monachorum, c. 7. It is also printed in *Documents . . . of the English Black Monks*, ed. W. A. Pantin, Camden 3rd series, xlv (1931), i. 273–4; C.-J. Hefele–H. Leclercq, *Histoire des Conciles*, v. 2, Paris 1913, 1342–4.

[5] W. A. Pantin, op. cit., *T.R.H.S.* 4th series, x (1927), 244.

[6] J. Hourlier, op. cit., 101. Sometimes, however, they were held more frequently than triennially.

[7] W. A. Pantin, op. cit., *T.R.H.S.* 4th series, x (1927), 227. In 1222, one president (the abbot of Gloucester) did not appear (D. Knowles, *The Religious Orders in England*, i, Cambridge 1948, 11). The power of the presidents of provincial chapters attracted the attention of canonists. Innocent IV said that the presidents did not possess an ordinary jurisdiction: they acted by virtue of a papal delegation of power (see J. Hourlier, op. cit., 183–4).

[8] *Documents . . . of the English Black Monks*, 86, and see also 64, 85, and W. A. Pantin, op. cit., *T.R.H.S.* 4th series, x (1927), 230.

[9] J. C. Dickinson, op. cit., 79.

Canterbury and York, ordering them to meet in a general chapter at Leicester on 8 November of the same year. The abbots of Welbeck and Croxton of the Premonstratensian order were to be invited to give help. The letter was given to the abbot of Leicester, who was to see that a copy of it reached every Augustinian house.[1] The date of the separation of the two provinces is uncertain. A licence of the pope issued on 28 June 1223, at the petition of the archbishop of York, decreeing that the black canons of the province of York should celebrate their chapter in their own province in future, may be the first grant about this.[2] Although every Augustininian house was supposed to keep a copy of the proceedings of the chapters, they have not often survived, and no evidence of the hearing of causes is known. The jurisdiction was never strong, and Mr. Dickinson considers that the regular canons, excepting the two congregations of St. Victor and Arrouaise, who continued to attend their own chapters, failed to solve adequately the problems of government.[3]

In most orders the general chapter was substituted for the *Curia Romana*: from its decisions there was no appeal.[4] It made laws and it adjudicated in disputes between houses within the order. Its position was not as authoritative with the Benedictines and Augustinians, who did not belong to specific congregations, but it exercised some legislative and judicial powers. During the thirteenth century, the religious orders conformed faithfully to the holding of annual general chapters,[5] and, as yet, the question of attendance had not become a serious problem.[6] There can be little doubt that all the chapters dealt with judicial business:[7] within the smaller orders quarrels were probably settled when the annual general chapters met; within the more numerous congregations new developments were necessitated.

---

[1] *Chapters of the Augustinian Canons*, ed. H. E. Salter, ix.
[2] Ibid., xi.
[3] J. C. Dickinson, op. cit., 89.
[4] *Statuta* 1134, 30; H. M. Colvin, op. cit., 197; A. Bruel, op. cit., 544 n.5, and G. R. Galbraith, op. cit., 75.
[5] J. Hourlier, op. cit., 164.
[6] It was, however, becoming a trouble with the Cistercians. With the Benedictines, attendance was poor (see W. A. Pantin, op. cit., *T.R.H.S.* 4th series, x (1927), 219).
[7] Since this article went to press, two important pieces of work on the Premonstratensian texts have appeared in print (see above, 23–4). I. J. van de Westelaken ('Premonstratenzer Wetgeving 1120–1165,' *Analecta Praemonstratensia*, xxxviii (1962), 7–42), considers that there were at least three codifications of Premonstratensian law, *PX*, the first, of before 1131, *PW*, the second, of 1140–65 (ed. R. van Waefelghem in 1913), and *PM*, the third, compiled between 1161 and 1165 (ed. E. Martène from Bibl. Nat. MS. latin 14,762). H. Marton ('Initia capituli generalis in fontibus historicis ordinis, and 'Status iuridicus monasteriorum *Ordinis* Praemonstratensis primitivus', ibid., 43–69 and 191–265), has seen a gradual development with no supreme and all powerful central authority from the very first, 1124–28.

The Judicial Activities of the General Chapters: II

W ith the growth of houses in size and number, judicial activities and problems became more evident, and the general chapter consequently developed into a complex organ which was capable of dealing with the new demands.[1] The records are not sufficient to show the smaller orders transacting judicial business and, indeed, their general chapters were probably less highly organised, but for the larger orders such as the Cistercians, and to a lesser extent the Premonstratensians, a jurisdiction can be seen at work. As records of the central government, the Cistercian *Statuta* are comparable with both the papal registers and with the papal law books or codes. They form the written law of the order, which was made in many instances like the Canon Law from questions and queries, and they record the operation of the judicial machinery, the activities of the judges and of the courts. Each Cistercian abbot had a copy of the year's *Statuta*. The records of the general chapter at Prémontré are apparently lost, but the letters of Gervase, abbot of Prémontré from 1209 to 1220, survive, and consequently they supply some information of an informal and unofficial kind about the conduct of lawsuits within that order.[2] For the other orders, except the Dominicans whose *acta* survive from 1220 onwards,[3] central records are either rare or non-existent. For instance, the documents referring to the general chapter of Molesme, which belong to the period before 1251, are few in number, and unfortunately the *statuta* do not survive in a collection save those of 1334.[4] The *diffinitiones* of Cluny have not been discovered from before 1259.[5]

[1] See J. Hourlier, *Le Chapitre Général jusqu'au moment du Grand Schisme*, Paris 1936, 55.

[2] H. M. Colvin, *The White Canons in England*, Oxford 1951, 194. The letters of Gervase are edited by C. L. Hugo in *Sacrae Antiquitatis Monumenta*, i, Étival 1725.

[3] G. R. Galbraith, *The Constitution of the Dominican Order 1216–1360*, Manchester 1925, 2, and *Acta Capitulorum Generalis Ordinis Praedicatorum*, ed. B. M. Reichert, Monumenta Ordinis Fratrum Praedicatorum Historica, iii, iv, v, Rome 1898–1900. The provincial records of the English Dominican province no longer exist (G. R. Galbraith, op. cit., 53).

[4] *Cartulaires de l'Abbaye de Molesme*, ed. J. Laurent, i (Paris 1907), 267, 269, and ii (1911), Appendix 6.

[5] R. Graham, *English Ecclesiastical Studies*, London 1929, 24, citing A. Bruel, 'Les chapitres généraux de l'ordre de Cluny depuis le XIIIᵉ jusqu'au XVIIᵉ siècle', *Bibliothèque de l'École des Chartes*, xxxiv (1873), 542–79, especially 554, 555 n. 1, 563, 569.

Cistercian lawsuits have been little studied.[1] A sixth of the cases which were recorded in the *Statuta* between 1198 and 1254, concern English houses. A search among the surviving cartularies of the English Cistercian houses, for the same period, has not produced a great number of cases, but it has often made it possible to trace a suit after its delegation, sometimes to its conclusion. The quarrel between Fountains (Yorks.) and Byland (Yorks.) about a mine, was delegated in 1225.[2] Both a Byland and a Fountains cartulary recorded the settlement, which it seems took place in 1226.[3] Similarly the suits between Combermere (Cheshire) and Dieulacres (Staffs.), Dieulacres and Croxden (Staffs.), Dieulacres and Hulton (Staffs.) Sawley (Yorks.) and Fountains, and Beaulieu (Hants) and Stanley (Wilts.), can be traced from delegation to a decision.[4]

The papacy had delegated its legal, judicial and executive responsibilities to these orders: the new congregations were then faced with the same difficulties as the papacy. Papal influence can be traced on some aspects of the administration of Cistercian legal affairs: in other ways, the Cistercians developed a system peculiar to themselves. The general chapter was the substitute for the *Curia Romana*, with the marked contrast that it was not a permanently sitting court. At Cîteaux the general chapter lasted five days: at Prémontré it was a three-day and sometimes a four-day session.[5] The general chapter had declared itself the highest court of the Cistercian order. It therefore reserved the settlement of difficult or important cases, the *causae maiores*, for its own cognisance, and it exercised the right of final decision where no satisfactory settlement could be made by its delegates. With the larger orders, the members of the general chapter were too numerous for affairs to be discussed rapidly, and sometimes difficult judicial problems arose.[6] These were the reasons for the origin of the *diffinitores*. The first four abbots of the Cistercian order were

---

[1] There are only the brief considerations of the subject by Dom J.-M. Canivez in 'Cîteaux', *Dictionnaire de Droit Canonique*, iii, cols. 776–81, and by J.-B. Mahn in *L'Ordre Cistercien et son Gouvernement des Origines au milieu du XIIIᵉ siècle*, Paris 1951, 211–16.

[2] *Statuta Capitulorum Generalium Ordinis Cisterciensis*, ed. J.-M. Canivez, Bibliothèque de la Revue d'Histoire Ecclésiastique, fasc. 9, 10 (1933–4), 1225, 34; (hereafter cited as *Statuta*).

[3] Byland Cartulary, B.M. Egerton MS. 2823, fols. 78ʳ, 78ᵛ; Fountains Cartulary, Bodleian MS. Rawlinson B. 449, fols. 147, 148.

[4] *Statuta* 1241, 57 and *The Chartulary of Dieulacres Abbey*, ed. G. Wrottesley, William Salt Arch. Soc., Coll. Hist. Staffordshire, New series ix (1906), 356, no. 172 (hereafter referred to as *Dieulacres Cart.*); *Statuta* 1246, 47, 1248, 30, and *Dieulacres Cart.*, 358, no. 175; *Statuta* 1249, 45, and *Dieulacres Cart.*, 356–7, no. 173; *Statuta* 1249, 47, and *The Chartulary of the Cistercian Abbey of St. Mary of Sallay in Craven*, ed. J. McNulty, Yorks. Arch. Soc. Rec. ser. xc (1934), no. 411 (Fountains Cartulary, B.M. Add. MS. 40009, fols. 195ᵛ, 196ʳ, 196ᵛ); *Statuta* 1213, 64, 1214, 40, 1215, 41, 1216, 53, and Beaulieu Cartulary, B.M. Cott. MS. Nero A XII, fols. 40ᵛ, 41ᵛ.

[5] J. Hourlier, op. cit., 178. At Cluny eight days was the maximum duration for a general chapter.

[6] *Statuta* 1216, 56; 1209, 38: 'Querela abbatis Sancti-Sulpitii (St. Sulpice-en-Bugey, dioc. Belley, France), contra abbatem de Casania (La Chassagne-en-Bresse, dioc. Lyon, France), filium suum committitur abbati Pontiniaci auctoritate Capituli terminanda'.

diffinitores by right.[1] They represent the papal 'auditores generales causarum sacri palatii', but unlike the auditors they acted in unison, and they had powers to pass judgment with a majority vote.[2] Most of the major cases concerned the relationship between mother and daughter houses. In 1226, the quarrel between the houses of Furness (Lancs.) and Waverley (Surrey) over the 'prioratus' of their houses, was committed to the abbots of Pontigny (dioc. Auxerre, France), Clairvaux (dioc. Langres, France) and L'Aumône (dioc. Chartres, France), who were to carry out an enquiry when they were present in the following year, and they were instructed to act as they saw fit. In the *Statuta* of 1232 it is recorded that the question was settled by the abbot of Cîteaux, when Furness was declared the mother house of the L'Aumône and Savigny convents in England, and Waverley was defined as the parent of the other houses.[3]

It is probable that the Cistercians consciously copied the papacy in dealing with cases by delegation, but it is noteworthy that all Cistercian cases, which came before the general chapter, were of first instance, and this factor may have influenced reciprocally the papal conduct of judicial affairs. Cistercians were appointed judges-delegate by the popes from the early twelfth century. Papal delegation became common during the pontificate of Innocent II (1130–1143). When Innocent II on 3 December 1130 appointed a bishop to hear a cause, he ordered him to take counsel of Stephen, abbot of Cîteaux, and Bernard, abbot of Clairvaux.[4] The following year, Stephen abbot of Cîteaux was appointed a judge-delegate.[5] One of the earliest cases of papal delegation to English judges took place during the course of the lawsuit between Bernard, bishop of St. Davids, and Urban, bishop of Llandaff, which was settled in 1131.[6] At this time there were only two Cistercian houses in England, Waverley (Surrey), which was founded in 1128, and Tintern (Monm.), which was established on 9 May 1131.[7] It is, therefore, impossible that causes were delegated by the general chapter to abbots in the English Cistercian province as early as this. Furthermore, it would appear that the general chapter was not yet sufficiently organised to dispense justice in this way.[8]

[1] See *Statuta* 1205, 68, where an important case about an abbey was committed to the abbot of Cîteaux and the first four abbots.
[2] *Statuta* 1230, 23—a cause which was committed to two judges, 'diffinitoribus definitivam sententiam reservantes'. The Cluniacs, Carthusians and monks of the order of Molesme had 'diffinitores' (see *Cartulaires de l'Abbaye de Molesme*, i. 269; E. M. Thompson, *The Carthusian Order in England*, London 1930, 95), and the Benedictines in the chapter at Abingdon in 1290, first appear to have elected 'diffinitores seu provisores', whose ordinances or provisions the abbots and proctors pledged themselves to observe (see W. A. Pantin, 'The General and Provincial Chapters of the English Black Monks, 1215–1540', *T.R.H.S.* 4th series, x (1927), 234).
[3] *Statuta* 1226, 14; 1232, 20.   [4] P.L. clxxix, col. 70 C–D.
[5] P.L. clxxix, col. 112 A–B (4 Nov. 1131), and (12 Feb. 1132)—papal confirmation.
[6] *Regesta Pontificum Romanorum*, ed. P. Jaffé, revised by S. Loewenfeld, 2nd ed., i, Leipzig 1885, no. 7511; *Liber Landavensis*, reproduced by J. Rhys and J. G. Evans, Oxford 1893, 65, and see also 30–67, 87–94, cited by M. Cheney in *E.H.R.* lvi (1941), 178; *Historia Novella*, ed. K. R. Potter, London 1955, 11.
[7] D. Knowles and R. Neville Hadcock, *Medieval Religious Houses*, London 1953, 116–17.   [8] See the first part of this article, above 18–22.

JUDICIAL ACTIVITIES OF THE GENERAL CHAPTERS: II

Perhaps the earliest instance of Cistercian delegation to English abbots comes from 1154–1155.[1] In that year, Ailred abbot of Rievaulx (Yorks.), gave judgment in a suit between John, abbot of Furness (Lancs.), and Richard, abbot of Savigny (dioc. Avranches, France), about the subjection and obedience of Byland (Yorks.), which had been delegated to him and the abbot of Waverley (Surrey). The abbot and convent of Furness had taken their suit to the general chapter.[2] The choice of Ailred as a judge-delegate is not surprising. Walter Daniel wrote of him that

'made aware of the facts, he was like a second Daniel in disentangling cases and coming to a prudent decision. When the Abbot (William) sent him to Rome on the famous case of the dissension at York he was received so graciously by the Lord Pope, and expounded the business and brought it to conclusion with such energy, that the esteem and admiration which he won after his return was widespread'.[3]

Ailred also acted as an arbiter, and in 1164 he attested the agreement between the religious orders of Cîteaux and Sempringham, which took place at Kirkstead (Lincs.).[4]

The early *Statuta* are incomplete, and they record no delegation of cases before the year 1190.[5] In that year eight lawsuits were transmitted to delegates for hearing.[6] Entry number 19 stated that delegation was ordered because a private settlement had proved impossible:

'Querela quae vertebatur inter abbatem Joyaci (Jouy-en-Brie, dioc. Sens, France), et canonicos Sancti-Jacobi (unidentified), *quia non potuit cum pace partium terminari committitur* abbatibus Quinciaci (Quincy, dioc. Langres, France), Scarleiarum (Les Écharlis, dioc. Sens), Secanae Portus (Barbeaux, dioc. Sens): ut quod minus actum erat plenius compleatur'.[7]

It is not until the 1230s that the recording of the delegation of quarrels becomes noticeably more orderly, and affairs are announced regularly by 'Querela etc.'.

---

[1] D. Knowles, *The Monastic Order in England*, Cambridge 1950, 263, dates this as 1151, but Sir Maurice Powicke in *The Life of Ailred of Rievaulx by Walter Daniel*, London 1950, lxiii and xcii, gives the date above. The case recorded in the Kirkstead Cartulary, B.M. Cott. MS. Vesp. E XVIII, on fol. 105ᵛ (and fol. 214ᵛ) may be earlier, but it is impossible to date it exactly. It cannot be much earlier than 1150 (the date of the foundation of Sibton), because Hugh, the first abbot of Sibton (Suffolk), was amongst those who were appointed arbiters.

[2] Sir William Dugdale, *Monasticon Anglicanum*, ed. Caley, Ellis and Bandinel, v. 352–3; 'Documents relating to Furness Abbey', ed. L. Delisle, *The Journal of the British Archaeological Association*, vi (1851), 423–4.

[3] *The Life of Ailred of Rievaulx by Walter Daniel*, 23.

[4] Ibid., lxiii and xciv; *Cartularium Abbathiae de Rievalle*, ed. J. C. Atkinson, Surtees Society, lxxxiii (1889), 181–3, and see below 181.

[5] See J.-A. Lefèvre, 'Pour une datation nouvelle des *Instituta Generalis Capituli*', *Collectanea Ordinis Cisterciensium Reformatorum*, Annus XVI (1954), 253–4.

[6] *Statuta* 1190, 19, 29, 41, 43, 58, 65, 69, 71.

[7] The italics are mine: a case in which only one of the parties was Cistercian, see below, 182.

In some cases, judges of the same filiation as each of the parties were appointed.[1] In 1195 it had been decreed, however, that the hearing of suits should not be committed to those who were daughter-houses of the parties, if others could be found.[2] The statement of J.-B. Mahn that from 1216 onwards judges were always three in number must be modified.[3] Evidence from the *Statuta* denies this. For example, of the suits which were sent to delegates in 1241, twelve went to commissions of two judges, and only two to commissions of three,[4] and in a case of 1245, for instance, a third judge was added.[5] A calculation which has been made from the *Statuta* between the years 1198 and 1254 shows that the abbots of Buildwas (Salop.) figured as judges in nineteen commissions. The abbots of Waverley (Surrey), a house which Ailred of Rievaulx described as hidden away in a corner ('in angulo'),[6] received twelve commissions, and Garendon (Leics.) comes next with eleven. The abbots of Fountains (Yorks.) and Rievaulx (Yorks.) received respectively nine and eight commands to hear causes.

In the Premonstratensian order, causes were delegated by the time of the abbacy of Gervase, an Englishman, that is 1209 to 1220.[7] Between 1209 and 1215, an English case was delegated by abbot Gervase and the general chapter at Prémontré to abbots Geoffrey of Newhouse (Lincs.), Adam of Croxton (Leics.) and Jordan of Bayham (Sussex),[8] and again, between 1209 and 1220, another English suit was committed to the same judges.[9] This was probably the same commission because the abbot and convent of Welbeck (Notts.) figure as the plaintiffs in both suits.[10] During the same period, the abbots of Newhouse (Lincs.) and Croxton (Leics.) were commissioned as delegates to deal with a suit between Lavendon (Bucks.) and St. Radegund's (Kent).[11] This case had been before the general chapter in the time of abbot Vermond of Prémontré (1203–1208), but there is no intimation of previous delegation.[12]

Apart from the Benedictines, there is no evidence of delegation among the other congregations. For the smaller orders it was probably unneces-

---

[1] J.-B. Mahn, op. cit., 211–12. I have investigated the question of delegation in greater detail in 'English Cistercian Cases and their Delegation in the First Half of the Thirteenth Century', *Analecta Sacri Ordinis Cisterciensis*, Annus XX, fasc. 1 (1964).

[2] *Statuta* 1195, 43.

[3] J.-B. Mahn, op. cit., 212. Three was the usual number of papal judges-delegate for a commission.

[4] *Statuta* 1241.

[5] *Statuta* 1245, 44.

[6] *The Life of Ailred of Rievaulx by Walter Daniel*, ed. F. M. Powicke, lxii, quoting from *Chronicles of the Reigns of Stephen, Henry II and Richard I* (R.S.), ed. R. Howlett, iii, London 1886, 184.

[7] See 'L'Obituaire de l'Abbaye de Prémontré', ed. R. van Waefelghem, *Analectes de l'Ordre de Prémontré*, v (1909), 12.

[8] Welbeck Cart., B.M. Harl. MS. 3640, fol. 130ʳ.

[9] Welbeck Cart., B.M. Harl. MS. 3640, fol. 129ʳ.

[10] There were, however, probably no general mandates.

[11] St. Radegund's Cart., Bodleian Library, MS. Rawl. B 336, fol. 42.

[12] 'L'Obituaire de l'Abbaye de Prémontré', op. cit., 11. H. M. Colvin (op. cit., 86) says that this case was before the general chapter in 1203–4.

sary. In England, the statutes of the Benedictine general chapter of 1277, provided that if any major quarrel or controversy arose between abbots of monasteries, or between abbots and their convents, it was to be referred to the visitors or to the presidents of the last chapter, who were to appoint neighbouring abbots to adjudicate, or, if it was necessary, the whole matter was to be sent to the general chapter.[1]

Cistercian subdelegation followed the papal arrangements. Between 1130 and 1148 Innocent II instructed certain judges-delegate:

'Si quis vero de vobis, certa prepediente causa, interesse non poterit, vos, qui adesse poteritis, idem iudicium terminate'.[2]

This was probably the first papal pronouncement about subdelegation. In the Furness–Savigny case, Godfrey, abbot of Garendon (Leics.), replaced the abbot of Waverley (Surrey) as a judge-delegate of Cîteaux.[3] By 1191 it was usual for the general chapter to appoint three judges, whereas all previous commissions except for one had been addressed to two. Clause 29 states 'Quod si unus ex ipsis interesse non poterit hoc reliqui duo nihilominus exequantur', and clause 39 of the 1204 *Statuta* gives a similar instruction: 'Quod si tres interesse non potuerint, duo nihilominus exequantur'.[4] These were, however, instructions addressed to specific judges, and as yet there had been no general decree. But in 1207 the general chapter declared that when a commission was addressed to three abbots, if the third abbot could not be present, the other two should attend to the commission alone; the third should, however, always present a letter of excuse.[5] In 1216 the general chapter again made a pronouncement about subdelegation for universal application, and repeated in the first paragraph of the *Statuta* that two judges could execute a commission which had been sent to three.[6] A general acceptance must have been accorded to this, for by 1228 it was deliberately stated in one case, that without the abbot of Meyra (dioc. Lugo, Spain), one of the judges-delegate, the other two were on no account to proceed.[7]

The use of arbiters was encouraged. When the abbot and convent of Dore (Heref.) quarrelled with the house of Strata Florida (Cardigan) about lands, pastures and woods, an arbitration was completed by the

---

[1] *Documents . . . of the English Black Monks*, ed. W. A. Pantin, Camden 3rd series, xlv (1931), 86, and see also 64, 85, and W. A. Pantin, op. cit., *T.R.H.S.* 4th series, x (1927), 230.

[2] *Corpus jur. can.*, C2. q5, c. 17, and see *The Letters of John of Salisbury*, ed. W. J. Miller and H. E. Butler, revised by C. N. L. Brooke, London 1955, nos. 14, 15.

[3] 'Documents relating to Furness Abbey', op. cit., 423–4.

[4] Cf. *Corpus jur. can.* C2. q5, c. 17, and I tit. xxix, cc. 3, 6; cf. also e.g. Magdalen College, Oxford, Selborne Charter 252: 'Quod si non omnes hiis exequendis potueritis interesse duo vestrum ea nichilominus exequantur'.

[5] *Statuta* 1207, 8; cf. Eye Transcript, B.M. Add. MS. 8177, fol. 149ʳ, and see J.-B. Mahn, op. cit., Pièces Justicatives nos. 16, 17.

[6] *Statuta* 1216, 1: 'Statutum est a Capitulo generali ut causae deinceps ad Capitulum generale delatae, tribus committantur abbatibus; et si omnes nequiverint interesse, duo nihilominus exequantur'.

[7] *Statuta* 1228, 21.

V

five abbots of Neath (Glam.), Tintern (Monm.), Margam (Glam.),
Whitland (Carm.) and Aberconway (Caern.) in 1209.[1] Combe (Warw.)
and Stanley (Wilts.), who had been given a settlement previously by the
abbots of L'Aumône and Tintern, delegates of the general chapter, com-
promised in 1244 on H., abbot of Garendon (Leics.) and Adam of Luton,
abbot of Woburn (Beds.), 'qui utriusque partis rationibus auditis et
causarum meritis diligenter discussis domini pre oculis habentes talem
sentenciam protulerunt'.[2] As with papal arbitrations, it was stipulated
that if either party broke the arrangement it should pay forty shillings to
the other.[3] At the exhortation of the judges, the abbots of Sawley (Yorks.)
and Dieulacres (Staffs.), a case between Furness (Lancs.) and Jervaulx
(Yorks.) was taken to arbiters. Jervaulx chose the abbot of Byland (Yorks.),
Furness the abbot of Stanlaw (Cheshire), and both parties agreed upon
Richard, prior of Roche (Yorks.), as the third arbiter.[4] In a suit between
the convents of Pipewell (Northants) and Combe (Warw.), which was
committed to the abbots of Waverley (Surrey), Woburn (Beds.) and
Bruern (Oxon.), arbiters were appointed. They were the Cistercian
abbots of Warden (Beds.) and Medmenham (Bucks.), and the suit was
settled in 1242.[5]

In the method of conducting their lawsuits, the Cistercians and
Premonstratensians emulated the Roman law procedure, which had been
assimilated and adapted by the papacy, and Cistercian court *acta* illustrate
the documentary as well as the procedural similarity.[6] The intention was
formulated and declared, followed by the parties' allegations.[7] The abbot
and convent of Combe (Warw.) alleged that Pipewell (Northants) had
acquired the 'villa' of Newbold, against the tenor of a previous composition, and to their prejudice. Pipewell countercharged by saying that
Combe molested them over some mills, and that they had erected a
grange contrary to the statutes of the general chapter.[8] Contumacy was
punished:

'Abbas de Landesio (le Landais, dioc. Bourges, France), quia mandato
Capituli generalis noluit obedire, in eo quod iudicibus sibi a Capitulo
delegatis tertio vocatus non venisset, tribus diebus sit in levi culpa, et
septem extra stallum suum'.[9]

[1] P.R.O. E 326/727.
[2] Combe Cartulary, B.M. Cott. MS. Vit. A I, fols. 60r, 60v, 61r.
[3] Ibid., fols. 60r, 60v.
[4] *The Coucher Book of Furness Abbey*, 2 pt. ii, ed. J. Brownbill, Chetham Society New Series, lxxvi (1916), 353: (the text of the charter is from P.R.O. Duchy of Lancs. Ancient Deeds 25/479). The parties bound themselves to abide by the settlement under penalty of 100 marks.
[5] Pipewell Cart., B.M. Cott. MS. Caligula A XIII, fols. 157v, 158r. Woburn was the mother house of Medmenham.
[6] B.M. Harleian Charters 44 A 14, 43 B 46, 43 B 47, 75 A 6, 75 D 11.
[7] B.M. Harl. Ch. 44 A 14; *Statuta* 1216, 63; and cf. 'Tancredi Bononiensis Ordo Iudiciarius', *Pillii, Tancredi, Gratiae Libri de Iudiciorum Ordine*, ed. F. Bergmann, Gottingen 1842, 271.
[8] Pipewell Cartulary, B.M. Calig. A XIII, fols. 158r, 158v, 159r, 159v.
[9] *Statuta* 1203, 23; cf. *Corpus jur. can.* I tit. xxix, c. 5, and II tit. i, c. 1.

174

Witnesses were interrogated, and their attestations formed an operative part in influencing the decision of the suit.[1] Ailred heard witnesses and altercations before he declared in favour of Savigny, who were consequently absolved from the charge of Furness.[2] A similar reliance was placed on documentary evidence, and documents were frequently inspected.[3] Quitclaims and compositions were made, and definitive sentences were passed.[4] In a suit between Pipewell (Northants) and Warden (Beds.), Warden quitclaimed all right and renounced a court settlement,[5] and when G., abbot of Bégard (dioc. Tréguier, Brittany, France), made a notification that he and the convent of Bégard conceded and quitclaimed to H. abbot and the monks of Kirkstead (Lincs.), all right and claim to certain lands and possessions in the soke of Gayton le Wold (Lincs.), he promised also to begin no further quarrel.[6]

The desire for simplicity in religious practice permeated Cistercian legal conduct, and gave it certain characteristics of its own, even though so much was borrowed from canonical procedure. The general chapter demanded that the conduct of cases should be kept simple. Elaborate procedure, long and muddling pleas, exceptions and legal subtleties, were condemned, and advocates were not to be used.[7] In line with this decree the abbot of Carracedo (dioc. Astorga, Spain), was punished in 1231 for not replying simply in front of the chapter and the definitors. Three days' 'levis culpa', one of them on bread and water alone, was imposed on him.[8]

Furthermore, because the Cistercian area of jurisdiction was so much smaller than the papacy's, a closer supervision could be maintained by the general chapter over each case. From the evidence of the *Statuta*, about four hundred cases were taken to the general chapter and were delegated between 1198 and 1254. Contrary to the papal arrangements there were no general mandates: a separate order was issued for each case, and a note was made among the *Statuta* for the year.[9] In some cases one judge announced the commission to the others. In 1199, the abbot of Croxden (Staffs.) was told to announce the delegation to his fellow judges, the abbots of Buildwas (Salop.) and Dore (Heref.), in a suit between the convents of Kemmer (Abbey-Cwmhir, Radnor, or Cymmer, Merioneth), and Aberconway (Carnarv.),[10] and in 1230 the abbot of Espina (dioc.

---

[1] Welbeck Cart., B.M. Harl. MS. 3640, fols. 129–30, and see H. M. Colvin, op. cit., 345–8.
[2] 'Documents relating to Furness Abbey', op. cit., 423–4.
[3] *Statuta* 1208, 36, 37; 1209, 31; B.M. Harl. Ch. 44 A 14; cf. P.R.O. E 135/21/33, E 135/4/17, and B.M. MS. Julius D II, fol. 75ʳ.
[4] B.M. Harl. Ch. 75 D 11; Pipewell Cart., B.M. Calig. MS. A XIII, fols. 158ʳ, 158ᵛ, 159ʳ, 159ᵛ, and Byland Cart., B.M. Egerton MS. 2823, fol. 78ʳ; cf. P.R.O. E 135/4/17.
[5] Pipewell Cart., B.M. Stowe MS. 937, fols. 93ᵛ, 94ʳ.
[6] B.M. Harl. Ch. 43 B 47.
[7] *Statuta* 1225, 1, and see also 1225, 12; 1231, 25, 26.
[8] *Statuta* 1231, 25.
[9] Only a very few mandates were enregistered in the papal registers. On the incompleteness of the early *Statuta*, however, see above 171 n. 5.
[10] *Statuta* 1199, 22.

Palencia, Spain), one of the judges, was instructed to inform his colleagues of the commission. The abbot of Espina was present at the general chapter.[1] Sometimes another abbot of the same country, who had not been appointed a judge, was ordered to tell the judges of their commission. For instance, in 1238 the abbot of Roche (Yorks.) was instructed by the general chapter to tell the abbots of Furness (Lancs.), Combermere (Cheshire) and Beaulieu (Hants), that they had been appointed to hear the suit between the convents of Byland (Yorks.) and Rievaulx (Yorks.).[2] Professor Cheney has drawn attention to the ways in which news was transmitted, and to the use of merchants as postmen, in an article on the abbot of Prémontré, and this was possibly another way in which mandates were conveyed.[3] These messengers presumably delivered some written order or mandate, and they were presumably charged with this duty when the delegates were not attending the general chapter, or that particular committee of it which dealt with the delegation of lawsuits.

No original Cistercian mandates, or copies of them, have come to light, and it might be argued that these instructions were conveyed orally, although this seems unlikely.[4] A document of Theobald, abbot of Cîteaux, and all the abbots of the general chapter, records the commitment of a suit to the abbots of Combe (Warw.) and Rewley (Oxon.). It is dated from the general chapter of 1290, and suggests that by this date the abbots had written authority on which to act.[5] Mandates, as noted in the *Statuta*, were stereotyped and can be placed in certain categories. The wording suggests papal influence. Sometimes the judges were instructed to terminate the suit within a certain time, before St. Andrew's day, before Christmas, before Easter or before Whitsun.[6] Very often the 'terminus ad quem' was the next general chapter.[7] Most causes were supposed to be terminated within a year. The annual compilation of the *Statuta* enabled the abbots to keep a trace of the suits which had been delegated, and to see that their common decisions were respected. The beginnings of the legal action might be delayed if the announcer failed to convey the commission to the judges. Punishment was usual for those who neglected to announce mandates. The abbot of Croxden (Staffs.) was penalized for this in 1200:

'Abbas de Crosquedam qui mandatum Capituli nuntiare neglexit,

---

[1] *Statuta* 1230, 29: 'Controversia quae est inter abbatem de Alcobatia (Alcobaça, dioc. Leira, Portugal) et abbatem de Carraceto (dioc. Astorga, Spain), committitur abbatibus de Spina (Espina, dioc. Palencia, Spain), de Nucharia (dioc. Messina, Sicily), et de Ursaria (Osera, dioc. Orense, Spain), fine debito terminanda. Abbas de Spina *qui presens est* hoc eis denuntiet'. See also e.g. 1241, 57, and 1252, 35: 'Abbas de Furnesio (Furness, Lancs.) hoc collegis suis denuntiet'. [2] *Statuta* 1238, 72.

[3] C. R. Cheney, 'Gervase Abbot of Prémontré: a Medieval Letter-Writer', *Bulletin of the John Rylands Library*, xxxiii (1950), 39–40.

[4] There is a cartulary copy of a Premonstratensian mandate printed in H.M. Colvin, op. cit., 345. [5] P.R.O. E 327/18.

[6] E.g. *Statuta* 1200, 52; 1208, 29, 30; 1221, 29; cf. *Corpus jur. can.* I, tit. xxix, c. 4 (Alex: III.) and *Les Registres de Grégoire IX*, ed. L. Auvray, Bibliothèque des Écoles Françaises d'Athènes et de Rome 2ᵉ série, ii, Paris 1907, nos. 2731, 3261.

[7] E.g. *Statuta* 1201, 20, 23; 1206, 13; 1207, 55; 1218, 64.

de commissione querelae inter abbates de Commirs (Abbey-Cwmhir, Radnor, or Cymmer, Merioneth) et Albae cornui (Whitland, Carm.), tribus diebus sit in levi culpa, uno eorum in pane et aqua. Abbas de Margan (Margam, Glam.) hoc ei denuntiet'.[1]

The abbot had been appointed a delegate in 1199 and told to inform his colleagues.[2] A similar penalty was imposed on the abbots of Margam (Glam.) and Coggeshall (Essex) in 1204.[3]

Judges were punished for failing to report to the general chapter and for neglecting to hear causes. In 1207 the general chapter allowed a year for terminating cases.[4] In 1213 certain judges, delegated by the general chapter, were instructed to report on their activities at the chapter of the following year, even if they had not fulfilled their commission.[5] It had also been stated in 1208 that mandates only expired when sentences were finally given,[6] and penalties of three or six days' 'levis culpa' were published for negligent judges-delegate.[7] This was a general pronouncement of the Cistercian chapter. The abbots of Sobrado (dioc. Compostella, Spain), and Osera (dioc. Orense, Spain), were reprimanded for not reporting in 1210, and were ordered to submit to three days' 'levis culpa', one of them on bread and water alone.[8] The abbots of Fountains (Yorks.), Garendon (Leics.) and Boxley (Kent), were not punished when a cause was recommitted to them in 1208, because some ambiguity had arisen in the instructions.[9] Similarly, in 1216 no punishment was decreed for the judges-delegate who had not terminated a case on account of a reasonable excuse.[10] In 1206 the abbots of Bordesley (Worcs.) and Buildwas (Salop.), who it was found had not executed the mandate of the general chapter, were punished. The case, however, was again committed to them, with the stern injunction that they should terminate it before Easter, or face six days on bread and water. The abbot of Waverley (Surrey) was to inform them of these decisions:

'Abbates de Bordelec (sic) et de Beldoas qui noluerunt exequi mandatum Capituli generalis, tribus diebus sint in levi culpa, uno eorum in pane et aqua. Interim vero eis committitur eadem causa usque ad

[1] *Statuta* 1200, 44, and see also 1202, 32; 1218, 54; 1235, 35; 1236, 25.
[2] *Statuta* 1199, 22. This would seem to be Kemmer (Abbey-Cwmhir, Radnor, or Cymmer, Merioneth) and not Cumber (Ireland). Canivez has given Kemmer in the first instance but not in the second.
[3] *Statuta* 1204, 25; cf. 1209, 58.
[4] *Statuta* 1207, 5. This is a contrast with the papal stipulations.
[5] *Statuta* 1213, 70, and see 1196, 21—Sawley (Yorks.) v. Furness (Lancs.).
[6] *Statuta* 1208, 9: 'Quando aliqua commissio fit abbatibus, donec finiantur querelae non expiret eorum iurisdictio quibus commissum est negotium, sed semper de ipsa querela ad ipsos recurratur'. Cf. *Regesta Honorii Papae III*, ed. P. Pressutti, i, Rome 1888, no. 1422, where the judges were ordered to proceed actively or to remit to Rome.
[7] *Statuta* 1208, 4: 'Abbates delegati a Capitulo qui super delegatione sua negligentes fuerunt, illi etiam qui eis obedire contempserunt, sex diebus sint in levi culpa, duobus eorum in pane et aqua'.
[8] *Statuta* 1210, 8.
[9] *Statuta* 1208, 31.
[10] *Statuta* 1216, 11.

Pascha terminanda; et si neglexerint ex tunc omni sexta feria sint in pane et aqua, donec Capitulo se praesentent. Abbas de Waverle hoc eis denuntiet'.[1]

From the number of second commissions it might be argued that the judges were unwilling to hear causes, but a year was not long for terminating suits.[2] When it is remembered that 'Ailred, in the course of each year, had the obligation of visiting Citeaux, Clairvaux, Woburn, Revesby, Rufford, Melrose and Dundrennan', the burden of serving as a judge as well, with the possibility of a visit to other houses, will be realised.[3] Many of these second commissions must have followed reports to the general chapter that the hearing had not been completed, although the judges were actively engaged on dealing with the suit. The phrase 'quibus anno praeterito commissa fuerta, iterum committitur', as in an example of 1209, when no punishment was decreed, shows the grant of a further period for terminating the cause.[4] Sometimes a cause was recalled and committed anew, as in 1247, presumably if the chapter was not satisfied.[5] Rebukes were issued when causes dragged on,[6] and in 1247, in a case between the convents of Stratford Langthorne (Essex) and Roche (Yorks.), which had been committed to delegates in 1246, the general chapter ordered that the hearing should be 'effectually proceeded with'.[7]

The new congregations jealously guarded and asserted their judicial rights. They recognised no other jurisdiction for the settlement of disputes between members of the order. The Cistercians acted vigorously in prohibiting appeals to other courts. The *Instituta* declared that abbots were not to appeal to any other court—'neque inde ad aliam audientiam appelare liceat'.[8] In 1190 when a cause was committed to two judges, it was ordered that if an appeal had been made to Rome it was to be renounced;[9] while clause 9 of the 1197 *Statuta* threatened excommunication to those Cistercians who tried to take their lawsuits outside the order. In the same year, a prior who had gone to Rome without licence of the general chapter, was removed from his office and convent.[10] Punishments for this offence were imposed in 1200 and 1205,[11] and in 1201 a general pronouncement was made by the chapter:

'De non eundo in Curiam romanam, antiqua sententia teneatur. Abbas vero qui eam scienter transgressus fuerit, si in propria persona

---

[1] *Statuta* 1206, 41, and see 1211, 39.
[2] Thirty-five second commissions are recorded in the *Statuta* for these years.
[3] D. Knowles, *The Monastic Order in England*, 262.
[4] *Statuta* 1209, 49.
[5] *Statuta* 1247, 25.
[6] *Statuta* 1252, 31; 1254, 21.
[7] *Statuta* 1247, 23; 1246, 43.
[8] *Statuta* 1134, no. LXX, pp. 29–30. For the date of the *Instituta*, see the first part of this article, above, 19–22.
[9] *Statuta* 1190, 71.
[10] *Statuta* 1197, 47. Permission was sometimes granted after a request had been made, however, to take business to Rome, see *Statuta* 1197, 44; 1225, 14; 1239, 49.
[11] *Statuta* 1200, 47; 1205, 37.

ierit, omni sexta feria ieiunet in pane et aqua, non celebret, et extra stallum abbatis maneat donec revertatur in sequenti Capitulo generali veniam petiturus'.[1]

An interesting entry appears among the *Statuta* for 1216:

'Abbates Mansiadae (Mazan, dioc. Viviers, Languedoc, France), et de Aqua bella (Aiguebelle, dioc. St. Paul-Trois-Châteaux, France), qui cum recepissent iudices delegatos a Capitulo generali et eorum praetermittentes iudicium in personam quae non est de Ordine, et promiserunt, tribus diebus sint in levi culpa, uno eorum in pane et aqua, et ad praedictos recurrant iudices qui causam pace terminent vel iudicio, quod de cetero non redeat ad Capitulum; duobus tamen iudicibus addatur tertius nempe abbas Cassaneae (La Chassagne-en-Bresse, dioc. Lyon, France)'.[2]

In 1223, with the expansion of Cistercian jurisdiction, the general chapter was still endeavouring to enforce its complete supremacy by disallowing contact with Rome, when the assertion 'Antiqua sententia de non mittendo ad Curiam tenatur', implies that it was not being respected everywhere.[3] It was likewise added that all those who tried to appeal would be excommunicated by the general chapter.[4] As late as 1296–7 a bull of Boniface VIII reiterated that the due chastisement of all persons belonging to the order, should be in the hands of the chief officers of the order, and that there should be no appeal from their judgments.[5] Evidence about Cistercian causes in England suggests that this decree was kept, and that the judicial authority of the general chapter was respected.[6]

The same provisions against taking lawsuits outside the order are found with the Premonstratensians and Carthusians. Innocent III in 1198, declared that the abbot of Prémontré with the counsel of religious, was to settle all differences and quarrels, and he forbade the Premonstratensians to take their causes elsewhere.[7] In 1310 (?) an appeal was made to the Holy See against Adam, abbot of Prémontré, and his chapter, concerning a subsidy, by Roger Heverburg, proctor of the abbot and convent of Bayham (Sussex), but it was natural that the papacy should be regarded as the final arbiter in the last resort.[8] Legislation was directed not against this fundamental theory but against unnecessary recourse to Rome. In 1149 there was an appeal by some Carthusian monks to Rome.[9]

---

[1] *Statuta* 1201, 2.
[2] *Statuta* 1216, 31, and see 1215, 28.
[3] *Statuta* 1223, 6.
[4] *Statuta* 1223, 1.
[5] *The Coucher Book of Furness*, 1 pt. iii, ed. J. C. Atkinson, Chetham Society New Series, xiv (1888), 552–3.
[6] That is to say there is, so far as I know, no evidence of cases between English Cistercians before 1254 coming before the papacy or its courts.
[7] P.L. ccxiv, cols. 297D–302C (27 July 1198).
[8] *Collectanea Anglo-Premonstratensia*, ed. F. A. Gasquet, i, Camden 3rd series, vi (1904), 16–17.
[9] E. M. Thompson, op. cit., 89–90.

V

Under Basil (1151–73), statutes were issued by the general chapter forbidding any house or person of the order to obtain letters from the Roman court against the decrees of the common chapter. No house was to 'presume to write to the person of the lord Pope' for its own or another's business, without the chapter's permission,[1] and in 1190 a bull of pope Clement III forbade any Carthusian prior or brother to appeal without the consent of the chapter.[2]

As yet another instance of judicial self-consciousness in the new orders in the second half of the twelfth century, agreements were made between the Cistercians and Premonstratensians, the Cistercians and Gilbertines, and the Cistercians and Carthusians, for the private settlement of suits. The concurrent rapid expansion of the Cistercians and Premonstratensians throughout northern France, prompted the composition on 11 October 1142 of an agreement between the two orders. It made provision for lawsuits:

'Si forte in aliquibus locis inter aliquos utriusque ordinis aliquid querimonie emerserit et inter eos per aliquos religiosos mediatores componi non poterit sine majori audientia differetur et ad audientiam alterius generalis capituli referetur'.[3]

A quarrel of certain Premonstratensians with some Cistercian abbots, was committed in 1194 to the abbot of Clairvaux for termination, and the *Statuta* provide further instances of judicial transactions between the two orders.[4] On at least two occasions quarrels between them were delegated to Cistercians for settlement.[5]

In England there seems to have been some doubt and confusion, however, as to how cases between members of the two orders should be treated; there was also possibly a desire in some instances to take them before the papal courts. In 1216 in the cathedral at Lincoln, the abbots of Louth Park (Cist., Lincs.), Revesby (Cist., Lincs.), Welbeck (Prem., Notts.) and Newbo (Prem., Lincs.), and the prior of Kyme (Augustinian, Lincs.), arbitrated in a suit between the convents of Kirkstead (Cist., Lincs.) and Barlings (Prem., Lincs.), which had been before papal judges-delegate, the abbots of Thornton (Aug., Lincs.) and Newsham (Prem., Lincs.), and the prior of Elsham (Aug., Lincs.).[6] H. abbot and the convent of Kirkstead brought another suit against the abbot and

---

[1] Ibid., 91.
[2] Ibid., 97.
[3] Kirkstead Cart., B.M. Vesp. MS. E XVIII, fols. 106ʳ, 106ᵛ. See also *Statuta* i. 35–7, where it is printed with slight variations; Watkin Williams, *S. Bernard of Clairvaux*, Manchester 1935, 233–4, and H. M. Colvin, op. cit., 29. The original MS. of this settlement exists among the archives of the Haute-Marne at Chaumont.
[4] *Statuta* 1194, 12: 'Querela Praemonstrati contra quosdam abbates Ordinis nostri committitur terminanda domino Claraevallis', and *Statuta* 1207, 54.
[5] *Statuta* 1249, 49; 1230, 33.
[6] Kirkstead Cart., B.M. Vesp. E XVIII, fols. 203ᵛ, 204ʳ; and see Easby Cartulary, B.M. Egerton MS. 2827, fols. 301ʳ, 301ᵛ, a suit between Easby and Byland, delegated by Honorius III on 25 May 1221.

convent of Barlings before judges-delegate (unnamed), contrary to the tenor of the composition which had been made between the two orders, but, with the assent of the parties, the suit was withdrawn from the cognisance of the judges. It was submitted to arbiters, the abbots William of Vaudey (Cist., Lincs.) and Adam of Croxton (Prem., Leics.), and prior John of Vaudey, and Thomas, canon of Newhouse or Newsham (Prem., Lincs.). The arbitration was agreed upon on 23 April 1219 in the church of St. Swithin at Lincoln.[1]

In 1225, a composition was made between the abbot and convent of Jervaulx (Cist., Yorks.) and the abbot and convent of St. Agatha's, Easby (Prem., Yorks.), about the pasture of Grisedale. At the settlement they agreed that in future no letters were to be impetrated from the pope or the king, and that if another controversy arose between them it was to be settled by two monks and two canons, or more if these could not make an arrangement. This composition was read to both chapters and approved by them.[2] The Cistercian–Premonstratensian agreement about boundaries and lands, was referred to when certain quarrels between Newminster (Cist., Northumb.) and Alnwick (Prem., Northumb.), and Newminster and Warkworth ('domus de werkeword ordinis Praemonstratensis'), about the grange of Sturton (Northumb.) and a salt pan at Warkworth, were settled.[3]

In 1164 an agreement was entered into by the religious of the two orders of Cîteaux and Sempringham, 'for the keeping of peace and charity'.[4] It was modelled on the Cistercian–Premonstratensian agreement. The most obvious source of dispute was the acquisition of lands. The agreement provided, therefore, that no one of either chapter might build a grange or a sheepfold within two leagues of a grange or sheepfold of the other order.[5] Quarrels were to be settled by three Cistercian abbots and three Gilbertine priors 'of wise counsel', who were to be appointed on account of the distance of the general chapter, presumably of Cîteaux. The hearing of a suit could not be taken to another tribunal until these judges had met at least twice and had failed to arbitrate.[6]

An agreement on a smaller scale, between the two neighbouring houses of Louth Park (Cist., Lincs.) and Alvingham (Gilb., Lincs.), took place in 1174. It stipulated that neither house was to hire or buy lands

---

[1] Kirkstead Cart., B.M. Vesp. E XVIII, fol. 106v. This appears to be the copy of a *form* of arbitration.

[2] Easby Cart., B.M. Egerton MS. 2827, fols. 180r, 180v, 181r. Among the witnesses were Stephen abbot of Sawley (Cist., Yorks.), Reginald abbot of Roche (Cist., Yorks.) and Adam monk of Byland (Cist., Yorks.).

[3] *Chartularium Abbathiae de Novo Monasterio*, ed. J. T. Fowler, Surtees Soc., lxvi (1878), 205–6. There appears to be no evidence elsewhere of a Premonstratensian house at Warkworth: see J. C. Hodgson, *A History of Northumberland*, v, London 1899, 195. Both Alnwick and Newminster possessed salt pans at Warkworth, and the reference is perhaps to a grange of Alnwick.

[4] R. Graham, *S. Gilbert of Sempringham and the Gilbertines*, London 1901, 128–9; *Cartularium Abbathiae de Rievalle*, op. cit., 181–3.

[5] R. Graham, op. cit., 129; parallel with the Premonstratensian arrangements.

[6] R. Graham, ibid., 130, citing Pipewell Cart., B.M. Stowe MS. 937, fol. 145v.

without the consent of the other. The settlement was to hold good in twenty Lincolnshire parishes, and arrangements were laid down in case the contract was broken. If the monks of Louth Park broke the pact, the abbots of Fountains (Cist., Yorks.), Kirkstead (Cist., Lincs.) and St. Lawrence, Revesby (Cist., Lincs.), were to enforce it, and failing them the Cistercian general chapter. If the prior and convent of Alvingham were at fault, the abbots of Kirkstead and St. Lawrence, and the priors of Haverholme (Gilb., Lincs.) and Sixhills (Gilb., Lincs.), were to compel them to make amends within forty days, and failing them the chapter of Sempringham, and then the bishop and chapter of Lincoln.[1]

The agreement between the heads of the Cistercian and Carthusian orders was negotiated in 1195: there had been quarrels between the two congregations. It provided that no Carthusian monk was to be received by the Cistercians without the consent of his prior and community, and that no Cistercian monk was to be accepted by the Carthusians unless his abbot and convent agreed to this.[2] As far as is known there was no specific provision about lawsuits between the orders: it is likely that if they arose they were privately settled.

Cases between Cistercian houses, and those of other orders, were supposed to come before the ordinary ecclesiastical courts, or the papal delegated tribunals, and not before Cistercian judges. There are, however, instances of people outside the jurisdiction coming before Cistercian courts. A proctor of a Benedictine house brought a case before the Cistercian general chapter in 1253, and expressed his consent to its delegation to Cistercian judges:

'Querela abbatis et conventus de Mazat (Mozac, dioc. Clermont, France), nigri Ordinis contra abbatem de Monte petroso (Montpeyroux, dioc. Clermont), nostri Ordinis, de Septem Fontibus (Sept Fons, dioc. Autun, France), et de Valle lucida (Vauluisant, dioc. Clermont), abbatibus committitur in plenaria Ordinis potestate pace vel, etc., quia in hoc consensit procurator dictorum abbatis et conventus de Mazat, qui dictam querelam detulit ad Capitulum generale, et quid inde, etc.'.[3]

Accusations of lay persons against Cistercian houses were sometimes heard by Cistercian judges. In 1216, count Simon de Montfort consented to come before the judicature of the order, and to submit to Cistercian judgment or arbitration.[4] Several English cases came before Cistercian tribunals. It must be supposed that if the non-Cistercian party did not

[1] R. Graham, *S. Gilbert of Sempringham and the Gilbertines*, 129–30; Bodleian MS. Laud 642, fol. 130ᵛ. As with Cistercian–Premonstratensian cases, some seem to have come before papal tribunals, e.g. P.R.O. E 135/6/13: there is no indication that the suit had been heard previously by the three abbots and three priors of each order.

[2] E. Margaret Thompson, op. cit., 86; *Annales Ordinis Cartusiensis*, ed. C. Le Couteulx, iii, Monstrolii 1888, 141.

[3] *Statuta* 1253, 20. There are also instances of cases between the Templars and Cistercians, and between the Cluniacs and Cistercians, coming before the general chapter: *Statuta* 1251, 48; 1249, 39.

[4] *Statuta* 1216, 61.

object, nothing would be done to prevent it. In 1203 the abbot and convent of Dore (Heref.) brought a case against a merchant of lord William de Braose before the general chapter, which was delegated to the abbots of Margam (Glam.) and Coggeshall (Essex),[1] and in 1207 the quarrel of a certain William with the abbot of Furness (Lancs.) was committed to the abbot of Savigny.[2]

At the same time as this development, there was a considerable increase in the number of Cistercian cases which came before the general chapter, at least from England. By the mid-twelfth century many Cistercian houses had acquired considerable land, in some cases removing villagers and villages, and in 1190 the general chapter forbade, probably with little effect, the further taking of land lest it should become a source of scandal.[3] The increase in the number of suits from about 1235 onwards corresponds with Cistercian agrarian development. Suits over lands, pastures, granges, sheepfolds, mills, rents and possessions, form the majority.[4] The abbot and convent of Bégard (dioc. Tréguier, Brittany, France), sought two and a half carucates of land in the soke of Gayton from the abbot and convent of Kirkstead (Lincs.).[5] The abbot and convent of Combe (Warw.) sued the house of Stanley (Wilts.) about pasture for six cows, two mills and certain rents.[6] The quarrel between Combermere (Cheshire) and Dieulacres (Staffs.) in 1252 concerned granges,[7] and part of the trouble between Dieulacres and Hulton (Staffs.), in the same year, was over sheepfolds.[8] In 1229, G. abbot of Cîteaux and the general chapter delegated a suit about mills to the abbots of Bordesley (Worcs.) and Woburn (Beds.).[9] A suit about a rent of three shillings and eight pence between the abbots and convents of Pipewell (Northants) and Combe (Warw.), was settled on 11 June 1242;[10] the same parties had previously disagreed about lands and tenements in 1225–6.[11]

Like the papacy, the general chapter had no permanent executive officers at its command. Local Cistercian abbots were appointed to execute and maintain sentences. In the Beaulieu (Hants) against Stanley (Wilts.) case, the abbots of Kingswood (Glos.) and Bruern (Oxon.) were ordered by the general chapter of 1216 to see to the execution of the sentence: they were to announce and report on what they had done at the next general chapter.[12] Sometimes the judges who had heard the case were

---

[1] *Statuta* 1203, 49.   [2] *Statuta* 1207, 62, and cf. 1210, 42.

[3] M. Beresford, *The Lost Villages of England*, London 1954, 152–3; *Statuta* 1190, 1; and see the stories of Gerald of Wales in 'Speculum Ecclesie', ed. J. Brewer, *Giraldi Cambrensis Opera* iv. 225–9, quoted by C. V. Graves in 'The Economic Activities of the Cistercians in Medieval England (1128–1307)', *A.S.O.C.*, Annus XIII (1957), 47–8.

[4] E.g. *Statuta* 1235, 33, 52—pastures: 1233, 41—granges: 1230, 25; 1250, 18—animals.

[5] B.M. Harl. Ch. 44 A 14.

[6] Combe Cart., B.M. Vit. A I, fols. 60ʳ, 60ᵛ.

[7] *Dieulacres Cart.*, 356, no. 172.

[8] Ibid., 356–7, no. 173.

[9] Pipewell Cart., B.M. Stowe MS. 937, fols. 93ᵛ, 94ʳ.   [10] Ibid., fols. 157ᵛ, 158ʳ.

[11] Ibid., fols. 156ᵛ, 157ʳ.   [12] *Statuta* 1216, 53.

empowered to enforce the sentence, and in 1209 the general chapter announced that abbots, who were chosen as judges-delegate, should arrange for the enforcement of their sentences.[1] Those who carried out sentences were granted certain powers by the general chapter: they could punish by excommunication.[2] Abbots who did not keep sentences might be threatened with deposition. Five times the abbot of Carracedo (dioc. Astorga, Spain) was ordered to pay a debt to the abbot of Bégard (dioc. Tréguier, Brittany, France): the fifth time he was threatened with deposition and this seems to have been effective.[3] The same elaborate precautions for the retention of compositions and decisions, were taken, as with the papacy. Chirographs were made.[4] Confirmations were sought and issued from the general chapter.[5] Penalties for non-observance were recounted in the final *actum*, and often the following clause was included:

'Sed si aliquis sive monachus sive conversus hinc inde convictus fuerit quod formam istius pacis transgressus fuerit absque retractatione penam sustineat in compositione inter Fontan' (Fountains, Yorks.) et Belland' (Byland, Yorks.) prius facta contentam et omni sexta feria per annum sit in pane et aqua',

or

'Si quis autem monachus vel conversus de Stanle (Stanley, Wilts.) vel de Bello loco regis (Beaulieu, Hants.) hanc formam pacis imposterum turbaverit a domo propria eliminetur non reversurus nisi de consensu utriusque domus'.[6]

In an instance where both parties objected to a sentence, they were ordered to come to the general chapter the next year, but meanwhile to obey it.[7]

There are intimations that sentences were not always observed. Disagreement sometimes broke out again, as was bound to happen with a certain number of cases.[8] In 1235 the abbot and convent of Neath (Glam.) complained that Margam (Glam.) was not observing a sentence.[9] In a 1279 settlement, which was made at Kirkstall (Yorks.) it was recorded:

'Et quia secundum jus canonicum nulla est jurisdictio sine cohercione, statuerunt dicti judices omnia tam in priorum judicum processu (1249–1251) quam in presenti sua ordinatione contenta ab omnibus utriusque

---

[1] *Statuta* 1209, 1; and see 1216, 16; 1229, 20.
[2] *Statuta* 1251, 73.
[3] J.-B. Mahn, op. cit., 215; *Statuta* 1209, 8; 1210, 7; 1211, 7; 1212, 16; 1213, 5.
[4] Pipewell Cart., B.M. Stowe MS. 937, fols. 93ᵛ, 94ʳ—(an out-of-court arrangement).
[5] *Statuta* 1216, 46, 53.
[6] Byland Cart., B.M. Egerton MS. 2823, fol. 78ᵛ; Beaulieu Cart., B.M. Cott. MS. Nero A XII, fol. 40ᵛ.
[7] *Statuta* 1254, 24.
[8] Beaulieu Cart., B.M. Cott. MS. Nero A XII, fol. 41ᵛ; Combe Cart., B.M. Vit. A I, fol. 68ʳ; Pipewell Cart., B.M. Calig. A XIII, fols. 158ʳ, 158ᵛ, 159ʳ, 159ᵛ.
[9] *Statuta* 1235, 31.

domus professoribus firmiter et perpetualiter observari, sub pena excommunicationis quam auctoritate a Capitulo generali sibi commissa in scriptis fulminarunt in quemlibet utriusque domus professum tam priorum quam posteriorum judicum ordinationem infringentem a nemine nisi a domino abbate Cisterc' absolvendum'.[1]

In spite of the smallness of Cistercian jurisdiction, the intense difficulties of communication meant that the strongest party might prevail against a judicial settlement which did not suit it. Cistercian houses were at a distance from one another, and the abbots who had been charged with enforcing the decision might be out of England when needed. The lack of permanent officials concerned with the execution of sentences probably contributed in part to the non-observance of some decrees, but such documentary evidence as remains would not justify a conclusion that the authority of the Cistercian general chapter was frequently disregarded.

The most obvious effect on the papacy of the holding of general chapters by many of the religious orders was that it lessened the increasing work of the papal court of justice and its subsidiaries. The general chapters appeared at the same time as a tremendous expansion was taking place in papal justice. The Cistercians borrowed much from the papal legal and judicial system. Cîteaux repaid its debt. In but one small way, the Cistercian jurisdiction produced suitable judges-delegate for the *ad hoc* papal courts: on a larger scale, the Cistercian judicial machine prolonged the time when the order had power to revive and influence the Universal Church.

[1] Fountains Cart., B.M. Add. MS. 40009, fols. 196ᵛ, 197ʳ, 197ᵛ, 198ʳ; *The Chartulary of the Cistercian Abbey of St. Mary of Sallay*, op. cit., no. 412.

VI

MONASTIC ARCHDEACONS

THIS paper seeks to examine the history and establishment of the four major monastic archdeaconries in England – St Albans, Glastonbury, Bury St Edmunds and Westminster – and to investigate the jurisdiction and administration of the monastic archdeacon.

I

The first stage in the establishment of an exempt area of this kind was the development of a religious cult and the land endowment of the church at the cult centre. The second stage, the confirmation (royal, papal, episcopal and popular) of the cult and of the lands, brought the precise definition of the territory and rights of the church. The four monasteries developed notably different rights at widely different times and exhibit various historical features. All had considerable pre-Conquest endowments, but the abbey of Westminster stands out from the three others as having no pre-Conquest cult, and hence no early sanctuary area where the peace of the saint operated. All the cults were associated with British or English saints, but at Westminster the post-Conquest cult of Edward the Confessor (and English kingship) followed the land endowment, which, ironically, had been made principally by the future recipient of the cult. Two of the cult centres, St Albans and Glastonbury, were probably on or near pagan religious sites, but whilst at St Albans the cult was clear-cut and the endowment followed, at Glastonbury the generally accepted venerability of the place brought gifts before a suitable cult was found, and even then, in contrast to the other three centres, there were several cults – St Patrick, St Benignus, St Bridget and St Indracht from the tenth century and the Holy Thorn and the Holy Grail from the late twelfth century – and the unsuccessful ones of Edgar and his father, Edmund, king of the West Saxons, which 'never got off the ground'. Certain distinctions can be made, too,

between the development of these two early cults, of St Alban at
St Albans in the first part of the fifth century and of St Patrick and
others at Glastonbury in the early tenth century, and those later
developed in the eleventh and twelfth centuries at Bury (St Edmund)
and Westminster. At St Albans and Glastonbury the royal territorial
endowment began very early and was associated, probably not totally
unhistorically, with Offa (757–96) at St Albans and with Ine (680–726)
at Glastonbury. Here the archidiaconal rights were later exercised over
comparatively large territorial areas, whereas at Westminster and Bury,
where the endowment was made between the mid-tenth and mid-
eleventh century, principally by Edward the Confessor and Cnut, the
area of the monastic archdeaconry was much more restricted.[1]

The confirmation and establishment of the land endowment – the
acceptance of the *seigneurie* of the saint[2] – was clearly necessary before
archidiaconal jurisdiction could be established. Ordinary archidiaconal
jurisdiction pre-supposes a reasonably advanced diocesan system.
Although the office of archdeacon was known by the ninth century, the
ordinary archdeaconry, as an established institution in all dioceses, was a
post-Conquest arrangement. This was probably the achievement of
Lanfranc, but territorialisation did not develop generally until the mid-
twelfth century.[3] There is no evidence of a monastic archdeaconry
before the eleventh century.[4] The existence of the monastic archdeacon
and acceptance of his (or his abbot's) position, as wielding very extensive
ecclesiastical powers, was to depend on the confirmation and acceptance

[1] On the two early cults at St Albans and Glastonbury, see W. Levison, 'St Alban and St Albans',
Antiquity, xv (1941), 337–59; C. A. Ralegh Radford in *The Quest for Arthur's Britain*, ed. G.
Ashe (London, 1968), pp. 119–38; H. P. R. Finberg, 'St Patrick at Glastonbury', *West-Country
Historical Studies* (Newton Abbot, 1969), pp. 70–88; and J. Armitage Robinson, 'William
of Malmesbury "On the Antiquity of Glastonbury"', *Somerset Historical Essays* (London, 1921),
pp. 1–25; and, for some pertinent remarks in general, Janet Nelson, 'Royal Saints and Early
Medieval Kingship', *Studies in Church History*, x (1973), 39–44. On sanctuary, see J. C. Cox,
The Sanctuaries and Sanctuary Seekers of Medieval England (London, 1911), esp. pp. 41, 86, 202–3
and 209–10; and for the land endowment of the four houses, see P. H. Sawyer, *Anglo-Saxon
Charters*, Royal Historical Society Guides and Handbooks, viii (1968) (hereafter cited as *Anglo-
Saxon Chs.*).
[2] See R. Génestal, 'La Patrimonialité de l'archidiaconat', *Mélanges Paul Fournier*, Bibliothèque
d'histoire du droit (Paris, 1929), p. 291; J-F. Lemarignier, *Étude sur les privilèges d'exemption
et de juridiction ecclésiastique des abbayes normandes*, Archives de la France Monastique, xliv
(Paris, 1937), 116. Génestal showed that the monastic archdeaconries were established generally
where the monks were also proprietors of the lands.
[3] F. M. Stenton, *Anglo-Saxon England* (Oxford, 1947), pp. 434 (on pre-Conquest archdeaconries)
and 668; and J. Scammell, 'The rural chapter in England from the eleventh to the fourteenth
century', *EHR*, lxxxvi (1971), 7, esp. n. 3, who cites all the evidence on territorialisation.
[4] U. Berlière, 'Les Archidiaconés ou exemptions privilégiées de monastères', *Revue Bénédictine*,
xl (1928), 116–22.

Monastic Archdeacons

of these privileged houses and their ecclesiastical liberties by the people
of the locality, by the diocesan, by the king and by the pope. The abbot
may have exercised these powers in person at first, but with the development of the corrective system, visitation, the courts and the law, he was
forced to delegate. The monastic archdeacon made his appearance in the
four abbeys in the years between 1071 and *c.* 1190, during the period of
the territorialisation of the ordinary archdeacon in the dioceses.

Bury St Edmunds

The area of the archdeacon's jurisdiction at Bury was small but
probably very ancient. It coincided with the *banleuca*,[5] which included
the abbey, the churches of St James and St Mary, three hospitals and
various chapels, the districts within the four crosses, Eyhtecros, Hold-
hawe, Weepingcross and a cross near Henhowe (or Heyecros).[6] The
documentary beginnings of the monastery's supreme powers over the
banleuca begin with Cnut's charter of 1028. The liberty of St Edmund
(8½ hundreds), which corresponded with West Suffolk, was territorially
enormous if compared with Glastonbury's liberty of the Twelve Hides
(about 2¼ square miles). The essential difference was that the Bury
monastic archdeacon had no jurisdiction there, but within the *banleuca*
he exercised secular and ecclesiastical powers, and Bury claimed an
exemption which Glastonbury never had. The very smallness of the
abbey of Bury's archidiaconal jurisdiction is more closely comparable in
extent with that of Westminster – over the immediate area, parts of the
palace, and the parish of St Margaret – to be explained, perhaps, by
their later endowment if compared with Glastonbury and St Albans.

There is no doubt that the archdeacons were monks, but from what
date is not clear. At Bury the office was, at least later, associated with the
extremely powerful one, within the town area, of sacrist of the abbey.
In Herman (*c.* 1070), author of the *Miracles of St Edmund*, we doubtless
have a monastic archdeacon and not a diocesan one.[7] The arch-

---

5 The *leuca*, or league, equalled the Gallic mile of 1500 paces and was slightly smaller than the
standard English mile. M. D. Lobel, 'The Ecclesiastical Banleuca in England', *Oxford Essays in
Medieval History presented to H. E. Salter*, ed. F. M. Powicke (Oxford, 1934), pp. 122–40.

6 See M. D. Lobel, *The Borough of Bury St Edmunds* (Oxford, 1935), p. 5, n. 8 and map of the
banleuca at the end. The four crosses, erected by the monks, are noted in a papal bull of 1172:
see W. Dugdale, *Monasticon Anglicanum*, ed. J. Caley & others (6 vols. in 8 parts, London,
1817–30), III, 99, and CUL. MS Ff 2. 29 (a fifteenth-century register of the liberties and jurisdictional rights of Bury), fo. 40.

7 *Ungedruckte Anglo-Normannische Geschichtsquellen*, ed. F. Liebermann (Strasburg, 1879), pp.
227, 231: the text of the *Miracles* is also in *Memorials of St Edmund's Abbey*, ed. T. Arnold, 3 vols.

deaconry appears to date from 1071, when Pope Alexander II came to Bury's rescue against the machinations of Arfast, bishop of Elmham, and the outlining of Bury's exemption might well account for the appointment of a monastic archdeacon at this time or soon after. It could be that Herman is in fact the first monastic archdeacon of Bury, whose office predates any occurrence of an archdeacon within Norwich diocese, and, by some years, the division of the archdeaconry of Suffolk into two, Suffolk and Sudbury, which has been attributed to Bishop Everard of Calne (1121–45).[8]

The importance of early documentation in the struggle for exemption from the diocesan is illustrated by the abbey of Bury.[9] The establishment of the see at Norwich in 1094 or 1095 obviated another immediate attack from that quarter, and the relations between the bishops of Norwich and the abbots of Bury seem to have been quite cordial.[10] This may serve to illustrate an early acceptance of Bury's sizeable rights (though confined in terms of the archdeaconry) and its peculiarly strong position *vis-à-vis* the crown. For of all four abbeys, the franchise of Bury was the greatest. The abbot had the return of writs, acted as coroner, held the shire court and had civil and criminal jurisdiction over the borough and its inhabitants;[11] and it could be argued that the abbot's spiritual powers as archdeacon within the

RS xcvi (London, 1890–6), I, 26–92. Thurstan and Tolinus appear to have been sacrists under the first post-Conquest abbot, Baldwin (Dugdale, *Mon. Angl.* III, 162 no. xxxii).

[8] See *Fasti Ecclesiae Anglicanae 1066–1300*, ed. D. E. Greenway, II (University of London, 1971), 61–9, esp. 61–2. The prior of Worcester exercised archidiaconal rights over the churches of the city belonging to the monks from at least 1092, according to R. R. Darlington, who treats Wulfstan's charter as 'beyond suspicion': *The Vita Wulfstani of William of Malmesbury*, Camden Soc. 3rd ser., XL (1928), p. xxxv, n. 2. At Durham, in 1093, William of St Calais committed the office of archdeacon to the prior: Simeon of Durham, *Historia Ecclesiae Dunhelmensis*, ed. T. Arnold, 2 vols. RS LXXV (London, 1882–5), I, 129.

[9] *The Pinchbeck Register*, ed. Lord F. Hervey (2 vols., privately printed, 1925) I, 3–4 (JL no. 4692); also printed in Migne, *PL*, cxlvi, cols. 1363–4. It is possible that this bull is a forgery, although the general and vague terms in which it is written are quite credible, and Bury certainly was accepted as having sizeable though ill-defined liberties early on (see Lobel, 'Banleuca', p. 129). Also the facts that the pope concerned in the issue was Alexander II (and it is difficult to see why a later forger should choose him), that the see was *not* established at Bury, and that the papacy was concerning itself with legislation about episcopal sees at this time, seem to me to make it convincing. V. H. Galbraith, 'The East Anglian See and the Abbey of Bury St Edmunds', *EHR*, XL (1925), 222–8; D. Knowles, 'The Growth of Exemption', *Downside Review*, L (N.S. xxxi, 1932), 209–11; and B. Dodwell, 'The Foundation of Norwich Cathedral', *TRHS*, 5th ser., VII (1957), 1–18, do not appear to doubt the bull on historical grounds. See also *PUE*, III, no. 8, and *Pinchbeck Reg.* I, 19–20.

[10] Jesus College, Cambridge, MS Q B 1 fo. 111v recites protests of Simon, bishop of Norwich, in 1263; of Henry, bishop of Norwich, in 1371; and of William, bishop of Norwich, in 1335 and 1344 against Bury's exempt jurisdiction, but in fact they could do little more than protest verbally.

[11] H. M. Cam, *Liberties and Communities in Medieval England* (London, 1963), pp. 186–95.

Monastic Archdeacons

borough were considerably less threatening to the diocesan than his secular powers in the $8\frac{1}{2}$ hundreds.

St Albans

Indirect evidence suggests an early origin for the archdeaconry of St Albans: otherwise it seems impossible to explain the alignment of the later archdeaconries within the see of Lincoln with the counties – Buckinghamshire, Bedfordshire, Huntingdonshire etc. – excluding Hertfordshire, the bulk of which formed the archdeaconry of St Albans, and whose remaining parishes, bordering Huntingdonshire, became absorbed in that archdeaconry after the death of Nicholas (who had borne the title of archdeacon of Cambridge, Huntingdon and Hertford) in 1110.[12]

However, the first occurrence of an archdeacon of St Albans is in 1129, at the time of the translation of St Alban by Abbot Geoffrey de Gorron (1119–46).[13] He thus precedes our first indication of the archdeaconry in the papal confirmation of 1157, where the liberty and archdeaconry of St Albans was defined as fifteen parishes: St Peter's, St Stephen's and Kingsbury in the town of St Albans, Watford, Rickmansworth, Abbots Langley, Redbourn, Codicote, St Paul's Walden, Hexton, Norton. Newnham, Barnet (all in Hertfordshire), and Winslow and Aston Abbots (both in Buckinghamshire).[14] During the thirteenth century the detached parts of the liberty and archdeaconry in Hertfordshire were absorbed into the hundred of St Albans (now called Cashio), with the exception of Caldecote adjoining Newnham. The central part of the archdeaconry consisted of an area about ten miles by ten miles in extent, roughly equivalent in size to that of Glastonbury.[15] It had, however, rather more parishes, some of

---

[12] *Fasti*, II, 50; Henry of Huntingdon, *Historia Anglorum*, ed. T. Arnold, RS LXXIV (London, 1879), 302. The Cambridgeshire archdeaconry was taken out of Lincoln with the foundation of the see of Ely in 1109.

[13] *Gesta Abbatum Monasterii Sancti Albani*, ed. H. T. Riley, 3 vols. RS XXVIII (London, 1867–9), I, 85–6.

[14] *PUE*, III no. 118; and see no. 459, Pope Celestine III's re-issue of the bull in 1193, where monks were specified for the office. At Evesham, however, it was a secular office from *c.* 1050 to the time of Thomas of Marlborough: D. Knowles, *The Monastic Order in England* (Cambridge, 1940), p. 606, n. 5.

[15] See for an outline indication *Map of Monastic Britain* South Sheet (Ordnance Survey, 1950); for more detail on the liberty and archdeaconry of St Albans, see the map in *Studies in Manorial History by A. E. Levett*, ed. H. M. Cam, M. Coate and L. S. Sutherland (Oxford, 1938), and for Glastonbury, O.S. 1-inch Map Sheet 165, on which the boundaries of the seven parishes can be clearly traced.

which were detached, unlike the sizeable Glastonbury parishes of Moorlinch and Middlezoy with their numerous chapelries. Situated at the far end of the enormous diocese of Lincoln, St Albans was in a strong position to resist the diocesan. It was not until the 1160s that Robert de Chesney challenged the extensive rights of the abbey, but was unsuccessful in the face of powerful papal bulls obtained by St Albans between 1122 and 1157.[16] The date of the transfer of the cathedral church from Dorchester to Lincoln in 1072 must have seemed a recent event to the monks of St Albans if they looked back at their long history; and St Albans liberty, one of the most powerful ecclesiastical liberties, grew rather than shrank during the Middle Ages. St Albans came nearer the exemption of certain major European houses than any other English community, and Abbot de la Mare's book of the fourteenth century shows no signs of St Albans relaxing its hold. Indeed the apogee of its pretensions was not reached until 1487, when John de Rothbury, archdeacon of St Albans, set out to claim episcopal powers for the abbot.[17]

Glastonbury

By the opening of the twelfth century Glastonbury probably exercised some jurisdiction over the seven large parishes which lay to its west, roughly between the rivers Brue and Parrett, but it is unlikely that there was any clear-cut definition of the jurisdiction. By 1129, William of Malmesbury was claiming ancient exemption for the monastery of Glastonbury.[18] In 1144 Lucius II confirmed to Glastonbury the surrounding islands – Beckery, Godney, Marchey, Panborough, Nyland and Farningmere;[19] and the vills of Street, Moorlinch, Butleigh, Shapwick and Zoy, with their churches and chapels.[20]

[16] See my article 'Papal Privileges for St Albans Abbey and its Dependencies' in *The Study of Medieval Records*, ed. D. A. Bullough and R. L. Storey (Oxford, 1971), pp. 64–5; and for the ordination of 1219, CUL. MS Ee 4.20 fo. 107v.

[17] Sayers, 'Papal Privileges for St Albans', pp. 72–8, 82.

[18] Lemarignier, *Privilèges d'exemption*, p. 200. It is doubtful, however, whether Malmesbury really accepted that the church of Glastonbury had been consecrated by Christ himself, and that consequently it could not be subject to the bishop, though he does repeat the story which was obviously in circulation at the time.

[19] Panborough was part of Meare, see G. B. Grundy, *The Saxon Charters and Field Names o Somerset*, Somerset Archaeol. and Natural History Soc. (1935), pp. 113–14. All the names suggest Saxon colonisation. 'Ey' or 'iey' means island.

[20] *The Great Chartulary of Glastonbury*, ed. A. Watkin, 3 vols., Somerset Record Soc. LIX, LXIII–IV (1947–52), no. 175 (hereafter cited as *Glastonbury Cart.*); Secretum = Bodleian, MS Wood empt. 1 (hereafter cited as S.) fos. 51v–2; and Trinity College, Cambridge, MS R 5 33 fos. 89v–90 ('Pie postulatio voluntatis'). This has some relationship to the spurious charter of

Monastic Archdeacons

Henry II's confirmation of 1154–89 added the churches of Pilton and Ditcheat.[21]

In about 1171, presumably after the death of the powerful Abbot Henry of Blois, Thomas, archdeacon of Wells, obviously fearing a rival archidiaconal jurisdiction, claimed possession of the churches. This led Abbot Robert of Glastonbury to make an agreement with the bishop that the churches of Glastonbury, Meare, Street, Moorlinch, Butleigh, Shapwick and Zoy, and three more, should form an archdeaconry to be administered by the abbot as archdeacon. In exchange for this concession, the church of South Brent was to be given to the archdeacon of Wells to form a prebend and the well-endowed church of Pilton to the bishop.[22] Such an arrangement, however, did not suit the community at Glastonbury and they appealed to Rome.

In 1189, when Henry de Soilli became abbot, he gave up the claim to archidiaconal jurisdiction over the three churches which had been added by Abbot Robert and relinquished Pilton, South Brent and Huish in return for an undisputed jurisdiction over the seven churches. The compromise was enshrined in Bishop Reginald's charter of 1191,[23] where the archdeaconry was clearly defined as consisting of the parishes of St John, Glastonbury, Meare, Street, Butleigh, Shapwick, Moorlinch and Zoy, which were to be exempt from the bishop's jurisdiction except in cases of appeal. Only the bishop could fulfil the essentially episcopal functions of institution, ordination, the dedication of churches and attending the solemn penitence of parishioners, but otherwise the monastic archdeacon of Glastonbury was to exercise full archidiaconal rights of visitation, induction and correction.[24]

The bounds of the Jurisdiction of Glastonbury, as described in 1334,[25] may have differed little from those accepted in 1191. It seems likely that

Ine, of supposedly 725 (*Anglo-Saxon Chs.* no. 250), which indicates the rights of the monks in the churches of 'Zoy', Brent, Moorlinch, Shapwick, Street, Butleigh and Pilton. It makes the extreme claim for them of excluding the bishop from any episcopal functions there. It seems likely that this charter was fabricated during the early years of the twelfth century, when what Finberg calls 'the fabulous tales of its antiquity' were circulated.

21 *Glastonbury Cart.* no. 302.
22 See Watkin in intro. to *Glastonbury Cart.* p. xxi; A. Morey, *Bartholomew of Exeter* (Cambridge, 1937), pp. 65–6; and *Calendar of the Manuscripts of the Dean and Chapter of Wells* I (Historical MSS Commission, 1907), p. 26.
23 Certainly post-1189 and before 27 November 1191, the date of the election of Bishop Reginald fitz Jocelin to Canterbury. If 1191, which Watkin seems to favour (p. xxi), this would fit closely into the historical background of Glastonbury's advancement.
24 *Glastonbury Cart.* no. 1; S. fo. 20; and Dugdale, *Mon. Angl.*, I, 28 no. xv. Also in Adam of Domerham: Thomas Hearne, *Adami de Domerham Historia de rebus gestis Glastoniensibus*, 2 vols. (Oxford, 1727), II, 345. 25 S. fo. 24.

the estate boundaries were settled at the time of endowment. The bounds of Zoy are given in Ine's charter of 725[26] and of Butleigh in Egbert's charter of 801.[27] Bounds are given for estates at Pennard in 681, possibly for Shapwick in 729 and at Baltonsborough in 744.[28] The only definition after the donations were made would have been caused by assarting in the thirteenth century. It seems likely, too, that the establishment of the parochial boundaries took place at the same time as the drawing of the estate boundaries and accorded with them.

The archdeacon of Glastonbury occurs in an unusual instance in 1215, when Jocelin, bishop of Bath and Glastonbury, who was also abbot of the house, and had hence appended Glastonbury to his title, issued a statute on the sequestration of vacant churches which naturally concerned his archdeacons. Here Thomas, archdeacon of Glastonbury, undoubtedly a monk,[29] appears in conjunction with the bishop's officers, the diocesan archdeacons of Wells, Bath and Taunton, as responsible for the seven churches.[30] The final establishment of the see at Bath and Wells in 1242 and the termination of the curious arrangement whereby two of the bishops of Bath were also abbots of Glastonbury (Savaric, 1193–1205, and Jocelin, 1206–42), with their cathedral at Glastonbury, removed the anomaly of a monastic archdeacon responsible to a diocesan who was also his abbot.[31] It also initiated prolonged attacks by the bishops of Bath and Wells. In the same year Glastonbury appealed to the pope, when a case from the archdeaconry was taken before the bishop.[32] Innocent IV's confirmations of Glastonbury's rights over the archdeaconry in 1245 and 1246 followed this case, but did not stop the attack.[33] Throughout the early fourteenth century

[26] *Anglo-Saxon Chs.* no. 251; H. P. R. Finberg, *The Early Charters of Wessex* (Leicester Univ. Press, 1964), no. 379; and see Grundy, *Saxon Charters and Field Names of Somerset*, pp. 116–18. Finberg cites the suggestion of Mr S. C. Morland that Zoy includes Weston Zoyland and Othery: if so, it would equate with the parish of Middlezoy which included these places as chapelries. The island and manor of Zoy or Sowy contained about 1850 acres of flood-free land and three main settlements: Michael Williams, *The Draining of the Somerset Levels* (Cambridge, 1970), p. 47. [27] *Anglo-Saxon Chs.* no. 270a; Dugdale, *Mon. Angl.*, I, 47 no. lxxxiv.
[28] *Anglo-Saxon Chs.* nos. 236 (Grundy, 75–7); 253 (Grundy, 114–16); and 1410 (Grundy, 61–4).
[29] For other Glastonbury archdeacons, all monks, see S. fo. 23v.
[30] *Councils and Synods*, ed. F. M. Powicke and C. R. Cheney, II, pt. 1 (Oxford, 1964), pp. 44–6.
[31] On Savaric Fitzgeldewin, Jocelin's predecessor, bishop of Bath and Glastonbury and also abbot of Glastonbury (1193–1205), see *The Heads of Religious Houses in England and Wales 940–1216*, ed. D. Knowles, C. N. L. Brooke and V. C. M. London (Cambridge, 1972), p. 52. Armitage Robinson in *Somerset Historical Essays*, p. 70, suggests that Jocelin abandoned the joint title of bishop of Bath and Glastonbury in 1219, but that is not the view of Knowles, etc.
[32] *Glastonbury Cart.* no. 12.
[33] *Ibid.*, nos. 9 and 180. His confirmation of the archdeaconry is also in Trinity College, Cambridge, MS R 5 33 fo. 93r-v (dat. 1245) and two pairs of it are referred to in the inventory of

Monastic Archdeacons

repeated attempts were made by the bishops to visit. Walter de Haselschawe (1299–1302), previously dean of Wells, tried to visit the church
of Weston Zoyland, but was prevented from entering either the
church or the manse of the rectory. Bishop John de Droxenforde
(1302–9) attempted to visit the church of Street, but his commissary
withdrew when he was shown the privileges of Glastonbury, declaring
to the assembled company, which included the abbot of Glastonbury:
'I see that you are not held to undergo our visitation, therefore I
withdraw.'[34] The full-scale visitation of the seven churches, mounted
by the commissaries of Bishop Ralph of Shrewsbury in 1334,[35] was the
occasion of an appeal to Rome and to the Court of Arches for tuition,
pending full investigation by the Holy See. Fifty years later, John,
bishop of Bath and Wells, confirmed Glastonbury's jurisdiction.[36]

The extraordinary persistence of the bishops of Bath and Wells
is to be explained by their proximity to the forum of confrontation,
and in particular by the convent of Glastonbury's lack of exemption
from episcopal control, which distinguished Glastonbury from the
other three monastic archdeaconries. In the circumstances of being
able to visit the monastery of Glastonbury, it was difficult for the
diocesans to believe that the seven parishes were exempt from their
control. There was no doubt, however, in the minds of the parishioners,
some of whom recalled in 1335 having seen the charter of Bishop
Reginald.[37]

Westminster

The charters used by Westminster in its establishment of an archidiaconal jurisdiction, and in its claims of liberty and exemption, were
the so-called charter of St Dunstan, the bull of Clement III (1189) and
the charter of Stephen Langton (1222).[38] The charter of St Dunstan
supposedly defined the precinct of St Peter's, marked by crosses and

Glastonbury deeds in the same register (fo. 78v); and see no. 6 where Alexander IV appointed
judges delegate to investigate the jurisdiction in 1261.
[34] S. fos. 24r-v, 25, and cf. *Calendar of the Register of John de Drokensford*, ed. Bishop Hobhouse,
Somerset Rec. Soc. I (1887), 159 (fo. 140v): stitched on to the original is a torn scrap of parchment, endorsed 'Visitatio Jurisd. Glaston.', and stating that at Street church, Bruton enquired
after the incumbents' exhibits, accepting that matters of conduct for the seven churches came
under the archdeacon of Glastonbury (see below pp. 190–1).
[35] S. fo. 24v. [36] Longleat Deed 10583.
[37] S. fos. 23, 25v. The jurisdiction of Glastonbury was accepted by the bishop at a visitation in
1385, see Hearne, *Domerham* I, 273, no. xxv.
[38] See W[estminster] A[bbey] M[uniments] Bk. I, fos. 138–9, and PRO. E 132/35 (nos. 3, 10,
15).

ditches (and hence the sanctuary area), within which priests and clerks were to be free from the payment of synodals and of Romescot. The charter is undoubtedly a forgery, as is the third charter of Edward the Confessor which mentions the immunity of the precinct and the cemetery of Westminster. Both belong to the batch of forgeries fabricated for the cause of the canonisation of Edward the Confessor in the 1140s, possibly by Osbert de Clare,[39] but there seems no reason to doubt the authenticity of the grant of Edgar which virtually outlined the archdeaconry, when he 'restored' an estate on the north side of the Thames between the Tyburn and the Fleet, to which Ethelred added a gift in 1002.[40] The canonisation of the Confessor on 7 February 1161 laid the way open for the bull of Clement III,[41] which spoke of the monastery precinct and of the church of St Margaret within the monks' cemetery, and the laymen and clerks within the same, as being free from the control of the diocesan, but the precise rights and area were not defined.

The charter of Stephen Langton of 1222 declared that the monastery of Westminster and the church of St Margaret, with its parish and all the chapels within the parish, with their tithes and appurtenances, and the clerks and laymen living within the parish should be exempt from all jurisdiction of the bishop of London. The boundaries of the parish of St Margaret were defined in 1222 as covering an area from the Tyburn to the Thames, along Watling Street (Oxford Street–High Holborn) to the hospital of St Giles, Holborn, and down to the Strand and Charing in one direction (excluding the church and cemetery of St Martin), and to the mound south west of Horseferry Road and down to the Thames in the other direction.[42]

Although an archdeacon of Westminster is not mentioned by name until 1246,[43] the office presumably existed before then, perhaps origi-

---

[39] *Anglo-Saxon Chs.* no. 104. See P. Chaplais, 'The Original Charters of Herbert and Gervase Abbots of Westminster (1121–1157)', *A Medieval Miscellany for D. M. Stenton*, ed. P. M. Barnes and C. F. Slade, Pipe Roll Soc., N.S. XXXVI (1960), 89–110. It was Tait who spoke of Westminster as a 'factory of forgeries' in 'An Alleged Charter of William the Conqueror', *Essays in History presented to Reginald Lane Poole*, ed. H. W. C. Davis (Oxford, 1927), pp. 158–9, n. 2.

[40] *Anglo-Saxon Chs.* nos. 670 (date much disputed but almost certainly not 951, as specifically dated, and probably after 959) and 903. See M. Gelling, 'The Boundaries of the Westminster Charters', *Transactions of the London and Middlesex Archaeol. Soc.*, N.S., XI, pt. 2 (1953), 101–4, who gives translations of the bounds and a map.

[41] *PUE* I, no. 262; and see D. Knowles, 'Parochial Organization', *Downside Review*, LI (1933), 514–15.

[42] WAM 12753: printed *Acta Stephani Langton*, ed. K. Major, CYS, L (1950), no. 54.

[43] Matthew Paris, *Chronica Majora*, ed. H. R. Luard, 7 vols. RS LVII (London, 1872–83), IV, 589.

Monastic Archdeacons

nating in the activities of Abbot Gervase (1138–c.1157) and the canonisation of Edward. The archdeacon exercised jurisdiction in the precincts, parish of St Margaret and parts of the palace, and was also the chief administrative officer of the sanctuary, although the sanctuary area at Westminster was not as extensive as the liberty or archdeaconry. At Bury, the *banleuca*, within which there was sanctuary,[44] was distinct from the liberty as a whole, but coincided with the archdeaconry. The sanctuary area at Westminster was about the same size, extending from King Street to Tothill Street down to Strutton Ground and Horseferry Road.[45] The sacred character of sanctuary to the medieval mind is well illustrated by the words of one of the writs of Abbot Gilbert demanding sanctuary, which states that the fugitive had sought 'the altar of St Peter and the body of King Edward'.[46]

The case of Westminster is closer to Glastonbury than to Bury and St Albans, although the house enjoyed exemption from the diocesan. This, however, was not clarified until Langton's settlement of 1222,[47] and the proximity to Westminster of the cathedral church of London meant that the bishop was never far away and had to be constantly reminded of the limitations of his power. Furthermore, the 1222 settlement had no reason to deal with the extent of the archdeacon's rights over the palace of Westminster and St Stephen's chapel which posed problems beyond that of control by the ordinary.

The rights of the palace of Westminster and St Stephen's chapel were extremely complex. The account of the serving of a citation on the countess of Warenne within the palace of Westminster, by the archdeacon of Norfolk and his official in 1420, refers to the palace as the 'most solemn' place of the kingdom, sited within the liberty of the church of Westminster. The crown defended Westminster's claims, declaring that no archbishop, bishop or other person, whosoever he might be, might exercise ordinary jurisdiction there, and the action of

---

[44] Lobel, *Borough*, p. 144. The evidence seems to suggest that it was a confirmation of an old custom, rather than an innovation, as Mrs Lobel suggests, when the burgesses sought that the borough as well as the abbey should be an asylum.

[45] N. H. MacMichael, 'Sanctuary at Westminster', *Westminster Abbey Occasional Papers*, XXVII (1971), 9–14; and see M. B. Honeybourne, 'The Sanctuary Boundaries and Environs of Westminster Abbey and the College of St Martin-le-Grand', *Journal of the British Archaeol. Assoc.*, XXXVIII, pt. 2 (1933), 316–33; I. D. Thornley, 'Sanctuary in Medieval London', *ibid.*, 293–315; and Lobel, 'Ecclesiastical Banleuca', pp. 123, 125.

[46] See J. Armitage Robinson, *Gilbert Crispin* (Cambridge, 1911), p. 37. During the course of the Peasants' Revolt of 1381, one fugitive was dragged from a pillar of St Edward's shrine, and, according to the Westminster chronicler, the failure of the revolt was due to St Edward's outrage at this insult (Thornley, 'Sanctuary', p. 299, n. 1).   [47] WAM 12753.

the Norwich officials resulted in their summary committal to the Tower of London on the grounds that they must have known of the abbot of Westminster's rights.[48] The Customary of St Peter's refers to the archdeacon as being permitted to go freely to the palace and the other parts of the 'vill' of Westminster in the exercise of his duties, holding chapters and courts.[49] The rights over St Stephen's chapel within the palace were disputed intermittently until the compromise of 1394, when the abbot secured the right of inducting the dean of St Stephen's on the king's presentation, arranging certain processions and giving licence for celebrating in the oratories within the palace. Presumably his archdeacon had the usual rights over the personnel of St Stephen's chapel resident within the palace of Westminster.[50]

II

There are few surviving records of the activities of the monastic archdeacons in England. St Albans has some miscellaneous court *acta*, dating from 1425 to 1446;[51] act books and a deposition book, covering the years 1515 to 1543;[52] and testamentary material from 1415.[53] At Westminster there are some forty deeds concerning the archdeaconry, of which three are original *acta* of the archdeacon.[54] For Bury there survives the important formulary-book of William of Hoo, sacrist and monastic archdeacon from 1280 to 1294,[55] and testamentary material

[48] WAM Mun. Bk. 1, fo. 139 (PRO. E 132/35 no. 20) and WAM 5977.

[49] *Customary of the Benedictine Monasteries of St Augustine, Canterbury, and St Peter, Westminster*, ed. Sir E. M. Thompson, 2 vols., Henry Bradshaw Soc., XXIII and XXVIII (London, 1902 and 1904), II, 95; and see PRO. E 132/35, no. 19, and below p. 196.

[50] WAM Mun. Bk. 1 fos. 127, 139; and fos. 118–24 (the composition of 1394).

[51] This is contained in fos. 71 to 76b *verso* of the first surviving register of wills, Register Stoneham, in the Hertfordshire County Record Office. It occupies sixteen pages, and was obviously erroneously bound up in the middle of William of Wallingford's probate of wills, which continue in the same hand. Furthermore, the entries for Stephen London have been copied where there were blanks – on fos. 71v, last entry, 72, continuation of previous entry, and end of 76a recto.   [52] Herts. County Record Office ASA 7/1, 7/2, 8/1.

[53] Archdeacon Hale gives 1408, and he had apparently seen wills dating from 1412, see W. H. Hale, *A Series of Precedents and Proceedings in Criminal Causes...from...1475 to 1640...from Act-Books of Ecclesiastical Courts in the Diocese of London* (London, 1847), p. xxxi, but they no longer exist, at least with the main deposit of records at Hertford.

[54] WAM 5981 has an impression of a fourteenth-century archdeacon's (John Borewell's) seal. E. H. Pearce, *The Monks of Westminster* (Cambridge, 1916), p. 4, n. 4, records that a die was made from Borewell's seal for ceremonial use, being handed to the archdeacon in chapter at his annual election. The office of archdeacon of Westminster continues, nominally at least.

[55] BL Harley MS 230, ed. A. Gransden, *The Letter-Book of William of Hoo Sacrist of Bury St Edmunds 1280–1294*, Suffolk Records Soc., V (1963). Jesus College, Cambridge, MS Q B 1 is a fifteenth-century Bury formulary related to this.

188

Monastic Archdeacons

from 1354. For Glastonbury there is some relevant material in the *Secretum* or personal register of Abbot Walter de Monington.[56] The reason for the lack of court records of the monastic archdeacon in England is apparently their uselessness in the post-Reformation period, following the dissolution of the abbeys and their archdeaconries. This explains the better survival of St Albans records, whose archdeaconry continued within the diocese of London from 1550, whereas Westminster's archidiaconal jurisdiction vanished with the extinction of the short-lived see of Westminster in the same year.

How did the monastic archdeacon compare with the diocesan archdeacon? It seems likely that the ordinary archdeacon had assumed the two basic functions of visitation and correction and certain administrative duties by the thirteenth century, and this is probably true of the monastic archdeacon, a detailed account of whose powers and duties, as accepted in the fourteenth century, is to be found in the *Secretum*. The archdeacon visits the parishes within his jurisdiction annually and enquires about the fabric and ornaments of the churches and the condition of both clergy and laity. He proceeds *ex officio*; he also accepts instance cases. His competence is over the whole field of ecclesiastical cases: marriage, perjury, breach of faith, adultery, cases concerning testaments, laying violent hands on clerks, usury, worshipping evil spirits, witchcraft and defamation; and he may accept instance cases from parties within the jurisdiction, and from plaintiffs outside, provided that the defendant is living or staying within his jurisdiction. He imposes punishments: penances, suspension from office, interdicts and excommunication; and he absolves from the same. He celebrates monthly chapters in the archdeaconry and he examines clerks for ordination.[57]

The process of archidiaconal visitation is only obliquely referred to in the monastic archdeaconries, but it was certainly exercised. Elias le clerk of Weston Zoyland recalled Brother Edmund Barri, archdeacon of Glastonbury in the 1290s, imposing penances for *comperta* revealed at

[56] Bodleian, MS Wood empt. 1 (cited as S.). If this book was made for Walter de Monington then ?1341-2, and not 1340-2 as dated by Watkin (*Glastonbury Cart.* pp. x–xi). Watkin, however, believes it to be associated with John de Breynton. Can there be an identification between the *Secretum* and the register of John de Breynton which is referred to in the Feodary?

[57] S. fos. 23–23v, 25v, 26, 26v, 28. Cf. the account in 'The Friar's Tale', *The Complete Works of Geoffrey Chaucer*, ed. W. W. Skeat (Oxford, 1894), p. 359, which is remarkably similar. Geoffrey Chaucer (born *c.* 1340) began writing *The Canterbury Tales* between 1386 and 1387. On the chapter, see Scammell, 'Rural Chapter', p. 1.

his visitation.[58] Visitation was the time, too, when records were 'exhibited', the clergy producing their title deeds, letters of ordination and dispensations. According to Lyndwood, archidiaconal visitation was annual.[59] At visitations the archdeacon took procurations, which were the payments made to support the visitor in lieu of board and lodgings, or he accepted hospitality. The archdeacon also held synods to supervise the clergy and instruct them, but it was in the chapters, or private sessions of them, that correction of the clergy usually took place.[60]

At St Albans the abbot celebrated a synod of his own clerics from the fifteen churches twice a year.[61] The right to hold synods was an essential part of the archidiaconal powers and William Thorne attacked Abbot Scotland of St Augustine's Canterbury as being too complaisant in agreeing that the priests of their churches should attend the primate's synod.[62] The method of holding a synod is described for the Bury jurisdiction. The dean is ordered to cite the priests, chaplains, and others in holy orders, numbering fifteen persons from St Mary's parish, fifteen from St James's, two each from the hospital of God and of St Saviour, and three each from the hospitals of St Michael and of St Peter. All then swore oaths to be obedient to the abbot and to the sacrist. The mass of the holy spirit was celebrated, the litany sung, a sermon preached and the gospel 'I am the good shepherd' read, followed by the hymn *Veni creator spiritus*, and then the priests exhibited their letters of orders. Lastly the synodal constitutions were declared, which all had to accept.[63]

Witnesses in a case concerning the archidiaconal jurisdiction of Glastonbury which came before the Court of Arches refer specifically to the archdeacon's right to examine clerks seeking ordination. If the archdeacon approved the candidates, they were presented to the bishop. Without any further examination the bishop then conferred orders on the candidates. William Hardi of Zoy confirmed the testimony of Sir John Tys, saying that this was the procedure when his son was ordained. Nicholas Thynne of Othery, possibly a clergyman and literate, remembered being present in Bruton church in 1319 for an ordination when one of the candidates, who had not been approved by the archdeacon, was refused ordination by the bishop.[64] A further witness, Richard

[58] S. fo. 23v; and for Edmund Barri, see Longleat MS 10590 fo. 36.
[59] Plentiful material and exhortations in *Councils* (e.g. II, pt. I, 128) show the willingness of the archdeacons to visit. See also X. I tit.xxiii c.6 (Alexander III) and Scammell, 'Rural Chapter', p. 15.   [60] Scammell, 'Rural Chapter', pp. 14–15.   [61] *Gesta Abbatum*, I, 158.
[62] *William Thorne's Chronicle of St Augustine's Abbey Canterbury*, trans. A. H. Davis (Oxford, Basil Blackwell, 1934), pp. 54–6.   [63] BL Harley MS 645 fo. 87r–v.
[64] S. fos. 25v, 26, 26v.

Monastic Archdeacons

Phelip of Moorlinch, recalled being present in the parish church of Zoy at Easter 1310, when a certain Thomas de Boteleigh, clerk, presented himself to the bishop of Bath and Wells in the chancel, duly robed for ordination to the priesthood. But not having been approved by the archdeacon of Glastonbury, Brother John of Worcester, he was refused ordination until he should be presented by the archdeacon to the bishop.[65] Institution belonged to the bishop of Bath and Wells in the jurisdiction of Glastonbury, but induction into corporal possession of the living was the right of the abbot and convent of Glastonbury and hence the monastic archdeacon.[66] Abbot de la Mare's formulary includes an example of the abbot ordering the archdeacon of St Albans to induct into a benefice in the exempt jurisdiction, and Archdeacon Alnwick inducted the vicar of Redbourn and the rector of Bushey in 1430.[67] Induction was apparently the occasion when the parson swore to inform the archdeacon of punishable (and lucrative) misdemeanours in the parish.[68] It was also the occasion for the archdeacon to levy a fee from the inducted man.

The jurisdiction of the archdeacon over the clergy, though possibly not older than his jurisdiction over the laity in spiritual cases, can be traced back only very tentatively to the Northumbrian Priests' Law.[69] But it quite clearly developed with the growth of the canon law and the concessions of royal government (especially the Conqueror's ordinance) from the late eleventh century onwards. Those clergy who fell short of the requirements were the obvious prey of the archdeacons, both ordinary and monastic, and there is nothing to distinguish between the activities of the two here, except that parochial clergy subject to the supervision of the monastic archdeacon were usually subject to his house as patron. Three St Albans cases reveal the condition of the clergy. 'Ex officio' *acta* before Archdeacon Alnwick in 1434 concerned John Mey, once chaplain of St Peter's church, St Albans, who agreed that he was guilty of revealing the confession of Robert Hyllary, clerk of the church, and also of public defamation; he was suspended from celebrating and later absolved.[70] A charge, doubtless brought at visitation,

---

[65] S. fo. 28. [66] S. fo. 25.

[67] CUL MS Ee 4.20 fo. 32v; and Reg. Stoneham fo. 74, 74v; and see *PUE*, III, no. 327.

[68] Scammell, 'Rural Chapter', pp. 16–17, citing Gerald of Wales; and see Reg. Stoneham fo. 74 for the parson's oath on institution.

[69] *English Historical Documents c. 500–1042*, ed. D. Whitelock (London, 1955), no. 53, pp. 434–9.

[70] Reg. Stoneham fo. 75b recto. Cf. A. T. Bannister, 'Visitation Returns of the diocese of Hereford in 1397', *EHR*, XLIV (1929), 288, another case of revealing a confession. Hyllary's confession was that the woman living with him was not his wife. Parish clerks were not supposed

by certain parishioners of Chipping Barnet against their rector, John Smyth, alleged that he was lax in hearing confessions, that he did not celebrate in the parish of East Barnet and the chapel of Chipping Barnet on Sundays and feast days, and that he did not ring the bells for mass. The rector defended himself, before Abbot Wheathampstead in his greater chamber, declaring that he supplied chaplains in his stead, and he countercharged that his parishioners did not pay their tithes.[71] There is no record as to whether the rector brought an instance case against the parishioners, but the countercharge shows the way in which archidiaconal business, based on the probe of visitation, may have snowballed.[72] Charges were brought against Nicholas Grene, vicar of Abbots Langley, for not serving his cure and for non-residence. He was finally deprived.[73]

From very early times a large part of the archdeacon's work was associated with the correction of sexual offences, such as incontinency, fornication and adultery. Two confessions of incontinency, made in the presence of Thomas Pyk, archdeacon of Westminster, may have originated from visitation returns and from *publica fama*.[74] They doubtless led on to correction, which entailed a penance. The penance usually consisted of a whipping. The archdeacon did not stop, however, at enforcing beatings for sexual offences. The physical assaults on guilty parishioners would be accompanied by fines. The amounts involved have left no record and the sources are reticent about penances. Before the Conquest, secular penalties were specified for almost all ecclesiastical crimes, including sexual offences, and these were usually fines. The 'pecunial torment', to which Chaucer referred, implies payment of fines on top of a penance which would have left no record. Later sources refer clearly to fines as well as penances in *ex officio* cases.[75] A frequent form of penance in the monastic archdeaconries entailed

to be married, but there seems no knowledge of that in this case: see C. E. Woodruff, 'Some Early Visitation Rolls preserved at Canterbury', *Archaeologia Cantiana*, xxxii (1917), 149.

[71] Reg. Stoneham fo. 71v. The vicar of Erdesley was brought before the bishop for allowing two women to help him celebrate and ring the bells: Bannister, 'Visitation', *EHR*, xlv (1930), 447.

[72] There is an example of an instance suit between Robert Smyth, farmer of the rectory of St Stephen's, and Sir John Forthe, vicar of St Stephen's and farmer of the rectory of St Julian, in the same register (Reg. Stoneham fo. 71), heard by the archdeacon.

[73] Reg. Stoneham fo. 72v.

[74] WAM 5974–5: recorded in documentary form and sealed by the archdeacon.

[75] See A. Gransden, 'Some late thirteenth century records of an ecclesiastical court in the archdeaconry of Sudbury', *BIHR*, xxxii (1959); R. Peters, *Oculus Episcopi. Administration of the Archdeaconry of St Albans 1580–1625* (Manchester University Press, 1963), p. 62. In S. (fos. 23v, 24), for example, the witnesses refer to the imposition of penances by the Glastonbury archdeacon, but never to what they actually consisted of.

Monastic Archdeacons

making an offering to the feretory of the shrine – usually imposed when clergy were involved. When William of Hoo imposed a penance on a rector for incontinency and for refusing purgation, thus admitting guilt, he required him to visit the shrine of St Edmund and offer one wax candle of three pounds' weight at the feretory, and to feed five poor men on the following Friday.[76] Similarly, offerings to the feretory of St Alban were ordered in early-sixteenth century cases of fornication in that archdeaconry.[77] Clearly these offences were seen as offences against the saint, who had to be recompensed and who alone could give absolution. More sinister than the payments connected with correction, but understandable and apparently common, were the payments made to the archdeacon to stay his hand.[78] The degradation of these physical punishments must have always been felt and commutation increasingly sought by those who could afford to pay.[79]

The sizeable marriage jurisdiction of the archdeacon has left little visible record. It is possible that at first the monastic archdeacon was concerned with correction and that the definite right to hear cases was not accorded to him until the twelfth century, when the law had developed considerably. In 1189 Pope Clement III licensed the abbot of Bury to hear matrimonial cases in parishes belonging to the monastery.[80] Did this mean that the abbot had at first not exercised this power, or that it had to be specified in the case of a monastic archdeaconry which had very early, and hence ill-defined, rights? In the case of an archdeaconry, like Glastonbury, which was defined later, the right was clearly there for the archdeacon to hear cases, subject to appeal to the bishop after sentence. For Glastonbury, when the bishop of Bath and Wells was attacking the jurisdiction in the fourteenth century, witnesses came forth from the parishes to tell of the cases which they remembered the archdeacon hearing between the 1290s and the 1330s. Thirteen of the seventeen cases concerned marriage and were apparently instance cases. Divorce[81] was granted on the grounds of precontract, bigamy, impotence, unlawful sexual inter-

---

[76] Jesus College MS QB1 fos. 25v–26.   [77] ASA 7/1 fos. 6, 7.

[78] Scammell, 'Rural Chapter', pp. 17–18. Doubtless the bribes which the archdeacons were counselled not to accept were usually for this purpose.

[79] For commutation, see Peters, *Oculus Episcopi*, pp. 29, 76, and B. L. Woodcock, *Medieval Ecclesiastical Courts in the Diocese of Canterbury* (Oxford, 1952), p. 75.

[80] *PUE*, III, no. 416.

[81] Divorce was only absolute, 'a vinculo matrimonii', as in our sense, if it could be proved that there had never been a valid contract; otherwise, it was a separation, 'a mensa et thoro', as for adultery. The word *divorcium*, however, was used indiscriminately.

course with a relative of the other party (usually daughter) before marriage, and adultery. Four of these cases hinged on precontract.[82] The case of Joan Kympton and Nicholas Brunne, which came before the archdeacon of Westminster, was a clear case of bigamy as Joan's husband, William Twyford, was declared to be still alive and hence her liaison with Nicholas was illegal.[83] A divorce was granted to Alice Cole of Weston Zoyland on the grounds of the impotence of her husband, and to Margaret Colin and to Elena on the grounds of their husbands having had intercourse with their daughters.[84]

These were instance cases between freemen and women which were brought before the archidiaconal court. In the case of St Albans, the archdeacon of the abbey was not allowed competence to deal with the matrimonial affairs of villeins – these belonged to the cellarer.[85] Although there is no direct evidence, jurisdiction over free tenants only is likely for the other monastic archdeaconries. In the whole area of marriage jurisdiction, however, we should be wary of interpreting all cases between parties as instance jurisdiction. As has been pointed out, the distinction between office and instance cases was fine and we may well imagine that some of these cases came to light as a result of visitation. On the surface we have defended suits, but underlying this may be clerical and communal instigation. The apparitor and the clergy were known to promote cases.[86] The sentence of divorce, pronounced *ex officio* in the conventual church of St Albans in 1428, is presumably an example of clerical instigation, and, if it really was *ex officio*, illustrates that the Church could not overlook adultery even if the offended partner could.[87] Cases of correction, of adultery for example, might well lead on to divorce between the offended party and the offender. Contrariwise, an instance case for divorce on grounds of adultery or bigamy would obviously lead to correction of the offender unless he managed to flee the archdeaconry.[88]

[82] S. fos. 25, and 25v–26.   [83] WAM 5989, 5990.
[84] S. fos. 23v, 25, 26. The reason for divorce is not given in the other Glastonbury cases on these folios, nor in a case before the archdeacon of St Albans: Jesus College MS Q B 1 fo. 124.
[85] *Studies in Manorial History by A. E. Levett*, p. 238.
[86] See Peters, *Oculus Episcopi*, p. 21; and for a clear case of initiation of proceedings by the parson, who, seeing his flock at work in the fields on a Sunday, summoned them to appear before the archdeacon's chapter: see R. Hill, 'A Berkshire Letter Book', *Berks. Archaeol. Journal*, XLI (1937), 23. For other instances of working on Sundays, which must always have roused the parson's wrath, see Gransden in *BIHR*, XXXII, and the numerous charges which occur in the records of the post-Reformation courts.   [87] Reg. Stoneham fo. 73.
[88] WAM 5989, 5990. WAM 5996 shows Peter Thebaud and Joan Malwayn, described as his wife, removing themselves from the city to the archdeaconry of Westminster to avoid answer-

Monastic Archdeacons

It seems likely that the profits from instance jurisdiction were considerably less than those from correction. Firstly the number of instance cases may well have been small.[89] Secondly, the profits probably went to the registrar and proctors and not to the owner of the jurisdiction.[90] No supporting evidence at all for the monastic archdeacons can be added to these suggestions, which have been made for the ordinary archdeacon during the later medieval period and beyond, and no accurate figures could be compiled without a run of the act books. The profits of correction of matrimonial and sexual offences are bound up with the profits of visitation. Protests were mainly against the profits from visitation and from correction, and the archdeacons were widely seen as enriching 'their own purses to the damage of poor people',[91] apparently from correction. There seems no way of estimating either, although the theory that the vigour of the archdeacons was based on their ultimate financial rewards seems outwardly acceptable.

There were also profits from the administration. The claim of the archdeacons of St Albans after 1539 to issue marriage licences, which was based on the rights of their predecessors, the monastic archdeacons,[92] was thought to be a lucrative one. By the sixteenth century, Archbishop Whitgift's table of fees for consistory courts stipulated half a mark for a licence to marry without banns, and it is possible that the fee was equally high during the medieval period.[93] No doubt, too, the certification of a marriage cost the parties something and marriages and the licences for them involved considerable profits.[94]

Controlling wills and testaments was basically an administrative function which brought profits. It is not known what probate fees were charged: probably they related to the value of the estate in

ing Margery Leget in a divorce case. They were, however, pursued by a letter of the commissary of the bishop of London. The definitive sentence of divorce pronounced by the archdeacon of St Albans between William Gosbyll and Elizabeth his wife in 'consistorio nostro' in 1446 on grounds of the adultery of William would have led to his correction, but there is no evidence of this because the records are so scanty (Reg. Stoneham fo. 71v).

[89] See Peters's figures for 1583 and 1588 (*Oculus Episcopi*, p. 51): 34 *ex officio*, 3 instance and 2 probate; and 17 *ex officio*, 1 instance and 1 probate.

[90] Woodcock (*Medieval Ecclesiastical Courts*, pp. 75–6) said that the archdeacon 'had no financial interest in the business of the court, apart from the fees charged for probate and small sums derived from the commutations of penance. Instance business could dwindle to zero without affecting his income'. He was, however, relieved of providing for his subordinates.

[91] Richard Burn, *Ecclesiastical Law* (4 vols., London, 1775), IV, 17 (William Lyndwood, *Provinciale* [Oxford, 1679], p. 224), citing Stratford's injunctions (Otto's injunctions printed on p. 16 of Burn imply the same). The extract continues 'it becometh not ecclesiastical persons to gape after or inrich themselves with dishonest and penal acquisitions'.

[92] Peters, *Oculus Episcopi*, pp. 11, 30–1.

[93] Burn, *Ecclesiastical Law*, II, 233. [94] e.g. WAM 5973.

question.[95] In the thirteenth century there are a number of complaints that they were excessive.[96] The account of the goods of William Paleys, weaver of Tothill Street, Westminster, made in 1468 on an estate amounting to £6 4s 3d, shows the property going into the hands of the archdeacon of Westminster.[97] Obviously he exacted his pound of flesh, which on the basis of a tenth would have been 12s 5d. When Thomas de Bykenor, knight, died in 1416 in the palace of Westminster, the archdeacon of Westminster examined and proved the will, and, out of the goods of the deceased in the palace amounting to £20, arranged for the obsequies and funeral. Doubtless he took his cut.[98]

Hale estimated the number of wills which were proved in the arch-deaconry of St Albans to have been roughly 380 between 1412 and 1439, hence about fourteen a year, and nearly 700 between 1505 and 1538, twenty-one a year.[99] The number of wills proved yearly between 1415 and 1470 averages twenty-eight a year.[100] Woodcock recorded probate fees for one year, 1505–6, for the Canterbury archdeacon. They amounted to £27 13s 4d,[101] and, although presumably in excess of those enjoyed by the archdeacon of St Albans, it may be noted that they came to nearly one-fifth of the archdeacon's total income. The proof of the will consisted of a note on the dorse and the addition of the archdeacon's seal,[102] and the registration of the will doubtless cost money.[103] At Bury there was considerable opposition to the arch-deacon's control of testamentary matters. His jurisdiction was felt to be extortionate, and in 1327 the abbot was forced to promise that no fee at all should be exacted either for probate, proclamation, acquit-tance or administration.[104] Whether this promise was kept can only be

---

[95] M. M. Sheehan, *The Will in Medieval England*, Pontifical Institute of Mediaeval Studies, Studies and Texts, VI (Toronto, 1963), p. 206 and n. 185, citing the provincial council of 1328, which stipulated that there was to be no fee on goods under 100s in value, and an incidence of a fee of 8d being charged in 1293 on an estate valued at 33s 8d.

[96] Woodcock, *Medieval Ecclesiastical Courts*, pp. 22–3; and see below.

[97] WAM 5983. [98] PRO. E 132/35 (no. 19), and WAM Mun. Bk. 1 fo. 139.

[99] Hale, *Precedents*, p. xxxi. It is difficult to know what he based these figures on, particularly as the dates do not accord with the registers. Reg. Stoneham, the first surviving register, begins in 1415 (and not 1408 as Hale states) and the earliest originals in the Herts. Record Office come from 1518 (a later copy) and 1540.

[100] My assessment is on Reg. Stoneham (1415–70), and on the basis of about six entries to a page (260 pp., 130 fos.).

[101] Woodcock, *Medieval Ecclesiastical Courts*, p. 75.

[102] Jesus College MS QB1 fo. 111.

[103] S. fo. 25v – Robert Kene of 'Lym' remembered the registering of the will of Robert Drove by the archdeacon, and that the same Drove had previously been divorced from his wife.

[104] Lobel, *Borough*, p. 43.

Monastic Archdeacons

surmised: if so, the archdeacon may have managed to levy sufficient sums from other sources.

The close watch which was normally kept on the administration of wills is an indication of the profits which could accrue to the owner of the jurisdiction. In 1304 the official of the archdeacon of London wrote to the archdeacon of Westminster asking him to summon peremptorily Alice, widow and executrix of Robert, the king's tailor, who had 'fraudulently transferred' to the archdeaconry of Westminster, to render account of her administration of the will, and also to answer Elias, rector of St Mary Aldermary, the rector of St James, Garlickhithe, and Geoffrey called Belchester, chaplain, on certain matters, probably bequests.[105] The archdeacon's concern was not confined to the legatees: he had his own interests. Master John de Faringdone had something to say about the profits from intestacy in the Glastonbury jurisdiction in 1334. He recalled the case of the intestacy of Richard Sencler of But- leigh, whose goods were sequestrated by the archdeacon of Glastonbury and converted to his own uses. The official of the bishop of Bath and Wells had attempted to claim Sencler's effects in Butleigh, but relaxed his sequestration order in 1333 when he saw Glastonbury's privileges.[106] The goods of intestates were claimed in most liberties, although pro- vision was made for claimants and dependants who came forward.[107] At Westminster, with its well-developed rights of sanctuary, the abbot and convent had a confirmed right to the sequestration of goods and chattels of felons and fugitives within their liberty as well as to those of intestates.[108]

The archdeacon was only entitled to deal with the testaments and prove the wills of freemen: the testaments of villeins were the concern of the manorial courts, and, in the case of St Albans, the cellarer might prove their wills in the halimote.[109] There is every indication, however, that this was a thriving jurisdiction, bringing many testamentary cases before the archdeacon,[110] and an immense amount of administration:

---

[105] WAM 5969.
[106] S. fo. 28. The witness who followed, Brother Walter de Kynwardesleye, also recalled the case and confirmed that the withdrawal of the bishop's claim took place 'half a year ago' in the hostelry of Glastonbury abbey.
[107] CUL. MS Ff 2 33, fos. 149v, 159v (and see Lobel, *Borough*, p. 44, and Bodleian MS Gough Suffolk 1 fo. 72); and Jesus College MS QB1 fos. 9, 22, 26v.
[108] WAM 6219, 6234. The letter of William Montacute to Abbot Lytlington shows that the archdeacon had power to sequestrate the goods of fugitives, at least *pro tempore* (WAM 9615). The petition of Thomas Sherman for the return of his goods declares that they were seized within the sanctuary by the sacristan and by the archdeacon (WAM 6222).
[109] *Studies in Manorial History by A. E. Levett*, pp. 208–10.   [110] S. fo. 26v.

certification, relaxation on completion, the grant of letters of administration in cases of intestacy, and excommunication of those who kept
goods from executors or who did not return their records on
completion.[111]

Other cases before the archdeacon concerned perjury, breach of oath,
laying violent hands on clerks, usury, witchcraft and defamation. One
case of perjury, recalled by witnesses as coming before the archdeacon of
Glastonbury, was between Elias le clerk of Weston Zoyland, formerly
parson there, and a certain Richard de Lokyngton.[112] Two cases of
breach of oath and perjury from 1425 and 1427 came before the archdeacon of St Albans.[113] Breach of faith was often closely associated with
debt. Debt cases showed the working of the two jurisdictions, secular
and ecclesiastical. A writ was procured against a plea of debt in the Bury
sacrist's court; and the archdeacon of Westminster recorded in 1389
that Johanna Socton, the defendant in a case before his court, had
petitioned the king for a writ of prohibition on the grounds that the
suit concerned chattels and debt which were neither matrimonial nor
testamentary.[114] Laying violent hands on clergy was apparently no rare
charge. Elias le clerk again figures as the plaintiff in a case before the
archdeacon of Glastonbury, alleging that William of Zoy had violently
assaulted him.[115] Sir John Tys, staying in Glastonbury and Meare, was
brought before the archdeacon's court *ex officio* on a charge of usury,[116]
and Alice Robat of Zoy on a charge of witchcraft.[117] Usurious practices
were possibly more common in city areas; communing with spirits in
the country.[118] In 1408 the sacrist of Bury's dean heard a case of defamation in which the plaintiff alleged that Isabella, a widow, had defamed
him by saying that he had stolen certain articles from her house. His
proctor demanded Isabella's excommunication.[119] Three cases of
defamation are recorded before William Alnwick, archdeacon of St
Albans.[120] In one of them, John Palmer and his wife and John Nodde
and his wife, all of Redbourn (Herts.), were put on their best behaviour,

---

[111] See Jesus College MS Q B 1 fos. 9, 22, 26v; CUL MS Ff 2 33 fos. 147, 149v, 159v; and WAM
6684.   [112] S. fo. 24.   [113] Reg. Stoneham fo. 72, 72v.
[114] Lobel, *Borough*, p. 43 (and BL Harley MS 645 fo. 265v – breach of faith?); and WAM 5992.
[115] S. fo. 23v, and see fo. 25v. Hale, *Precedents*, cites a case of a layman breaking a priest's arm in
church (3 no. 11); and see *EHR*, XLIV (1929), 288, 449.
[116] S. fo. 24; and as a witness on fo. 25v.
[117] S. fo. 24. Eleanor, wife of Humphrey, duke of Gloucester, took sanctuary at Westminster
following a charge of treason and black magic (MacMichael, 'Sanctuary', p. 13).
[118] See e.g. Hale, *Precedents*, nos. 159, 238, 504; and *EHR*, XLIV, 287 – the chaplain of Kilpeck.
[119] Jesus College MS Q B 1 fo. 39r-v.
[120] Reg. Stoneham fos. 72v, 74, 75b *recto*.

after purgation, and under penalty of forty shillings, not to slander one another publicly or privately.

The archdeacon's traditional role as an excommunicator is amply illustrated. John Stowe, archdeacon of Westminster in 1388, notified William, priest of St Margaret's, within the jurisdiction, of the major excommunication of John Broke, a skinner, for the non-payment of a debt.[121] William Alnwick protected the convent of St Albans' table by ordering the vicars of the churches in the city to proclaim the excommunication of those who had killed several of their swans in 1426.[122] Monastic archdeacons, as the ordinary archdeacons, and, indeed, all ecclesiastics with jurisdictional powers, excommunicated for contumacy, the most persistent problem of the medieval court. All archdeacons called upon their fellows to publish excommunications.[123] In 1304 the archdeacon of Westminster was asked by the official of the archdeacon of London to announce an excommunication in his churches, and in 1310 the archdeacon of London's commissary asked the archdeacon of Westminster to publish the excommunication of Brother John of London, called 'le Bevere', for an offence committed within the archdeaconry of London.[124] The relaxation of sentences of excommunication entailed further administrative work.[125]

The monastic archdeacon never apparently tried to establish his own jurisdiction and separate court as did the diocesan archdeacon *vis-à-vis* the bishop.[126] This is the essential difference. The description of the archdeacon of Glastonbury as 'monk of the house and commissary of the abbot' crystallises his position as delegate of the abbot, which is found also in the other abbeys. Yet the monastic archdeacon, while functioning as the delegate of the abbot, might be extremely influential.[127] There seems little doubt that the office of archdeacon in a monastery had become a distinctly legal one by the thirteenth century. Monastic archdeacons acted as judges delegate and commissaries,[128] examining witnesses, defining boundaries and trying cases.[129] By the fourteenth century men of some scholastic quality were selected for the office,[130]

[121] WAM 5979. [122] Reg. Stoneham fo. 72.
[123] e.g. WAM 6684 (and Lib. Nig. Quat. fo. 124v). [124] WAM 5986, 6047.
[125] BL Harley MS 645 fo. 188; and Jesus College MS QB1 fos. 20v–21.
[126] Pointed out for Bury by Lobel, *Borough*, p. 42.
[127] See e.g. WAM 5965, where the archdeacon of Westminster acts as commissary of the abbot in a 1325 case about the fruits of the archdeaconry of Coventry.
[128] e.g. BL Egerton Ch. 409 and WAM 5976. [129] WAM 1262, 5982, 6113, 6684, 13536.
[130] B. Harvey, 'The Monks of Westminster and the University of Oxford', *The Reign of Richard II*, ed. F. Du Boulay and C. Barron (Athlone Press, 1971), p. 123.

and several monastic archdeacons were used as proctors before the papal curia.[131] At Westminster in 1371 the archdeacon was appointed papal conservator for Bindon by the abbot of his house, who was papal conservator for the Cistercian order in England as a whole, and, in a case some fifty years earlier, the defendant before the *auditor litterarum contradictarum* alleged that he could not litigate in England against Robert, archdeacon of Westminster, on account of his power there.[132] Robert had already claimed papal exemption from excommunication and suspension. How could a simple rector hope to fight such a man on equal terms?

By the fourteenth century the archdeacon of Glastonbury had a commissary,[133] as did the archdeacon of St Albans by the mid-fifteenth century. William Albon, commissary at St Albans in 1441, when Stephen London was archdeacon, followed him in the office in 1446.[134] The last archdeacon of St Albans (prior to the dissolution of the house in 1539), Thomas Kyngesbury, had a commissary, Christopher Leysey, whose business is indistinguishable in the Act Books from the archdeacon's.[135] Within his archdeaconry, the archdeacon was served by a dean (at Bury at least) and by apparitors.[136] In 1391 the archdeacon of Westminster appointed an apparitor: previously he had used the chaplain of St Margaret's church for citing and excommunicating within the archdeaconry.[137] There is some evidence that it was the apparitor, too, from amongst the archdeacon's henchmen, who meted out the punishments with his rod.[138]

In terms of remuneration it is difficult to compare the position of the monastic archdeacon with that of the ordinary archdeacon. A document of 1601 among the St Albans records says that the archdeacon and the register had 'in times past' several pensions of the abbot which since the dissolution are 'detained and not paid'.[139] It is not clear whether these sums were alternatives or supplements to fees, but it is quite possible that the archdeacon received certain fixed monetary payments, and that the court perquisites and fees from correction and the administra-

[131] William Amondesham, archdeacon of Westminster in 1414, proctor of the abbot of Holy Cross, Waltham (WAM 5988), and cf. William Colchester, proctor of Westminster in 1382 and possibly monastic archdeacon at the same time (WAM 18478D, and F).
[132] WAM, 5999, 6000.　　　[133] *Glastonbury Cart.* no. 68: by name, Walter Broun, clerk.
[134] Reg. Stoneham fos. 35–6, 36–50 and 50–60.　　　[135] ASA 7/1 fo. 1a *verso*.
[136] Lobel, *Borough*, p. 42; and BL Harley MS 645 fo. 266.　　[137] WAM 5979, 5981, 5989.
[138] Scammell, 'Rural Chapter', p. 18, referring to Rochester diocese (the sub-apparitor) and *Registrum Hamonis Hethe*, ed. Charles Johnson, 2 vols., CYS, XLVIII–XLIX (1948), I, 441–2.
[139] *Records of the Old Archdeaconry of St Albans: A Calendar of Papers 1575 to 1637*, ed. H. R. Wilton Hall, St Albans and Hertfordshire Archit. and Archaeol. Soc. (1908), no. 156.

Monastic Archdeacons

tion went straight into the common monastic fund. The tenacity with which the monks defended their rights as monastic archdeacons might be explained by the value of the parishes within the archdeaconries as much as by the profits of archidiaconal jurisdiction. There is evidence of the profitability of the sacrist's rights within the parishes as well as the borough at Bury, where the geographical area was small. At Westminster, where similarly the archdeaconry was small, the monastic archdeacon may have relied mainly for his profits on the sanctuary rights, although those over the palace must have been lucrative, particularly from the wills of gentry who did not quite qualify for the jurisdiction of the Prerogative Court of Canterbury.

Both Glastonbury and St Albans had a considerable number of subject parishes, Glastonbury seven and St Albans fifteen, and these merit closer investigation. The wealth of Glastonbury throughout the Middle Ages was proverbial and was equalled by no other house from the time of Domesday to the Dissolution (when its net income was £3311).[140] The estates of the Jurisdiction included particularly profitable marshland, mills and fishponds in the seven parishes, and it may be that the ecclesiastical profits compare well with the income in economic and seigneurial terms. The *Taxatio* shows the richest church, Zoy, to be worth £33 3s 8d. Moorlinch came next at £20 13s 4d, followed by St John's, Glastonbury, and Street, £16, and £16 13s 4d, and Shapwick, £15 6s 8d. The other two, Butleigh and Meare, were assessed at under £15.[141] The surveyors of 1539 recorded the payment of fifty-three shillings from the six churches (Glastonbury excluded), being the procurations and synodal payments payable 'allwayes' to the archdeacon. In pensions, Glastonbury received £7 from Moorlinch; £1 from Shapwick; £1 from Butleigh; £3 from Street; and £2 13s 4d from Middlezoy. The tithes of hay belonging to the parsonages of Shapwick and Moorlinch and of Meare were worth annually the considerable sum of £86; the tithes belonging to the parsonage of Glastonbury £72, and the tithes of corn and hay of Butleigh and Baltonsborough were leased to Elizabeth Adams for £12 and for £8 10s yearly. The total sum from the Glastonbury parsonages

[140] D. Knowles, *The Religious Orders in England* III (Cambridge, 1959), 473–4.
[141] On the estates of Glastonbury in the twelfth century, see M. Postan, *Essays on Medieval Agriculture and...the Medieval Economy* (Cambridge, 1973), pp. 249–77. Some of the grievances of Glastonbury against Bishop Jocelin were that he had despoiled mills and fishponds. A papal ordination stated that the fishpond of Meare was to be shared (Cambridge, Trinity College MS R 5 33 fo. 42v). *Taxatio Ecclesiastica...Nicholai IV*, ed. S. Ayscough and J. Caley (1802), p. 198.

amounted to £315 3s 4d, of which £176 10s came from archidiaconal sources; and the total sum from the spiritualities in Somerset amounted to £354 18s, of which £193 16s 4d was provided by income of various kinds from the seven churches.[142]

The net income of St Albans, according to the *Valor*, was £2102, thus putting it in fourth place. It had considerably improved its position since the Domesday survey, when its position was tenth.[143] For St Albans the *Taxatio* estimates a sum of £297 2s from the archdeaconry.[144] According to the King's Books, six of the livings were worth between £40 and £50 (between £8 and £18 at the time of the *Taxatio*) and the archdeacon was entitled to 48s from procurations and to 48s 2d from synodals.[145] As with Glastonbury, appropriation had continued relentlessly over the years: Hexton was assigned to the sacrist in 1243 and Norton to the monks' ale in 1258. The scriptor had a portion in Redbourn; the chamberlain pensions in Redbourn, Abbots Langley and Winslow; and the infirmarer in St Peter's, St Albans – possibly appropriated in 1252. This last church, with its chapels, was estimated in the *Taxatio* as worth £60, of which the vicar received £5 and the infirmarer £5 6s 8d. The next most valuable living in the thirteenth century was Winslow, worth £18, with its chapels of Horwood and Grandborough, followed by Redbourn (£17 6s 8d), Rickmansworth (£16) and Watford (£12). There were some distinct changes in value between the 1290s and the 1540s, but the position of overall wealth from these churches did not change – roughly double that accruing to Glastonbury, which, on a basis of twice the number of churches, levels out.

In conclusion, the main profits made by the monastic archdeacons probably came from the shortcomings of people, although the evidence to clinch this is simply not available. The archdeacon's operations were built upon fear and terror which the structure of society reinforced. Efficiency seems to have been the keynote of the ordinary archdeacon's activities. Indeed, the most remarkable feature of archidiaconal administration over the whole medieval period was its relentless efficiency,[146] and it is difficult to see the monastic archdeacon with his

---

[142] Dugdale, *Mon. Angl.* I, 15.

[143] Knowles, *Religious Orders*, III, 473–4.   [144] *Taxatio*, p. 37.

[145] John Ecton, *Thesaurus Rerum Ecclesiasticarum* (London, 1742), pp. 375–6. Peters (*Oculus Episcopi*, p. 10, n. 6) gives the considerably higher figure of £3 14s for procurations in the 1570s (from Act Book VII).

[146] See Scammell, 'Rural Chapter', pp. 1–21, and M. Bowker, 'Some Archdeacons' Court

Monastic Archdeacons

smaller archdeaconry as less exacting than his diocesan counterpart. Courts in medieval England were frequented by specific social classes. When the jurisdiction of Glastonbury was attacked, the house appealed immediately to the pope. When Bishop Grosseteste commissioned his archdeacons to inquire into the morals of *all* people within his diocese, it caused loud protest from the gentry who did not accept correction from the archdeacon.[147] But the archdeacon's inquisitions into the affairs of the majority of men and women had to be tolerated. The peasants knew his court as the corrective ecclesiastical counterpart to the manorial court, and even the freemen knew little of the world of king's and bishops' courts, and of appeals to other *fora*. Instance cases brought by freemen came before the archdeacon, who also drew money from this group by providing them with essential administrative documents, for which the Church had created a need – a licence to marry, perhaps, or probate of a will. There was a fair amount of truth in the Chaucerian phrase that before the bishop caught them with his crook they were all down in the archdeacon's book.

Coupled with the profits from correction, from administration and, to a lesser extent, from instance cases, were the additional assets from the subject churches and from land-ownership in the parishes. The parishes forming the archdeaconries may not have been excessively rich, but the livings were substantial. Pensions were paid from them, the livings were gradually appropriated and the manors forming the parishes were intensively farmed. Sowy island and its surrounding moors, for example, increased dramatically in value in the mid-thirteenth century due to drainage, and so consequently did the value of its church.[148] The jurisdictional quarrels between Wells and Glastonbury were also economic disputes. The great monasteries of Glastonbury, St Albans, Bury and Westminster had been well endowed. No unworthy gifts had been bestowed on their saints. The patrimony of the saints brought money from pilgrims,[149] from the rights of jurisdiction and from the lands. They were trusts to be handed down intact. Economic advantages ensured that tradition was maintained.

Books and the Commons' Supplication against the Ordinaries of 1532' in *The Study of Medieval Records*, ed. D. A. Bullough and R. L. Storey (Oxford, 1971), esp. pp. 287–90, 311–12.

[147] Cited by Scammell, 'Rural Chapter', pp. 18–19; and cf. Peters, *Oculus Episcopi*, pp. 80–1, and Bowker, 'Some Archdeacons' Court Books', esp. pp. 308–16, who argues that it was when heresy cases became more frequent, bringing gentry before the archidiaconal courts, that protests were made. [148] Williams, *Draining of the Somerset Levels*, pp. 47–51.
[149] Knowles, *Religious Orders*, III, 249, n.1 records the total of *c.* £1142 in offerings to St Thomas of Canterbury in 1220. *[See over for Addenda.]*

ADDENDUM to pp. 179-80: Antonia Gransden ('Baldwin, abbot of Bury St Edmunds, 1065-1097', *Proceedings of the Battle Conference on Anglo-Norman Studies 4* [1981] 67) has resuscitated the notion that Herman was not a monastic archdeacon but a diocesan one in the service of Arfast, bishop of Elmham (1070-2) and then at Thetford, challenging Liebermann's view. It is true that we know — from Herman's own pen, indeed — that he dictated and wrote the letters for Arfast at the time of his attempt to set up his see at Bury (*Memorials* i 62). However, we also know that Herman was closely associated with Bury and with Abbot Baldwin, who had commissioned him to write the 'De Miraculis' which was not completed until after Baldwin's death in 1097 (ibid. i 27). The evidence styling Herman archdeacon is, not surprisingly, late, and comes from the fourteenth century and the hand of Henry of Kirkstead, monk and antiquary of Bury, on the one surviving manuscript of Herman's work (Cotton MS Tib. B II), but it seems to me to confirm that Herman was mentioned as archdeacon in earlier Bury sources. Whether Herman was in fact the first Bury archdeacon cannot be proven, but some time after 1071, when it was clear that an episcopal see was not to be established at Bury, a monastic official of this kind would have become necessary. To my mind, Liebermann's view is the more plausible.

An Evesham manuscript
containing the treatise known as 'Actor et Reus'
(British Library Harley MS 3763)

In an article published in 1962,[1] Professor Kuttner identified an earlier recension of the *Actor et Reus* than that edited by Wahrmund in 1899[2] and argued that it originated in the Anglo-Norman school in the early years of the pontificate of Pope Innocent III.[3] He also established two forms of the dialogue (from which Wahrmund's vulgate text was developed), text A and text B. Text A was found in Bodleian, MS Selden supr. 87, fol. 149rb-150ra (=S) and Worcester Cathedral MS F 159, fol. 66ra-vb, 68ra (first half column), and 67ra-rb (= W). Text B appears in MS Selden supr. 87, fol. 182va-183vb (=S) and Vat. lat. 2343, fol. 84va-86ra (=V). In the case of text A, S and W were found to

---

[1] S. Kuttner, 'Analecta iuridica Vaticana', *Collectanea Vaticana in honorem Anselmi M. Card. Albareda* I (Studi e Testi 219; Città del Vaticano 1962) 415-52: section 8 (431-43) concerns the *Actor et Reus*. — This note was written during a visit to the Institute of Medieval Canon Law in the summer of 1976 and owes much to the kindness and encouragement of Professor Kuttner.

[2] 'Actor et Reus', ed. L. Wahrmund, AKKR 79 (1899) 403-24, 603-28.

[3] For the argument, see Kuttner, 'Analecta', principally 433, 438-41.

vary towards the end, with sections in W that are absent in S, perhaps representing additions to the original; while B, which omits the introduction, was clearly written in the same school and on the same case as A.[4] From these variants, Dr. Kuttner demonstrated that the work 'consisted at first of two separate series of adversative *allegationes*' which, after several substantial revisions, were combined into a single dialogue and came to form the vulgate text of Wahrmund (= w).

In the manuscript tradition, Harley MS 3763, fol. 31va-39ra (= E) can be immediately placed with w, for which Wahrmund used (i) Vat. Ottob. lat. 16, fol. 80v-95v (= A), (ii) Palat. lat. 666, fol. 167r-74r (= D), (iii) Paris lat. 4603 fol. 167r-74v (= B) and (iv) Paris lat. 4604, fol. 81v-84v (= C) to establish his text. E has the same opening as w: 'Quidem impetrauit' — this is also found in text A, to which W belongs. Like w, E uses the plural form of text B for the defendant's statements 'Nos etc.', and the indirect form for the plaintiff's *replicatio*: 'Quod allegatum est a parte aduersa'. It provides the pope's name as Gregory in the mandate which commences the argument, and gives the additional information that it is addressed to Robert de Stanley.[5] The church of St Nicholas occurs in both w's and E's copy of the mandate, although the plaintiff changes from G. in w to T. in E. E, moreover, mentions the name of Master Odo the Spaniard, who appears in w as Hocco or Hoceo and as Odo Pictaviensis.[6]

E, however, includes two forms which are missing from w but occur in text B (SV).[7] They are the 'Nos autem non sumus gauisi' introduced on the part of the defendant, and the 'Si proponatur proximus dies ... cum presens est respondere tenetur' which appears in two forms — 'Si proponatur primus dies peremptorius' and 'Si secundus dies ponatur peremptorius'. S provides a shortened version of the 'Nos autem', but the differences do not appear to be significant, nor is there any noticeable difference in the citation of authorities from Code, Digest and *Extra*. The differences between E and w suggest no more than that E represents an intermediary stage in the compilation of the vulgate, retaining certain forms which, in the long term, were of no great importance.[8]

An analysis of the composition of Harley MS 3763 (201 folia) is now appropriate in order to consider E in relation to the rest of the manuscript. The whole

---

[4] The omission of the introduction and the plural form of address (see below) removes the possibility of an Urtext; Kuttner, 'Analecta' 438.

[5] Probably fictional, but possibly a Robert, abbot of the Cistercian abbey of Stanley in Wiltshire. An R. abbot of Stanley occurs on 7 October 1221 (*Charters and documents ...* of *Salisbury*, ed. W. R. Jones and W. D. Macray [RS 97; 1891] 114) who, D. Knowles, C. N. L. Brooke and V. London (*The heads of religious houses, England and Wales 940-1216* [Cambridge 1972] 142) suggest might be identified with Ralph who occurs as ex-abbot in 1224.

[6] E fol. 37r. See Kuttner, 'Analecta' 441 n. 3; H. Kantorowicz, *Studies in the glossators of the Roman law* (Cambridge 1938, repr. 1969) 29 n. 2; and 'Actor et Reus' 617 and n. 2. Nothing more has as yet been discovered about Master Odo of Spain.

[7] See Kuttner, 'Analecta' 437.

[8] E omits the *explicit* and ends: 'Ubi pena non est statuta a lege uel a canone arbitrio iudicis est infligenda, ut C. de iudiciis l.iiii. Excipiuntur tamen tres casus ... super illa decretale extra de officio et potestate iudicis delegati c. De causis' (X 1.29.4).

volume is a composite work concerning the rights and privileges of the Benedictine abbey of Evesham in Worcestershire, compiled over a period of at least
two centuries,[9] and incorporating legal material as follows:[10]

(a) The Ombersley case, fol. 3r-21v.
Documents in the case over Ombersley church (Worcs.) between Tedisius
de Lavania, canon of Beauvais, and William de Chirinton, clerk, of Worcester
diocese, which came before a papal auditor in 1284.[11] The abbot and convent
of Evesham were the patrons of Ombersley.

(b) A tract on the canonical position of clerks and monks, fol. 21v-29r.
fol. 21v-2v: 'Hec sunt irregularitates que impediunt promouendos'.
fol. 22v-9r: 'Hec sunt irregularitates que detiniunt iam promotos'.

(c) Various forms, mainly forms of libels, exceptions against libels, and some
acta, fol. 29v-30v, 41r-44v.
fol. 29v(i): Dilatory exceptions in a case of violence between John de Arundel[12]
and William, priest.
fol. 29v(ii): Dilatory exceptions made in the course of two days' pleading
in a testamentary case between Ralph Cokeyn and the executors of the will
of Robert de Worvesl'.
fol. 30r: Exceptions against, and replies to, the libel in a case between A.
and Beatrice, relict of Robert, clerk, over the wardship of a nephew and $4\frac{1}{2}$
marks of silver.
At foot of fol. 30r: (in another hand) Suspension by the dean of Christianity
of the Vale of Evesham of Robert le Noreys, chaplain, in 1308, for palpable
offence.[13]
fol. 30v: A case before judges delegate, the dean of Lincoln, Master Peter, the
bishop's official, and J. Soton, treasurer of Lincoln.[14]
fol. 41ra-va: Sixteen exceptions against the libel in a testamentary case, put
forward by Simon de Collesham, proctor of Master William de Clifford, rector
of 'Brungton', in a suit against Master Simon of Huntingdon, W. Crochemen
and W. of Bedford, executors of the testament of Master Richard Crochemen,
formerly rector of 'Brungton'.
fol. 41va-42rb: A matrimonial case. Mabel Prat of 'Ilmed' constitutes Master
Simon of Ely, her proctor, in a case against Hervey Dyer. The case went on

---

[9] N. R. Ker, *Medieval libraries of Great Britain* (2nd ed. London 1964) 81, appears to
assign the manuscript to the fifteenth century, but the legal material is definitely in a thirteenth-century hand.
[10] G. R. C. Davis, *Medieval cartularies of Great Britain* (London 1958) 44 no. 382, describes
folios 3-57 as concerning Ombersley, thus obscuring all the procedural material and the
Actor et Reus.
[11] Material in *Register of Bishop Godfrey Giffard*, ed. J. W. Willis Bund (The Worcestershire
Historical Society; London 1902) 107, 264, 284, 299. A William de Chyryton was elected
abbot on 30 August 1316 and died on 13 December 1344 (Harley MS 3763, fols. 176v, 177r).
[12] A John de Arundel occurs on 24 February 1300 as an executor in a case about a testament before the dean of Evesham (Harley MS 3763, fols. 186v-187r).
[13] Cf. the various legal notes and jottings, some in the same hand, on fols. 30v, 31r, 43v-44r.
[14] J. Soton is fictional — there is no gap in the list of the treasurers of Lincoln cathedral.
Similarly no trace has been found of a Master Peter, official.

appeal from the archdeacon of Ely to the bishop, and to the papal court and for the tuition of the court of Canterbury.

fol. 42rb: Other formularized documents concerning marriage cases, including Richard Cardoun *v.* Amicia Quintyn.

fol. 42vb: Thomas and Richard Bernard of 'Langeley', executors of the will of Thomas de E. *v.* Edmund de Heye.

fol. 43ra-vb: 'Nota libellum presentationis beneficio occupato'. This is a case which was heard by N. de G., bishop of Lincoln.[15] (The names of the parties are formularized, and change even within those forms.)

fol. 43vb: 'Acta ad contestand' precise' in the conventual church of St. Mary de Pratis outside Northampton on the Friday after the feast of St. Matthew the apostle 1284, from the previous Thursday, before Oliver Sutton, bishop of Lincoln, in a case between P. de V. (sic), rector of the church of C. (sic) *v.* G. de V. (sic), clerk.[16]

At foot of fols. 43v-44r: Libel over unjust excommunication: Joan Bonpayn of Evesham *v.* William Morand, chaplain.

fol. 44ra: P. de Ilmedon *v.* J. rector of the same.

fol. 44rb: 'Libellus in causa reconventionis' before the official of the court of Worcester (R. de Nasinton)[17] between O. de Hay, rector of the church or chapel of 'Meldona', and Stephen de N., acting as rector.

fol. 44va(i): A case before the dean of Christianity of Oxford, commissary of the official of the bishop of Lincoln, which went on appeal to the papal court and for the tuition of the see of Canterbury.

fol. 44va(ii): 'Libellus in causa defamationis'. P. de Ilmedon (again) *v.* W. clerk.

fol. 44va-vb: 'Libellus spoliationis' of the proctor of Richard de Vessy, rector of 'Forde' (diocese of York) *v.* Master G. de Clif, clerk.

(d) Procedural treatises, fol. 31ra, 31rb, 31va-9ra, 39ra-40vb, 44vb.

fol. 31rb: The preface to *Scientiam*. This is preceded by some notes in medieval French on the court Christian and the royal dignity (fol. 31ra) and followed by extracts from 'De noui operis nunciatione' (=Dig.39.1), and an argument at the foot of the folio to support the view that ecclesiastical judges should not defer to a royal prohibition, citing X 2.1.3.

fol. 31va-9ra: The *Actor et Reus*.

---

[15] Fictional.

[16] Oliver Sutton was bishop of Lincoln from 1280 to 1299. There is no record that I can find of this case. See *The rolls and register of Bishop Oliver Sutton* II, ed. R. M. T. Hill (Lincoln Record Society 43; Lincoln 1950) index, for the parish church of St. Mary extra castrum at Northampton. There was no conventual church dedicated to St Mary at Northampton. Should Leicester, perhaps, be substituted for Northampton? They may, however, be imaginary instances. Since St. Matthew's day (21 September) fell on a Thursday in 1284, probably 14-22 September is intended.

[17] Nassington is a common name and I have not been able to identify any such person, but there was a J(ohn) de Nassington, official of York, in 1316, a Thomas de Nassington, official of Master John de Grandisson, archdeacon of Nottingham, in 1311, and a William de Nassington, official of Durham, *sede vacante*, in 1345; see A. B. Emden, *A biographical register of the University of Oxford to 1500* II (Oxford 1958).

fol. 39ra-40vb Unidentified. 'Quidam uocauit aduersarium suum ad iudicium, aduersarius die proximo ante dies feriatos insidiose opposuit sibi exceptionem excommunicationis, ex isto themate oriuntur tres questiones . . . contra ff. de furtis l. quia' (=Dig. 47.2).

fol. 44vb: Treatise by an unidentified Egidius.[18] 'Quibus modis possunt positiones actoris repelli'. 'Ut autem rei aduocatus instruatur . . . si vero non sufficiunt in totum petere debet actor dilationem sibi dari ad probandum per alios probationes'. A further note, in a later hand, citing C.3 q.5 c.15.

The rest of the manuscript can be sectionalized as follows:

fol. 54v-57r: Form of coronation and consecration of a king of England.

fol. 45r-54v, 58r, 59r-67v, 70v-76r, 77v-94v, 153v-63v, 180r-98v: Charters relating to Evesham properties, tenants, and other business of the house.

fol. 68r-v: Knights and free tenants of Evesham abbey.

fol. 95r-149v: Transcripts of Evesham's privileges. Papal privileges (fol. 95r-115v); Royal privileges (fol. 119r-149v).

fol. 150r-53v: Transcripts of the customs of Evesham.

fol. 169r-79r: Extracts from the *Gesta Abbatum* [printed in *Chronicon abbatiae de Evesham*, ed. W. D. Macray RS 29 (London 1863)].

From the foregoing précis, it will be noticed that the *Actor et Reus* in E is directly preceded (apart from a later jotting) by the preface and first paragraph, 'Quid actor agere debeat', of the *Ordo Scientiam*,[19] a treatise common enough in English and continental collections of law books, and quite widely used in the English church courts. Professor Kuttner has pointed out that *Scientiam* also occurs in the Worcester MS (W) and in Troyes MS 936 no. 7, where it precedes immediately the *Actor et Reus*. In the latter manuscript, the *Actor et Reus* is apparently then followed by another 'Summa que vocatur Actor et reus'.[20] In the Evesham manuscript, the scribe presumably intended to copy *Scientiam* before copying the *Actor et Reus*, because the prologue begins on the recto, while the *Actor et Reus* begins at the top of the verso of the same folio which begins a new gathering.[21] In the Troyes manuscript, the *Ordo* begins 'Scientiam celestem appetunt naturaliter' as opposed to the usual 'Scientiam omnes appetunt'.[22] No particularly distinctive features are apparent in E. It follows the usual form of opening, recording that it is G. who has prepared these notes (on the *actor, reus* and judge) at the suggestion of his colleagues from the work of Master P. Puerellus.[23] The reason why the scribe desisted

---

[18] This is neither Aegidius de Fuscarariis nor Master Aegidius whose treatises were edited and printed by L. Wahrmund in *Quellen zur Geschichte des römisch-kanonischen Processes im Mittelalter*, vols. 1 and 3.

[19] It continues to p. 2 line 21 of the printed edition (Wahrmund, *Quellen* II.i [1913]) 'et recisius tempus concedatur', stopping short in the middle of the second paragraph.

[20] 'Analecta' 437. Kuttner has commented on the need for further investigation of the genesis of *Scientiam* and has shown that (in the Worcester manuscript) it predates 1234, citing decretals from the *Compilationes antiquae* and not the Decretals of Gregory IX, see 'Analecta' 434 n. 3.

[21] The end of the gathering is fol. 44v. The gathering is of fourteen folios. It includes the whole of the *Actor et Reus* but not all of the procedural material.

[22] Kuttner, 'Analecta' 437 n. 4.

[23] Occurring in other manuscripts as Master Peter Pencrell, Penerell and Peneressi (possibly Penella, Coimbra, Portugal) and distinguished by Professor Kuttner, 'Bernardus Com-

from completing the copying of *Scientiam* and turned to the *Actor et Reus* cannot be investigated profitably. Whether his exemplar contained both treatises is again unascertainable, but it seems likely; although it was clearly not the Worcester MS (W) that he used, as that represents an earlier redaction. Had the redaction E affinities with text A, it would be tempting to associate it with the prominence of Evesham in its case for episcopal exemption at the papal court in 1202-06, and the legal interest which was epitomized by the house's proctor, later abbot, Thomas of Marlborough. Marlborough went to Bologna during the preparation of the abbey's case to improve his arguments and to hire counsel and could well have been acquainted with the *Actor et Reus* at the time of its production. But E is definitely part of the vulgate series of manuscripts of the *Actor et Reus* and hence cannot be this early.

Accepting a date of after 1234 (and probably before 1241)[24] for the composition of the unified vulgate (w), the question of when E was copied into the Evesham book must be determined. In the manuscript, E is placed between formularized legal material, part possibly real and part imaginary, one case of which bears the date 1284. The composer has provided libels and exceptions to libels, mainly for use in testamentary and matrimonial cases, but has also included some cases dealing with occupied benefices and spoliation. The testamentary and matrimonial material must have been useful to the dean of the Vale of Evesham and his officers, who exercised an ancient (and, after 1206, reinforced) jurisdiction over the parishes of the Vale, on behalf of the abbey.[25] The material relative to benefices, on the other hand, would have been appropriate to the convent in its dealings in the courts with other religious houses and litigants, as would the *Scientiam*, had it been completed, and the *Actor et Reus*.

In 1284, too, the church of Ombersley (Worcs.) was in dispute between Tedisius de Lavania, Pope Adrian V's cousin, and William de Chirinton, clerk, who had been presented to Ombersley by the abbot and convent of Evesham as the patrons, and who was in possession of the benefice at the time of the dispute. If it is difficult to envisage the use of a fifty-year-old treatise in a case before an auditor of the Rota, in which a papal nominee was involved, it is, perhaps, possible to see the abbey's clerk, the dispossessed William de Chirinton resorting to it. For, in spite of the fact that the *Actor et Reus* was by the 1280s hardly original, it was still useful and 'it is certain that the unified treatise was read and re-copied in the Bolognese school, down to the time of

---

postellanus Antiquus', *Traditio* 1 (1943) 317, as Master Peter of Spain, the younger, who taught at Bologna and later at Padua in the twenties of the thirteenth century. He was author of 'Notabilia' on the 'Compilatio Quarta' (as distinct from Peter of Spain, the elder, who published glosses on the 'Compilatio Prima' and was active in the seventies of the twelfth century), and is, perhaps, to be identified with M. Pedro Salvadores, whom Gregory IX consecrated in 1235 as bishop of Porto (Portugal).

[24] The terminal date of Gregory IX's pontificate.

[25] Thomas of Marlborough himself had been dean of the exempt jurisdiction of the Vale, the first non-secular to hold the office. Harley MS 3763, fol. 186r-7r contains material on the office, powers and duties of the dean, and on his jurisdiction. I hope to investigate the history and development of this jurisdiction more fully elsewhere.

Johannes Andreae (d. 1348) and beyond'.[26] Indeed, it might be argued that this kind of text-book treatise, because of its very humdrum nature, was precisely the one that would remain in use. Fashioned and re-fashioned over the first forty years of the thirteenth century, its arguments must have been familiar to several generations of advocates and proctors.

ADDENDA: For this and other treatises, see now L. Fowler-Magerl, *Ordo iudiciorum vel ordo iudiciarius. Repertorium zur Frühzeit der gelehrten Rechte* (Ius Commune 19, 1984).

To pp. 79-80 n.23:   L. Mayali identifies him as Master Peter Peverel and suggests that he was English ('Johannes Bassianus—Nachfolger des Vacarius in England?', *ZRG* Rom. Abt. 99 [1982] 324-5).

---

[26] Kuttner, 'Analecta' 443. Books which were left to Evesham in 1392 by Prior Nicholas Herford included the Decretum, two copies of the Liber Extra, the Clementines, the Institutes and Johannes Androw (sic) on the Decretales (Harley MS 3763, fol. 180r-v).

VIII

A Judge Delegate Formulary from Canterbury

THE JUDGE DELEGATE formulary printed below is found in Cotton MS. Julius D. ii of the British Museum,[1] a manuscript which has attracted the attention of scholars. Dr. Rose Graham made use of fos. 157–161 in an article entitled 'A Papal Visitation of Bury St. Edmunds and Westminster in 1234',[2] and F. W. Maitland brought to light fos. 143v–147v, the earliest *Registrum Brevium* which is known.[3] But the formulary has escaped notice or at least comment, although, as we shall have reason to observe later, the formulary and the *Registrum* are intricately connected.[4]

The revolutionary decretal of Innocent III, which enacted that every step taken before and by the ecclesiastical judge should be made the subject of a written minute or protocol, is probably responsible for this type of formulary.[5] Innocent's decree was made in the 1215 Lateran Council. It is suggested therefore, that this species of formulary dates from after 1215. There are five known English examples of this kind, none of which has been precisely dated before 1215.[6] The purpose of their composition was to provide for a distinct legal need. It was essential that the necessary forms should be made known to the judges, and through them transmitted to the clerks. The work was of a private nature, comparable with decretal collecting, and its aim was to assist the judge.

The care with which specific letters and forms are included in this

[1] Folios 150r–154r. It is quite a long formulary and is complete. The folios measure 13·6 cm. across by 18 cm. down.
I am indebted to Miss Kathleen Major, Dr. Pierre Chaplais and Mr. G. D. G. Hall in the preparation of this note and edition.
[2] *Eng. Hist. Rev.*, xxvii (1912), 728–39.
[3] 'The History of the Register of Original Writs' in *The Collected Papers of F. W. Maitland*, ed. H. A. L. Fisher (Cambridge, 1911), ii. 110–73, especially p. 130.
[4] The compiler of the Cotton Catalogue of 1802 thought that fos. 150–154 were a continuation of the 'Forma Brevium': 'Forma brevium cursualium ad justiciarios constituendos in Hibernia, tempore Henrici III—a fol. 143b usque ad f. 147b.—et rursus a f. 150 ad f. 154.' [*See Addenda.*]
[5] c. 11. X. II. 19, canon 38 of the Fourth Lateran Council: C.-J. Hefele and Dom H. Leclercq, *Histoire des Conciles d'après les Documents Originaux* (Paris, 1907–52), V ii. 1363–4.
[6] The five are Brit. Mus., Cotton MS. Julius D. ii, fos. 150r–154r, Baltimore (Walters Art Gallery) MS. W. 15, fos. 79v–81v (unfortunately only part of this is in print, see *Oxford Formularies* (Oxford Hist. Soc., new ser. v, 1942), ii. 271–7), Lambeth Palace MS. 105, fo. 271v, Brit. Mus., Royal MS. 15 B. iv, fos. 65v–66r, and Bodleian, MS. Laud Lat. 17, fos. 223v–224v. [*See Addenda.*]

formulary shows definitively that it was devised for the use of judges delegate, or for their clerks. The writer concentrates on all the aspects of a case which would interest a judge: citations, punishment for contumacy, forms of commission and excuse for the judge, the treatment of witnesses, sentences and their execution. There is nothing about libels, exceptions or interrogatories, for instance, or other such subjects on which the parties would most want information.

The two circumstances of provenance and date give this formulary its particular interest. It is not known where any of the four formularies which have been noted by Professor Cheney came from or where they were composed,[1] whereas this formulary was definitely composed at Canterbury, in the monastic chancery of St. Augustine's or of Christ Church.[2] The whole manuscript Julius D. ii has long been attributed with a weight of authority to St. Augustine's abbey, seeing that it contains charters and privileges of that house,[3] but it is a collection of a miscellaneous and composite character which has been several times re-sewn and the folios re-distributed. Folios ccxxvi–cccxli in a later medieval foliation of the thirteenth-century manuscript, Brit. Mus., Add. MS. 46352, have been identified as originally forming the central part of Julius D. ii.[4] Likewise fos. 148r–149v of Julius D. ii do not belong in their present position. Folio 149v is a blank and the material and hand of fo. 148r onwards bear no relation to the *Registrum Brevium* which these folios now separate. Indeed fo. 148r contains a letter of Henry III ordering his bailiffs to protect the lands and possessions of the monks of Holy Trinity (or Christ Church) Canterbury. It is therefore certain that fos. 148r to 149v were misplaced when the book was sewn. An examination of the manuscript shows that the formulary is inextricably connected with the *Registrum Brevium*. The last letter of the *Registrum* series is on fo. 150r, the first folio of the formulary, which commences immediately afterwards. The hand of the end of the *Registrum Brevium* commencing half way down fo. 145r is the same as that in which the formulary is entirely written: this hand, a distinctive one, does not occur anywhere else in the book. The gathering in which most of the formulary is contained, begins on fo. 144r in the middle of the Register of Original Writs and ends on fo. 153v. The last folio of the formulary (154r) is the beginning of a new gathering,

---

[1] C. R. Cheney, *English Bishops' Chanceries 1100–1250* (Manchester, 1950), pp. 119–30, especially p. 125: see above p. 198, n. 6 for the list.

[2] The evidence for its coming from the third religious house of the city, St. Gregory's, depends solely on the use of the prior's name in several instances. In view of the more salient arguments in favour of a St. Augustine's or Christ Church origin this attribution has not been considered further.

[3] N. R. Ker, *Medieval Libraries of Great Britain* (1941), p. 27 and revised card catalogue in the Bodleian Library; G. R. C. Davis, *Medieval Cartularies of Great Britain* (1958), p. 23.

[4] Davis, p. 24. This book belonged to John Twyne (father and son), Sir Edward Dering and Sir Thomas Phillipps: nothing is known of the ownership of Julius D. ii before it reached the Cotton collection.

and it is followed by entries relating to St. Augustine's, which are of a later date and could have been copied here after the formulary was written. It is the beginning of the first gathering in which the *Registrum Brevium* is included that suggests most strongly a St. Augustine's provenance, for fo. 143r consists of the end of a list of St. Augustine's properties. This folio is in a different hand from the first hand in the *Registrum Brevium*, but it is also a hand of apparently thirteenth-century date, so that if the formulary and *Registrum* come from somewhere else they must have arrived at St. Augustine's soon after their composition.

The *Registrum Brevium* is prefaced by a writ of Henry III issued at Canterbury. There is otherwise no clue in the contents as to where it was compiled,[1] and there would be no reason to doubt that both the *Registrum Brevium* and the formulary came from St. Augustine's, if it were not for the evidence contained within the formulary. In the first place throughout the formulary there is no mention of St. Augustine's, whereas the prior and precentor of Holy Trinity (i.e. Christ Church) and the penitentiary of Canterbury appear frequently as the judges. Walter the prior of Christ Church is mentioned twice. The cathedral church is constantly mentioned as the meeting place of the court, and 'S.' and 'T.', archbishops, are presumably Stephen Langton and Theobald. It seems strange that a St. Augustine's monk, supposing he were writing such a formulary, should deliberately choose to use the names of ecclesiastics from other houses, always excepting his own and strongly favouring Christ Church, especially since it is likely that the author was working from original charters.[2] In this context also, the inclusion of the last document in the formulary, a confirmation by the prior and convent of the cathedral church, which would only be of use in that chancery, would seem to be an added argument in favour of a Christ Church origin for the formulary.

The date of the formulary can be given fairly precisely. 'H.' pope, 'W.' prior of Holy Trinity, and 'S.' archbishop of Canterbury, appear to be Honorius III who occupied the papal throne from 1216 to 1227, Walter, prior of Christ Church from 1213 to 1222, and Stephen Langton who was archbishop of Canterbury from 1207 to 1228. The formulary must have been composed therefore after 1216. There is strong evidence of the writer's familiarity with Tancred's *Ordo Judiciarius*, a work which was written in about 1216 and which became popular in England soon after.[3] The *terminus ad quem* presents a more difficult problem. A date,

[1] Unfortunately it is not known where Henry III was in Canterbury on 10 Nov. 1227, the date of the commencing writ.

[2] No documents corresponding to this case seem to have survived, although the mention of a confirmation of 'T.', sometime archbishop of Canterbury, may link up with one of Theobald's charters (see below p. 211).

[3] Compare e.g. Tancred in *Pillii, Tancredi, Gratiae libri de judiciorum ordine*, ed. F. C. Bergmann (Göttingen, 1842), p. 133: 'Attamen delegati iudices in prima citatione consueverunt tenorem commissionis sibi factae in literis citationis totum de verbo ad verbum inserere et reo, qui ad iudicium vocatur, transmittere . . .'— with the opening sentence of the formulary.

10 November 1227, is affixed to the first document in the *Registrum Brevium*. This would suggest that the formulary dates from after 1227, but not from long after, for it is unlikely that the hand is later than the first half of the thirteenth century.

In the complete work thirty major forms, and many minor variations, are treated by the writer. Of these some, as far as can be ascertained, are not to be found elsewhere, for instance the letter of absolution after sentence for contumacy, the form of letters concerning sick witnesses, the summoning of a cleric who has not carried out the mandate of the judges, and the various forms of arbitration over disputed jurisdiction. They do much to elucidate and explain the Romano-canonical procedure of the delegated courts. The formulary appears unusual because of the few other surviving formularies with which it is comparable, yet within the rather rigid boundaries set by formulary writing, there is little spark of originality and no incursion into judicial theory. The formulary was composed for business use and reference, and the work was no labour of love for the author or perhaps his scribe. At the end of the formulary he wrote: 'Explicit. Expliceat. Ludere scriptor eat.'

British Museum, Cotton MS. Julius D. ii fos. 150r–154r

Notes on the method of transcription

Abbreviations have been extended[1] except where the correct extension appears doubtful as in place names. Following modern custom 'v' is substituted for 'u' and 'j' for 'i' where appropriate. A distinction has also been made between 'c' and 't' according to the modern usage. The medieval punctuation and use of capitals have not been reproduced, but the passages which the scribe wrote in red have been printed in italics. The different forms have been numbered and separated into paragraphs.

(1) [*fo. 150r*] *Tenor literarum domini pape inseri debet in primis literis citatoriis destinandis reo vel alicui alii vel aliis quibus officium citationis a delegatis fuerit demandatum. Si ipsi reo talis erit forma.* Prior et precentor et penitentiarius ecclesie talis dilecto sibi in Christo H. capellano salutem in domino. Mandatum domini pape suscepimus sub hac forma: Honorius episcopus servus servorum dei dilectis filiis priori precentori penitentiario ecclesie talis salutem et apostolicam benedictionem. Conquerente nobis R.*[2] accepimus quod dilectus filius noster H. capellanus super quodam equo et rebus aliis injuriatur eidem etc. Quocirca etc. Testes autem etc. Quod si non omnes etc. Datum etc. Hujus igitur auctoritate mandati discretionem tuam rogandam duximus ac monendam quatinus predicto R. infra xv. dies post harum literarum susceptionem satisfacias, alioquin tibi mandamus quatinus compareas coram nobis apud Cant' in majori

[1]The expression 'etc.' has been retained where it occurs in the MS., but it has not otherwise been used.

[2]R.* denotes places in the MS. where R. is followed by 'c' with overwritten 'u' probably indicating a further name or office.

ecclesia in crastino sancti Laurentii[1] prefato R. responsurus et juripariturus.[2] Ut autem scias quid a te jam dictus R. petiturus est, noveris quod petit a te unum equum quem dato pretio a te comparavit, item petit a te fenum talis prati, item sellam calcaria et frenum talis pretii salvo sibi jure addendi vel minuendi. *Per hoc quod dicit rebus aliis potest reus conveniri super multis que minora debent esse primo nominato.* Quocirca etc. Testes etc. Quod si non omnes etc. Datum etc. *Omnia ista et quicquid apponitur in literis domini pape interseri debent in literis citatoriis.* Discretionem tuam etc. *Hoc apponi debet quando apponitur in literis domini pape.* Ammonitione premissa. *Alioquin non est necesse hoc apponi.* Ut autem scias etc. *Hec clausula petente actore est apponenda, alioquin non est necesse ut apponatur, et si plena facta fuerit editio in citatoriis poterunt denegari indutie deliberatorie reo cum comparuerit. Ista autem predicta citatio debet probari coram judicibus per duos vel plures testes.*

(2) *Si vero alii quam reo officium citationis injunctum fuerit, sub hac forma fiat citatio.* Prior precentor et penitentiarius priori sancti Gregorii vel decano vel capellano sancti Pauli Cant'[3] salutem in domino. Mandatum domini pape suscepimus in hec verba: Honorius episcopus servus servorum dei dilectis filiis priori et conjudicibus suis salutem et apostolicam benedictionem. Conquerente nobis R. etc. accepimus quod dilectus filius noster H. capellanus super quodam equo et rebus aliis injuriatur eidem. Quocirca etc. Testes autem etc. Quod si non omnes etc. Datum etc. Hujus igitur auctoritate mandati tibi mandamus quatinus admoneatis prefatum H. quod infra xv. dies post literarum nostrarum susceptionem eidem R. satisfaciat, alioquin cites eum vel citari facias quod coram nobis compareat[4] apud Cant' in majori ecclesia in crastino beati Laurentii responsurus [*fo. 150v*] prefato R. et juripariturus, et quicquid inde feceris nobis predictis die et loco per literas tuas patentes cures intimare. *Vel.* De citatione facta nos predictis die et loco per literas tuas patentes certificare non omittas. Ut autem predictus H. sciat quid ab ipso jam dictus R. petiturus est ei facias intimari, scilicet equum etc. ut prius. Quatenus admoneas etc. *Hoc intellige quando apponitur in literis domini pape.* Ammonitione premissa. *Alioquin non est necesse hoc apponi.* Ut autem predictus H. sciat etc. *Hoc intellige ut supra.*

(3) *De secunda citatione.* Prior precentor penitentiarius Cant' capellano H. salutem in domino. Meminimus tibi dedisse in mandatis quod compareres coram nobis in crastino sancti Laurentii apud Cant' in majori ecclesia R.* responsurus et juripariturus, set quia dictis die et loco nec per te nec per sufficientem responsalem coram nobis non comparuisti vel noluisti comparere, tibi auctoritate domini pape qua fungimur in hac parte edicto iterato mandamus quatenus compareas[5] coram nobis apud Cant' in majori ecclesia in crastino sancti Egidii[6] predicto R. secundum formam tibi alias editam vel secundum formam in primis citatoriis contentam responsurus etc. *Vel si hec clausula,* 'Ammonitione premissa', *in literis domini pape apposita fuerit tunc dicatur:* discretionem tuam iterato admonemus quatenus infra viii. dies post literarum istarum susceptionem eidem R. satisfacias, alioquin tibi iterato edicto mandamus quatenus coram nobis compareas etc. ut prius. *Hanc vero citationem debet actor*

---

[1] In the cathedral, probably on 11 Aug.

[2] MS. parituri.

[3] This church was in the patronage of St. Augustine's abbey. See E. Hasted, *The History and Topographical Survey of the County of Kent* (Canterbury, 1778–99), iv. 492.

[4] MS. comparea.   [5] MS. comparas.   [6] 2 Sept.

probare coram judicibus per duos testes vel plures. *Secunda vero citatio potest fieri peremptoria ex causa scilicet ubi vertitur periculum anime et ubi res que petitur in brevi peritura est, etiam tunc apponatur hec clausula.* Et hunc diem tibi constituimus peremptorium.

(4) *Si reus debeat citari ab alio quam a delegatis, sic.* Prior precentor et penitentiarius Cant' priori sancti Gregorii vel decano vel capellano sancti P. Cant' salutem in domino. Meminimus tibi dedisse in mandatis quod citares vel citari faceres H. capellanum quatenus coram nobis compareret in crastino sancti[1] N. apud Cant' in ecclesia tali R.* responsurus et juripariturus, set quoniam predictis die et loco coram nobis non comparuit auctoritate domini pape qua fungimur in hac parte tibi mandamus quatenus predictum H. iterato admoneas quod infra viii. dies post literarum nostrarum susceptionem prefato R. satisfaciat, alioquin cites eum iterato vel citari facias quod coram nobis compareat in crastino sancti Egidii apud Cant' in tali ecclesia predicto R.* secundum formam alias sibi editam responsurus etc. Et quid inde feceris per literas tuas patentes nos dictis die et loco certificare non omittas. *Hec citatio debet probari coram judicibus per literas citantis.*

(5) *De tertia citatione que debet esse peremptoria.* Prior et conjudices H. capellano salutem in domino. Meminimus nos iterato edicto te citasse vel tibi dedisse in mandatis quod coram nobis compareres R.* responsurus et juripariturus, set quoniam coram nobis non comparuisti ne predicto[2] R. in jure suo deesse videamur, tibi auctoritate domini pape qua fungimur in hac parte mandamus quatenus compareas coram nobis apud Cant' in tali ecclesia in crastino sancti M., jam dicto R. secundum formam in primis citatoriis contentam responsurus et juripariturus, et hunc diem tibi constituimus peremptorium. *Vel aliter.* Tales judices capellano sancti P. salutem. Quoniam H. capellanus iterato vocatus edicto coram nobis non comparuit R.* responsurus et juripariturus, auctoritate domini pape qua fungimur in hac parte tibi mandamus quatenus cites vel citari facias prefatum H. quod compareat coram nobis tali die et loco eidem R. secundum formam alias editam responsurus et juripariturus, et hunc diem ei constituas peremptorium. Et de citatione taliter facta nos predictis die et loco certifices. [*fo. 151r*] *Hec citatio debet probari per literas citantis.*

(6) *De secundo peremptorio.* *Secundum peremptorium conceditur ex causa scilicet ad convincendum [sic] malitiam alicujus contumacis, vel quoniam contumax est persona illustris, alioquin post primum peremtorium puniri potest.* Tales judices H. capellano salutem in domino. Meminimus[3] edicto peremptorio te citasse tibi dedisse in mandatis quod coram nobis compareres tali die et loco R.* responsurus et juripariturus, set quia coram nobis non comparuisti tibi quantum de jure possumus deferre cupientes, tibi auctoritate domini pape qua fungimur in hac parte mandamus quatenus compareas coram nobis apud Cant' in tali ecclesia tali die prefato R. secundum formam in primis citatoriis contentam responsurus et juripariturus. Sciturus pro certo quod sive veneris sive non secundum quod jus dictaverit vel secundum quod justum fuerit in causa tali procedemus vel faciemus vel contumaciam tuam gravem habemus et molestam vel graviter canonice te puniemus. *Vel aliter.*[4] Tales judices priori sancti Gregorii vel decano vel capellano sancti P. Cant' salutem in domino. Meminimus H. peremptorie vel edicto peremptorio citatum fuisse quod coram nobis

---

[1]MS. sancto.   [2]MS. predito.
[3]MS. meminus.   [4]Not in red.

compareret tali die et loco R.* responsurus et juripariturus, set quoniam coram
nobis non comparuit licet in ipsum propter ipsius contumaciam possemus
animadverti vel punire eidem tamen quantum de jure possumus deferre cupientes, auctoritate domini pape qua fungimur in hac parte tibi mandamus quatenus
eundem H. iterato peremptorie cites vel citari facias quod coram nobis compareat
tali die et loco predicto R. secundum formam in primis citatoriis editam responsurus et juripariturus. Sciturus pro certo quod sive venerit sive non etc.
ut supra.

(7) *De contumacia punienda.* Tales judices H. capellano salutem in domino.
Meminimus iterato edicto peremptorio te citasse quod coram nobis compareres
R.* secundum formam tibi in primis citatoriis editam responsurus et juripariturus, set quoniam id efficere non curasti vel coram nobis comparere noluisti
vel non comparuisti, ne multiplicata contumacia tua remaneat inpunita te ab
ingressu ecclesie suspensum scias vel suspendimus te ab ingressu ecclesie, vel
interdicimus tibi celebrationem divinorum vel ab officio et beneficio te scias esse
suspensum, nihilominus tamen auctoritate domini pape qua fungimur in hac
parte tibi mandamus quatenus coram nobis compareas tali die et loco prefato
R. secundum formam tibi alias editam[1] et nobis de contumacia tua vel inobedientia responsurus et juripariturus. *Vel aliter.* Tales judices capellano sancti
Pauli Cant' salutem in domino. Quoniam peremptorie citatus coram nobis tali
die et loco non comparuisti ne inpunitas delicti intentionem tribuat tibi delin-
quendi auctoritate qua prius te excommunicationis vinculo innodamus, vel
scias te a nobis excommunicatum esse vel excommunicationis vinculo innodatum.
*Iste autem citandus est quia si non comparuerit pro contumacia augmentata augmen-
tabitur et pena. Vel aliter.* Tales judices H. capellano salutem. Quoniam peremptorie coram nobis tali die et loco non comparuisti tibi iterato mandamus et
peremptorie quatenus coram nobis tali die et loco compareas R.* responsurus
et juripariturus, et nisi die illo coram nobis comparueris ab illo die scias te ab
ingressu ecclesie suspensum esse vel excommunicationis vinculo innodatum.
Vel aliter. Tales judices decano Cant' salutem. Quoniam H. peremptorie
citatus vel iterato peremptorie vocatus coram nobis non comparuit auctoritate
etc. tibi mandamus quatenus eundem H. ab ingressu ecclesie suspendas, vel
excommunices vel excommunicatum denunties nisi tibi prestiterit sufficientem
cautionem quod coram nobis tali die et loco comparebit R.* secundum formam
sibi prius editam responsurus et juripariturus. Et quid inde feceris nobis
predictis die et loco per literas tuas patentes cures intimare vel non reddas
certiores.

(8) *Alia pena si petatur res mobilis vel actio fuerit realis.* Tales judices decano
Cant' salutem. Quoniam H. capellanus multotiens peremptorie citatus [*fo. 151v*]
coram nobis non comparuit ne contumacia ipsius remaneat inpunita auctoritate
qua prius tibi mandamus quatenus R.* in possessionem talis ecclesie vel talis
fundi vel talium decimarum causa rei servande inducas, quam ecclesiam vel
terram prefatus R. petit coram nobis et quoniam parum[2] prodest in possessionem
mitti nisi missus teneatur,[3] tibi mandamus auctoritate qua fungimur quatenus
jam dictum R. in possessione tali tuearis et defendas contradictores si qui fuerint
per censuram ecclesiasticam compescendo. *Quacumque hora reus venerit dum-*

---

[1] 'responsurus et juripariturus' here but deleted.
[2] MS. par.
[3] The scribe should have written 'tueatur' possibly.

modo infra annum possessionem suam recuperabit, si vero non venerit infra annum post annum sic missus verus efficietur possessor. Tales judices decano Cant'. Quoniam H. capellanus multotiens et peremptorie citatus coram nobis non comparuit gravem habentes contumaciam ejus et molestam auctoritate qua ut[1] prius tibi mandamus quatenus R.* mittas in possessionem bonorum ipsius H. causa rei servande pro modo debiti declarati. Petit enim jam dictus R. ab ipso H. x. marcas vel equos duos et runcinum unum quos comparavit ab eo pro iiii. libris volumus etiam et mandamus quod missum tuearis et defendas contradictores si fuerint per censuram ecclesiasticam compescendo. *Vel sic.* Tales judices decano Cant'. Noveris quod R.* petit coram nobis auctoritate domini pape ab H. capellano x. marcas vel duos equos eidem detinet et reddere contradicit contra fidem prestitam temere veniendo. Prefatus vero H. legitime citatus et peremptorie noluit comparere, nolentes igitur contumaciam ipsius totiens multiplicatam clausis oculis pertransire auctoritate qua ut[2] prius tibi mandamus quatenus eundem R. in possessionem bonorum ipsius H. pro modo debiti declarati inducas, contradictores si qui etc. ut prius.

(9) *Forma literarum absolutionis.* Tales judices decano Cant'. A memoria tua non credimus excidisse qualiter H. capellanus pro contumacia sua ab ingressu ecclesie auctoritate nostra suspendisti vel excommunicatum denuntiasti vel excommunicasti. Nunc vero penitentia ductus vel rubore confusus ad cor rediens munus absolutionis sibi petit humiliter exiberi. Cum igitur nemini penitenti venia sit neganda eum a sententia que tenebatur tibi remittimus absolutum mandantes quatinus in locis in quibus excommunicatus fuerat eum denunties absolutum, quod enim nostro parebit mandato nobis sufficientem prestitit cautionem. *Vel aliter.* Tales judices decano Cant' salutem. Qualiter auctoritate nostra H. capellanus pro contumacia sua ab ingressu ecclesie sit suspensus vel sententia excommunicationis innodatus tuam credimus discretionem non latere, nunc vero ad nos accedens nobis humiliter supplicavit ut eidem absolutionis munus faceremus exhiberi judicio sisti[3] sufficientem offerens cautionem. Cum igitur sancta mater ecclesia nulli gremium suum claudat vel veniam deneget, ad se venienti prefatum H. ad te remittimus mandantes quatenus eidem secundum formam ecclesie munus absolutionis facias selempniter [*sic*] exhiberi. Et quid ex inde feceris nobis per literas tuas cures intimare.

(10) *Forma restituende possessionis.* Tales judices decano Cant' salutem. Discretionem tuam credimus non latere qualiter tibi dederimus in mandatis quod pro contumacia H. mitteres R.* in possessionem talis terre vel decimarum causa rei servande, ut jam dictus H. tedio affectus coram nobis compareret eidem R. responsurus et juripariturus. Cum igitur prefatus H. tedio jam affectus vel rubore confusus vel timens sibi dispendium gravius imminere coram nobis comparuerit tali die et loco, petens sibi restitutionem fieri ecclesie sue vel decimarum ac judicio sisti sufficientem offerens cautionem, tibi auctoritate qua ut[4] prius mandamus quatenus jam dicto H. possessionem suam cum [*fo. 152r*] perceptis fructibus plenarie restituas in quam jam dictum R. ob contumaciam alterius causa rei servande induxisti.

(11) *Forma commissionum in una causa.* Prior talis magistro H. salutem in domino. Quoniam congnitioni cause que vertitur coram nobis et conjudicibus nostris auctoritate domini pape tali die loco inter H. capellanum ex una parte et R.* ex alia super uno equo et rebus aliis interesse non possumus, tibi vices

---

[1]MS. et.   [2]MS. et.   [3]MS. sist.   [4]MS. et.

nostras quantum ad diem illum committimus ratum et gratum habituri quod a vobis predictis die et loco mediante justitia actum fuerit reservatis nobis de jure reservandis. Idem conjudicibus nostris et partibus significamus. *Vel aliter in pluribus causis.* Prior talis loci magistro H. Pictavens'[1] salutem in domino. In omnibus causis que vertuntur coram nobis et conjudicibus nostris auctoritate domini pape inter quoscumque in crastino sancti N. in ecclesia Christi Cant' tibi vices nostras committimus, ratum habituri et gratum quod per te dictis die et loco actum fuerit mediante justitia reservatis nobis de jure reservandis, vel sententiis diffinitivis tamen nobis reservatis. Idem conjudicibus nostris et partibus significamus. Item committimus etiam tibi potestatem acta et citationes sigillo tuo sigillandi. *Vel aliter.*[2] Viris venerabilibus[3] de Boxel' et Faveresham abbatibus W. prior talis loci[4] salutem. Quoniam urgentibus ecclesie nostris negotiis vel impediente corporis nostri infirmitate vel imbecillitate, cognitioni cause que vertitur coram nobis auctoritate domini pape tali die et loco inter H. capellanum ex una parte et R.* ex altera super uno equo et rebus aliis interesse non possumus, vices nostras magistro H. Pictavens' committimus reservatis nobis de jure reservandis ratum habituri et gratum quod dictis die et loco mediante justitia factum fuerit per eundem. Idem partibus significamus.

(12) *Excusatio judicis.* Talibus judicibus prior talis conjudex eorum[5] salutem in domino. Quoniam congnitioni cause que vertitur coram nobis auctoritate domini pape inter H. capellanum ex una parte et R.* ex altera super quodam equo et rebus aliis interesse non possum, habeatis me quantum ad totam causam vel ad diem talem excusatum et ideo quod vestrum est non expectata presentia mea in jam dicta causa faciatis.[6] Idem partibus significo.

(13) *Forma procurationis ex parte actoris ad diem.* Viris venerabilibus priori sancte Trinitatis et conjudicibus suis H. capellanus salutem in domino. Quoniam ventilationi cause que vertitur coram vobis auctoritate domini pape tali die et loco inter me ex una parte et R.* ex alia super quodam equo et rebus aliis interesse non possum, magistrum H. Picta. procuratorem meum predictis die et loco mediante justitia actum fuerit. Idem parti adverse significo. *Si vero debeat componere vel transigere, sic.* Ratum habiturus et gratum quicquid per eum actum fuerit sive componendo sive transigendo vel aliis quibuscumque modis secundum quod viderit expedire. Promitto etc. Idem etc.

(14) *Commissio eisdem judicibus.* Talibus conjudicibus suis prior sancti Gregorii Cant' salutem in domino. Quoniam congnitioni cause etc. interesse non possum vices meas vobis ad totam causam vel quantum ad diem vel usque ad sententiam committo, ratum habiturus et gratum quicquid per vos actum fuerit. Idem partibus significo etc.

(15) *Forma procurationis ex parte rei.* Talibus judicibus R.* salutem in domino. Quoniam ventilationi cause que vertitur coram vobis auctoritate domini pape inter etc. tali die et loco interesse non possum, magistrum H. Pictav' procuratorem meum constituo ad totam causam vel ad diem talem[7] ratum habiturus et

---

[1] Of Poitiers ? A brother Hamon Picte of Romney was seneschal of St. Augustine's abbey in 1277, see *William Thorne's Chronicle of St. Augustine's Abbey Canterbury*, trans. and ed. A. H. Davis (Oxford, 1934), pp. 266–7.

[2] Not in red.

[3] MS. venerabibus.

[4] Walter, prior of Christ Church, see below, p. 210, n. 3.

[5] 'conjudex eorum' written above 'talis salutem' with an omission mark.

[6] MS. ficiatis.   [7] MS. 'constituo' deleted.

gratum quicquid de predicta causa predictis die et loco actum fuerit per eundem et pro eo judicatum solvi promitto. Idem parti adverse etc. *Si opus fuerit transactionem, dic sicut prius ex parte actoris.*

(16) *Forma revocandarum.* Abbati de Boxel' et conjudicibus suis prior talis et sui conjudices salutem in domino. Mandatum domini pape [*fo. 152v*] suscepimus sub hac forma: Honorius etc. Cum igitur ab H. capellano qui jam dictas literas impetravit acceperimus quod R.* ad vos alias literas impetraverit contra eum super eadem causa que coram vobis vertitur, que posteriores usu et tempore esse dinoscuntur nec de literis ipsius H. faciunt mentionem, auctoritate qua prius discretionem vestram duximus rogandam ac monendam quatenus si ita est a congnitione et executione cause que vertitur inter tales desistatis.

(17) *Si dubitetur quorum sit jurisdictio, sic.* Abbati de Boxel' et conjudicibus suis prior talis et sui conjudices salutem in domino. Ad memoriam reducimus nos vobis scripsisse ut ab agnitione [*sic*] cause que vertitur inter tales desistere curaretis, set quoniam ut accepimus dubitatum est a vobis utrum nostra vel vestra sit jurisdictio vel que litere sint priores vel que sint revocatorie, discretionem vestram rogandam duximus ac monendam quatenus die tali compareatis una nobiscum apud talem locum ut quorum sit jurisdictio inter nos discernamus. *Vel.* Ut secundum quod jus dictaverit super tali discussione inter nos discernamus, partes etiam idem de mandato nostro comparebunt. *Sciendum autem quod jus dictat quod debeant eligi arbitri qui discernant quorum debeat esse jurisdictio, et ideo ponitur hec clausula secundum quod jus dictaverit etc. Si debeant arbitri judices omnes scribere debent aliquibus ut arbitrium in se suscipiant et quorum sit jurisdictio vel que sint revocatorie discernant.*

(18) *Item sub qua forma judices scribere electis in arbitros qui quorum sit jurisdictio debent discernere.* Abbas de Boxel' et conjudices sui prior talis et sui conjudices dilectis fratribus in Christo magistro T. et H. Pictavens' salutem in domino. Noveritis quod H. capellanus literas domini pape contra R.* ad nos abbatem scilicet de Boxel' et conjudices nostros ex una parte super causa tali impetravit, R.* vero ad nos priorem scilicet et conjudices nostros alias literas contra eundem H. et super eadem re impetravit, cum igitur pro varietate literarum diversarum causarum fines confundi consueverint, *vel*, cum igitur pro varietate literarum partibus non commodum set dispendium consueverit pervenire, ut partium laboribus parcamus et expensis de communi assensu partium in vos de quorum discretione fiduciam plenam optinemus, compromisimus ut vos inspectis literis domini pape et auditis audiendis quorum sit jurisdictio vel que litere sint revocatorie discernatis. Et nos quod a vobis rationabiliter provisum fuerit observabimus et faciemus inviolabiliter ab omnibus observari. Conveniatis[1] igitur apud Cant' secundum formam predictam processuri et vos dabimus in mandatis partibus quod coram vobis tali die et loco comparebunt et quid sententialiter vel per sententiam provideritis nobis per literas vestras curetis intimare.

(19) *Sub qua forma isti arbitri debeant rescribere.* Viris venerabilibus abbati de Bexel' et conjudicibus suis et priori Cant' et conjudicibus suis tales arbitri salutem in domino. Convenientes apud Cant' die tali mandatum vestrum vel quod nobis mandastis secundum quod dominus monstravit curavimus adimplere, partibus igitur in presentia nostra constitutis dictis die et loco visis ac intellectis literis utriusque partis, tandem post multas altercationes prudentum virorum

---

[1] MS. Coveniatis.

usi consilio pronuntiavimus literas R.* tanquam priores tempore quod per datam earum congnovimus prejudicare vel prevalere literis ipsius H., presertim cum in literis posterius impetratis nulla fiat mentio de primis. Prior igitur Cant' et sui conjudices quorum jurisdictionem esse pronuntiamus secundum quod jus dictaverit in causa ipsa procedant.

(20) *Forma litterarum ad compulcionem testium.* Prior talis et sui conjudices decano tali salutem in domino. Cum veritatem occultare sicut et dicere falsum nunquam peccatum mortale reputetur, auctoritate domini pape qua fungimur in causa que vertitur coram nobis inter H. capellanum et R.*, tibi mandamus quatenus testes quos predictus H. tibi nominabit admoneas et indu[*fo. 153r*]cas quod tali die et loco coram nobis compareant in predicta causa peribituri testimonium veritati. Et si forsan videris quod predicti testes vel aliquis de testibus timore gratia vel odio vel amore se subtraxerit, ne veritas indiscussa permaneat eosdem testes per censuram ecclesiasticam compellas. Et quid ex inde feceris nobis per literas tuas predictis die et loco cures intimare.

(21) *Forma litterarum[1] pro expensis testium.* Prior talis et sui conjudices decano Cant' salutem in domino. Noveris quod H. capellanus produxit coram nobis tales testes peribituros testimonium veritati in causa que vertitur inter ipsum et R.*, qui veniendo ad nos vel apud nos moram faciendo occasione ipsius non modicas fecerunt expensas. Cum igitur secundum canonica ac civilia jura venturis ad judicium testibus expense debeant inveniri, tibi auctoritate qua prius mandamus quatenus eundem H. admoneas et inducas quod eisdem testibus sumptus et expensas exibeat competentes quas idem testes occasione ipsius fecisse dinoscuntur, et eundem H. ad id si necesse fuerit per censuram ecclesiasticam compellas.

(22) *Forma litterarum de testibus valitudinariis.* Tales judices archidiacono et decano London' salutem in domino. Ne pro defectu probationum causa inter H. capellanum ex una parte et R.* ex alia nobis auctoritate domini pape delegata indiscussa relinquatur, vobis de quorum discretione fiduciam optinemus auctoritate qua fungimur mandamus quatenus ad R. et W. B. cives Lond' valitudinarios vel senie ac debilitate confectos, ut audivimus quos predictus R. testes nominavit, personaliter accedatis inquirentes diligenter si coram nobis apud Cant' possint comparere in predicta causa perhibituri testimonium veritati. Et si videritis quod ipsedicte infirmitate etate vel debilitate ad nos venire non possint, tunc demum ipsos juratos diligenter examinetis inquirentes de circum-stantiis et de aliis que ad jam dictam causam dinoscuntur pertinere et dicta eorum fideliter inscriptum redigatis et attestationes eorum sub sigillis vestris signatas nobis destinetis. Litis contestationem vobis sigillis nostris signatam transmittimus et prefiximus diem parti adverse quo coram vobis debeat com-parere juramenta testium audituri.

(23) *Forma sententiarum pro actore.* In nomine patris et filii et spiritus sancti amen. *Secundum quosdam debet preponi forma litterarum domini pape ex integro, sic.* Nos priores mandatum domini suscepimus sub hac forma: Honorius episcopus etc. Nos igitur sancte Trinitatis et sancti Gregorii Cant' priores congnitores cause que vertitur inter H. capellanum ex una parte et R.* ex altera super equo etc. auctoritate domini pape nobis delegata vel commissa partibus tum per se tum per procuratores comparentibus, lite legitime contestata testibus productis attestationibus rite publicatis auditis et intellectis utriusque partis allegationibus

---

[1]MS. *littarum.*

prudentum virorum usi consilio pronuntiamus R. actorem intentionem suam sufficienter probasse. Unde H. capellanum per sententiam diffinitivam condempnavimus ad restitutionem equi etc. vel talis terre vel xx. marcarum predicto R. faciendum, reservata nobis de consensu partium legitima taxatione expensarum.

(24) *Sententia pro reo preponatur forma litterarum*[1] *domini pape.* In nomine patris et filii et spiritus sancti amen. Nos sancte Trinitatis et sancti Gregorii Cant' priores a domino papa in causa tali inter R.* ex una parte et H. capellanum ex altera super tali terra vel ecclesia vel xx. marcis partibus coram nobis tum per se tum per procuratores constitutis, lite etc. testibus etc. Attestationibus etc. auditis etc. prudentum virorum etc. pronuntiamus R. actorem in probatione intentionis sue defecisse. Unde H. capellanum reum ab impetitione ipsius R. per sententiam diffinitivam absolvimus reservata[2] nobis de consensu partium legitima taxatione expensarum. *Sententia semper debet fieri in scripto nisi modica fuerit causa vel nisi de consensu partium secus fiat.*

(25) *Forma litterarum*[3] *pro exsecutione sententie.* [*fo. 153v*] Prior talis et sui conjudices decano tali salutem in domino. Noveris quod nos auctoritate domini pape procedentes in causa que vertitur inter H. capellanum ex una parte et R.* ex altera super uno equo vel terra tali vel xx. marcis vel ecclesia tali vel decimis talibus, condempnavimus vel adjudicavimus ei possessionem talis terre vel ecclesie H. quia in probatione intentionis sue defecit ab impetitione ipsius predictum R.[4] absolventes. Cum igitur ea que per sententiam diffinitivam sunt decisa effectui debeant mancipari tibi auctoritate qua prius mandamus quatenus jam dictum R. in possessionem talis terre vel talis ecclesie vel decimarum talium auctoritate nostra inducas, et quia non[5] sufficit aliquem in possessionem inducere nisi inductus tueatur, tibi auctoritate qua prius mandamus quatenus si qui fuerint contradictores per censuram ecclesiasticam ut desistant compellas. *Si vero petantur denarii, sic.* Mandamus quatinus ipsum R. in possessionem bonorum ipsius H. secundum modum debiti declarati inducas.

(26) *De sententia diffinitiva perpetuo observanda, sic.* Tales judices omnibus Christi fidelibus presentes literas inspecturis salutem in domino. Rerum gestarum memoria provide literis continetur ne transitu temporis ea que semel terminata sunt iteratis retrogrationibus perturbentur. *Vel sic.* Temporales actus de facili supplantare solet ruina temporis nisi vere firmentur apicibus sigillatis. *Vel sic.* Acta solempniter delet oblivio nisi firmentur stabili literarum firmamento. Hinc est quod universis ac singulis innotescat nos mandatum domini pape suscepisse sub hac forma: Honorius episcopus etc. Hujus igitur auctoritate mandati in causa tali ordine judiciario procedentes partibus tum per se tum per procuratores constitutis coram nobis, lite legitime contestata testibus productis attestationibus rite publicatis auditis et intellectis utriusque partis allegationibus prudentum virorum usi consilio, per sententiam diffinitivam condempnavimus talem reum ad restitutionem talis ecclesie vel terre vel decimarum vel xx. librarum tali actori faciendum, reservantes nobis potestatem compellendi si qua partium contra predictam sententiam venire presumpserit. Et ut hec nostra sententia futuris temporibus inviolabiliter observetur eam presenti scripto sigillorum nostrorum appositione communito confirmamus. Datum tali die anno pontificatus domini N.[6] pape xxv.

[1] MS. *litterum.* [2] MS. *reseruta.* [3] MS. *littarum.*
[4] MS. has 'ab' here. [5] MS. 'v̄o' apparently: the sense demands 'non'.
[6] No pope N. (or H.) had a reign of this length. Apparently a fictitious instance is provided.

(27) *Forma litterarum pro expensis.* Tales judices decano tali salutem in domino. Mandatum domini pape suscepimus sub hac forma: Honorius episcopus etc. Hujus igitur auctoritate mandati in dicta causa ordine judiciario per omnia observato procedentes per sententiam diffinitivam condempnavimus H. capellanum. Cum igitur victus victori secundum canonicas et legitimas taxationes condempnari debeat in expensis, tibi mandamus auctoritate qua prius quatenus predictum H. capellanum admoneas et inducas si opus fuerit per censuram ecclesiasticam compellas ut infra festum sancti Michaelis proximo sequentis x. marcas nomine expensarum jam dicto R. refundat, ad quarum solutionem predictum H. condempnavimus.

(28) *Vocatio ejus qui mandatum judicum non adimplet.* Tales judices decano Cant' salutem. Meminimus nos tibi dedisse in mandatis quod H. pro contumacia sua ab ingressu ecclesie suspenderes vel excommunicatum denuntiares vel citares quod coram nobis compareret. Set quoniam ut audivimus mandatum nostrum non curasti adimplere inobedientiam tuam gravem habemus et molestam, nolentes igitur quod mandata nostra vel edicta delusoria a quoquam inpune reputentur cum quasi arriolandi sit peccatum superibus [*sic*] repugnare et quasi celus ydolatrie nolle adquiescere, auctoritate qua prius tibi mandamus quatenus compareas coram nobis in crastino sancti Egidii apud Cant' nobis super inobedientia [*fo. 154r*] tua responsurus et hunc diem tibi constituimus peremptorium.

(29) *Sub qua forma debeat se quis excusare ne mandatum delegatorum exequatur.* Talibus judicibus decanus Cant' salutem. Mandatum vestrum jam dudum recepi in quo continebatur quod talem citarem vel excommunicarem vel suspenderem vel denuntiarem sententia excommunicationis innodatum. Set quoniam propter potentiam ipsius vel timorem vel trucidatus[1] corporis mihi minatur irrogare vel aliquod hujusmodi si mandatum vestrum curem adimplere quod mihi dedistis in mandatis non dum adimplevi. Cum igitur mandati vestri executio tali vel talibus debeat demandari quorum potentiam vel officium talis citandus vel excommunicandus non possit cohibere vel ne per insolentiam ipsius ecclesiastica censura enervetur, discretioni igitur vestre preces porrigo affectuosas quatenus me ab hoc honore si placet absolventes hoc officium alii delegetis qui sciat et possit mandatum vestrum[2] adimplere. Scituri pro certo quod nec per malitiam nec per excusationem frivolam a mandati vestri executione peto excusari.

(30) *Sub qua forma fieri debent confirmationes ab ecclesia cathedrali de rebus viris religiosis collatis.* Omnibus Christi fidelibus presentes literas inspecturis priori et conventui de Ledes W. prior[3] et conventus ecclesie Christi Cant' salutem in domino. Justis religiosorum desideriis consentire piisque eorum postulationibus clementer annuere religionis honestas et fraterne karitatis unitas nos hortantur. Quocirca ecclesiam vel ecclesias vel decimas nomine proprie exprimendas quas vobis vel talibus in proprios usus venerabilis pater noster S. Cant' archiepiscopus[4] contulit et carta sua confirmavit, quantum in nobis

---

[1] MS. truciatus.

[2] 'vestrum' written above 'adimplere', with an omission mark.

[3] Walter was prior of Christ Church Canterbury from 1213 to 1222; see *Christ Church, Canterbury*, ed. W. G. Searle (Cambridge Antiq. Soc., Octavo ser., xxxiv, 1902), p. 159.

[4] Presumably Stephen Langton, archbishop from 1207 to 1228. No confirmation of his to Leeds priory is known to survive, see *Acta Stephani Langton*, ed. K. Major (Oxford, 1950).

est confirmamus predictas donationes sicut juste et canonice facte sunt firmas et ratas habentes et hoc per presens scriptum sigilli nostri appositione roboratum protestamur. *Vel sic.* Quoniam sine vere cultu religionis nec karitatis unitas potest subsistere nec domino gratum servitium exhiberi[1] conveniens est religioni quam profitemur religiosas personas diligere et earum quieti ac utilitati salubriter providere. Ea propter vestris justis postulationibus inclinati donationes ecclesiarum vel decimarum quas vobis venerabilis pater noster S. Cant' archiepiscopus vel talis comes vel miles vobis fecit sub hac forma: S. dei gratia Cant' etc. *Et tota forma carte vel confirmationis in litteris istis apponatur.* Hujus igitur carte vel confirmationis tenorem coram nobis legi facientes predictas donationes sicut juste et canonice facte sunt quantum in nobis est confirmamus. Et in hujus rei testimonium presenti scripto sigillum nostrum duximus apponendum. *Vel sic.* Decet nos et a rationis tramite non discordat ad commodum et profectum religiosorum intendere et quod eisdem largitione pontificum oblatione fidelium collatum est ratum et firmum habere. Quocirca pias donationes ecclesiarum vel decimarum factas a quibuscumque priori et conventui sancti N. de Ledes quantum in nobis est ratas habemus et acceptas quarum nomina in literis confirmationis felicis recordationis T. quondam Cant' archiepiscopi[2] eisdem priori et conventui super hoc confectis prospeximus evidenter contineri. Nos igitur predictis donationibus prefate confirmationis assensum nostrum prebuisse et consensum presenti scripto sigillo nostro roborato protestamur. Explicit. Expliceat. Ludere scriptor eat.

ADDENDA

To p. 198 nn.3,4: See now for comments on the Register and an edition, *Early Registers of Writs,* ed. E. de Haas and G.D.G. Hall (Selden Soc. 87, 1970) pp. xxxiii–xl, and 1-17.

To p. 198 n.6 end: For additions, see now above Study II 47 and fol.

---

[1] MS. 'c̄o' here: a false start.
[2] There is a confirmation of Archbishop Theobald of the possessions of Leeds priory. See A. Saltman, *Theobald, Archbishop of Canterbury* (1956), p. 371, charter no. 148. Dr. Saltman has dated it 1150 to 1161: it is contained in a fragment of a Leeds cartulary (Maidstone, Kent Archives Office, MS. U/120, Q/13, fo. 2v).

IX

Papal Privileges for St. Albans Abbey and its Dependencies

A FOURTEENTH-CENTURY book of benefactors, richly decorated in the St. Albans *scriptorium*, reveals the existence of 172 papal privileges for the abbey. The greatest benefactor, Adrian IV, is shown with the ring, cup, chasuble called 'Adrian', and the relics of the Theban legion, which he gave to the abbey, while other popes from Calixtus II to Honorius III, together with Adrian I (772–95), are depicted holding letters variously sealed with blue, gold, and silver *bullae*, hanging from green, blue, red, and orange cords.[1] Few of these privileges survive in the original, but ample material from cartulary copies,[2] chronicles, and the papal registers, permits a detailed examination of the privileged position of St. Albans and its dependencies at four different stages. I shall consider successively the early privileges forming the basis of St. Albans' exemption from the bishop of Lincoln, conceded by the papacy between 1122 and *c.* 1180; the report of a visit to the papal curia in 1256–7, when Alexander IV was petitioned to renew the most important of the old privileges and to grant certain indults to accord with St. Albans' changing needs; the fourteenth-century letter-book of Abbot Thomas de la Mare, which includes a detailed discussion by Master Richard de Wymundeswolde of the implications of a privilege granted by Pope Clement III to Abbot Warin; the indults and personal documents of the 1420s and 1430s, the

---

[1] B.M. Cotton MS. Nero D vii, ff. 7–11; the text of the manuscript is printed in W. Dugdale, *Monasticon Anglicanum*, ed. J. Caley and others (London, 1817–30), ii. 218–19.

[2] I wish to thank His Grace the Duke of Northumberland for permission to use the Tynemouth cartulary in Syon House; His Grace the Duke of Devonshire for permission to use the St. Albans cartulary at Chatsworth; and His Grace the Duke of Rutland for permission to use the Belvoir cartularies and connected muniments in his collection.

cost of such documents, the confirmation of elections, and the position of the cells.

I. Amongst English Benedictine houses the great abbey of St. Albans held a unique position throughout the Middle Ages, because of its possession of the remains of Alban, the protomartyr of England. The cult of Alban goes back to the first part of the fifth century, and Bede relates the cure of the sick and frequent miracles at St. Albans in (?)731. Supposedly the tomb was then lost until a miraculous discovery of the relics on 1 August 793. Levison points out that it is unlikely that the tomb was ever lost between 731 and 793, but that King Offa, with whom the legend is connected, may well have erected a new church and shrine there in that year. During Offa's visit to Rome, Pope Adrian I is said to have canonized Alban and granted the abbey some privileges, and it was on this occasion that the king was assumed to have made the celebrated grant of Peter's Pence to the papacy. The rank of St. Albans among the foremost English Benedictine abbeys had thus been established well before the Norman Conquest and, like other abbeys which were important before 1066, it maintained this position thereafter. On 1 August 1129 the fragments of Alban were again translated to a new and more magnificent shrine, and on 25 June 1177 the relics of the newly invented St. Amphibalus, who had allegedly shared martyrdom with Alban, were discovered at Redbourn some four miles away.[1] St. Albans now had a full complement of martyrs, whose blood as it were was used to write the abbey's privileges.[2]

---

[1] For the whole of this paragraph, see W. Levison, 'St. Alban and St. Albans', *Antiquity*, xv (1941), 337–59, esp. 344 and 350–2. 'Amphibalus' was fabricated by Geoffrey of Monmouth, who misunderstood Gildas's account of the cloak in his description of the martyrdom of St. Alban. After 1129 the feast of the translation of St. Alban was celebrated on 2 Aug. because 1 Aug. was another important festival, that of St. Peter ad Vincula.

[2] Cf. C. R. Cheney, 'Magna Carta Beati Thome: another Canterbury Forgery', *BIHR* xxxvi (1963), 11, citing *Patrologia Latina*, ed. J. Migne, ccxv, col. 1048, where Innocent III says that St. Thomas wrote a special privilege for Christ Church 'as it were in his blood'. St. Albans was also associated with St. Oswyn after Robert de Mowbray made Tynemouth priory its dependency, and a bull 'Religione ac pietate' of 1156 ordered the bishop of Durham and his archdeacon to see that the feast of St. Oswyn was observed in the parishes of his diocese (*PUE* iii, no. 111).

The earliest authentic papal document for the house, 'Religione ac pietate', dates from 25 November 1122 and was granted by Calixtus II. It concerns the celebration of St. Alban's feast and grants an indulgence of twelve days to those visiting the abbey within the octave.[1] In conjunction with this grant Calixtus II issued on the same day a solemn privilege 'Ad hoc nos', which granted papal protection to the abbey and confirmed its possessions both past and future.[2] St. Albans' second basic privilege 'Officii nostri nos', which was obtained from Celestine II in 1143, confirmed the previous bull of Calixtus II, took the house under the protection of St. Peter—a special relationship for which it was to pay one ounce of gold to Rome yearly—and granted *episcopalia*, although ordinations were to be undertaken by the diocesan bishop (not by any catholic bishop as at Bury).[3] This, together with Eugenius III's bull 'Pie postulatio voluntatis' of 1147, which specifically detailed the dependencies of St. Albans,[4] laid the foundation of the abbey's privileges before the accession of Adrian IV in 1154, a pope who succeeded to the papacy at a time when papal confirmations were much sought after.

The exact nature of Adrian IV's relationship with St. Albans is obscure. It is unlikely that in his youth he was rejected as a novice in the house, but it is probable that he came from the town or its region and that his father had entered the monastery there.[5] It

---

[1] *PUE* iii, no. 6. In some ways this was a confirmation of an indulgence to all penitents who should come to St. Albans 'ad praedictam festivitatem', which had been issued by Bishop Robert Bloet of Lincoln (*Gesta Abbatum Monasterii Sancti Albani*, ed. H. T. Riley (R.S., 1867–9), i. 92). Adrian IV issued another 'Religione ac pietate' in 1156 (*PUE* iii, no. 102).

[2] *PUE* iii, no. 5 (the last clause of this document is really an abbreviation of no. 6).

[3] Ibid., no. 43. Cf. *The Pinchbeck Register*, ed. Lord F. Hervey (privately printed, 1925), i. 3–4, 19–20 (*PUE* iii, no. 8).

[4] *PUE* iii, no. 68.

[5] The life of Adrian by Boso (in *Le Liber Pontificalis*, ii, ed. L. Duchesne, Bibliothèque des Écoles Françaises d'Athènes et de Rome, ser. 2, no. 3, 2nd edn., Paris, 1955) and the account of William of Newburgh, are to be preferred to that given by Matthew Paris, with whom the story of his rejection originates (*Gesta Abb.* i. 124–32). R. L. Poole in *Studies in Chronology and History* (Oxford, reprint, 1969), p. 293, argues that Adrian had been at the house of Austin canons at Merton before entering the Augustinian community of regular clerks of St. Rufus at Avignon, on the seemingly incontrovertible evidence of the final clause in one of John of Salisbury's letters (*The Letters of John of Salisbury*, ed. W. J. Millor and H. E. Butler, revised C. N. L. Brooke (Nelson's Medieval Texts, 1955), no. 50).

is possible that on his election to the papacy he had taken the name of Adrian in deference to the pope who was held to have canonized Alban, and that he retained a particular devotion to the saint and his birthplace. Although much remains undetermined about Adrian IV, it is certain that he gave to St. Albans a splendid array of privileges, twelve in all, together with similar documents for the cells of Sopwell, Wymondham, Belvoir, and Tynemouth, and that none of these can be deemed forgeries.[1] His two most important bulls for St. Albans—the 'Incomprehensibilis' of 1156 and the 'Religiosam vitam eligentibus' of 1157—were essentially the means by which the abbey secured independence from the diocesan.[2]

Firstly, following these two bulls, the abbey could invite any catholic bishop to conduct ordinations and consecrations.[3] Throughout the medieval period various bishops, some of whom were resident at St. Albans, were called upon to ordain and consecrate, for example the bishop of Down (Ireland) in 1203 and 1214, and the bishop of Lichfield in 1427.[4] A bishop was also necessary to bless the chrism and holy oils, for which Abbot Robert de Gorron alleged the bishop of Lincoln and his archdeacons had taken payment.[5] On Maundy Thursday 1204 Herlewin, bishop of Leighlin,

[1] Adrian issued only two (? three) bulls for Bury. Dr. Chaplais has drawn attention to a bull of Adrian IV for Westminster (*PUE* i, no. 69; supposedly based on *PUE* i, no. 21, of Innocent II), which he suspects as a forgery ('The Original Charters of Herbert and Gervase Abbots of Westminster (1121–57)', p. 96 n. 6 in *A Medieval Miscellany for D. M. Stenton*, P.R.S., N.S. xxxvi, 1962). It seems possible to me that 'Religiosam vitam' may have acted as the prototype here to which were added the tell-tale embellishments. The texts of the St. Albans bulls are late, but they cannot be regarded as forgeries on textual grounds, and historically they stood up to immediate scrutiny in the Lincoln case (see below, p. 64). It was St. Albans' good fortune that it did not have to resort to forgeries but was able to get the real thing at a time when written evidence was becoming essential. On this point, see E. Searle, 'Battle Abbey and Exemption: the Forged Charters', *EHR* lxxxiii (1968), 468.
[2] *PUE* iii, nos. 100, 118. 1157 was the date of Battle's first showing of William II's charter confirming ecclesiastical exemption (Searle, op. cit., p. 457).
[3] On monastic exemption in Normandy to 1140, see J.-F. Lemarignier, *Étude sur les privilèges d'exemption et de juridiction ecclésiastique*, Archives de la France Monastique, 44 (Paris, 1937), and for England, see D. Knowles, 'The Growth of Exemption', *Downside Review* l (N.S. 31, 1932), 201–31, 396–436.
[4] 'Annales Sancti Albani a.1200–1214' in *Anglo Normannische Geschichtsquellen*, ed. F. Liebermann (Strasbourg, 1879), pp. 167–8, 171–2; and 'Chronicle of the Reign of Henry VI from St. Albans' in *Annales Monasterii S. Albani a Johanne Amundesham*, ed. H. T. Riley (R.S., 1870–1), i. 15. R. Vaughan, *Matthew Paris* (Cambridge, 1958), p. 15, comments on the residence of John, bishop of Ardfert, and Richard, bishop of Bangor, for periods in the 1240s.   [5] *PUE* iii, no. 105.

who had been a monk of Christ Church Canterbury, consecrated the oil and chrism at the high altar at St. Albans in the presence of Abbot John and the whole convent.[1] Secondly, the abbot and monks could not be summoned to a diocesan synod nor could they be compelled to obey its decrees. Thirdly, the monastery was free from the bishop's excommunication and from general interdicts. Fourthly, the abbot had rights of wearing some or all of the *pontificalia* ('Religiosam vitam' granted mitre, ring, sandals, and gloves, while the reissue of Celestine III added tunic and dalmatic). Fifthly, the monastery was exempt from episcopal visitation and correction, though this privilege was not defined in this specific way until the late twelfth century ('Religiosam vitam' forbade anyone exercising the 'episcopal office', and in 1170 the house was stated to be under no bishop except the pope).[2] Finally, the pope stipulated that in future a profession of obedience should be made only to the Church of Rome. It appears that such professions had been made not to the diocesan but to the metropolitan, until the time of Abbot Richard d'Aubigny, who made his profession to Bishop Robert Bloet of Lincoln.[3] As for the blessing of the abbot, Celestine II's privilege had stated that this should be by the diocesan (place not specified), whereas 'Incomprehensibilis' now stated that it should be by a bishop of their choice, presumably in the abbey church.[4] In 1214 it was Eustace, bishop of Ely, who blessed Abbot William before the high altar at St. Albans.[5]

In 'Religiosam vitam' the area of the liberty of St. Albans was defined with some precision, and the fifteen churches which constituted it are named—St. Peter's, St. Stephen's, and Kingsbury in

[1] 'Annales Sancti Albani a. 1200–1214', pp. 167–8.
[2] *PUE* iii, nos. 169, and 170, reissued by Clement III in 1188 (*Chronica Majora*, ed. H. R. Luard (R.S., 1872–83), vi, no. 33) and by Celestine III in 1193 (*PUE* iii, no. 457).
[3] *Gesta Abb.* i. 71–2.   [4] *PUE* iii, nos. 43, 100.
[5] 'Annales Sancti Albani', p. 171. Knowles, 'Growth of Exemption', p. 214, describes 'Incomprehensibilis' as 'a bull of privileges equalling or surpassing that of any other monastic house'. He might have included 'Religiosam vitam eligentibus' with it, which was virtually reissued or confirmed by Alexander III (*PUE* iii, no. 135), Clement III (St. Albans Cart., Chatsworth, ff. 38–9ᵛ; and Small Belvoir Cart., Belvoir Castle Add. MS. 98, pp. 89–91, including 'Incomprehensibilis'), Celestine III (*PUE* iii, no. 459, including 'Incomprehensibilis'), and by Honorius III in 1219 (Large Belvoir Cart., Belvoir Castle Add. MS. 105, ff. 13ᵛ–14ᵛ). The confirmation of Clement III and subsequent reissues I consider to be the 'great privilege', see below, p. 65.

62   *Papal Privileges for*

the town of St. Albans, Watford, Rickmansworth, Abbots Langley, Redbourn, Codicote, St. Paul's Walden, Hexton, Norton, Newnham, Barnet (all in Herts.), and Winslow and Aston Abbots (both in Bucks.). This document, too, speaks of the archdeacon who was to administer the liberty on behalf of the abbot, and whose office was filled by monks of the abbey.[1] Besides being lord of the liberty, the abbot of St. Albans was also lord of the hundred of St. Albans. By the fourteenth century the liberty, and consequently the hundred, had grown and had been to some extent rationalized, and by the end of the Middle Ages the liberty contained twenty-six parishes.[2] The early land endowment of St. Albans had established the liberty. Grants had been made to the saint in the remote past; tradition had accorded Offa the position of founder of the abbey's liberties, and Norman kings had confirmed them.[3] Popes, too, had confirmed St. Albans' liberties and possessions in increasingly exact terms, and it was in this now defined area of the liberty that the privileges of exemption from episcopal visitation and control were to be used to the full.

With the death of Adrian IV, the stream of privileges did not cease to flow, and favour continued to be shown by Alexander III, who granted St. Albans some forty-three privileges and in addition important documents for the cells of Binham, Hatfield Peverel, and Hertford, which confirmed their possessions and took them under the protection of the papal see.[4] Alexander also confirmed certain churches to Belvoir and a tithe arrangement with Thetford,

[1] Celestine III's reissue of 'Religiosam vitam' (*PUE* iii, no. 459) actually specifies monks for the office, and it seems likely that they had in fact always filled it. The first occurrence of an archdeacon appears to be in 1129 at the time of the translation of St. Alban. The authority for this is the *Gesta Abb.* (i. 85–6), but there is no particular reason to doubt the existence of a monastic archdeacon before the liberty and archdeaconry were clearly defined.

[2] For an account of the changes, see *VCH, Hertfordshire*, ii. 319 f. For maps of the liberty, see the endpapers of P. Newcome, *History of the Abbey of St. Albans* (1793), and A. E. Levett, *Studies in Manorial History*, ed. H. M. Cam and others (Oxford, 1938); and for the liberty at the end of the Middle Ages, see R. Peters, *Oculus Episcopi* (Manchester, 1963), introduction.

[3] See P. H. Sawyer, *Anglo-Saxon Charters* (Royal Historical Soc., 1968), nos. 136 and 138 (of Offa, probably spurious), and nos. 150–1, 888, 912, 916, 1228, 1235, 1488, 1497, 1517, 1532; and *Regesta Regum Anglo-Normannorum*, ii, ed. C. Johnson and H. A. Cronne (Oxford, 1956), nos. 218*a* (p. 396), 314*c* (p. 399), 400*a* (p. 404), 512, 595, 1203.

[4] The documents for the cells are *PUE* iii, nos. 136, 147, 256.

and upheld the rights of St. Albans over the dependency of Tynemouth against the bishop of Durham, who was attempting to
assert normal diocesan rights by excommunicating the prior of
Tynemouth (a monk of St. Albans), by consecrating chapels and
cemeteries in churches belonging to St. Albans, and by taking
synodalia from their churches.[1] The rest of Alexander's grants fall
into four main groups: confirmations of churches and possessions,
and exemption from paying tithes in certain areas;[2] documents of
protection addressed to influential clerics;[3] confirmation of the
old privileges in the reissue of 'Religiosam vitam' and further
definition of the fact that no one might issue sentences of excommunication or interdict against St. Albans;[4] and a host of documents concerning *episcopalia*, of which the most important was
'Cum vos et' of 1170. This said that no one except a legate might
suspend or excommunicate the priors of St. Albans' cells; that in
the parishes where the abbey did not have episcopal rights it was
to appoint priests and present them to the bishop, who was to
admit them if suitable;[5] that the bishop was not to exact procession
dues within its confines and parishes; and that in abbatial vacancies the prior and chapter of St. Albans might exercise authority
over the dependencies.[6] In parishes where St. Albans did not have
episcopal rights, no one was to build a church or oratory without
the consent of the diocesan and St. Albans,[7] but in proprietary
churches in the liberty the clerics were to be answerable to the
abbot alone in both spiritual and temporal matters,[8] and it was the
archdeacon of St. Albans who inducted, and not the bishop of

[1] *PUE* iii, nos. 138, 167, 174–6, 178–81, 184, 190, 203, 239–40, 245, 330, and
332.
[2] Ibid., nos. 152, 168, 171, 255, 326, and nos. 133–4, 205, 246.
[3] Ibid., nos. 177, 191, 206.   [4] Ibid., nos. 135, 165–6.
[5] Further defined in 'Qui ad universorum' of 1171 (ibid., no. 182) and 'Qui pro
defensione', addressed to the bishops (ibid., no. 328) and by Clement III (ibid.,
no. 404).
[6] Ibid., no. 170—confirmed by Clement III in 1188 (*Chron. Maj.* vi, no. 33) and
by Celestine III in 1193 (*PUE* iii, no. 457).
[7] 'Ad officii nostri' of 1173 (ibid., no. 204), confirmed by Celestine III in 1193
(ibid., no. 454).
[8] 'Erga prelatos suos' of 1171–81 (ibid., no. 329) and 'Merito debent dignitatis'
of 1171–81 (ibid., no. 325) and its confirmations of 1188 and 1193 (*Chron. Maj.* vi,
no. 31 and *PUE* iii, nos. 450 and 458), and 'Cum ab ecclesia' of 1173 (ibid., no.
200).

Lincoln's archdeacons.[1] The relationship between these parishes and St. Albans was equivalent to that between St. Albans itself and the pope, who was its only bishop,[2] while the parishioners of its cells were protected from their diocesans to some degree, although only in temporal concerns.[3]

It has been held that Alexander III favoured St. Albans and other great Benedictine houses in their struggles against the bishop. When the Lincoln case opened St. Albans flourished the privileges of Calixtus II, Eugenius III, Adrian IV, and Alexander III.[4] The king demurred to the section of Celestine II's privilege which concerned the vills and liberties of St. Albans, and during the hearing of the case it was obvious that the abbey had stolen a march on the bishop, who could produce no privileges—his cupboard was bare—and who had to fall back on the argument of prescription, that is, the traditional practice of the diocese.[5] It was undoubtedly St. Albans which triumphed in the settlement before the king, his bishops, abbots, and magnates, completed in 1163. For the grant of £10 p.a. the bishop, Robert de Chesney, was forced to surrender his claim over the abbey itself and the fifteen churches of the liberty.[6] It may be asked why the Lincoln party were so slow in pressing their claims before the popes and for that matter before the king. An answer to this seems to lie firstly in the prompt action of St. Albans (when Abbot Robert died on 23 October 1166 the house was more than 600 marks in debt from his efforts),[7] and secondly in the fact that the assumption of powers by the abbot of St. Albans had led to a firmly established jurisdiction at a remote end of the diocese of Lincoln, to the south and east of

---

[1] This may be inferred to have developed from the establishment of the liberty and archdeaconry in or before 1157, see above, pp. 61–2. *PUE* iii, no. 327 'Cum ad tuenda' (1171–81), repeated by Clement III in 1188 (*Chron. Maj.* vi, no. 35) outlines (and the above documents) the duty of the bishop to induct when the abbot and convent had presented to him.   [2] See *PUE* iii, no. 169.

[3] Ibid., no. 172, 'Dilecti filii nostri', confirmed by Lucius III (*Chron. Maj.* vi, no. 27)

[4] See L. F. Rushbrook Williams, *History of the Abbey of St. Alban* (London, 1917), pp. 72–5, for an account of the case.

[5] H. P. King, 'The Life and Acts of Robert de Chesney' (London M.A. thesis, 1955), also gives an account of the case.

[6] *The Registrum Antiquissimum of the Cathedral Church of Lincoln*, i, ed. C. W. Foster (L.R.S. vol. 27, 1931), no. 104, and see also *Reg. Antiq. Linc.* ii (L.R.S. vol. 28, 1933), no. 321 (*Cal. Charter Rolls 1327–41* (H.M.S.O., 1912), p. 149).

[7] Williams, *Abbey of St. Alban*, p. 76.

which lay the powerful diocese of London and the archdeaconry of Middlesex, and the Middlesex parishes of the archbishop of Canterbury's peculiar of Croydon. From 1163 onwards the abbot's rights of exemption from episcopal interference in the liberty were beyond question and, although challenged, the rights of the cells to be extra-diocesan had been clearly declared by the popes. On Easter Sunday 1163 Abbot Robert de Gorron celebrated mass in the abbey church in pontificals and made plain his position as a mitred abbot,[1] and at the Council of Tours in May of the same year he took the first seat among the English abbots—in the words of 'Religiosam vitam': 'sicut Beatus Albanus (Anglorum) prothomartyr esse dinoscitur, ita et abbas monasterii ipsius inter abbates Angliae primus omni tempore dignitatis ordine habeatur . . .'.[2]

II. In 1256 Master William de Sancto Edwardo, clerk, and Brother William de Horton,[3] proctors of St. Albans, set out for the curia with instructions to negotiate for certain documents. There are two accounts of the business which was expedited: the fuller is in the *Gesta Abbatum*[4] which contains two more impetrations and bulls; the other account is in the Wymondham Cartulary,[5] which is considerably more corrupt and was probably taken from another source or perhaps indirectly from the *Gesta*. Firstly the proctors sought the renewal of the 'great privilege', undoubtedly 'Religiosam vitam' as reissued by Clement III, Celestine III, and Honorius III, which they seemingly effected with difficulty.[6] The immediate occasion of their visit, however, was not this, but the desire of St. Albans to appropriate Hartburn church (Northumb.) to

---

[1] *Gesta Abb.* i. 158. The final settlement took place on 8 Mar. 1163, as Foster says, and Easter Sunday fell on 24 Mar.   [2] *PUE* iii, no. 118, and *Gesta Abb.* i. 177.

[3] William de Horton occurs as a papal chaplain in 1259 (*CPL* i. 364). He was cellarer of Tynemouth by 1244, was to become (?)prior (*temp.* Hen. III) and finally prior of Wymondham in 1264 (*Chron. Maj.* vi. 90; J. Brand, *History of Newcastle upon Tyne* (1789), ii. 82; and Dugdale, *Monasticon*, iii. 325). His appointment as prior of Wymondham possibly accounts for the copying of these transactions into the Wymondham Cartulary, and the note at the end 'Hec sunt adquisita domini Willelmi prioris de Wymondham' might well refer to him, since he was concerned in the acquisitions, rather than to William of St. Albans, prior from 1257 to 1262.

[4] i. 350–5.   [5] B.M. Cotton MS. Titus C viii, ff. 74–5.

[6] Honorius's confirmation of 20 Feb. 1219 appears in the Large Belvoir Cart., ff. 13ᵛ–14ᵛ. Printed in Dugdale, *Monasticon*, ii. 232–3, num. xxi (from the Binham Cart. B.M. Cotton MS. Claudius D xiii); and see *CPL* i. 63 and *Gesta Abb.* iii. 163, and for confirmations by Archbishops Kilwardby and Sudbury (St. Albans Cart.,

go towards expenses on hospitality. On hearing rumours of the death of the rector of Hartburn, Hugh de Florentino, the abbot of St. Albans had presented Robert de Sotingdona,[1] a royal clerk. When the church, which belonged to the cell of Tynemouth and hence indirectly to the abbey, was found not to be vacant after all, the abbot commissioned William de Horton, the cellarer of Tynemouth, to arrange for its future appropriation with Walter Kirkham, bishop of Durham (1249–60). Kirkham agreed that on the death of the present rector two-thirds of the proceeds from the church should go to St. Albans, while the remaining third was to be used for establishing a vicarage. At the time of these transactions Horton himself visited the church of Hartburn, and, on the same occasion witnessing as it happened the sudden death of the rector, took possession of the church despite the presence of armed men. A successful request was made to Sir Hugh Bolebec, to whom the armed men presumably belonged, to surrender the right which he claimed as patron of the church by grant of the abbot and convent of St. Albans.[2] But it was at this point that Master John de Camezano, nephew of the former pope, Innocent IV, and his *auditor litterarum contradictarum*, endeavoured to exchange Wingrave church (Bucks.) for Hartburn.[3] Innocent IV had already promised the appropriation of Hartburn and St. Albans was determined to resist John de Camezano's challenge. John de Camezano now got a mandate to the abbot of St. Augustine's, Canterbury, to act as judge delegate and try the case. The case, perhaps not unexpectedly, was returned to Rome and came before the English cardinal, John of Toledo, to whom the St. Albans proctors, William de Sancto Edwardo and William de Horton, had commendatory

Chatsworth, ff. 53–6). This was confirmed at the petition of King Richard II and St. Albans, by Pope Boniface IX as late as 1395 (*CPL* iv. 516) and by Nicholas V in 1447 (*CPL* x. 353–4).

[1] Robert de Shottindon occurs as a royal justice from 1254 to 1257, when he died at Hertford while on circuit (E. Foss, *The Judges of England* (London, 1848–57), ii. 474, and B.M. Cotton MS. Caligula A xii, f. 58ᵛ).

[2] See *Gesta Abb.* i. 346–9.

[3] For John de Camezano, see P. Herde, *Beiträge zum Päpstlichen Kanzlei-und Urkundenwesen im 13. Jahrhundert*, 2nd edn. (Kallmünz, 1967), pp. 22–4. He was in possession of the church of Wingrave in 1256 (*Les Registres d'Alexandre IV*, ed. B. de La Roncière and others (Bibl. des Écoles Françaises d'Athènes et de Rome, ser. 2, no. 15, Paris, 1895–1959), i, no. 1445).

letters from the king, and also to the royal proctors, Master
Robert de Barro and Master Finatus.[1] Cardinal John's ordination,
dated at Anagni on 10 July 1256, confirmed Hartburn church to
St. Albans but said that St. Albans was to give to John de Camezano
a yearly pension of 25 marks until an alternative benefice of not
less than 80 marks value became vacant.[2] The abbot and convent of
Waltham, St. Albans' conservators, were instructed by Alexander
IV on 23 July of the same year to carry out the sentence.[3] The
church of Wingrave had figured in the history of the appropriation
of Hartburn and now together with Coniscliffe (Durham) it was
to be the subject of further instructions to St. Albans' proctors,[4]
for we read in the account of the curial business that the pope
agreed to the appropriation of these two churches, and that he
issued executory letters about this.[5] The papal document allowing
the appropriation ('Et si ecclesiarum') was addressed by Alexander
IV to St. Albans on 13 January 1257.[6]

A large section of the business naturally concerned further
definition and revitalization of St. Albans' exemption. The pope
stated that obedience from churches, which St. Albans or its cells
held 'in proprios usus', was to be to them and not to the diocesans
of the places where the churches were situated. This was the indult
which was granted on 6 February 1257 by Alexander IV on their

[1] *Chron. Maj.* vi, nos. 160–1 (the latter dated 11 Apr. 1256). Henry III had also
written to the pope and to Master John de Camezano on the matter of the church of
Hartburn (ibid., nos. 157–9). The proctors' letters of appointment are dated from
St. Albans on 10 Apr. 1256 (St. Albans Cart., Chatsworth, ff. 51–3).

[2] For Cardinal John of Toledo, see my *Papal Judges Delegate in the Province of
Canterbury 1198–1254* (Oxford, 1971), pp. 24–5. A vicarage was established at
Hartburn by 1260 (*CPR, 1258–66*, p. 96).

[3] St. Albans Cart., Chatsworth, f. 34^r-v (and see ff. 51–3 for Cardinal John's instrument and account of the case); see also *Reg. Alex. IV*, i, no. 1445.

[4] *Gesta Abb.* i. 350. The monk, William de Sancto Edmundo, seems to have been
part of their number by this time. He had served as a proctor at the curia with
William de Sancto Edwardo as early as 1252. In the September of that year they
received letters of credit for 50 marks (*Chron. Maj.* vi, nos. 108–9). According to the
Gesta Abb. (i. 331) he had been sent to Rome to deal with the Wymondham affair,
while Master William de Sancto Edwardo was to deal with the appropriation of St.
Michael's church Kingsbury (effected in 1252) (St. Albans Cart., Chatsworth,
ff. 45^v–46, and *CPL* i. 281). *

[5] The clause concerning the appropriation of Wingrave and Coniscliffe is missing
from the account in the Wymondham Cartulary but it appears in the account in the
Gesta Abb.

[6] St. Albans Cart., Chatsworth, f. 35. The mandate of induction is in *CPL* (i. 343).

* In 1249 the archdeacon of Norfolk had attempted visitation of Wymondham; see *Papal
Judges Delegate*, 280.

petition.[1] The next concession was a confirmation of the exemption granted by Innocent IV that, contrary to his general ruling in the Council of Lyons of 1245, they should not be forced to answer before ordinaries 'ratione delicti seu contractus'.[2] Two documents from Alexander address St. Albans apparently on this matter, one dated at Anagni on 7 October 1256,[3] the other dated 1257.[4] This exemption went hand in hand with the following one, that neither St. Albans nor its priors should be summoned more than two days' journey from their diocese to make answer in lawsuits which had been initiated by papal letters.[5] The age-old privilege which exempted St. Albans from any adverse decrees or constitutions of legates or *nuncii* was restated in 'Exigentibus vestre devocionis' of 26 October 1256.[6] Finally the abbot of St. Albans was empowered to dispense the monks from any irregularities,[7] the priors of the cells were to enjoy the liberties and immunities of the mother house, and in churches where St. Albans did not have episcopal rights, priests were to be appointed by it, presented to the diocesan, and assigned portions. These priests were to answer to St. Albans in temporal matters and to the diocesan in spiritual matters, according to the tenor of St. Albans' privileges.[8]

A further section of the transactions related to certain indulgences which the pope was asked to grant or confirm. Firstly, he conceded an indulgence of one year and forty days' enjoined penance to all penitents visiting St. Albans on the feast of the Saint and in the following week (eight days). Roughly contemporaneous with this must have been Alexander IV's grant, made on 11 December 1256, of an indulgence but with a lesser period of time (forty days), to

---

[1] *CPL* i. 341.

[2] c. 1. 6. V. 7, in *Corpus Iuris Canonici*, ed. E. Friedberg, 2nd edn. ii (Leipzig, 1881).

[3] St. Albans Cart., Chatsworth, f. 33ᵛ.   [4] *CPL* i. 344.

[5] See the ruling of Innocent III in the Fourth Lateran Council (c. 28. X. I. 3, in *Corpus Iuris Canonici* ii), and compare a similar undated indult for Bury St. Edmunds from Alexander IV, which refers to a previous exemption for them from his predecessor, Pope Innocent IV (*Pinchbeck Reg.* i. 17–18, and same document on pp. 46–7). This grant was to be valid for five years.

[6] St. Albans Cart., Chatsworth, f. 34.

[7] Ibid., f. 48: a document of Urban IV ('Quia ex apostolica': Viterbo 1 Apr. 1262) is in part a confirmation of this.

[8] See above, p. 63. This application and concession is not included in the account in the Wymondham Cartulary but only in the *Gesta Abb.* (i. 351).

those going to the house of St. Mary de Pré on the feast of the Blessed Virgin or during the following eight days.[1] The St. Albans document accords with a later document of Pope Nicholas IV of 17 June 1290 for the house, which granted a similar period of time to Alexander's.[2] The earliest known grant of this kind to the shrine had been that of Calixtus II, who had allowed twelve days.[3] Thus the grant had grown almost thirty-four fold—a sign of the popularity of this kind of document—and by the time of Boniface IX (1389–1404) a relaxation of seven years and seven periods of forty days' enjoined penance was made to penitents who visited the parish church of St. Peter in St. Albans on principal feasts, those of St. Peter ad Vincula and the Dedication, during the octaves of some of them, and the six days of Whitweek.[4] A second form of indulgence granted three periods of forty days to those contributing towards the fabric of the church,[5] and the pope confirmed all indulgences and remissions which had been granted by archbishops and bishops 'ab principio mundi usque in hodiernum diem'. These included one year and forty days granted by the bishop of Sora (Italy) to those going to the monastery on separate days out of devotion, or contributing to the fabric, a similar grant from the bishop of Trebinje in the province of Ragusa, a grant of forty days from the bishop of Rochester,[6] and of 140 days from the pope himself.

Another group of documents which were sought concerned financial exactions. Foremost among these was an indult which stated that the obligations which had been imposed upon the cells of Tynemouth and Belvoir by the bishop of Hereford, Peter d'Aigueblanche, and Master Rostand (Masson), were to be revoked, since 'one and the same body should not be doubly

---

[1] Dugdale, *Monasticon*, iii. 356–7, num. v.

[2] *CPL* i. 513.

[3] See above p. 59, and *PUE* iii, no. 6 (cf. Bury which was granted twenty days: ibid., no. 8).

[4] *CPL* v. 276.

[5] Cf. Alexander IV's two grants to St. Mary de Pré (dated 13 Sept. and 23 Dec. 1256) of forty days' indulgence to those helping towards the repair of the buildings (Dugdale, *Monasticon*, iii. 356, num. iv and 357, num. vi).

[6] Cf. ibid., ii. 236, num. xxiii, a later grant by Thomas of Ingoldisthorpe, bishop of Rochester—this cannot be before 1283 (see *Handbook of British Chronology*, ed. F. M. Powicke and E. B. Fryde, 2nd edn. (Royal Hist. Soc., 1961), pp. 247–8).

IX

70   *Papal Privileges for*

afflicted'. This doubtless refers to the 1255 mission of the papal collectors who imposed a payment of 500 marks on St. Albans itself, and provoked Matthew Paris to write: 'Alas! For shame and grief! These and other detestable things emanated at this time from the sulphurous fountain of the Roman church.'[1] Money was directly, or indirectly, the subject-matter of some of the other privileges, including tithes. The usual complement concerned possessions—the goods of the monasteries were confirmed and an indult stated that any alienations of land which had been made by their predecessors might be revoked, oaths, pacts, and confirmations notwithstanding. No one from the monastery, without the consent of all or the seals of the convents, was to obligate St. Albans or the priors of the cells to any merchants: nor were they to be compelled to confer benefices or give pensions unwillingly, a reference to reservations[2] and provisions.[3]

Further grants were sought and made to the abbot. He might in future have a portable altar to take about with him, on which he or a deputy could celebrate and administer the sacrament to his household. The date of this grant was 6 January 1257 from the Lateran.[4] It was also requested that the abbot might give solemn blessings after the 'Agnus Dei' outside and through the streets, to which the curial officials replied that the St. Albans proctors unnecessarily sought this privilege, because they already had one which allowed solemn benedictions of all kinds, and no one in a position to object had questioned this.[5]

[1] See *Councils and Synods*, ed. F. M. Powicke and C. R. Cheney, 2 vols. (Oxford, 1964), ii, pt. i. 501–3, for the council held at London in Oct. 1255 in this connection; *Gesta Abb.* i. 382–3; and *Chron. Maj.* v. 524, for Matthew Paris's remarks.

[2] Cf. similar indults of Innocent IV, 'Monasterii vestri profectibus' and 'Monasterio vestro quod', dated from Genoa on 1 June 1251, and 'Devocionis vestre precibus', dated at the Lateran on 31 Oct. 1253 (St. Albans Cart., Chatsworth, ff. 45–6ᵛ): presumably it was a confirmation of these.

[3] See canon no. 3 among the decrees of the Council of Lyons (Mansi xxiii) which is obviously referred to in one of the points of petition.

[4] St. Albans Cart., Chatsworth, f. 34ᵛ, and cf. B.M. Arundel MS. 34, f. 13ʳ⁻ᵛ, a later grant of this kind of 1423, and *Gesta Abb.* iii. 437, a grant to Abbot John de la Moote (1396–1401).

[5] Cf. previous documents, the 'Dignum arbitramur et' of Alexander III of 1181 (*PUE* iii, no. 337)—blessing not specifically mentioned here—of Clement III of 1188 (St. Albans Cart., Chatsworth, ff. 37ʳ⁻ᵛ, and B.M. Cotton MS. Nero D i f. 159ᵛ, and *Chron. Maj.* vi, no. 34), and the reissue of 'Religiosam vitam' by Celestine III in 1193 (*PUE* iii, no. 459).

The last section of the curial business, according to the account in the Wymondham Cartulary, concerned the impetration of conservatorial documents, to safeguard all the privileges which had been granted, for a term of five years.[1] The vogue for getting conservatorial documents began during the pontificate of Innocent IV. An example of the appointment of a conservator to protect a particular document is provided in the affair of the appropriation of St. Michael's church, Kingsbury, when the abbot of Waltham was required to see this put into effect in 1252 and to uphold the sentence.[2] The conservatory document provided an insurance cover and became a frequent part of curial business. In all probability the abbot of Waltham (Augustinian, Essex) was one of the conservators who were granted in 1257. He appears as a conservator of the privileges of St. Albans at the end of the thirteenth century in connection with the Datchet case,[3] and in the late fourteenth century as conservator of the privileges of St. Albans and her cells, when he had to deal with certain 'men of Satan' who had assaulted the monks of Tynemouth, burnt their houses and stolen their goods.[4] The abbots of Bury, Westminster, and Reading, are mentioned in the same source as conservators of St. Albans, and it is not difficult to account for their appointment.[5] The abbot of Waltham, though at first sight not the most obvious choice, had much to recommend him. He was only some fifteen miles from St. Albans, not quite so accessible as the prior of Dunstable, but unlike the prior of Dunstable he did not have his own powerful liberty and was therefore obviously more acceptable as a conservator. The requests of St. Albans had thus for the most part been granted and the conservatory letters had been issued, so that the abbey's position was assured, but in point of fact it was St. Alban who proved to be the best conservator of its privileges in the thirteenth century, just as he had been its most powerful advocate with the papacy in the twelfth century.[6]

[1] Clause 26 in the Wymondham Cartulary: in the *Gesta Abb.* account it is not placed last.   [2] St. Albans Cart., Chatsworth, f. 46, and *CPL* i. 281.
[3] St. Albans Cart., B.M. Cotton MS. Otho D iii, f. 160.
[4] Tynemouth Cart., Syon House Muns. D. xi. 1, ff. 116ᵛ–118ᵛ.   [5] Ibid., f. 116.
[6] In the fifteenth century the relics of St. Alban were used against dearth, and were allegedly no less powerful in bringing changes in the weather ('Chron. of the Reign of Henry VI from St. Albans', pp. 36, 38, 63).

III. The third part of our investigation concerns Abbot Thomas de la Mare's formulary or letter-book, and in particular the section of that book which records the elucidation by Master Richard de Wymundeswolde of certain doubtful points in the privilege which had been granted in the time of Clement III to Abbot Warin and St. Albans.[1] Abbot Thomas de la Mare, some of whose brilliance and power is captured in the magnificent monumental brass in which he is arrayed in full pontificals and which remains in the abbey today, was elected to rule over St. Albans in 1349. He survived until 1396 and was said to have reached the age of eighty-eight when he died. It is recorded that he entered the monastery in the time of Abbot Hugh of Eversdon (1309–27),[2] was sent by him as a monk to Wymondham and was later appointed prior of Tynemouth, an office which he held by 1340.[3] The documents which are included in the formulary or letter-book range in date from 1342 to 1391, and it is stated that the core of the collection was drawn up in 1382 by Brother William Wyntershulle, chaplain to Abbot de la Mare. The primary interest of the formulary is that it is composed of real documents.[4]

Here the privileges of the abbey and liberty can be seen in operation in the latter part of the fourteenth century. The abbot orders the archdeacon of St. Albans to induct into a benefice in the exempt jurisdiction,[5] and grants him a general commission for absolving.[6] The visitors of the exempt jurisdiction order the archdeacon to cite on their behalf.[7] The abbot seeks chrism from the bishop of London;[8] he grants a licence to William de Saxeby, rector of Bushey (in the exempt jurisdiction), to be absent from his cure for two years;[9] he warns the vicar of St. Peter's in the town of St. Albans to reside.[10] He sends a commission to the bishop of 'Lambrensis' (?Lycostomen, under the patriarch of Constantinople)[11]

---

[1] C.U.L. MS. Ee 4. 20 (Wymundeswolde's section is on ff. 114-18ᵛ).

[2] See *Gesta Abb.* ii. 373.

[3] See Dugdale, *Monasticon*, ii. 197–8, and *Gesta Abb.* ii. 371 ff.

[4] See W. A. Pantin, 'English Monastic Letter-Books', *Historical Essays in honour of James Tait*, ed. J. G. Edwards and others (Manchester, 1933), p. 220.

[5] C.U.L. MS. Ee 4. 20, f. 32ᵛ.   [6] Ibid., f. 35.

[7] Ibid., f. 44.   [8] Ibid., f. 87ᵛ.   [9] Ibid., f. 87.   [10] Ibid., f. 89ᵛ.

[11] Robert, bishop of Lambrensis (1366–94), see *Handbook of British Chronology*, p. 267, and W. Stubbs, *Registrum Sacrum Anglicanum*, 2nd edn. (Oxford, 1897), p. 197.

to come to St. Albans and to confer sacred and minor orders on 17 December 1384.[1] A similar licence to the archbishop of Damascus from Abbot de la Mare refers to the blessing of chrism, the consecration of altars and churches and the ordination of clerks.[2] The abbot writes to the bishop of London about an exchange between the incumbent of Barnet (in the exempt jurisdiction) and the incumbent of Littleton (Middx.), in the bishop's diocese,[3] and he collates to the chapel of St. Julian.[4] He notifies the king of the appointment of a coroner within the liberty.[5] The prior of St. Albans is granted a commission to visit the priory of Hertford,[6] and sent to provide a prioress for the cell of Sopwell.[7] Articles of inquiry are transcribed for use when visiting a monastery,[8] and the oaths to be taken by the abbot of an exempt monastery and by the prior of a cell on his appointment are included.[9] Reading all this, and details about parish churches, deaneries, legal settlements and the ordination of vicarages, one is strongly reminded of the average diocesan's work.

The section of the book between folios 107 and 119, which constitutes a separate quire, consists of a section on compositions between St. Albans and the diocesans of Norwich, Lincoln, and Durham, a section on portions and the ordination of vicarages, and the section concerned with the interpretation of Clement III's privilege for St. Albans. It reflects, therefore, other aspects of St. Albans' jurisdiction: namely the establishment of the rights of the mother house and cells *vis-à-vis* the ordinaries and the general move towards the appropriation of churches, which had happened in the mid thirteenth century, followed by the ordination of vicarages and the provision of portions. To find a basis for their activities, both past and present, the abbots returned to a study and analysis of some of their early privileges. That Abbot Thomas de la Mare chose to do so at this time suggests either that certain rights of St. Albans were under attack, and had therefore to be established and authenticated, or that the abbot was seeking to expand his jurisdiction.

[1] C.U.L. MS. Ee 4. 20, f. 49ᵛ. [2] Ibid., f. 82ᵛ.
[3] Ibid., f. 83ᵛ, and cf. 67ᵛ. [4] Ibid., f. 59. [5] Ibid., f. 40.
[6] Ibid., f. 33. [7] Ibid., f. 35. [8] Ibid., ff. 71–2ᵛ.
[9] Ibid., f. 73ʳ⁻ᵛ.

74   *Papal Privileges for*

Shortly after his election Abbot de la Mare petitioned the pope, Clement VI, for certain grants, firstly that he might present one of his monks to the priory of Tynemouth,[1] secondly that he might appropriate Appleton church in order to send monks to Oxford (the monastery of St. Albans being in financial straits because of the Black Death)[2] and finally that he might have an indult to choose a confessor.[3] According to the St. Albans chronicler, papal claims were made to present to the priory of Tynemouth because the vacancy became known through the promotion of Thomas de la Mare to St. Albans, although the abbot of St. Albans had long had the right of electing the prior of the dependency.[4] This right had been clearly stated in the composition between St. Albans and the bishop of Durham, which was made by judges delegate in May 1247. The abbot was to appoint the prior of Tynemouth (the prior of St. Albans might do so in an abbatial vacancy), to remove him if it was necessary, according to his privileges, and to present him to the bishop of Durham, to whom the prior was to show obedience for his parish churches.[5] The bull 'Religionis zelus sincerae', allowing Abbot de la Mare to appoint, was obtained on 11 August 1349, and thus the rights over Tynemouth were saved, but it was expensive.[6] The second request, which was for the appropriation, was granted saving the rights of the bishop and the archdeacon, and is said to have cost the abbot £200.[7] The effects of the Black Death had made appropriation very desirable and had caused a lack of priests—the subject of two later indults to Abbot de la Mare, dated 28 February 1351 and 7 June 1363. These permitted the abbot to promote monks of twenty to twenty-five years of age to holy orders.[8] Mention has been made of the growing financial

---

[1] *Calendar of Entries in the Papal Registers: Petitions to the Pope, 1342–1419*, ed. W. H. Bliss (H.M.S.O., 1896), i. 172 (hereafter cited as *Cal. Pet.*); and see *Gesta Abb.* ii. 391–2.
[2] *Cal. Pet.* i. 171–2. Nicholas IV had allowed appropriation in 1291 (St. Albans Cart., Chatsworth, ff. 50ᵛ–51), but this presumably had not taken effect.
[3] *CPL* iii. 329 (not in *Cal. Pet.* i. 173 as stated). This is really of no particular note here except that it was granted on the same day as these documents and that this kind of indult was becoming more frequently sought, see below, p. 78.
[4] *Gesta Abb.* ii. 390–4.   [5] C.U.L. MS. Ee 4. 20, f. 108, and *Gesta Abb.* i. 390.
[6] *CPL* iii. 314.   [7] *Gesta Abb.* iii. 386.
[8] *CPL* iii. 383 (St. Albans Cart., Chatsworth, ff. 49ᵛ–50), and *Cal. Pet.* i. 425. See also C.U.L. MS. Ee 4. 20, f. 82. 7 June 1363 is the date of the petition, which is marked 'Granted'.

plight of St. Albans, which Abbot de la Mare attempted to remedy in part by obtaining a perpetual indult to the effect that the abbot-elect need no longer go to the curia for confirmation. This had hitherto been a fruitful source of papal income. In the long term this was a great saving to St. Albans, but immediately it probably added to the abbey's financial difficulties and debts.[1] His abbacy also witnessed considerable discontent from the townsmen, culminating in the Peasants' Revolt.[2] Another challenge to Abbot de la Mare's authority came apparently from within the abbey, from the prior, John de la Moote, who was to succeed de la Mare as abbot in 1396, and who is said to have obtained certain bulls which were to the Abbot's detriment.[3]

These circumstances presumably account for the abbot seeking the opinion of Master Richard de Wymundeswolde, a highly successful English proctor at the papal curia, a D.C.L. in 1338 and an advocate of the curia by 1343. The opinion must have been given by the spring of 1356, for he died early in that year at Avignon. It is interesting that de la Mare chose to employ a famous secular lawyer and not one of St. Albans' monks at Oxford.[4]

The articles of inquiry and Wymundeswolde's opinions were as follows:

(1) whether St. Albans and its priories might be classified as fully exempt. The reply affirmed that there was no doubt on this matter as the words of the privilege definitely showed.

(2) whether the abbot might summon any catholic bishop to celebrate in the monastery or in a church or cell subject to it, without having sought a licence from the bishop of the diocese in question. This point was more open to doubt and therefore more fully argued, the authorities of Hostiensis, Johannes Andreae, and

---

[1] *CPL* iv. 293–4, 517–18; and see below, pp. 80–1. Henceforth St. Albans was to pay the papacy 20 marks yearly for this concession.

[2] See *Gesta Abb*. iii. 285 ff. and 370. In **1357** Abbot de la Mare had obtained a licence to crenellate and in the 1360s a new gateway and walls were erected against the townspeople (*CPR, 1354–8*, p. 574, and *A Guide to St. Albans Cathedral* (Royal Comm. on Historical Monuments, H.M.S.O., 1952), p. 28).

[3] *Gesta Abb*. iii. 463.

[4] See A. B. Emden, *A Biographical Register of the University of Cambridge to 1500* (Cambridge, 1963), and A. B. Cobban, *The King's Hall within the University of Cambridge in the Later Middle Ages* (Cambridge, 1969), p. 54 n. 2 and p. 199 nn. 1 and 12.

others were cited, and it was decided that when a bishop was summoned to a place fully exempt, the diocesan's permission was not necessary.

(3) whether such a bishop might ordain any suitable clerks, who had letters dimissory from their diocesans, or only clerks and monks who were fully subject to the abbot. The bishop might ordain any suitable clerks.

(4) whether, if the bishop ordains those not subject to the abbot, their diocesans might intervene or coerce the bishop in any way. To this it was answered that there could be no coercion because both the place and the ordaining bishop were exempt from the diocesan.

(5) whether priors of priories and cells which were subject to the monastery, not having sought licence from the diocesan in whose diocese they were, might require bishops to celebrate orders in their cells in the same way. Here some definition was needed: it seemed that if it meant that the priors were acting without the licence of the abbot the answer was no, otherwise, with abbatial approval, it was in order.

(6) whether the abbot might institute monks in vacant churches and chapels, which were fully subject, united, or appropriated to the monastery, in which perpetual vicars and secular clerks were usually instituted. It seemed firstly that he could not, because such a right was not specifically conceded, but on the other hand it was not specifically prohibited either and the abbot had definite pontifical powers to change the status of benefices.

(7) whether the abbot might tax, augment, or split up the portions of vicars, when it seemed to him to be a legitimate action. Here it seemed that he might not split up vicarages but that he might augment and tax them.

(8) whether the abbot might authorize exchanges between the incumbents of benefices which were fully subject to him. The authorities of Johannes Andreae and Hostiensis appeared in favour, but against them it was alleged that a dispensation was needed. However, the pope had given pontifical jurisdiction to the abbot and these powers related to jurisdiction and not to episcopal orders.

(9) whether the abbot might unite etc. churches, priories, and cells, over which he had episcopal jurisdiction. First of all it seemed that he might not, because the power was not expressly mentioned in the pope's concession, but on the other hand it might be said that he could, as argued in the answer to question eight.

(10) whether the bishop of the diocese might, without licence of the abbot, ordain those within the jurisdiction of the abbot, and if he should do so whether he would incur a penalty. On the one hand it might be answered in the affirmative, because although they were exempt generally, they were still subject to the bishop to get orders and chrism, but on the other hand there was a negative answer, because the said clerks were like the clerks of another diocese and the bishop could not ordain them without the licence of their superior, in this case the abbot.

(11) whether the abbot might receive *munera* when visiting the cells or priories, and churches, especially when it was the custom, and if he should do so whether he would incur a penalty. It seemed that the abbot might not because the *Decretales* prohibited such tributes and all authorities (Johannes Andreae and the Novels) seemed to agree on this, and there was now a law that he could not receive any gift unless a procuration in money as stated in the *Extravagantes* of Benedict XII, and there was thus accordingly a penalty if he did. But for a solution to this question one had to consider the power of the abbot in the place he was visiting. If he had free administration of the fruits of the place, he might receive *munera*; if, however, he did not have free disposal of the fruits, it did not seem that he could receive gifts at a visitation but only a tax.

(12) whether the abbot might grant general indulgences to those over whom he had episcopal jurisdiction. The answer was in the affirmative, because the abbot had all pontifical rights as stated in the answer to the first point on which there was no doubt.

(13) whether the abbot might make a journey through the province giving solemn blessings anywhere throughout the whole kingdom;

(14) whether a legate *a latere* or his delegate might excommunicate, suspend, or put under an interdict the abbot or monks, without a special licence from the apostolic see;

(15) whether the abbot and monks were bound to keep the decrees of legates of the apostolic see; and finally

(16) whether the abbot might convert churches 'in proprios usus', where he had rights as patron and where the churches were served by secular clerks alone, saving a reasonable delay until provision was made for the priest.

The opinions on the last four points have not survived, if indeed they were recorded, but from the evidence on the other points St. Albans and Abbot de la Mare had reason to be well satisfied with Wymundeswolde's assessment.

IV. From the mid fourteenth century the indult became the most common papal document. The numerous grants of these privileges to individuals reflect the change in social conditions since the period when the abbey as a community had obtained for itself bulls confirming possessions and establishing rights. The most common indults or dispensations were to choose a confessor who might grant absolution enjoining a salutary penance, except in cases which were reserved to the Holy See, or who might give plenary remission to those who were penitent at the hour of their death. Such indults were granted to monks of St. Albans, some of them resident in the cells,[1] and in at least one instance to a nun of St. Mary de Pré,[2] as well as to superiors, including the prior of Tynemouth and the prioress of Sopwell.[3] Many of these were granted by Martin V, a considerable proportion of them in 1423, and it is recorded that the fee was ten *grossi* for an indult for one person and twelve for two persons.[4] Indults to have a portable altar were granted to John Wheathampstead, John Stokes, Adam Thoby, John Langley, and John Hatfield—all monks of St. Albans— between 1415 and 1423.[5] Three of these, Adam Thoby, John Langley, and John Hatfield, acquired indults for confessors at the same time.[6] On 20 October 1423 Martin V issued a general indult

---

[1] *CPL* iii. 326, 409, 437, 444; iv. 487; v. 42; vii. 307–9, 311, 318, 340, 342; and viii. 36, 432.   [2] Ibid., xii. 701.   [3] Ibid., vii. 307–8.   [4] Ibid., vii. 308–9.
[5] Ibid., vi. 358, 363; vii. 306, 316.   [6] Ibid., vii. 306, 309, 316, 318.

to the abbot and convent of St. Albans allowing them to use portable altars, because some of the monks were frequently called away from the monastery to attend to business in London, while yet others were at the *studium generale* at Oxford.[1] Other indults were sought by monks of St. Albans, who were priests, to receive and retain any benefice, to exchange for similar or dissimilar benefices, to hold a benefice with cure which was normally assigned to secular clerks, and other permutations of these.[2] Sixtus IV granted John, abbot of Wymondham, a dispensation to receive *in titulum* for life, with the said or any other monastery of the same order, any two benefices with or without cure which were customarily held by secular clerks, and to resign them simply or for exchange as often as he pleased.[3] On the same day, 30 January 1481, he dispensed Richard Harman, monk of St. Albans, to receive and retain any benefice.[4]

Details survive of the payments made to procure a general indult to have a portable altar, which was conceded to St. Albans by Martin V on 20 October 1423; for two other indults of the same date to eat meat from Septuagesima Sunday until Quinquagesima Sunday except on days when meat was expressly forbidden, and to let to farm their tithes to laymen;[5] as well as for a confirmatory bull of Eugenius IV of 1431 which confirmed Abbot John's institution of a common chest whose funds might be used in time of need.[6] For the three indults of Martin V, it cost in the one instance 8 and in the other two instances 10 florins for the minute; 3 *bol(endini)* for the charter; for the scriptor 8 and in one instance 10 florins; for the bull (sealing) 22 florins, 8 florins 8 *grossi*, and 11 florins respectively; for the registration, 8 florins and in one instance 10; finally 2 *grossi* for the clerk doing the registration. Additional expenses of 6 *grossi* were paid to the clerks of the lord secretary for writing the minutes. The total sums in English money were as follows: for the

---

[1] B.M. Arundel MS. 34, f. 13 (not in *CPL*).
[2] *CPL* v. 156; vi. 79; ix. 266, 271, 456, 459; xi. 526; xii. 508; xiii (2), 562.
[3] Ibid., xiii (2), 790.
[4] Ibid., and see p. 796 and xiii (1), 156.
[5] B.M. Arundel MS. 34, f. 14. Cf. *CPL* iv. 501, an indult of Boniface IX of 2 Oct. 1395 allowing this. Martin's indult refers to a previous bull of Boniface VIII, perhaps wrongly.
[6] B.M. Arundel MS. 34, ff. 12, 13, 14, 56ᵛ (see also *CPL* viii. 327).

indult about meat eating £7. 14*s*.; for the indult about the leasing
of tithes £5. 9*s*. 4*d*.; and for the bull concerning the portable altar
£6. 18*s*. 10*d*. In addition to these sums there were other costs since
the abbot fell ill with dysentery, while at Rome petitioning, and
had to purchase a plenary indulgence, and on his recovery gifts for
the pope. The confirmatory bull of Eugenius IV was more expensive
and cost £9.[1] The seven bulls which Abbot John de la Moote
obtained through his proctor, Master John Fraunceys, between
1396 and 1401, had cost him £44. 6*s*. 8*d*.; Fraunceys received 10
marks and Peter de Bosco, bishop of Dax (France), a payment for
his 'benevolence' in the curia, which was almost certainly a 'benevolence' connected with these impetrations.[2]

These amounts were extremely small, however, if compared with
one source of expenditure. A decree of the Fourth Lateran Council
had stated that the heads of exempt houses were to present themselves in person at Rome for confirmation after election. The first
two abbots elected after the decree avoided the trip on the plea of
advanced age, but there were still the expenses of proctors to pay,
and Abbot John de Berkhamstead made the journey in person in
1291, perhaps to cut the costs.[3] A detailed expense-sheet of money
paid out at Rome for Abbot John de Maryns's confirmation in 1302
records an expenditure of 3,000 florins (or 1,250 marks)[4] for obtaining a private audience with the pope—this might be advantageous
for the convent but was still expensive—and sums paid out to the
examiners, the referendary, the impetrator, the scribe, the papal
corrector, the scribe for the second time, the bullators, the registrar,
the copiers, and the notaries, for the actual letters and for gifts,
bringing a total expenditure of 2,561 marks sterling.[5] The account

---

[1] B.M. Arundel MS. 34, f. 77ʳ⁻ᵛ; and see *Amundesham Annales* i. 149–65, 276,
289–91.

[2] *Gesta Abb.* iii. 436–7, 455–6.

[3] In general, see R. Vaughan, 'The Election of the Abbots at St. Albans in the
Thirteenth and Fourteenth Centuries', *Proc. of the Cambridge Antiquarian Society*,
xlvii (1954), 1–10.

[4] The editor of the *Gesta Abb.* in the R.S. edition (H. T. Riley) states that this
was probably equal to 5000 marks 'as 4 florins are throughout made to equal 1 mark'
(ii. 56 n. 4).

[5] *Gesta Abb.* ii. 56–8: printed in translation in G. G. Coulton, *Life in the Middle
Ages*, 2nd edn. (Cambridge, 1930), iv. 282. The expenses of Abbot Hugh of Eversdon's confirmation in 1308, the next in the line, were said to be heavy because of his

of the expenditure on his election feast, to which the monastic
servants were made to contribute, and at which herons, bitterns,
cygnets, peacocks, and sucking pigs were served, is followed by a
note of the money borrowed from Florentine merchants presumably
to pay for all this.[1] The expenses of Abbot Richard of Wallingford
who was at the papal court for confirmation in 1326 were also
heavy.[2] Those of Abbot de la Mare in 1349 were detailed as eighty
florins for the confirmation documents and 126 florins for the bull
which allowed twenty monks to be ordained in their twentieth
year.[3] He also took the opportunity of impetrating indults of
plenary remission for ten persons, of whom some were his own
monks, some seculars, for which he paid 108 florins.[4] In 1382 Abbot
de la Mare set in train a process to gain exemption from the requirement that the abbot should visit the curia on election, and suppli-
cated that the abbot-elect should be confirmed in England.[5]
Apparently Evesham abbey already had a bull to this effect, and
when approached by St. Albans for permission to borrow it, the
Evesham monks insisted that it should not leave their abbey but
should be copied there.[6] When in 1478 the Benedictine abbey of
St. Peter at Westminster sought a similar exemption, they referred
to the grants already made to Waltham abbey and to St. Albans.[7]

By the mid fifteenth century one of the most resented rights of
the abbot of St. Albans was his power to appoint and remove the
priors of dependencies at will, and to post the monks from place
to place.[8] Difficult monks had frequently found themselves sent to
Tynemouth; at least one monk of St. Albans ended a miserable
existence in chains at Binham, and in 1380 the abbot of St. Albans
had removed the prior of Wymondham from his office, citing the

---

lack of Latin and his consequent fear of going to the papal court in person (Vaughan,
'Election of the Abbots', pp. 10–11).
    [1] *Registrum Abbatiae Johannis Whethamstede*, ed. H. T. Riley (R.S., 1872–3), ii.
330–3, 335–8, 342–3.   [2] *Gesta Abb.* ii. 186–91.
    [3] Ibid., pp. 387–8. For the indult concerning ordination, see above p. 74, and *Cal.
Pet.* i. 425. For Clement VI's bull confirming Abbot Thomas de la Mare, see Dugdale, *Monasticon*, ii. 238, num. xxix.
    [4] *Gesta Abb.* ii. 388.   [5] Ibid., pp. 146 ff.
    [6] Ibid., pp. 160–1; and see *CPL* iv. 293–4, reference to Innocent III's and Urban V's
grants to Evesham.   [7] *CPL* xiii (1), 201.
    [8] *Gesta Abb.* i. 226. In *c.*1330 the nuns of Sopwell had tried to elect their own
prioress but were swiftly thwarted by the abbot of St. Albans (*VCH, Herts.* iv. 423).

privileges which allowed him to do so.[1] The papacy's scheme for erecting the exempt religious houses *vis-à-vis* the diocesans was no longer valid in the social context of fifteenth-century society. In 1487 Abbot William Wallingford sought the ultimate mark of ecclesiastical autonomy for the abbot by asking the pope to endow him with the episcopal powers of ordination and confirmation. John de Rothbury, the archdeacon of St. Albans, was dispatched to Rome to negotiate on his behalf, but the claim was too extreme and on 11 August he returned to St. Albans having been unsuccessful.[2] Even the powerful mitred abbot of St. Albans, who had within his exempt area the full jurisdictional powers of a bishop, was not to gain the sacramental powers which were reserved exclusively to the bishop's office. Instead of countenancing such proposals for the abbot's aggrandizement, fifteenth-century popes were prepared to reduce his authority. Indults were sought by and granted to priors conceding that they should not be removed or recalled by the abbot, or any other person, without reasonable cause. In 1444 Eugenius IV granted such an indult to Richard Hall prior of Belvoir;[3] in 1456 Calixtus III confirmed William Albon in his office as claustral prior of St. Albans (which office was revocable at the pleasure of the abbot) and stated that he was not to be removed by the present abbot or his successors;[4] and in 1482 William Dixwell, prior of Binham, got a similar concession from Sixtus IV.[5] William Somerton, prior of Binham, who sought not to be removed by the abbot from his post, was arrested on his return from the continent and his papal letters were seized and given to the abbot of St. Albans— who 'only knows what the bulls contained'.[6] The extreme authority of the abbot over his monks was finally flouted in 1448 when, at the time of Wymondham's erection into an abbey, Nicholas V granted an indult to Richard Langley, Edmund Shenley, William Gondred, and William Wubeche, all monks of St. Albans, to transfer

---

[1] Dugdale, *Monasticon*, iii. 309; and *Gesta Abb.* iii. 124, 128.
[2] *Reg. Whethamstede*, ii. 287–9.   [3] *CPL* ix. 453.   [4] Ibid., xi. 88–9.
[5] Ibid., xiii (2), 806. This was really a letter of rectification, because the indult which Dixwell had got on his election had wrongly stated that Binham was in the diocese of Lincoln. As prior of Hertford, he is stated to have spent £11. 16*s*. out of an expenditure of £90. 10*s*. on legal and travelling expenses, perhaps applying for a similar indult (*VCH, Herts.* iv. 420).
[6] Dugdale, *Monasticon*, iii. 350, num. xiii; and *Gesta Abb.* ii. 140.

to the new abbey without licence of the abbot of St. Albans or any other.[1] Two of them, however, seem subsequently to have regretted their act and sought reinstatement at St. Albans.[2]

The priory of Wymondham, which had been founded by William d'Aubigny and put under St. Albans by him, was the first dependency to gain exemption from the overlordship of St. Albans. The bull which constituted it an abbey, named the prior, Stephen London, as first abbot, and declared that the monastery was in future to be subject to the bishop of Norwich and no longer answerable to St. Albans or liable to the annual payment of one mark of silver. The patron was to present to the ordinary the person who had been elected abbot by the convent, and the bishop of Norwich and the abbots of Westminster and Bury were to defend Wymondham against any interference from St. Albans or any other persons.[3] Trouble was not long in developing between Wymondham and its new overlord, the bishop of Norwich. As subject to St. Albans, Wymondham had enjoyed a fair amount of exemption from the diocesan. Now all this was to change. In 1463 Walter Lyhart, bishop of Norwich, excommunicated Wymondham because it had refused to obey his mandate and pay forty shillings annually. He had already, according to Wymondham, snatched the papal letters concerning the exemption from the abbot's hand, had carried them away and was believed to have torn them up.[4] The pope, Pius II, ordered the bishops of Ely and Exeter to inquire into Wymondham's alleged exemption from the bishop.[5] In fact the composition of 1228 had clearly stated that Wymondham was to pay the bishop forty shillings in lieu of visitation.[6]

Three of St. Albans' other dependencies were suppressed, Beadlow in 1428 to provide for the monks at Oxford, Wallingford in 1528 to provide for Cardinal College, and St. Mary de Pré (which

---

[1] *CPL* x. 46 (printed in *Reg. Whethamstede*, ii. 62–3, with additional material on 63–5); and see *Reg. Whethamstede*, i. 137–8 and 146–7, for these and some others from other cells. Cf. the case of Robert Morpath, monk of St. Albans, whom Nicholas V rehabilitated in 1449. He had obtained the perpetual vicarage of Aldworth (Berks.) without seeking a licence from his abbot (*CPL* x. 49).

[2] *Reg. Whethamstede*, ii. 63–4.

[3] *CPL* x. 19–20, and Dugdale, *Monasticon*, iii. 338–9; and *CPL* x. 51. See also *Reg. Whethamstede*, i. 148–52, for an account of the withdrawal.   [4] *CPL* xi. 489–90.

[5] Ibid., pp. 495–6.   [6] C.U.L. MS. Ee 4. 20, f.107.

84   *Papal Privileges for St. Albans Abbey and its Dependencies*

had been a nunnery since the first part of the fourteenth century) also in 1528.[1] Such suppressions needed the consent of the papacy and documents were applied for to this effect. The authorization of the unification of Beadlow with St. Albans cost the mother house forty shillings.[2] The hospital of St. Julian was annexed to St. Albans in 1505.[3] Of the remaining dependencies Redbourn survived until 1535, Hatfield Peverel until 1536, Sopwell until 1537, Hertford until 1538, and Binham, Belvoir, Tynemouth, and St. Albans itself, until 1539.[4] The old papal privileges had remained powerful enough to prevent the fragmentation of the cells although the hierarchical position of the abbot of St. Albans was challenged when the economic structure of feudal society began to crumble. The relationship between St. Albans and its dependencies had naturally changed since the establishment of the ties in the eleventh and twelfth centuries, and this was reflected in the growing tendency by the late thirteenth and early fourteenth centuries for the cells to seek their own privileges from the papal curia.[5] Yet documents were still issued in the early fifteenth century which spoke of St. Albans and its cells as one entity, although society was no longer tolerant of such a powerful complex.[6] Basically the old privileges remained good until the whirlwind events of 1538–9, which, destroying the old religious houses, destroyed their privileges with them. Against this sort of lightning destruction the privileges and indulgences of the saints and popes were useless, just as the impression of the papal seal, which was fixed to the summit of the tower of the great church of St. Alban, had proved to be ineffectual in the thunderstorms of the early thirteenth century.[7]

---

[1] B.M. Arundel MS. 34, f. 33^{r–v}, and Dugdale, *Monasticon*, iii. 277, num. v (the supplication by Abbot John Wheathampstead), 282, num. ix; and 361–2, num. xi. Clement VII confirmed Wolsey's suppression of Wallingford and its annexation to Cardinal College although no mention had been made in the Pope's earlier faculty for the suppression that Wolsey was holding the abbey of St. Albans *in commendam*. The bull, dated 31 May 1528, is P.R.O., Papal Bulls (S.C. 7), 63/14; it is reproduced in Plate 1.

[2] B.M. Arundel MS. 34, f.56, and Dugdale, *Monasticon*, iii. 243.

[3] D. Knowles and R. N. Hadcock, *Medieval Religious Houses* (London, 1953), p. 303.

[4] See ibid. for dates.   [5] e.g., Large Belvoir Cart., f. 12^{r–v}.   [6] Ibid., ff. 19^v–20.

[7] Cf. *Gesta Abb.* i. 313, and Vaughan, *Matthew Paris*, p. 189.

Bull of Clement VII to Cardinal Wolsey, 31 May 1528

X

The Earliest Original Letter of Pope Innocent III for an English Recipient

AMONG THE ARCHIVES of the marquess of Bath at Longleat, MS. 961 is an early letter of Pope Innocent III, dated 25 May 1198. Only four originals have been listed in the *Calendar* for the first year of Innocent's pontificate. Two of them are in favour of the archbishop of Rouen, dated 3 and 4 June, and survive at Rouen. The other two are for English recipients: a general mandate at Levens Hall for the Cistercians, specifying Byland, and dated *c.* 29 July, and a grant at Lambeth in favour of Bury, dated 1 December.[1] The Longleat document is thus the earliest original letter of Pope Innocent III addressed to an English recipient, so far discovered. Possibly it has escaped notice on account of incorrect attribution to Innocent II or Innocent IV. There is no doubt, however, that it is attributable to Innocent III, for whom the issue of a document from St. Peter's is recorded on the same day, 25 May 1198, ordering the chapter of Milan to restore a prebend in their cathedral and a house to Otto, bishop of Tortona (Terdona).[2] The closest in date (27 May) among the recorded original letters of Innocent III is Archives Nationales, Paris, L 236 n.7 (with the incipit 'Non absque dolore').[3]

Diplomatically the letter at Longleat has some interesting features. A simple grant or confirmation, it does not bear comparison with the elaborate privileges of this pope for the great religious houses, but is rather an example of the common hybrid document, which bore features of both the *littere*

---

[1] *The Letters of Pope Innocent III (1198–1216) concerning England and Wales: a Calendar with an Appendix of texts*, ed. C. R. Cheney and Mary G. Cheney (Oxford, 1967), nos. 27, 29, 36 and 63. For corrections and additions to this list (none, however, for the first year, and incorporating no further originals), see the same authors, *ante*, xliv (1971), 98–115. For details of the Bury papal licence, see *Original Papal Documents in the Lambeth Palace Library: a Catalogue*, comp. J. E. Sayers (*Bull. Inst. Hist. Research*, Special Supplement vi, 1967), no. 14.

[2] *Regesta Pontificum Romanorum ab 1198 ad 1304*, ed. A. Potthast (2 vols., Berlin, 1874–5, repr. Graz, 1957), no. 211, and *Die Register Innocenz' III*, i, ed. O. Hageneder and A. Haidacher (Publikationen der Abteilung für Historische Studien des Österreichischen Kulturinstituts in Rom, Graz-Köln, 1964), no. 187. Innocent IV was at the Lateran on 8 kal' June in his first year (Potthast, no. 11401) and the scribes of Innocent II did not employ the pontifical year in their dating.

[3] *Schedario Baumgarten*, i, ed. G. Battelli (Vatican City, 1965), no. 9 (cf. nos. 10 and 11 for the abbot and convent of St. Victor, Paris ('Cum a nobis') and for the Templars ('Cum vos tamquam')).

cum serico and the *littere cum filo canapis*,[1] and which provided the papal clerks with the bulk of their work. The incipit 'Cum a nobis' is a very common one for a simple confirmation of this kind,[2] and Hageneder and Haidacher record seven examples of the more specific 'Cum a nobis petitur— effectum' in the papal register for the first year.[3] 'Cum a nobis petitur— effectum' appears in an original confirmation for the prior and convent of Durham, dated 23 April 1199, and elsewhere.[4] The pope's name is in elongated letters (the German *gitterschrift*). There are neither tittles nor broad ligatures, but only simple abbreviations—the plain dash and the hook contraction mark—as in Lambeth Papal Document no. 14 and Durham, Dean and Chapter 3.1 Pap. 8. The document measures 20·4 cm. (breadth) × 15 cm. (right-hand height), and the *plica* 2·5 cm., an average size for a simple privilege of the period.[5] There are no papal marks on the face and no papal endorsements. The distinctive features of the hand are the orna- mental capital 'I' of the initial letter of the pope's name. Such ornamen- tation was usual and is unique to each individual scribe.[6] In this case it is a very long tailed 'I', with three 'notches' in the stroke which forms the right-hand outer side of the letter. There is no inking within the letter, as was sometimes the practice.[7] Other notable features are the use of the two types of elongated 'N' in 'Innocentius' (the Durham confirmation also employs the two), the pronounced backward tail strokes of the capital letters 'C' and 'E',[8] the tilted angles of some letters, and the somewhat faltering strokes of those with long ascenders—'l', 'b' and 's'—which might suggest an elderly scribe and possibly one who had been trained in Celestine III's chancery. It is known that Innocent III, contrary to the practice of his predecessors, did not prolong the terms of appointment of Celestine's chancellor on his accession, but it is doubtful whether he could have made

[1] Herde's 'mischform': see P. Herde, *Beitrage zum päpstlichen Kanzlei- und Urkundenwesen im dreizehnten Jahrhundert* (2nd edn., Kallmünz, 1967), pp. 59–60, discussing a document of 21 May 1198 (*Schedario*, no. 8). The inconsistency in the use of forms at this date doubtless lay behind Innocent III's almost fanatical interest in forgery and his consequent declarations on the subject.

[2] E.g. *Schedario*, nos. 10 and 13.

[3] *Die Register Innocenz' III*, nos. 124, 134, 154, 198, 217, 285, 293.

[4] Durham, Dean and Chapter 3.1 Pap. 8 (Cheney, *Calendar*, no. 102).

[5] See for example *Die Papsturkunden der Schweiz von Innozenz III bis Martin V ohne Zürich*, ed. A. Largiadèr (2 vols., Zurich, 1968–70), i, no. 202, which measures 17·5 × 13·5 cm., and Lambeth Palace Library, Papal Documents no. 14, 18·5 × 14 cm., and Durham 3.1 Pap. 8, 17·6 × 14·1 cm.

[6] This is demonstrated by Public Record Office, S.C. 7/35/4 and 9, two bulls for Waltham, where the same device is used for the capital 'I', and the documents are clearly written by the same scribe.

[7] The ascenders of the 'b' and 'h' in 'fratribus' and 'hospitalis', in the first line only, have little backward 'tails'—a flourish to suggest an intermediary privilege?

[8] British Library, Cotton Charter viii. 24, a superb great bull (a facsimile of which is to be found in the back pocket of the Cheneys' *Calendar*), has a similar 'E' in 'Ego', and see L. Delisle, *Mémoire sur les Actes d'Innocent III* (Paris, 1857), p. 30, for examples in the lower case.

X

a clean sweep of the chancery scribes.[1] There is no *gemipunctus* before the addressees' name, which is the case in many papal letters issued in the eleven-nineties, but this is no sure indication of a scribe from Celestine's chancery, for there are examples of the *gemipunctus* in some of Celestine's documents.[2]

Little is known about the recipients of the letter, the lepers of St. Giles Hospital, Maldon (Essex). The hospital had been founded, possibly in the spring of 1164 by King Henry II, for a warden, a chaplain and leprous townsmen or burgesses of the borough of Maldon, and it enjoyed all forfeitures for bread, beer, flesh and fish which were not fit to be consumed.[3] The bull is addressed to the brothers and confirms to them the church of St. Giles Maldon, with the cemetery. It was endorsed at Maldon, sometime apparently in the late twelfth century, 'de ecclesia et cimiterio cum omnibus pertinentiis'.

The hospital is scheduled as an ancient monument. It stands about 900 yards south-west of All Saints' church in the parish of St. Peter's. Substantial parts of the ruins are of late twelfth-century date, incorporating some Roman brick.[4] Thus the bull appears to have been acquired on the completion of the quite sizeable leper church, which may have included some common offices at the west end (now no longer standing), although it was usual for lepers to be provided with separate accommodation. We know virtually nothing more about the hospital, its administration and its inmates.

In 1402 King Henry IV took the wardenship of the hospital into his own hands on the grounds that Robert Manfeld, clerk, previously provost of St. John's, Beverley, and keeper of the writs and rolls of the Common Bench from 1397,[5] had failed to sustain a chaplain and lepers there. Roger Wodhale was appointed warden in 1403—presumably enough lepers were found for his ministrations.[6] The hospital was appropriated to the Premonstratensian abbey of Beeleigh in 1481, after an attempt in the late fourteenth century to convey it to Bicknacre, an Augustinian house in the vicinity, had failed. On

---

[1] A search among the original letters of Celestine III has failed to reveal an identical hand, although Brit. Libr., Harley Charter 43.A.29 is a possible candidate for comparison, but it includes only one tironian 'et', which makes comparison difficult. Cotton Charter xii. 39 has some similarities (notably in the 'ets'), but not consistently enough to postulate the same scribe. Early letters of Innocent III have also been examined, but the same scribe has not been identified.

[2] E.g. in Lambeth P.D. no. 13.

[3] See the accounts in *Medieval Religious Houses: England and Wales*, comp. D. Knowles and R. N. Hadcock (2nd edn., 1971), pp. 327, 376; *Victoria County History of Essex*, ii. 188; and P. Morant, *The History and Antiquities of the County of Essex* (2 vols., 1768), i. 336. In general on hospitals see R. M. Clay, *The Mediaeval Hospitals of England* (1909).

[4] *Royal Commission on Historical Monuments: Essex*, ii (1921), pp. 177–8; photographs between pp. 176 and 177.

[5] On his career, see *A Biographical Register of the University of Oxford to A.D. 1500*, comp. A. B. Emden (3 vols., Oxford, 1957–9), ii. 1213–14.

[6] W. Dugdale, *Monasticon Anglicanum*, ed. J. Caley, H. Ellis and B. Bandinel (6 vols., 1817–30), VI. ii. 735–6.

X

18 February 1481, Henry Bourchier, earl of Essex, was given licence to appropriate the hospital, its land (about ninety acres), and the advowson and patronage to the abbot and convent of Beeleigh, in mortmain.[1] The families of Bourchier and Amory had presented to the wardenship, but it was in effect mainly the Crown who seems to have exercised this right.[2] Through the two lines of the Bourchier family (earls of Essex and earls of Bath, and their common ancestor, Sir William Bourchier, count of Eu),[3] the property and the title deeds passed eventually to the Thynnes, who were created marquesses of Bath in the eighteenth century. Deeds of the Bourchier family are recorded at Longleat.[4]

Longleat MS. 961
INNOCENTIUS episcopus servus servorum dei. Dilectis filiis fratribus hospitalis de Meldon' salutem/ et apostolicam benedictionem. Cum a nobis petitur quod iustum est et honestum tam vigor equita/tis quam ordo exigit rationis ut id per sollicitudinem officii nostri ad debitum perducatur/ effectum. Eapropter dilecti in domino filii vestris precibus annuentes. ecclesiam sancti Egidii de/ Meldon' cum Cimiterio et omnibus pertinentiis suis sicut ea iuste ac pacifice possidetis de/votioni vestre auctoritate apostolica confirmamus et presentis scripti patrocinio communi/mus. Nulli ergo omnino hominum liceat hanc paginam nostri confirmationis in/fringere. vel ei ausu temerario contraire. Si quis autem hoc attemptare presumpse/rit indignationem omnipotentis dei et beatorum Petri et Pauli apostolorum eius se noverit/ incursurum. Dat' Rom' apud sanctum. Petrum. viii kal' Iunii Pontificatus nostri anno Primo;[5]

Holes for strings of *bulla: bulla* not surviving.
Measurements: 20·4 cm. × 15 cm. *Plica* 2·5 cm.
Endorsed: *de ecclesia et cimiterio cum omnibus pertinentiis* (in a late twelfth-century English hand).

[1] *Calendar of Patent Rolls 1476–85*, p. 235. The principal endowment of the hospital was the manor of Jenkin Maldon. And see R. C. Fowler and A. W. Clapham, *Beeleigh Abbey* (1922), pp. 45–6.
[2] Dugdale, *Monasticon Anglicanum*, VI. ii. 735–6.
[3] See *The Complete Peerage*, comp. G. E. C[okayne] and others (13 vols., 1910–59), ii and v, entries for Bath, Bourchier, Essex, Eu and FitzWarin.
[4] See A. J. Horwood in Hist. MSS. Comm., *3rd Rept.* (1872), p. 200; then catalogued as F 4 nos. 181 and 182.
[5] Punctuation and capitalization have been kept as in the original, but the use of 'c' and 't' and 'u' and 'v' has been standardized. The ends of the lines are indicated by the symbol /.

XI

English charters from the third crusade*

MARC BLOCH wrote of the 'cross-examination' of documents,[1] of what they might reveal if we knew the right questions to ask. In a volume offered to a scholar who has looked at evidence so searchingly and who has considered the relationship between chronicle and charter so perceptively,[2] it seems fitting to investigate the English charters of the third crusade. In its beginnings, the science of diplomatic, as defined by Mabillon, concerned the distinguishing of genuine charters from spurious and was occupied primarily with tests on originals. None of the charters considered below survives in the original. We start, therefore, with severe limitations and caution must be exercised as we sail into uncharted seas. But, if no originals survive, then the copies must be exploited and the study of diplomatic moved into new areas of investigation, using the sources of charters in chronicles and in cartularies or registers. Exponents of the study of diplomatic in recent years have shown the aridity of concentrating so exclusively on form and 'rules' and have advocated the cross-examination of documents that exhibit exceptions. It is in the explanation of these variations that a new and vigorous approach to documents lies, for diplomatic must be concerned with the production of the document in its original historical context and with the content as much as with the form.[3] In the makeshift arrangements of an army campaign, systematized documents can hardly be expected from any source. Nowhere can the peculiarities of documents issued in exceptional circumstances be better illustrated than by examining the English charters of the third crusade.

---

* I should like to thank Mr J. B. Gillingham of the LSE, who read this article at an early stage and made many helpful suggestions, but he is, of course, in no way responsible for the opinions expressed in it.
[1] *The Historian's Craft*, trans. Peter Putnam (Manchester, 1954), pp. 64–5.
[2] See especially 'Charter and chronicle: the use of archive sources by Norman historians', in *CG*, pp. 1–17.
[3] See H. Fichtenau, 'La situation actuelle des études de diplomatique en Autriche', *BÉC*, CXIX (1962), pp. 5–20, esp. 17–18.

Only eight charters of Richard I which are likely to be authentic survive from the crusade: two in a chronicle (Roger of Howden), three in registers or cartularies and three in notarial copies, two of these being in a register. When Richard I left on the third crusade, the royal chancellor, William Longchamp, remained in England. Accompanying Richard was the vice-chancellor and keeper of the king's seal, Roger Malus Catulus. It was clearly Richard's intention to have an active 'field' chancery with him. However, the calamitous drowning of the vice-chancellor off Cyprus on 24 April 1191, when the great seal was lost but was recovered,[4] made the 'chancery' arrangements very makeshift indeed. Owing to the tragedy, Master Philip of Poitou, the king's clerk of the Chamber, came to prominence and was concerned with the drawing up of two, and perhaps four or five and possibly more, of the eight acceptable royal charters that were issued from the Holy Land between 6 August 1191 and 10 January 1192. Schooled in the ducal chancery of Poitou, his practices were apparently often at variance with those accepted for the English chancery both during the last years of Henry II and under Richard I. It is not the purpose of the present paper to comment on these differences. Until the *acta* of Henry II and of Richard are assembled we can make no judgements, but it is necessary to examine these charters briefly in order to consider their possible influence on other English charters issued during the campaign.[5]

Just eighteen days after the death of Roger Malus Catulus, Master Philip drew up and sealed a document on the day of Richard's wedding to Berengaria, 12 May 1191, at Limassol. The document concerned Berengaria's dower settlement.[6] Whether Master Philip had any part in the issue of the writ appointing the archbishop of Rouen, Walter of Coutances, as justiciar, is unknown. Walter left Messina in the early summer of 1191, taking with him this writ said to have been sealed with the great seal and with a smaller seal or signet of Richard.[7] Bearing in mind the importance of the appointment, the

---

[4] *Chronicles and memorials of the reign of Richard I*, ed. W. Stubbs 2 vols. (RS, xxxviii, 1864–5) I ('Itinerarium peregrinorum et gesta regis Ricardi' by Richard canon of Holy Trinity London), p. 184; H. E. Mayer, 'Die Kanzlei Richards I. von England auf dem Dritten Kreuzzug', *MIÖG*, LXXXV (1977), p. 27, and Landon, app. A on the seals of Richard I. In spite of its recovery, the loss of the seal provided a pretext for a second seal and the requirement (after May 1198) that all deeds issued under the first seal were to be confirmed, otherwise they would be regarded as void (C. Fagnen, 'Essai sur quelques actes Normands de Richard Coeur-de-Lion', *École nationale des Chartes. Positions des thèses* (1971), p. 74).

[5] Fagnen ('Actes Normands') has considered the Norman acts but the English documents await detailed diplomatic analysis by Professor J. C. Holt.

[6] Landon, p. 49 no. 358.

[7] *Giraldi Cambrensis Opera*, IV, ed. J. S. Brewer (RS, XXI, 1873), p. 426. See also Pierre Chaplais, *English Royal Documents King John – Henry VI 1199–1461* (Oxford, 1971), p. 24. The date of the writ appointing him is unknown: it was probably of *c.* 20–3 Feb. 1191; see Landon, p. 46 nos. 351–2.

English charters from the third crusade

affixture of some personal mark of authentication by the king seems highly likely. More important, from the point of view of the 'field' chancery, is the fact that Walter of Coutances, a man with much experience in Henry II's chancery, was now no longer available, leaving Master Philip of Poitou as the chief clerk for the duration of the campaign.

The first document supposedly issued by Richard from the Holy Land, the only document purporting to be an original, was exposed by Bautier in 1956 as a forgery, being one of the celebrated 350 charters in the 'Collection Courtois'.[8] It stated that it was issued from Acre on 3 August 1191 and commended certain royal servants to Giacomo de Jhota, a Pisan merchant, for the purpose of borrowing large sums of money.[9] In its form it is not unskilful.[10] The story of the Courtois forgeries is one of great interest. In 1839 Louis Philippe designated a gallery at Versailles for the history of the crusades and the French crusading families that had taken part. Immediately on the opening of the exhibition in 1840, and throughout the following year, a flood of French families came forward with claims forcing the exhibition to close pending enquiry into their entitlement. Most of the documents that were produced were requests for loans of large sums of money, 500, 600, 700 and 1,000 marks 'at least' (as is exactly the case in the above example). To consider the numerous claims, Louis Philippe appointed a judge, whose adjudications resulted in the admission of more than 250 families into the ranks of the French nobility, their titles depending on the acceptance of charters that had been fabricated and sold by Courtois and Letellier. The seals on a few of the documents in the 'Collection Courtois' (including possibly the document attributed to Richard which bears traces of sealing) are apparently authentic but show signs of re-affixing. That the forgers had access to an original, on which these fabrications were based, is clear, but that it was this particular document can be rejected immediately. The 'Collection Courtois' is a flamboyant example of the desire of rising nineteenth-century families to claim medieval origins but as historical evidence for the third crusade and for diplomatic purposes it is totally worthless.

Chronologically the first document that is probably genuine is a dispatch

---

[8] 'La collection des chartes de croisade dite "collection Courtois"', *Comptes-rendus des séances de l'Académie des Inscriptions et Belles Lettres* (1956), pp. 382–6, and see Mayer, 'Die Kanzlei Richards I.', p. 29.

[9] Landon, p. 52 no. 359; pd H. Geraud, 'Le Comte-Évêque', *BÉC*, v (1843–4), p. 36 doc. 4.

[10] Bautier's description of the colouring by candle flame and the washing and ironing of the parchment ('"Collection Courtois"', p. 383) invites comparison with the activities demonstrated to the French court in the 14th century by the celebrated forger the Demoiselle Divion, see L. C. Hector, *Palaeography and Forgery* (Borthwick Papers, St Anthony's Hall Publications no. 15, 1959), pp. 9–10, citing Toustain and Tassin, *Nouveau Traité de Diplomatique*, VI, pp. 185 fol.

to the king's justiciar (Walter of Coutances), dated 6 August 1191 at Acre[11] and found in *Epistolae Cantuarienses*.[12] It gives an account of the conquest of Cyprus and of the king's arrival at Acre and capture of the city and ends with an exhortation to the justiciar to promote the king's interests. The document terminates with the 'Teste me ipso' clause. By 1 October the king was at Jaffa where he caused to be written two letters, one to N. and the other to the abbot of Clairvaux: these letters recounted the course of the battle of Arsouf, which had been fought on the previous 7 September, and the capture of Acre, and deplored Philip Augustus's desertion of the crusade. They are to be found in the chronicle of Roger of Howden and, although they are doubtless corrupt and unproductive for analysis, their authenticity is certain. Both letters end with 'Testibus nobismetipsis apud Jopen'' and the date of the day and month.[13] Two subsequent letters, dated from Acre on 11 October and addressed to the archbishop, podestà, consuls and citizens of Genoa, in which the king implored Genoese help, have been queried as forgeries. They survive in a notarial copy of 22 June 1301 in the archives of the republic of Genoa where they are described as sealed.[14] But Dr H. E. Mayer, in a paper on Richard's crusading 'chancery', has argued that their unconventional diplomatic stems from their association with Master Philip of Poitou as they exhibit certain features found in other documents which are known to have come from him.[15] The Genoese documents are in the form of neither writ nor writ-charter and have little in common with the style of two documents (a mandate (*littere*) and a *carta*) issued at Messina in January and in February 1191.[16] The opening address is curious: 'viris venerabilibus et amicis karissimis archiepiscopo[17] potestati consulibus et consilio aliisque bonis hominibus[18] Ianuensibus ad quos presens scriptum pervenerit salutem' – unlikely but not impossible[19] – and the request is reminiscent of the form used in papal documents for addressing

---

[11] Walter of Coutances probably reached England about 27 June. He did not claim his title of justiciar until early October 1191, but it was presumably he (not Longchamp) whom Richard had in mind (see F. West, *The Justiciarship in England 1066–1232* (Cambridge, 1966), pp. 73–5).

[12] *Chronicles and memorials of Richard I*, ed. Stubbs, II, p. 347. Landon, p. 52 no. 360.

[13] *Chronica Magistri Rogeri de Houedene*, ed. W. Stubbs, 4 vols. (RS, LI, 1868–71), III, pp. 129–33, where the witness clause is given as 'Teste nobismet', possibly a mistaken extension of T' or Test'; *Foedera*, I(1), pp. 54–5; listed in Landon, p. 55 nos. 361–2. H. F. M. Prescott, 'The early history of "teste me ipso"', *EHR*, XXXV (1920), pp. 214–17: 217 records this use.

[14] Pd *Codice diplomatico della Repubblica di Genova*, ed. C. Imperiale, III (Fonti per la Storia d'Italia...per il medio evo LXXXIX, 1942), pp. 19–22 no. 7; Landon, p. 56 nos. 363–4.

[15] 'Die Kanzlei Richards I.', pp. 22–35. For a full discussion, see H. E. Mayer and M. L. Favreau, 'Das Diplom Balduins I. für Genua und Genuas Goldene Inschrift in der Grabeskirche', *QFIAB*, LV–LVI (1976), pp. 89–92.

[16] PRO, DL 10 nos. 44, 45 (Landon, nos. 347, 350).

[17] 'archiepiscopo' omitted in the second document (Landon, no. 364).

[18] 'viris' for 'hominibus' in the second document (Landon, no. 364).

[19] PRO, DL 10 no. 44 has 'ad quos presens carta pervenerit salutem'.

English charters from the third crusade

crowned heads ('rogantes attentius quatinus') rather than of the 'mandamus (vobis) et (firmiter) precipimus' of the English royal writ.[20] Not much attention can be paid to the royal title ('Ricardus dei gratia rex Anglie dux Normandie Aquitanie comes Andegavensis') because of the presumed notarial extensions of 1301, but the opening of each, 'Quoniam vos super' and 'Noverit dilectio vestra', find to my knowledge no parallels and the 'testibus nobis ipsis' compares only with the letters included in Howden and two other examples.[21] It is difficult to imagine why anyone would have wished to forge the Genoese documents. Mayer's suggestion that Master Philip was the author is attractive but it is not proved.

On 13 October 1191, two days after the issue of the Genoese documents, Richard I authorized a charter for the Pisans, confirming all the rights and privileges which Guy, king of Jerusalem, and Sibyl, his wife, and the brethren of the Temple had granted to them. This charter included an imposing list of witnesses: Guy, king of Jerusalem, the duke of Burgundy, count Henry, Garnier de Nablûs, master of the hospital of St John of Jerusalem, Robert de Sablé, master of the Temple of Jerusalem, and Geoffrey de Lusignan. It was dated at Acre in the house of the Temple on the 3rd of the Ides of October in the year 1192 according to the Pisan reckoning (which began the year on the preceding Lady Day, 25 March).[22] The charter formed the subject of a short note by R. L. Poole and has been widely regarded as a beneficiary's charter.[23] The text survives in two notarial copies, one of which, dated 24 April in the year 1249 on the Pisan reckoning, notes its inspection at Acre in the church of St Peter of the Pisans and describes the pendant wax seal. It is a vivid and unmistakable description of the two-sided English royal great seal, the obverse showing the king crowned and enthroned, holding in his right hand the sword and in his left the 'palla rotunda cum lilio', the reverse bearing the equestrian figure with sword in the right hand and on the left arm a shield.[24] The notary of 1249 commented on the existence of a legend which he had been unable to read on account of its age.[25] Mayer has demonstrated that the invocation and the arenga, as they survive in the texts, belong to the notarial copy and were not necessarily found in the original, and has produced intricate

---

[20] Cf. PRO, DL 10 nos. 44, 45, and BL, Add. Ch. 33649. Mayer, however, persists in calling them writs.

[21] Cf. 'Rex Anglie' in DL 10 no. 44 (23 Jan. 1191). The plural 'testibus' is logical, in view of the use of the plural throughout the document under Richard, but by no means as common as the singular. I note only two further examples in Landon, nos. 345, 11 Nov. 1190 issued at Messina, and 525, 30 Sept. 1198 issued at Dangu.

[22] Landon, p. 56 no. 365; pd Giuseppe Müller, *Documenti sulle Relazioni della Città Toscane coll' Oriente Cristiano e coi Turchi* (Florence, 1879), pp. 58–9 no. 35.

[23] 'Léopold Delisle', *PBA*, v (1911–12), p. 220.

[24] Landon, plates between pp. 172 and 173.

[25] Müller, *Documenti*, p. 59. The notarial documents are in Florence and in Pisa.

arguments to connect the unorthodox style with drafting by Master Philip.[26] There remains, however, the peculiarity of the adoption of the Pisan mode of dating, which Mayer has seen as a possible concession to the Pisans to ensure the charter's acceptance and enforcement. There is also a scintilla of doubt in the lack of a definite association of Master Philip with the charter, either in a 'Dat' per manum' clause, which might be expected, or as a witness. On these two points the argument for a beneficiary's charter does not seem quite dead.

The final two charters are clearly associated with Master Philip: the first confirming Norman property to Morehius le Diveis, to be held of the bishop of Évreux, was dated 'per manum Magistri Philippi clerici nostri' on 10 January 1192 at Jaffa. It survives in the cartulary of Évreux. Among the witnesses were Robert, earl of Leicester, Geoffrey de Lusignan and Hugh le Brun.[27] The second charter, apparently issued on crusade, has the place-date 'Frankenef' which it has been suggested was the name of the ship on which the king embarked. The grant was in favour of Chichester cathedral (it is found in the bishop's Liber B) and confirmed the church of Seaford to the common fund. The great seal was appended to it and it was witnessed by Master Philip. The text is heavily abbreviated and tantalisingly short in the final protocol. It reads:

Ricardus dei gratia Rex Angl' etc. Omnibus ad quos etc. Noverit universitas vestra nos ratam habere concessionem quam Seffridus episcopus fecit commune ecclesie Cic' de ecclesia de Safford prout carta eius rationabiliter testatur et eam presenti scripto et sigilli nostri appositione confirmamus. Teste etc. M. Philippo apud Frankenef'.[28]

Definite problems remain, but whether we accept Mayer's argument for Master Philip's authorship of some of these charters or not, the cross-currents of influence on Richard's documents are obvious. It is impossible to conjecture, however, how many charters were issued by Richard and how many of these were drafted by Master Philip. The number surviving is very small and of the eight two may not be genuine. How do they compare with the charters issued by lesser lords on the campaign? To see these charters in context it is necessary to consider first the arrangements made by crusaders before leaving England.

The lords and their subtenants who took the crusading vow had to raise money for the journey. Whether taking the cross or making the journey as a

[26] 'Die Kanzlei Richards I.', pp. 31–5.
[27] Landon, p. 60 no. 366, cal. *Calendar of Documents preserved in France*, I (918–1206), ed. J. H. Round (London, 1899), pp. 103–4 no. 309 (from the cartulary of the see of Évreux, G 6 fo. 9, Trans. 161).
[28] Landon, p. 69 no. 367; Chichester Liber B (West Sussex Record Office, Ep VI/1/2) fo. 26 no. 128. I am very grateful to Mrs Patricia Gill, County Archivist, for supplying me with a xerox copy of this charter. See also *The Chartulary of the High Church of Chichester*, ed. W. D. Peckham (Sussex Rec. Soc., XLVI, for 1942/3), p. 29 no. 128.

English charters from the third crusade

pilgrim, there was the need for ready cash. Grants to religious institutions appear often to have been for this purpose. Roger de Mowbray raised substantial amounts of money from Fountains abbey to enable him to go to the Holy Land in 1177; and in 1269 John, earl of Richmond, confirmed to Fountains the vill of Ainderby for a yearly payment of 26d, the monks giving him a down payment of £40 towards his journey to Jerusalem.[29] On taking the cross for the third crusade, Walter le Nair gave to the nuns of Swine two bovates in Skirlington, which Roger his father held, with the toft, in return for five marks towards his journey, and William son of Aldelin raised ten marks in the same way.[30]

Landowners had also to make arrangements for the administration of their estates and for their dependants during their absence, safeguarding the succession in the event of sudden death. John de Penigeston appointed his brother 'keeper of his land and heir' ('custos terre et heredis mei') and also attorned him to testify if necessary to a bequest to Nostell of which John had been a witness.[31] A desire not only to leave one's house in order but also to elicit prayers from the religious led to the ratification of charters. In 1198 Walter de Scoteny confirmed to Drax that all the land possessed by the priory in Roxby should be free of forinsec service. This was done in readiness for his journey to Jerusalem.[32] Complaints of the canons of Nostell in the late 1150s against Henry de Lascy for not putting them in seisin of certain lands and churches before he set out for Jerusalem showed the attitude of the religious to those who did not make these arrangements.[33] Fulk of Rufford, on the other hand, in c. 1190 granted the hospital of St Peter, York, 12d yearly from the town of Rufford, laying 12d on the altar of St Leonard as seisin of his gift upon the approach of his journey, probably to Jerusalem.[34]

The taking of crusading vows also made insurance for dependants necessary. In c. 1188 Ralph de Chall made an agreement with Easby to ensure provision for his wife and daughter in the event of not returning from 'his journey (peregrinacio) to Jerusalem'. Presumably Ralph had taken the cross.[35] 'On the day when he took his way with King Richard to Jerusalem', Roger, son of Richard Touche, knight, granted his daughter the manor of Over Shitlington on her marriage, with provision for its succession.[36] These charters were drawn

---

[29] *Charters of the Honour of Mowbray 1107–1191*, ed. D. E. Greenway (Recs. of Social and Economic History, n.s., I, Brit. Acad., 1972), no. 111 and pp. xxxi–xxxii. *EYC*, V, p. 242, cf. VII, no. 89 (1231–43).
[30] *EYC*, III, nos. 1409, 1641, and cf. XI, no. 68.
[31] *Ibid.*, III, no. 1787. [32] *Ibid.*, VI, no. 78.
[33] *Ibid.*, III, no. 1503. [34] *Ibid.*, I, no. 556.
[35] *Ibid.*, V, no. 215. In 1154–9 a traveller to Jerusalem arranged for the payment of 2s p.a. to his heirs if he did not return (*ibid.*, VIII, no. 102).
[36] *Ibid.*, III, no. 1748.

up in normal circumstances by English scribes. When they affected the religious they were registered in the cartulary of the house. They reflected a concern to avoid, if possible, the need for transacting written record while on crusade.

The cartularies of the Hospitallers and of the Templars, so far as they have survived, include to my knowledge no examples of gifts, grants or quitclaims that were made by either great or small men while on crusade, although the sizeable Hospitallers' cartulary (BL, Cotton MS Nero E vi) is notable particularly for its numerous gifts by lesser persons.[37] By the 1190s the Hospital of St John of Jerusalem was well endowed in all the English counties, including Sussex, where it had lands in Sedlescombe, Shoreham and Sompting; and Gilbert de Balliol, for example, who is associated with one of the following charters, had given to the Hospitallers an acre of land near the church of Helion Bumpstead (Essex).[38] Although the military order of the Templars had been founded for the protection of pilgrims on the journey to the Holy Places, none of its recorded documents appear to be surrenders or gifts of lands that were made on pilgrimage or on crusade. Besides the knights, chaplains, and manual workers of the order, there were also associates and temporary members who might be received into the community for the duration of the crusade or on the point of death, as was the case with William the Marshal.[39] These entrants must have been expected to make some donation but no record of such survives. Furthermore an examination of the cartulary of the church of the Holy Sepulchre, Jerusalem, reveals only endowments of local privileges, lands, houses, tithes, mills, and sales and other transactions which were made by residents in the Holy Land, and nothing of gifts offered by travellers or by crusaders.[40]

The historical and diplomatic interest of charters from the third crusade of lesser men than the king lies in their rarity. Howden's list of the crusaders who died at Acre or at Jaffa or on the journey included some of the greatest men in the land – Robert, earl of Leicester, William Ferrers, earl of Derby, and Nigel de Mowbray among the barons, Ranulph de Glanville, the ex-justiciar,

---

[37] Nor are there any similar documents in the general collections of the orders: *Cartulaire général de l'ordre du Temple* (1119?–1150), ed. Marquis d'Albon, 2 pts. (Paris, 1913–22), and *Cartulaire général de l'ordre des Hospitaliers de St.-Jean de Jérusalem*, ed. J. Delaville le Roulx, 4 vols. (Paris, 1894–1905), I (1100–1200).

[38] BL, Cotton MS Nero E vi, vol. II fo. 350v: pd *The Cartulary of the Knights of St John of Jerusalem in England Secunda Camera, Essex*, ed. M. Gervers (Recs. of Social and Economic History, n.s., VI, Brit. Acad., 1982) no. 454.

[39] *The Records of the Templars in England in the Twelfth Century*, ed. B. A. Lees (Recs. of Social and Economic History, IX, Brit. Acad., 1933), p. lxi.

[40] 'Cartulaire de l'église du Saint Sépulcre de Jérusalem', ed. T. L. M. E. Rozière, *PL*, CLV, cols. 1111–1262.

English charters from the third crusade

and Baldwin, archbishop of Canterbury, among the ecclesiastics.[41] There also perished Ralph de Alta Ripa, archdeacon of Colchester, and John de Morwick, canon of York.[42] As was customary, a number of clerks accompanied the army, and there would have been no shortage of persons to draw up charters. Yet there is virtually no charter evidence. Only one 'crusading' charter to come from the English feudal baronage (secular and ecclesiastic) has so far been traced but that is another of the celebrated Courtois forgeries from the crusading galleries at Versailles. In 1903 it was described but not edited by G. de la Morandière who pointed out its peculiarities, especially the description of John as 'Johannes Hosmundi', and commented on the fact that the seal confused the Osmund family with the Stutevilles.[43] The issue from Acre on the morrow of Whitsunday (3 June) 1191 and the matter of the charter – security for a loan of 100 *libri* of silver borrowed from Giacomo de Jhota and other citizens of Pisa – show its immediate similarity to the 'royal' forgery discussed above. The charter's historical veracity in other respects for the genealogy of the Stuteville family is without the confines of this paper. Clay appears to have accepted, acting on Lewis Loyd's report, its details of descent and some of the information given may be veracious.[44] But although such charters from baronial families may once have existed this is not a survivor of them.

Two charters of lesser knights, found in English cartularies, appear to be above suspicion and provide more scope for historical and diplomatic analysis.[45] They cast an interesting light on the intricacy of feudal relationships and the way in which the local crusading contingents were formed and maintained. The close ties between the local lord and his men illuminate the diplomatic of these charters, explaining by whom they were drawn up and how they were sent back to England, for the charters concern gifts not to the religious of Outremer but to local English religious houses whose archives ensured their survival. Both charters may be regarded in a broad sense as codicils to testaments.[46]

---

[41] *Gesta regis Henrici secundi Benedicti abbatis*, ed. W. Stubbs, 2 vols. (RS, XLIX, 1867), II, pp. 147–50; *Chronica...Rogeri de Houedene*, III, pp. 87–9; and see West, *Justiciarship*, p. 65.

[42] See *Fasti*, I, p. 19, and *York Minster Fasti*, ed. C. T. Clay, 2 vols. (Yorkshire Archaeol. Soc., Rec. Ser., CXXIII–CXXIV, 1958–9), I, pp. 69, 83, 91, II, pp. 23–4.

[43] *Histoire de la maison d'Estouteville* (Paris, 1903), p. 66, citing BN, MS Latin 17803 B pièce 37, 17803–5. I am very grateful to Dr R. C. Watson for locating this book for me in the library of the Victoria and Albert Museum and for pursuing the reference (? wrong) in the BN.

[44] *EYC*, IX, p. 35 n. 4, and see pp. 7 and 27.

[45] It is unlikely that they are solitary survivors.

[46] M. Sheehan, *The Will in Medieval England* (Pontifical Institute of Mediaeval Studies, Studies and Texts VI, 1963), pp. 137, 146 n. 2, has examples of *post obit* gifts: in one instance (137), if a man died on pilgrimage the land was to go to the abbey, but if not it was to be returned to him.

They share certain features that suggest a common origin. Information on drawing up 'crusading' wills shows, not surprisingly, 'national' influence. To be effective in one's homeland it was essential that the document should be cast in an accepted and conventional form as otherwise its validity might be questioned. In 1219 Barzella Merxadrus, an Italian, used a notary to draw up his will, which was done in his tent at Damietta. When Count Henry of Rodez added a codicil to his will at Acre in October 1222, he had it drawn up in the house of the hospital, where presumably a southern French clerk was available, and confirmed that the will he had made in his native land was to remain effective.[47]

John of Hessle's charter, which was discovered by the Reverend J. C. Dickinson, is copied into a fragment of a North Ferriby cartulary, now in the Bodleian Library, Oxford.[48] It recorded that John had given a furlong called 'Westdayle', outside the grove of Hessle towards the west, to the Temple at Jerusalem. Although he was in the Holy Land and the gift appears superficially to be a concession to the Temple of the Lord at Jerusalem, it was in fact a gift for the support of the canons at North Ferriby. The 'community' at North Ferriby, consisting probably of no more than three canons, and founded by Eustace fitzJohn, was a cell of the Austin canons of the order of the Temple of the Lord at Jerusalem, and not as once supposed[49] a preceptory of the Templars.[50] The charter was given into the hands of Petrobricius, prior of the Temple at Jerusalem, but there can be no doubt that an exemplification of it was returned to North Ferriby, where it came in time to be recorded in the cartulary.

Dated at the siege of Acre it must presumably be assigned to June or July 1191. After Richard I's arrival on 8 June the siege was pressed more vigorously and on 12 July the garrison surrendered. It is not known whether John of Hessle returned to England from Palestine, but if he did he must have died shortly afterwards.[51] He may indeed have been dead by 1192 and if so the likelihood must be that he perished at Acre.[52] No reasons for drawing up the charter are given, but it may reasonably be supposed to have been effected at the beginning of the siege when fears for survival would have been most acute. The named witness to this charter (present with others unnamed and with John

---

[47] For these examples see L. and J. Riley-Smith, *The Crusades. Idea and Reality 1095–1274* (London, 1981), pp. 174–6, taken from L. V. Savioli, *Annali Bolognesi* (Bassano, 1789), II(2), pp. 419–20, and *Cartulaire...des Hospitaliers*, ed. Delaville le Roulx, II, pp. 308–9.
[48] MS Add. C 51, fo. 5v (8 fos. only, but including 26 charters of Hessle).
[49] *MA*, VI(1), pp. 589–90.
[50] *MRHEW*, p. 148; *VCH Yorks.*, III, p. 241; and *EYC*, III, p. 501.
[51] *EYC*, XII, no. 28.
[52] *Ibid.*, no. 29, the next charter in the cartulary, in which John is recorded as dead, could be as early as 1192.

of Hessle at the siege of Acre) is Roger, parson of Howden (Yorks. E.R.). Roger seems to have left the Holy Land before the last week of August 1191, perhaps with the French detachment and the king of France.[53]

The charter formed the subject of a note by Lady Stenton in the *English Historical Review* for 1953 because it provided conclusive evidence that Roger the parson of Howden had been on the third crusade, from which fact Lady Stenton deduced further evidence for Roger's authorship of the *Gesta regis Henrici secundi Benedicti abbatis* – a major source for the third crusade – that text being the first draft of the chronicle which goes under Howden's own name[54] and is also the source for two of Richard I's letters discussed above.[55] Antonia Gransden has doubted that Roger the parson of Howden is the same person as Roger of Howden the chronicler, and doubt spread to other quarters, but David Corner has demonstrated convincingly that Roger of Howden wrote the whole of the *Gesta* and has maintained that since that work contains 'vivid details of the crusade in which Roger, the parson of Howden, played a part, it is highly probable that Roger of Howden, the chronicler, was Roger, the parson of Howden'.[56]

Roger parson of Howden's presence on the third crusade was doubtless with the Yorkshire and Lincolnshire contingents of whom we hear in some detail in the *Gesta*. The deaths of Nigel de Mowbray, Simon de Wale, Walter de Scrope, Walter de Kyme and Walter de Ros and two members of the Camville family are recorded at Acre. Most of these families had lands that spanned the Humber and the two counties and Howden itself lay no more than fifteen miles from Hessle and from North Ferriby in the East Riding. Roger's acute interest in the Yorkshire and Lincolnshire contingents appears to account for the northern emphasis in his list of casualties and it is not altogether surprising that when removed from the situation of battle his 'revised' chronicle did not repeat all the names of the dead.[57]

The overlords of John of Hessle at Hessle were the Tisons. There is some doubt as to whether the tenancy in chief was held by the Stutevilles and their Wake descendants or by the Mowbrays. It has been suggested, however, that the Tison interest in Hessle (and also in South Ferriby, Lincs.) formed part of the ten knights' fees which Roger de Mowbray granted as an under-tenancy to Robert de Stuteville III in the 1150s or 1160s as a compromise in the disputes between the two families.[58] Between *c.* 1164 and 1183 Robert de

---

[53] D. M. Stenton, 'Roger of Howden and "Benedict"', *EHR*, LXVIII (1953), p. 580.

[54] *Ibid.*, pp. 574–82. The charter is printed on pp. 576–7 and also in *EYC*, XII, no. 28 (and noted in *EYC*, IX, pp. x–xi, and 19).

[55] See above p. 198.

[56] 'The *Gesta Regis Henrici Secundi* and *Chronica* of Roger, parson of Howden', *Bulletin of the Institute of Historical Research*, LVI (1983), pp. 126–44, esp. 126, 130.

[57] Stenton, 'Roger of Howden', p. 579 n. 2.   [58] *EYC*, XII, p. 51.

Stuteville III confirmed a gift of John of Hessle to North Ferriby which seems
to clinch the issue. John of Hessle's generosity to North Ferriby thus predates
his setting out on the third crusade[59] and four gifts and two confirmations to
North Ferriby cannot be precisely dated but are likely to belong to the period
before 1190, perhaps forming part of his preparations for the crusade.[60]

There is no indication as to whether any of the Tison family left for the third
crusade. William Tison died before 1180 leaving four daughters as co-heiresses
who married into the families of Flamborough, Beauver (two of them) and
Steeton.[61] Robert de Stuteville III had died in 1183 and there is positive
evidence that William de Stuteville, Robert's heir and successor, did not go
on the third crusade for he acted as the king's justice at Lincoln in October
1191.[62] His younger brother, Osmund, however, joined the crusade and
perished, as the *Gesta* records, at Jaffa.[63]

Absence of John of Hessle's overlords may account for Roger the parson
of Howden being the chief witness to the charter. The circumstances of the
drawing up of the charter can only be surmised but the warranties suggest a
lack of certainty and some doubt about its eventual enforcement. The detailed
warranty clause committed John and his heirs to stand by the gift, pledging
land of equal value if that were not possible. It was followed by a penal or
sanction clause, both relatively rare in the late twelfth century, and finally the
impression of John's seal is mentioned as corroboration. For added security
the charter was placed in the Temple. Lady Stenton suggested that this livery
of the charter may have been substituted for the actual livery of seisin which
was clearly impossible in the circumstances. She also suggested that Roger may
have been the draftsman of the deed but not its scribe on account of the
occurrence of the French phrase 'devers le west' three times.[64] This phrase,
however, is not uncommon in English charters of the period – for instance in a
charter of 1176 and in another of 1193–1203[65] – and nothing in the charter
is inconsistent with an English origin. Indeed everything points to English
drafting, probably by Roger. The construction 'Sciatis me', which is used
here, dominated in the Clare charters of the central years of the twelfth
century.[66] The opening address 'Omnibus sancte matris ecclesie filiis tam
presentibus quam futuris' is common and perfectly acceptable, occurring in
both lay and ecclesiastical charters of the period, possibly more frequently in

---

[59] *Ibid.*, IX, no. 18. John also confirmed his father's (Ivo de Karkeni's) gift of the church of Hessle
to Guisborough before 1183 (*ibid.*, no. 102, and see p. 187 and no. 103).
[60] *Ibid.*, XII, nos. 22–7.
[61] *Ibid.*, p. 5.
[62] *Ibid.*, IX, p. 10.   [63] *Gesta Henrici secundi*, II, p. 150.
[64] 'Roger of Howden', p. 577.
[65] *Charters of...Mowbray*, no. 127; *EYC*, v, no. 146.
[66] *Earldom of Gloucester Charters*, ed. R. B. Patterson (Oxford, 1973), p. 21 n. 15.

English charters from the third crusade

the latter.[67] An ecclesiastical origin for the charter from a cleric travelling with the crusaders (with a limited experience of charter drafting) seems extremely likely, and it may not be totally irrelevant that the two uses of 'versus (*or* deversus*) le West' cited above are both from the Cistercian abbey of Fountains in Yorkshire. The notion of Lady Stenton that the French was inserted by the scribe is unconvincing: scribes would not have meddled with charters in this way. There can be little doubt that the instrument of the transmission of the charter back to Yorkshire was Roger. The charter was then copied into the North Ferriby cartulary and the gift was confirmed by John of Hessle's son, Robert, who used the same phrase 'vers le west' in contrast to the Latin heading to the charter in the cartulary.[68] There is no indication that the gift of John to North Ferriby was not respected.

John of Hessle's charter invites comparison with a charter of Robert of Icklesham, found in the cartulary of Battle abbey.[69] This charter is conspicuous by its abnormal address 'Sciant tam presentes quam absentes' and states that Robert of Icklesham (Sussex)[70] on a pilgrimage and in danger of death, when the Christian army was at Jaffa, mindful of the health of his soul, conceded to the monks of Battle a yearly rent of half a mark of silver from a virgate of land in Barnhorne in Bexhill, Sussex.[71]

As Robert of Icklesham's charter was issued at Jaffa, it must have been drawn up at some date between September 1191 and the autumn of 1192, when the English forces returned home; most probably in the seven weeks between 10 September, when the army arrived in Jaffa, and the end of October. During this time the main Christian army rested while Richard tried to negotiate a peace. Probably about 7 October 1191, Richard himself was forced to return to Acre to induce some deserters from the Christian army to rejoin him and on the 13th he came back to Jaffa by sea, escorting the two queens, Berengaria and Joan.[72] Richard left Jaffa with the main force on 31 October, but a garrison and the sick and wounded remained, of whom Robert of Icklesham may have

---

[67] *Facsimiles of Early Cheshire Charters*, ed. G. Barraclough (Oxford, 1957), nos. 2, 10; *EYC*, v, no. 122; C. N. L. Brooke, 'Episcopal Charters for Wix Priory' in *A Medieval Miscellany for Doris Mary Stenton*, ed. P. M. Barnes and C. F. Slade (PRS, n. s., XXXVI, 1960), nos. 5, 6.

[68] Fo. 6: noted *EYC*, XII, p. 59.

[69] Lincoln's Inn, MS Hale 87, fo. 68r (pd below p. 213). The charter was cited by L. F. Salzman in 'Some Sussex Domesday tenants. II. The family of Dene', *Sussex Archaeol. Collections*, LVIII (1916), p. 180, but he did not recognize its significance and rarity.

[70] The new town of Winchelsea was constructed within the parish of Icklesham, see M. W. Beresford and J. K. S. St Joseph, *Medieval England, An Aerial Survey* (2nd edn, Cambridge, 1979), pp. 238–41.

[71] The location is known only from the heading in the cartulary and other external evidence.

[72] H. E. Mayer, *The Crusades*, trans. J. Gillingham (Oxford, 1972), pp. 144–6, J. B. Gillingham, *Richard the Lionheart* (London, 1978), ch. 10, and 'Itinerarium', pp. 260–90, give general accounts of the period from the battle of Arsouf to the king's departure from Jaffa at the end of October.

been one. Richard was ill at Jaffa in August 1192, prior to sailing for home, but the words 'quando exercitus Christianorum moratus est apud Japhe' of Robert of Icklesham's charter suggest a date rather of September or October 1191. Robert may indeed have died on the crusade or on the journey home, after the departure of Richard I from Acre on 9 October 1192 and the dispersal of the English. He was certainly dead by 29 October 1194, by which time his widow, Sybil, had taken a second husband, Richard de Cumbe.[73]

The witnesses to Robert's charter, Geoffrey and H. de Balliol, whom he accompanied to the Holy Land, were his overlords at Barnhorne.[74] This branch of the Balliol family came from Bailleul-sur-Eaulne, department of Seine-Maritime (arr. Neufchâtel, cant. Londinières), while the Scottish Balliols' roots were in the Bailleul in the department of the Somme (arr. Abbeville).[75] Geoffrey de Balliol was the heir of Gilbert (? fl. 1166) and Geoffrey's heir in turn was another Gilbert. A charter of Henry II confirmed to St Mary, Eu, the church of Le Bosc-Geoffroy and certain tithes in Normandy and England given by Geoffrey de Balliol with the assent of Gilbert his heir.[76] The H. de Balliol of our charter might be the Henry who acted as one of the sureties for the count of Flanders in a treaty with Richard I in June or July 1197, when Ralph count of Eu pledged for Richard, but Henry seems more likely to have been one of the Balliols from the Somme.[77]

The Balliols were tenants of Eu in Sussex. In 1166 Gilbert de Balliol held three knights' fees in the rape of Hastings of the old feoffment of the count of Eu. The Eu *carta* refers to four further knights' fees, held by Gilbert's father, now belonging to the bishop of Chichester.[78] These are apparently the same knights' fees in the bishop's manor of Bexhill, three of which Bishop Hilary had given to Geoffrey de Balliol and his son Osbert in probably 1150 × 1161. The fourth fee, which was held by Hamund of Icklesham (and in which it was

---

[73] Salzman, 'Family of Dene', esp. pp. 180–1, citing *Feet of Fines...of Sussex*, I (Sussex Rec. Soc., II, 1903), no. 2.

[74] Osbern who held Barnhorne manor in 1086 was perhaps a member of the Balliol family, see *VCH Sussex*, IX, ed. L. F. Salzman (1937), p. 118.

[75] Lewis Loyd, *The Origins of Some Anglo-Norman Families* (Harleian Soc. CIII, 1951), p. 11. For the Scottish Balliols, see *A History of Northumberland* (issued under the direction of the Northumberland County History Committee) VI (Newcastle, 1902), pp. 14–87, esp. 15–31 and the genealogy on 72–3.

[76] Loyd, *Origins*, p. 11.

[77] Landon, pp. 118–19. There is also a Hugh who witnessed a charter of Wiscard Leydet of ?2 Aug. 1197, issued at Rouen? (*ibid.* p. 121). This is probably the Hugh who, in company with Thomas de St Valéry, was ordered by King John in 1201 to do what harm they could to the count of Eu in the approaching war. John, having quarrelled with the Lusignans, had confiscated the English possessions of the counts of Eu: GEC, V, pp. 160–1; cf. *History of Northumberland*, VI, p. 31 and n. 7.

[78] *The Red Book of the Exchequer*, ed. Hubert Hall, 3 pts (RS, XCIX, 1896), I, pp. 203, and 198–200 (the bishop).

English charters from the third crusade

stated specifically that there was no dwelling-house of Hamund), was quitclaimed to the bishop by the Balliols.[79] It is possible that Hamund lost his fee to the bishop at this time and this might explain subsequent events at Bexhill, in which Barnhorne lay, presuming, as is likely, that Robert of Icklesham was descended from Hamund.

The manor of Bexhill formed part of the ancient endowment of the bishopric at Selsey but seems to have been lost to the bishops after the removal of the see to Chichester in 1075. At some time it had been granted to John count of Eu who, on 14 November 1148, restored the vill, with the churches and 'omnia membra sua' and appurtenances, to Bishop Hilary. This restoration was confirmed both by King Stephen (who confirmed the manor with the hundred and churches and appurtenances)[80] and by Pope Eugenius III on 26 November 1149 in a letter which interestingly specifies 'the vill called Bexhill with the churches and the hundred, Icklesham and Wickham and all their appurtenances'.[81] There seems little doubt that Icklesham and Wickham (a manor in Icklesham parish) were connected anciently with Bexhill as detached portions.

Presumably Hamund's fee at Icklesham descended to Robert of Icklesham, overlordship of the rape of Hastings descending with the Eus and then after 1268 with the earls of Richmond, counts of Brittany.[82] Robert's granddaughter, Sybil, had the patronage of the church which she granted to Battle abbey some time between 1227 and 1247 and was therefore presumably lady of the manor there.[83] The manor was not granted to Battle with the church but descended to the Herringods by her marriage to Nicholas Herringod from whom it passed to the Finchs in Edward III's reign.[84] An eighteenth-century transcript states that the manor had formerly (i.e. before 1469–70) belonged to William Wilcheres and it has been tied up, probably wrongly, with one of the seven fees held by Humphrey de Wilcheres of the count of Eu in 1166.[85]

It is unlikely that the count of Eu was on the third crusade. Ralph d'Exoudun, a younger son of Hugh VIII, sire de Lusignan, and brother of Hugh le Brun, count of la Marche, married in 1191 Alice, daughter of Henry

[79] *ABC*, no. 23.
[80] *RR*, III, no. 183; *Chartulary...of Chichester*, no. 161; and *MA*, VI(3), p. 1171 no. 49. The original of John count of Eu's charter does not survive: it is to be presumed that it gave the details as in the papal letter.
[81] *PUE*, II, no. 60.   [82] *GEC*, X, pp. 811–12.
[83] Univ. of London Library, Fuller Collection I/28/4, ed. 'Charters of Battle Abbey' (reproduced by the Library, 1979) no. 24. Possibly in or before 1237 (21 Henry III, Hilary term), see BL, Add MS 5679, fo. 269.
[84] *Ibid.*, fo. 268v.
[85] *Ibid.*, fo. 269, citing Pelham deed H no. 9. I have not been able to trace this deed and Dr Marie Clough informs me that the whereabouts of the Pelham deeds is unknown. *Red Book of the Exchequer*, I, p. 202. *VCH, Sussex*, IX, p. 187 makes this deduction.

(II) count of Eu, and heiress to the Eu estates after the death of her brother as a minor in 1186.[86] The chronicles make no mention of Ralph d'Exoudun's participation with the English or French contingents on the crusade, although this silence does not, of course, rule out the possibility.

The rent of half a mark from a virgate in Barnhorne in Bexhill which troubled Robert of Icklesham, perhaps on his death-bed, recalls the whole story of the dispute between Gilbert de Balliol and the monks of Battle over the possession of the Barnhorne estate. The suit had come before the king's court at Clarendon when it was the occasion of the justiciar Richard de Lucy's[87] snide remark to Gilbert, who had protested against the validity of certain concessionary charters of his ancestors on the grounds that they were not sealed: 'It was not the custom in the past for every petty knight to have a seal'. When Gilbert was forced to surrender the manor to the abbey, repercussions were felt by an even smaller knight, Robert of Icklesham, who, together with his mother, Matilda, seized a meadow, complaining that the men who had defined the boundaries at the time of the dispute had taken more than was just. Robert's complaint to the king's court was dealt with by the justices at Winchester who re-examined the boundary assessors and found Robert guilty of a false plea. Robert's hasty retreat, which is vividly described in the Battle chronicle – 'when he heard this, he took flight secretly, sparing neither his spurs nor his horse, nor pausing till he reached home all a tremble' – was to avoid the penalty for a false plea of being forced into a formal quitclaim without compensation.[88] The secondary plea to the king's court, like the association of Robert of Icklesham with his overlords on crusade, illustrates the inter-dependence of society.

Robert's suit against the abbey appears to date from the 1170s and, after Odo succeeded to the abbey of Battle in 1175,[89] he, with the assent of Ralph parson of Icklesham, his brother Stephen, his mother Matilda and Ralph his heir released to the abbey all claim to land in Barnhorne.[90] Among the witnesses were Henry, his father's brother, and Samson of Guestling, his mother's brother. This relaxation was probably closely associated with a final concord between Robert and the abbot of Battle which is referred to in Ralph's confirmation of his father's renunciation of the rent while in the Holy Land.[91]

The circumstances of the composition of Robert's charter are clear. Sudden

---

[86] GEC, v, pp. 160–1.

[87] On de Lucy, see West, *Justiciarship*, pp. 37–9.

[88] *The Chronicle of Battle Abbey*, ed. and trans. E. Searle (OMT, 1980), pp. 213–21. On Robert's hasty retreat, see p. 220 n. 1 citing R. C. van Caenegem, *Royal Writs in England from the Conquest to Glanvill* (Selden Soc., LXXVII, 1958/9), pp. 43–4.

[89] *Heads*, p. 29.

[90] Thomas Thorpe, *Descriptive Catalogue of the...Muniments of Battle Abbey* (1835), p. 40.

[91] Battle cartulary, Lincoln's Inn, MS Hale 87, fo. 68r.

English charters from the third crusade

illness, fear of death – which in any case had perhaps determined Robert of Icklesham's crusader's vow in the first place – caused him to contemplate religion and the religious. The wrong, if there had been one, was against the monks of Battle. Past injuries had to be remedied. For this reason this charter did not concede a new gift to the orders of the Templars or the Hospitallers, nor did it add more to the property of Robertsbridge, Otham or Lewes to which Robert of Icklesham and his family had been small benefactors, but settled the account at Battle.[92]

The drawing up of the charter, its composition and writing raise several questions. There would have been no lack of scribes and persons capable of drafting charters on the crusade. Clerks of all ranks from the archbishop downwards attended the king; the nobility were accompanied by their households and the list of the named dead includes clerks and stewards.[93] Also the feudal monarchs of the Latin kingdom had a chancery, though not comparatively advanced, and a chancellor, and within Jaffa itself there was a church of the Latin rite, with parochial status and attendant clergy, and a royal castle with a chaplain.[94] Indeed on 26 October 1191, with the army at Jaffa, Guy king of Jerusalem, at the request of King Richard, confirmed a privilege of the Genoese which was dated by Girard the king's chaplain, possibly from the castle chapel.[95]

The style of the charter is characteristically English and the construction 'Sciant...quod' extremely common. The substitution of 'absentes' for the usual 'futuri' (which I have not found elsewhere) is unusual but a necessary adjustment to the particular requirement of the charter that the monks of Battle should be made aware of Robert's concession. Similarly the present tense 'do eis et concedo', which is not common but not unacceptable,[96] expresses the urgency of the matter and would seem to scotch any suggestion that the charter might have been committed to memory and then written down later in England. The use of 'la Bataille' rather than 'de Bello' is interesting. By the late twelfth-century French place-names became relatively common in English charters of the nobility and 'La Bataille' is found in at least one other

---

[92] *VCH Sussex*, IX, p. 187, citing *Feet of Fines...of Sussex*, I (Sussex Rec. Soc., II), no. 131. He witnessed the foundation charter of Otham (later fused with Bayham), *MA*, VI(2), p. 991 no. 1.

[93] *Gesta Henrici secundi*, II, pp. 147–50.

[94] See B. Hamilton, 'A medieval urban church: the case of the crusader states', *SCH*, XVI (1979), p. 162 and esp. nn. 18, 20; and J. L. La Monte, *Feudal Monarchy in the Latin Kingdom of Jerusalem 1100–1291* (Cambridge Mass., 1932), pp. 122–35 on the chancery and the 'pitifully small' number of charters. These were kept in the archives of the religious houses.

[95] R. Röhricht, *Regesta Regni Hierosolymitani* (MXCVII–MCCXCI) (Burt Franklin, New York, n.d.: originally published in *Oeniponti*, Innsbruck, 1893–1904), I, no. 702.

[96] Cf. H. E. Salter, *Facsimiles of Early Charters in Oxford Muniment Rooms* (Oxford, 1929), no. 93.

twelfth-century source.[97] Its absence from the monastic cartulary (except in this instance), where formal Latin documents prevailed, is hardly surprising. Although French was used in the chanceries of Outremer and flexibility of language was imperative in a society where many transactions had to be written in Arabic by local Saracen scribes and then translated,[98] it is unlikely that the influence on these single words and phrases was from so far afield. The draftsman and scribe of the Icklesham charter was perhaps a clerk of the Balliols, and certainly a man not used to the framing of monastic charters. The diplomatic of the charter appears more correct in 'English' terms than that of Master Philip's documents, but the phrase 'exercitus Christianorum' compares with the 'exercitus Christianus' of the two Genoese letters.[99] There is no sealing clause, so whether the charter was sealed, and if so, how and with whose seal, must remain open questions.[100] The original's omission from the later thirteenth-century Battle cartulary (now Huntington library, Battle abbey papers vol. 29) might suggest that it did not long survive. It was certainly not among the Bexhill charters in Battle abbey to reach the hands of the bookseller, Thomas Thorpe.

The named witnesses, the Balliols, were probably the necessary instruments in the charter's transmission back to England. The return of the charter to Sussex, where it was confirmed by Robert's heir, Ralph of Icklesham, with the assent of his mother Sybil, and other relatives, and where it came to rest in the abbey of Battle, is likely to be associated with them and for this reason we might hazard the guess that the draftsman of the charter was their clerk. The charter illustrates the ties between men in a tenurial and feudal sense which bound their arrangements in matters large and small. It was at Battle, too, where King Richard I, the Eus and the Sussex Balliols were all commemorated, that arrangements were made also for Robert of Icklesham's and his family's commemoration.[101]

This limited investigation has served to show the flexibility of diplomatic, the variety of influences and the cross-currents that existed in the world of Coeur de Lion. According to Mayer, Master Philip of Poitou 'broke the

[97] See *VCH, Sussex*, IX, p. 97.
[98] La Monte, *Feudal Monarchy*, p. 125, and C. Clermont-Ganneau, 'Deux chartes des croisés dans des archives arabes', *Recueil d'archéologie orientale*, VI (Paris, 1903/5), pp. 1–30.
[99] See above pp. 198–9.
[100] It is possible that the copyist may have omitted the sealing clause, but, as the witness-clause is given, it seems unlikely. The seals of the kings of Jerusalem (e.g. of Guy de Lusignan) and of the Antioch princes were of lead, doubtless because of both the Byzantine influence and the unsuitability of wax, which, however, was used by some of the nobility, for example, Humphrey de Montfort, seigneur of Beirut, see Clermont-Ganneau, 'Deux chartes', and G. Schlumberger, F. Chalandon and A. Blanchet, *Sigillographie de l'Orient Latin* (Paris, 1943).
[101] *Feet of Fines...of Sussex*, I, no. 433; and see Battle cartulary, Lincoln's Inn, MS Hale 87, fo. 69r.

English charters from the third crusade

monotony of the English writ and writ-charter':[102] he also, if responsible for all the eight charters described above, used many features that were strange to Richard's royal chancery. That Richard's 'field' chancery produced documents of composite influence is doubtless due to the particular circumstances. The knights' charters, too, exhibited peculiarities, but basically the influences on them were English and conservative.

APPENDIX

BATTLE CARTULARY, LINCOLN'S INN, MS HALE 87, FO. 68R

Carta Roberti de Iclesham de relaxacione redditus dimidie marce de^a una virgata in Bernore

Sciant tam presentes quam absentes quod ego Robertus de Iclesham in peregrinacione mea et periculo mortis constitutus quando exercitus Christianorum moratus est apud Japhe memor salutis anime mee redditum quem michi conventus monachorum de la Bataille solitus est annuatim reddere scilicet dimidiam marcam argenti do eis et concedo quietum et liberum amodo deinceps. Testibus Galfrido de Baillol, H. de Baillol et aliis.

[102] Mayer, 'Die Kanzlei Richards I.', p. 34. ^{a} pro *deleted and* de *substituted.*

ADDENDA

To p. 196 n.5:   J.C. Holt and R. Mortimer, *Acta of Henry II and Richard I Handlist* (List & Index Soc. spec. ser.21, 1986) have two additions (nos. 361-2) to the charters issued from Messina listed in Landon.

To p. 198 n.13:   On 'teste me ipso' etc. see J.C. Holt, 'Ricardus Rex Anglorum et Dux Normannorum' in *Magna Carta and Medieval Government* (Hambledon Press, 1985) 79-81.

XII

The Medieval Care and Custody of the Archbishop of Canterbury's Archives

SYSTEMS OF KEEPING archives in the middle ages paid great attention to security and ease of finding. More harm has been done to medieval documents in the modern age than perhaps in any other, and it is within living memory that seals have been cut off documents, gall used on them, and slices chopped off them to facilitate mounting on paper, thus obscuring endorsements. Furthermore, documents have been sewn up in books and both medieval methods of storing documents and the catalogues which were made to describe them, have been discarded.

Maximum security measures were used in storing charters in the middle ages. Frequently, documents were placed with such valuables as plate, seal matrices and ecclesiastical ornaments and vestments, often in a chest encased in iron bars and well secured with multiple locks. The chest was then put in a well guarded place, usually close to the high altar of the church.[1] Reference is made in 1274 to two tallies being 'in a little bag of leather which is in a chest standing behind the high altar of the church [of St. Paul, London] in which other things of the Lord [Bishop] are deposited . . .'.[2] It is well known that charters were frequently copied into gospel-books to give them added force, and transactions and promises were made on the high altar of the church endowing the document with a special sanctified authority. More frequently, a room or treasury was provided close to the high altar, and in the eastern part of the church, to which the public and laity had no easy access, and guards and night-watchmen were provided to watch out against thieves.[3]

---

[1] My thanks are due to Miss Diana E. Greenway who helped me on many points in the preparation of this paper. Cf. H. Peek and C. Hall, *The Archives of the University of Cambridge* (Cambridge, 1962), pp. 1–6; R. Dunning, 'The muniments of Syon abbey; their administration and migration in the fifteenth and sixteenth centuries', *ante*, xxxvii (1964), 105.

[2] *The Register of Thomas de Cantilupe*, ed. R. G. Griffiths and W. W. Capes (Canterbury & York Soc., 1906–7), ii. 182–3, cited by C. Jenkins, 'Some thirteenth century registers', *Church Quarterly Rev.*, xcix (1924–5), 89.

[3] See an early reference to the treasury at St. Paul's containing documents in 1111 × 1127 in *Early Charters of the Cathedral Church of St. Paul, London*, ed. M. Gibbs (Camden 3rd Ser., lviii, 1939), p. xxxvi and no. 273, and C. Oman, *English Church Plate 597–1830* (Oxford, 1957), p. 36.

Archbishops and even kings did not scorn to use the treasury at Christ Church, Canterbury. Gervase of Canterbury says that Henry II's will was, by order of the king, to be diligently reserved in three places in the kingdom to ensure its safety, 'videlicet in ecclesia Cantuariae, in cofris suis, et in thesauro Wintoniae'.[1] By Lanfranc's time the monks' endowments were separated from the archbishop's, but there is not known to have been any separation of the conventual and archiepiscopal archives as early as this.[2] The privileges of archbishop and convent may have been assigned severally for the first time as a result of a mandate from Gregory IX to the legate Otto in 1238, following an incident of forgery during the archiepiscopate of Edmund Rich.*[3] With some documents there can never have been a clear-cut differentiation; some of the archbishop's documents must have always remained with the monks and vice versa. For the main archival collection, however, there was certainly a division by 1277–80 when the archbishop's charters were listed separately. After that, frequent references occur to 'your' and 'our' archives,[4] and separate catalogues continue to be issued for both collections.[5]

At least by the thirteenth century the archbishop's charters were kept in *vasa*. The *vas* seems to have been quite a large storage unit, capable of holding from one up to forty-three charters and other containers such as a *hanaper* or wicker basket.[6] The word itself is applied to all sorts of cases from reliquaries to vessels containing food, to beehives, military baggage and agricultural and hunting implements, and Pliny and Cassiodorus use *vasarium* to mean archives and records.[7] *Vas* has given rise to the modern words vessel and vase, and a *vasculum* (a receptacle still so named and used by botanists for carrying specimens) was a smaller edition. The *vas* seems to have been particularly favoured by Canterbury archivists. The seventeenth-century Canterbury antiquarian William Somner copied a fourteenth-century catalogue of the Christ Church charters which were described as being kept in *vasa*: 'Archivum Ecclesie Christi Cantuariensis, sive descriptio, atque supervisio, omnium chartarum et munimentorum,

[1] *The Historical Works of Gervase of Canterbury*, ed. W. Stubbs (Rolls Ser., 1879–80), i. 300 (hereafter cited as Gervase).
[2] F. R. H. Du Boulay, 'The Archbishop as Territorial Magnate', in *Mediaeval Records of the Archbishops of Canterbury* (1962), p. 53 sqq.
[3] *Cal. Papal Letters*, i. 174; *Registres de Grégoire IX (1227–41)*, ed. L. Auvray, etc. (École Française de Rome, 1896–1955), no. 4371; Gervase, ii. 132, cited by C. R. Cheney, 'Magna Carta Beati Thome: another Canterbury forgery', *ante*, xxxvi (1963), p. 18 n. 5. See below p. 106 & n. 4.   * Read: Edmund of Abingdon
[4] E.g. *Literae Cantuarienses*, ed. J. B. Sheppard (Rolls Ser., 1887–9), i, no. 283; *Registrum Roberti Winchelsey*, ed. Rose Graham (Canterbury & York Soc., 1952–6), ii. 1326 (Canterbury, Dean & Chapter Archives, roll no. 14).
[5] See below p. 97, n. 1, p. 100, n. 1, and Canterbury, D. & C. Archives, Register I (Hist. MSS. Comm., *9th Rept.*, app., pp. 74–5) cited by Du Boulay, p. 59 n. 35.
[6] See *Table of Canterbury Archbishopric Charters*, ed. Irene J. Churchill (Camden Miscellany, xv, 1929), pp. 1–19 (hereafter cited as *Archbishopric Charters*).
[7] *Ibid.*, p. ix; C. T. Lewis and C. Short, *A Latin Dictionary* (Oxford, 1879), p. 1959; J. H. Baxter and C. Johnson, *Medieval Latin Word-List* (Oxford, 1934), p. 448.

quae in vasis tam Borealibus quam Australibus Armarii Chartophylacis Facta per Joh. de Glocesteria et Joh. de Eastria, A.D. MCCCLXX.— Custodes'.[1] The thirty *vasa* were placed in the great almery, which was divided into two parts with fifteen in each part.[2] An almery or press, containing nine vertical and seven horizontal rows, and sixty-three drawers of varying depths, made in the early fifteenth century, survives in the Aerary of St. George's Chapel, Windsor, and the *vas* was probably a wooden drawer, similar to those contained therein.[3] Most of the documents were folded, although at Windsor charters could be kept flat in the 'royal' drawer because it was bigger,[4] and careful arrangements were made for protecting the seals by the manufacture of little leather or cloth bags. Sometimes little cuts of old vestments were used. Archbishop Winchelsey, writing to the prior of Canterbury in 1304, comments on a certain document from which the seal has been separated, owing to the negligence of the keepers, and is lying loose, although intact.[5] Great care was taken over the preservation of documents and seals, and if the documents were regarded as of extreme importance, they were copied in considerable numbers. If they were inspected by other groups or persons, who had an interest in them, strict precautions were taken to see that they were not damaged or removed.[6]

An adequate finding-list or catalogue soon became a necessity. The archival expansion of the thirteenth century brought re-organization and listing.[7] From this period onwards, there survive several catalogues, of which the most famous is undoubtedly the Durham *Repertorium Magnum* of *c.* 1456, which is still the basis for finding documents there. Three previous catalogues of the Durham muniments survive, one of *c.* 1340 (Durham, Misc. Ch. 426), one of *c.* 1380 (Bodleian Libr., MS. Carte 177) and the *Repertorium Parvum* of *c.* 1400.[8] In 1323 a kalendar of the royal archives was made by order of Walter de Stapledon, bishop of Exeter and treasurer of the exchequer. Stapledon says in his preface that before 1323 the documents had been transferred 'from person to person and from place to place, as from the Wardrobe to the Chancery, from the Chancery to the Exchequer, and thence to the Receipt of the Exchequer, and per-chance to unfit persons'. The king then had them put away in definite

---

[1] Hist. MSS. Comm., *5th Rept.* (1876), p. 435, Canterbury, D. & C. Archives, MS. C. 232, cited in *Archbishopric Charters*, p. vi, n. 2.

[2] *Archbishopric Charters*, p. ix, n. 3.

[3] *The Manuscripts of St. George's Chapel, Windsor Castle*, ed. J. N. Dalton (Windsor, 1957), frontispiece, and introduction by M. Bond, p. xxx.

[4] *Ibid.*

[5] *Reg. Winchelsey*, ii. 1326.

[6] See *William Thorne's Chronicle of St. Augustine's Abbey Canterbury*, trans. A. H. Davis (Oxford, 1934), pp. 118–19.

[7] See V. H. Galbraith, 'Press-marks on the deeds of Lewes priory', *Sussex Archaeol. Collections*, lxv (1924), 196–205.

[8] W. A. Pantin, *Report on the Muniments of the Dean and Chapter of Durham* (printed for private circulation in 1939), pp. 1–10, gives a detailed and exciting description of the keeping of the medieval muniments.

places, distinguished by alphabetical letters and provided with a repertory or kalendar.[1]

Two catalogues describe the contents of the archbishop of Canterbury's muniment room in about 1277, and in 1330. The first list, included in the great Canterbury archiepiscopal cartulary Lambeth MS. 1212, and to which a fourteenth-century hand has added a title 'Capitula Cartarum Regiarum in Thesauraria Archiepiscopi inventarum', contains royal charters up to 8 May 1277.[2] There are no papal bulls after the pontificate of Gregory X, who died on 10 January 1276.[3] The list therefore must be later than May 1277, and a close study of the other charters might give a more exact date. Miss Major dated the hand which wrote the greater part of the book as of c. 1260–70, but this includes the Edward I charters, and Professor Du Boulay has shown that consequently it must be later.[4] The internal evidence, however, would suggest strongly that the list was compiled soon after 1277. For if not, why did it not include the charters of 8, 9, 11, and 12 Edward I (1280–4) which have been added, and appear in the 1330 list, but are not numerated?[5] Robert Kilwardby was translated to the cardinal-bishopric of Porto on 12 March 1278, and, after the short reign of Robert Burnell, whose election was quashed, Archbishop Pecham was appointed in 1279; provided on 25 January, consecrated on 19 February, he received the temporalities on 30 May.[6] Probably the compilation of the list can be rightly associated with Pecham's arrival on the scene and the usual stock-taking consequent upon a vacancy. It was due to Pecham that the manors were grouped in six large bailiwicks and manorial organization considerably improved.[7] He it was, too, who instructed his proctor to get back the property of the see, including *vasa*, jewels, ecclesiastical plate, books, and records, which Robert Kilwardby had taken to Rome: 'Tertio, ut bona ecclesiae nostrae inventa penes bonae memoriae praedecessorem nostrum per camerarium occupata in pecunia numerata, in vasis, monilibus, ornamentis ecclesiasticis, libris et processibus judicialibus ac registralibus nobis restituantur . . .'.[8] This collection may not have included the registers of the see, as has been suggested,[9] but the removal of certain of the muniments may have occasioned a check-list or catalogue.

[1]Public Record Office, *Lists & Indexes No. XLIX*, p. i: printed in *Antient Kalendars and Inventories of the Treasury of His Majesty's Exchequer*, ed. Sir F. Palgrave (3 vols., 1836), i. 1–155. A photograph of the Aquitaine section is reproduced in New Palaeographical Soc., *Facsimiles of Ancient MSS.*, 2nd ser., ii (1913–30), plate 115.

[2]Lambeth Palace Libr., MS. 1212, pp. 4, 68.

[3]*Ibid.*, p. 231.   [4]Du Boulay, p. 57.

[5]Lambeth Palace Libr., MS. 1212, pp. 4, 70–2.

[6]*Handbook of British Chronology*, ed. Sir F. M. Powicke and E. B. Fryde (2nd edn., 1961), p. 211.

[7]Du Boulay, p. 63.

[8]Lambeth Palace Libr., Reg. Pecham fo. 152v (*Registrum Epistolarum Johannis Peckham*, ed. C. T. Martin (Rolls Ser., 1882–5), ii. 550).

[9]I. J. Churchill, 'The Archbishops' Registers', in *Mediaeval Records of the Archbishops of Canterbury* (1962), p. 11.

Pecham's many complaints of the state in which Archbishop Boniface of Savoy had left all the archbishop's buildings, suggest an orderly mind,[1] and it is possible that he provided a new treasury at Canterbury for the archives, but this is a point to consider later.

The first of the two lists details the contents of fourteen *vasa*, containing some 290 charters. The numbers of the *vasa* are given in the right hand margin, and the charters belonging to each *vas* are bracketed together. The first seven *vasa* contained royal charters arranged chronologically by kings from William I to Edward I. *Vasa* eight and nine housed charters of others than the kings, baronial charters etc., ten and eleven were filled with compositions, and twelve to fourteen with papal bulls from Innocent II to Gregory X.[2] At some point the pages which list the papal bulls were separated from the rest of the catalogue, although this has not been noted before. They may be written by the same scribe.

We come now to consider the exact nature of the list. A. J. Collins described it as a 'table or index'.[3] Numbers of the charters are given in the left hand margin and these correspond with numbers in the text of the cartulary, so that charter number one of William I bears a number one in the margin on the page where it is transcribed in full. The royal charters start a new numeration with each king as do the papal bulls with each pope, so that one has to look for William I/1, William I/2 etc., Celestine III/1, Celestine III/2 etc.[4] The originals of these charters are also endorsed with corresponding numbers and Collins has traced thirty-one of these, at Lambeth among the Cartae Miscellaneae and the Papal Bulls, and bound up in MS. 959.[5] Another careful search has produced only one more document, which is in fact a duplicate, and bears what looks very like a Christ Church endorsement and not an archiepiscopal one.[6]

The list is more than a contents list or index to the register book, in that it enabled the searcher to find in which *vas* the document was kept. It also provided details about copies of charters, which are included in the book, but are not numerated because they are not kept with the rest in the *vasa*, but are elsewhere, at Dover and South Malling for instance.[7] It was obviously designed to some extent to provide the clerks of a peripatetic household with a knowledge of the whereabouts of the originals.

By 1330 the contents of the treasury had expanded to some 365 charters

---

[1] Reg. Pecham fo. 172 (*Reg. Epistolarum Peckham*, i. 203), fo. 152v (*ibid.*, ii. 551), fo. 210v (*ibid.*, p. 716), fo. 152v (*ibid.*, iii. 828), cited by Jenkins, *ubi supra*, p. 79.

[2] Lambeth Palace Libr., MS. 1212, pp. 1–11, with a later continuation on pp. 12, 226–32.

[3] A. J. Collins, 'Documents of the Great Charter', *Proc. British Academy*, xxxiv (1948), 237.

[4] A parallel system was used at Bury St. Edmund's abbey; cf. Lambeth Palace Libr., Papal Documents nos. 2, 14, 24, 37, 44, 48, 51–2, 59, 62, 65, 73, 88.

[5] See appendix below, and Collins's photographs at the end of his article, 11 a–c.

[6] Lambeth Palace Libr., C[artae] M[iscellaneae] X/109 (see appendix below). Cf. VI/119–21, 123–37, 140–8, further examples of Christ Church endorsements.

[7] Lambeth Palace Libr., MS. 1212, pp. 6, 106, 7, 118.

which filled thirty-two *vasa*, according to the second list of the archbishop's charters, which is now amongst the miscellaneous books of the exchequer in the Public Record Office.[1] Although the royal charters occupied the first twelve *vasa*, they were no longer kept chronologically. The first *vas* contained those of Stephen, the second William the Conqueror, the third Henry I, the fourth Henry II, the fifth Henry II's son Henry, the sixth Henry III, the seventh William Rufus, the eighth Richard I, the ninth John, and the tenth, eleventh and twelfth respectively the charters of Edward I, II, and III, though those of Edward III are not recorded.[2] Then follow the charters of others than the kings, roughly arranged according to place and subject.

A significant omission from the list of 1330 is the collection of papal bulls. It was not unusual for bulls to be kept separately. At St. Paul's the bulls occupied a separate bag;[3] at Westminster they had a separate chest.[4] According to Mr. Kingsford, the papal privileges and indulgences and royal charters were kept separately at Stanley, and the confirmations of papal bulls at Robertsbridge never have press-marks, which suggests that they were probably kept apart, perhaps in the custody of the abbot.[5] At St. Mary's, York, the papal bulls occupied several chests in a certain chamber, as the endorsements reveal.[6] In an interesting letter to Archbishop Mepham, dated 22 October 1329, Prior Henry of Eastry states that one of the bulls, which had been listed in MS. 1212 as in the twelfth *vas*, a privilege of Pope Innocent II concerning Dover, for which the archbishop had been asking, has been seen by him within the last year 'in archivis archiepiscopalibus vestris apud Cantuariam'.[7] Much could have happened between 1328 and 1330, but this passage suggests that the bulls had not yet been physically separated from the rest of the archives.

All the original charters which can be tied up with MS. 1212 can also be linked with entries in the 1330 list. But this list merely describes and groups the charters and records which were in each *vas*; it does not give a number to each charter. A charter of Richard de Clare, earl of Gloucester and Hertford, bound up between pp. 190 and 191 of MS. 959, however, is endorsed with a note that it is to be found in *vas* sixteen and this corresponds with its place as noted in the 1330 list. It has a registration mark xiii which connects with MS. 1212, both contents list number and registration number, and the note 'scribitur in libro', and was then in *vas* ten.[8]

[1] *Archbishopric Charters*, pp. 1–19 (P.R.O., E 36/137).
[2] *Ibid.*, p. 7, and see appendix below.   [3] P.R.O., S.C. 7/15/23.
[4] J. Armitage Robinson and M. R. James, *The Manuscripts of Westminster Abbey* (Cambridge, 1909), p. 95.
[5] Hist. MSS. Comm., *De L'Isle and Dudley MSS.*, i, p. xviii & n. 2, and as C. L. Kingsford says, cf. Galbraith, p. 204, on the deeds of Lewes Priory where the documents from Cluny were kept in the custody of the prior.
[6] Lambeth Palace Libr., Papal Documents nos. 38–9, 64, 101.
[7] *Lit. Cant.*, i, no. 283.
[8] Lambeth Palace Libr., MS. 1212, pp. 11, 142, and see appendix below.

Other original deeds which survive and which correspond with entries in the list of 1330, and which are not to be found in MS. 1212, date from after the compilation of MS. 1212 with two exceptions, documents concerning King John's peace with the clergy and barons, and a certificate of the bishop of Exeter dated 1275.[1] Two charters of Edward II, a charter of Archbishop Robert Winchelsey relaxing an interdict on the town of Dover, the process against Llewellyn, prince of Wales, and a document of the prior and convent of Christ Church, which was registered in Pecham's register and dated 1285, are all later than the convents of MS. 1212.[2] It seems as if the charter of the bishop of Exeter and John's charters were overlooked when the scribe came to make the earlier inventory or list.

The second inventory or list was made at the beginning of Archbishop Simon Mepham's reign in 1330, and is dated by the scribe. It will be asked why a second list was made of the contents of the treasury in 1330. This was shortly after Simon Mepham became archbishop. He was elected on 11 December 1327, consecrated on 5 June 1328 and provided with the temporalities on 19 September 1328.[3] It may be another example of an inventory made soon after the accession of a new archbishop. According to William de Dene in his *Historia Roffensis*, the archbishop wanted a reputable household, and extreme scrupulousness was shown by his brothers Edmund and Thomas in gathering together a suitable collection of clerks and servants, which proved to be a difficult task, since it was said that they sought not men but angels for this duty.[4]

When Archbishop Reynolds died at Mortlake on 16 November 1327, he left in the custody of his clerk, John de la Chambre, ornaments of the chapel and other goods in nine chests numbered A–I, and of these, chest E contained a *hanaper* with five branches of coral, certain muniments and rolls, chest F diverse bulls and other muniments, chest G diverse charters concerning the liberties of the archbishop and other quires of certain tracts of authors, chest H two books, one red and the other black, one Geoffrey of Monmouth's *History of the Britons*, possibly either the thirteenth- or fourteenth-century copy now bound up in Lambeth MS. 454,[5] and the other a *Vitae Clericorum*, rolls and other muniments, and chest I diverse muniments, three little knives, two of jasper, one pastoral staff of little or no value, one book of sermons and one quire, also of sermons. These were delivered to Archbishop Mepham on 25 October 1328 by

[1] Lambeth Palace Libr., CM I/43, MS. 959 charter between pp. 150 and 151 (*Archbishopric Charters*, p. 15 col. 2), CM XI/7 and 25. See appendix below.

[2] Lambeth Palace Libr., CM XI/79, 80 (*Archbishopric Charters*, p. 6 col. 2), XI/57 (Reg. Winchelsey fo. 88 and *Archbishopric Charters*, p. 14 col. 1), MS. 959 charter between pp. 194 and 195 (*Archbishopric Charters*, p. 15 col. 1), Reg. Pecham fo. 113 (*ibid.*, p. 9 col. 1). See appendix below.

[3] *Handbook of British Chronology*, p. 211.

[4] *Historia Roffensis*, in H. Wharton, *Anglia Sacra* (1691), i. 368.

[5] The first copy (the 14th-century one) commences on fo. 28, and belonged to Archbishop Sancroft, whose name is inscribed on it, and the second begins on fo. 124.

order of the king, who had taken possession of the property for a year to cover Reynolds's debts.[1]

There arises here the question of the location of the treasury of the archbishops. It does not seem as if the collection described above as among Reynolds's possessions at his death, can possibly be regarded as more than a personal collection of specific charters, taken out of the treasury for various reasons, or indeed made or received in a certain place and not registered or filed. Prior Henry of Eastry describes the royal charters which Reynolds showed him and several of the Christ Church monks at Maidstone, including a charter of Henry II relating to Dover priory which is recorded in both lists and still survives,[2] and Winchelsey apparently had some documents at Lambeth.[3] In 1282 an outgoing letter, dated from Mortlake, was not despatched, and according to a later annotator of the register, it lay in Archbishop Pecham's archives 'quasi perdita' until his twelfth year, 1290 to 1291.[4]

The first mistake would seem to be to accept that the documents were always kept together. The earliest list of charters, as noted above, contains some charters which have not been given numbers because the originals are in other places. A group of Wrotham charters are recorded on pp. 121–4 of the cartulary and in the additions to the list. Against the registration of them is written: 'All these charters, the chirograph and confirmation of the king (dated 12–13 September 1284), concerning the manor of Wrotham are in a certain pyx in the treasury of Saint Gregory's at Canterbury'. All the numbered charters in the *vasa* can be assumed to be in one place. If these were in the archbishop's treasury, and that treasury was at St. Gregory's, it might surely be assumed that such an emendation was unnecessary. By 1330, however, four of the charters in question were back with the main collection in the treasury in *vas* twenty, and a charter which had been at South Malling was also there in *vas* nineteen. A note of this kind must surely mean that the documents were not in the normal place, but in an unexpected one.

Furthermore, it would be incorrect to infer that the main collection was always in the same place. Professor Jenkins drew attention in 1925 to a letter in Pecham's register, dated 26 January 1281, where the archbishop, writing from Dereham in Norfolk, states that he does not have with him the privileges mentioning his rights of tuition, and that he will go to Canterbury and cause a search to be made through his archives 'in aede sacra'.[5] This, as Jenkins thought, would seem to mean the cathedral and it is highly likely that the privileges of the see were kept in the cathedral church, while

---

[1] P.R.O., S.C. 6/1128/7, 8, cited by Du Boulay, p. 60.

[2] *Lit. Cant.*, i, no. 283, Lambeth Palace Libr., CM XI/9.

[3] *Lit. Cant.*, i, no. 61.

[4] Jenkins, *ubi supra*, p. 93, citing Reg. Pecham fo. 47v (*Registrum Johannis Pecham* (Canterbury & York Soc., 2 pts., 1908–10), i. 101).

[5] Jenkins, *ubi supra*, p. 90, citing Reg. Pecham fo. 26 (*Reg. Epistolarum Peckham*, i. 172).

the more routine and less precious documents, and presumably some of the more private ones, were kept at some other place or places. Jenkins also drew attention to a marginal note made later on in the register, where it is noted that an original document of 1285, recording the revocation of an appeal made by the prior and chapter of Canterbury over the election of Walter Scammel as bishop of Salisbury, 'residet . . . in apud (sic) sanctum Gregor' Cant' in Thesauraria domini Archiepiscopi sub sigillo capituli Cant' '.[1] Miss Churchill, writing in 1929, linked the two references together and argue that 'aedis sacra' equalled the archbishop's treasury at St. Gregory's, not apparently allowing for any migration or separation of the documents.[2] This interpretation has been accepted ever since,[3] and no attempt has been made to discover if and when the documents were moved.

The answer may lie in the Canterbury cartulary. The Wrotham additions suggest that at least until 1284 the main part of the treasury was not at St. Gregory's. Its likeliest location would seem to be either the cathedral or the archbishop's palace. The whole argument for the archbishop's treasury being at St. Gregory's has hitherto depended on the marginal note of 1285 in Pecham's register, mentioned above. All references in later archbishops' registers, however, speak merely of the 'treasury of the archbishop', with no note of its whereabouts.[4] It is possible to see the note in Pecham's register in a different light. The scribe surely would not have mentioned the place unless there was likely to be some confusion. It may be that soon after 1284, Archbishop Pecham decided to provide himself with a new central treasury at St. Gregory's, transferring the main bulk of the documents there and that the treasury was in the process of being moved when the scribe made the note.

The first apparent unlikeliness of the archbishop's treasury being moved to St. Gregory's can, to some extent, be dispelled by the peculiar position which that priory held in relationship to the archbishop. The house was founded by Archbishop Lanfranc in 1084–5, and by him it was well endowed with relics.[5] We are told that the bodies of St. Edburg, St. Mildred, and St. Ethelburga, the sister of St. Edburg, were brought from Lyminge, 'praesidente Lanfranco archiepiscopo', to the church which the archbishop had constructed a short while before, and that Lanfranc, in his foundation

---

[1] Jenkins, *ubi supra*, p. 90, citing Reg. Pecham fo. 112v (*Reg. Pecham*, ii. 216–18). The document is listed as in *vas* 15 in 1330.

[2] *Archbishopric Charters*, p. vii.

[3] By Audrey Woodcock in *Cartulary of the Priory of St. Gregory* (Camden 3rd Ser., lxxxviii, 1956), p. xi; Rosemary G. Barnes, 'Lambeth MS. 1212 and the White Book of Canterbury', *ante*, xxxii (1959), 58, citing Reg. Pecham fo. 112v, and Du Boulay, p. 59. Kathleen Major (*Acta Stephani Langton* (Canterbury & York Soc., 1950), app. II), does not comment on the whereabouts of the archbishop's archives.

[4] *Archbishopric Charters*, p. viii, citing Lambeth Palace Libr., Reg. Langham fo. 96, Reg. Courteney fo. 182, and Reg. Arundel ii fos. 91v–92. Reg. Reynolds fo. 4 has 'the treasury of the archbishop at Canterbury'.

[5] *Cartulary of the Priory of St. Gregory*, p. ix.

charter gave to St. Gregory's the major part of the relics of his saintly predecessors which had been in Christ Church.[1] In 1145 this church was burnt.[2] The convent was under the special protection and patronage of subsequent archbishops. Theobald mentions it in his will, and Archbishop Winchelsey bequeathed the canons 300 marks to celebrate mass for his soul and those of his parents, the residue to be applied to their own uses.[3] In 1181, judges delegate of the pope caused the archbishop and the abbot of St. Augustine's to be summoned before them in the church of St. Gregory, which according to the St. Augustine's chronicler William Thorne, writing in the fourteenth century, 'being situated just under the walls of the city is regarded as a sort of parlour of the archbishop'.[4] During the troubles between Archbishop Baldwin and the Christ Church monks in 1189, the prior of St. Gregory's was used as a mediator, being sent by the convent to offer the archbishop a procession on his return to the city, and being despatched back to the monks as a peacemaker by the archbishop.[5] On 21 November 1238 Archbishop Edmund Rich* chose to consecrate Richard Wendene as bishop of Rochester at St. Gregory's, and in 1239 certain Christ Church malefactors were ordered to receive their penances from the penitentiary of the archbishop and the official at St. Gregory's, so that it is possible to envisage certain documents of the archbishop being accommodated there.[6] When, in 1289, Pecham instructed the archdeacon and commissary of Canterbury to order the abbot of St. Augustine's to produce certain privileges in some suitable and safe place, in or near Canterbury, they chose the church of St. Gregory's,[7] and by the fourteenth century the church was used for some sessions of the consistory court, and for the sitting of the archbishop's court.[8] In 1329 the great seal of England was deposited at St. Gregory's.

Memorandum, that on Wednesday the eve of the Ascension, to wit 31 May, in Queen Isabella's chamber in the priory of Christ Church, Canterbury, wherein the said queen was lodged, in her presence and in the presence of J. bishop of Ely and Sir Roger de Mortuo Mari, earl of March, and of others, Sir Bartholomew de Burgherssh carried the king's great seal in a bag sealed with the seal of H. bishop of Lincoln, the chancellor, and delivered it by the king's order to Master Henry de Clyf, together with a letter under the king's privy seal directed to the said Master Henry concerning the custody of the great seal; and Master Henry received the seal thus sealed, and carried it with Sir William de Herlaston there

---

[1] *Cartulary of the Priory of St. Gregory*, p. 1, cited by R. W. Southern, *Saint Anselm and his Biographer* (Cambridge, 1963), p. 266.

[2] Gervase, i. 130.

[3] *Cartulary of the Priory of St. Gregory*, p. xi; *Reg. Winchelsey*, ii. 1340 (from Canterbury, D. & C. Archives, Chart. Antiq. W. 218).

[4] *Thorne's Chronicle*, p. 117.

[5] Gervase, i. 451.   * Read: Edmund of Abingdon

[6] *Ibid.*, ii. 135, 153.

[7] *Thorne's Chronicle*, p. 307.

[8] *Cartulary of the Priory of St. Gregory*, p. xi; *Thorne's Chronicle*, p. 354.

then present to St. Gregory's priory, and they there opened the seal, and caused writs to be sealed therewith.

Memorandum, that on Sunday, the feast of Whitsuntide, to wit 11 June, the king, with H. bishop of Lincoln, his chancellor, Sir Henry de Percy, and other magnates in his company, returned from parts beyond sea to the port of Dover, and on Tuesday following Master Henry de Clyf, keeper of the great seal, at Canterbury, at the ninth hour, in the said chancellor's hall in St. Gregory's priory, Canterbury, wherein the chancellor was lodged, in the presence of Sir Ralph Basset of Drayton, Master Hugh de Camera, archdeacon of Lincoln, Master Walter de Seton, Sir Hugh de Burgh, Sir Henry de Edenestowe, and Sir Thomas de Evesham, clerks, and of others, delivered the seal to the said bishop in a bag sealed with the seals of the aforesaid Master Henry and of Sir William de Herlaston, and the bishop thus received the seal from the Master Henry, and caused writs to be sealed therewith on the same day after dinner.[1]

It also appears that in 1330 a certain Richard atte Notebeame, canon of St. Gregory's, had broken into the treasury at night, and, clothed in a secular habit, had carried off goods of the monastery, and of certain persons who had deposited possessions there.[2] It is possible, therefore, to imagine at this date a large treasury at St. Gregory's, and a place in which the archbishop could well have kept his own seal and muniments. The burglary of 1330 might even have provided the immediate occasion for the compilation of the list of archbishop's charters in that year.

If it is difficult to accept that St. Gregory's was the central place of deposit for the archbishop's archives in the period before 1285, there is one other possibility, and one which should not be immediately discarded. It is inconceivable that either Christ Church or St. Augustine's should have held the archbishop's archives *in toto*, but is it not more than likely that the first place of deposit would have been the archbishop's own palace at Canterbury? Unfortunately there is no evidence for the disposition of the thirteenth-century building, but at least in 1349 when Islip became archbishop, the palace was described as consisting of great hall, small chamber of the lord archbishop, great chamber, kitchen for that chamber, a great room called the hall of St. Thomas next to the lord's chamber, a chamber next to the great hall, two other chambers between the great hall and the great chamber, great kitchen, great gate and stables.[3] Certainly the bishop of Winchester had a treasury in his palace at Wolvesey, where he kept money, plate, books and documents, and outside the treasury door was a chest belonging to Robert of Maidstone, and containing writings and diverse other memoranda and notes. Outside the steward's chamber, too, there

---

[1] *Cal. Close Rolls 1327–30*, pp. 547, 549.
[2] *Lit. Cant.*, i, no. 330.
[3] R. Willis, *The Architectural History of the Conventual Buildings of the Monastery of Christ Church in Canterbury* (1869), app. VII, printing Canterbury, D. & C. Archives, Reg. 12, fo. 76v.

was another coffer containing 'rolls and tallies of various kinds connected with his accounts'.[1]

None of the archiepiscopal rolls have endorsements, and by their very nature they were not regarded with the same reverence as title deeds and evidences. Professor Galbraith comments that the obedientiary rolls at Lewes have no numbers and were thus presumably not in any system, being kept by the particular obedientiary responsible.[2] The archbishop's rolls were probably strewn about the different manor houses, with a proportion of them in the care of the steward, and probably at Canterbury, in the palace.[3]

Accepting, however, that in or about 1285 the major part of the archiepiscopal charters were deposited by the archbishop at St. Gregory's, we are confronted with the question of who looked after them. Little is known of the early history of the archbishop's household. The first archbishop who is known to have had a treasurer is Archbishop Edmund Rich*(1233–40), but nothing further has been found out about this man, Robert de Bath, or his office.[4] No such officer has been traced for Boniface of Savoy or Robert Kilwardby, but the records are sparse and as yet relatively unsearched. Pecham's treasurer, Thomas, rector of Chartham, is specifically referred to as treasurer of Canterbury to distinguish him from the treasurer of the archbishop's chamber, Master Roger Burd or Burt. He was granted full powers pertaining to that office, but unfortunately they are not detailed. This was one of the archbishop's first appointments in 1279.[5] It is not clear whether he continued to hold office under Winchelsey. In 1322 Archbishop Reynolds appointed John de Ryngwode, rector of Saltwood, as treasurer 'of his church of Canterbury',[6] and this title appears to have been one to distinguish him from the personal treasurer. But no clear picture can be built up of either the treasury and its clerks or of the chancery and its officials. Whether the chancellor, who had charge of the seal, had custodial duties over any of the archives is unclear.

At least from the early fourteenth century certain letters were to be found at Lambeth, but it was probably not yet regarded as a more important place of deposit than any other of the manor houses. The letter of 1322 from the convent of Christ Church to the bishop of Coventry and Lichfield, who had written asking for evidence of the legality of his election, in which it is said that certain processes, decrees and muniments are at Lambeth, suggests that this was due to the fact that Winchelsey had confirmed several episcopal elections there.[7] During the Revolt of 1381, Lambeth itself was burned, the archbishop beheaded, and probably some

[1] Jenkins, ubi supra, pp. 88–9.
[2] Galbraith, ubi supra, p. 199.   * Read: Edmund of Abingdon
[3] Decima L. Douie, Archbishop Pecham (Oxford, 1952), p. 59.
[4] C. H. Lawrence, St. Edmund of Abingdon (Oxford, 1960), p. 154; Lambeth Palace Libr., Estate Document no. 1193.
[5] Douie, p. 60.
[6] I. J. Churchill, Canterbury Administration (1933), i. 548; Reg. Reynolds fo. 128v.
[7] Lit. Cant., i, no. 61.

documents, like manorial rolls, went up in the flames.[1] By 1471 there is evidence of the archbishop's registry being in the great gateway, presumably the gatehouse built by Chichele, and some while before that it seems that it was in a room opposite the dwelling house of the janitor, which was in the gate.[2] Chichele's gateway was re-built by Cardinal Morton. According to tradition, the great chamber over the gate was used as the cardinal's audience chamber, and one at least of the rooms in this tower was used as a registry. In 1495 muniments from here were produced in a lawsuit, and there is reference to the archives being in boxes, cases or chests.[3] The tower was used as a place for storing the records in the eighteenth century, and until 1857 the records of the prerogative court of Canterbury were kept somewhere there. There is no evidence of the registers ever having been kept elsewhere than at Lambeth, and they have not been out of custody except for a short period during the Second World War when they were deposited for safety in the gaol at Shepton Mallett. But it seems likely that in the fourteenth century, when the archbishop's archives were in the treasury at Canterbury, on the death of an archbishop the separate quires and gatherings of registers would have been amassed together by the officials and taken to Canterbury to deposit. At some point then, in the fifteenth century, the registers were moved to Lambeth, perhaps with the building of the great 'document' gate, for this it seems mainly to have been, of Archbishop Chichele (1414–43), or that of Archbishop Morton.[4] It may not be too imaginative to suppose that the rest of the archives were moved from the archbishop's treasury to Lambeth, as it became the most favoured archiepiscopal residence, and before the events of 1535–6 brought such havoc to Christ Church, Canterbury, where the archbishop's documents had once been given shelter. At any rate, the sources are silent about any dispersal of the archbishop's treasure and documents from St. Gregory's in 1536. And when the rich jewels, precious stones, gold and silver from St. Thomas's shrine were being rattled off to London and the archives of Christ Church, St. Augustine's and St. Gregory's were being scattered and lost, the archbishop's muniments may have for some time been safely put away in their new home at Lambeth. Their trials were to come in the seventeenth century.

---

[1] Du Boulay, p. 65.

[2] C. Jenkins, 'Cardinal Morton's Register', in *Tudor Studies Presented to Albert Frederick Pollard* (1924), pp. 30–1; Lambeth Palace Libr., Reg. Morton fos. 237–8.

[3] Lambeth Palace Libr., Reg. Morton fos. 237–8, 232.

[4] In the 16th century the prior and convent of Durham transferred their registers to a separate 'Register House', see Pantin, p. 2.

APPENDIX

The Surviving Contents of the Archbishop's Treasury

Class, and finding and registration number, according to the two lists	Where registered (in the Canterbury cartulary, Lambeth MS. 1212, unless otherwise stated)	Place in 1277–80 list (Lambeth MS. 1212)	Where located in 1277–80	Place in 1330 list (P.R.O., E 36/137)	Where located in 1330	Surviving documents (Lambeth Palace Library press marks)
Royal charters (Hen. I), ii	p. 18	p. 1	vas 2	p. 3 col. 1*	vas 3	{ CM XI/1, CM X/109†
Royal charters (Hen. II), i	p. 25	p. 2	vas [3]	p. 3 col. 2*	vas 4	{ CM XI/2, CM XI/3
Royal charters (Hen. II), ii	p. 26	p. 2	vas [3]	p. 3 col. 1*	vas 4	CM XI/4
Royal charters (Hen. II), iiii	p. 26	p. 2	vas [3]	p. 3 col. 1*	vas 4	CM XI/13
Royal charters (Hen. II), viii	p. 29	p. 2	vas [3]	p. 3 col. 2*	vas 5	CM XI/9
Royal charters (Henry, son of Hen. II), i	p. 30	p. 2	vas [3]	p. 3 col. 2*	vas 8	CM XI/6
Royal charters (Ric. I), ii	p. 32	p. 2	vas [4]	p. 4 col. 1*	vas 8	CM XI/5
Royal charters (Ric. I), iii	p. 33	p. 2	vas [4]	p. 4 col. 1*	vas 8	CM XI/8
Royal charters (Ric. I), ix	p. 36	p. 2	vas [4]	p. 4 col. 1*	vas 8	CM XI/20
Royal charters (Ric. I), x	p. 37	p. 2	vas [4]	p. 4 col. 1*	vas 9	CM XI/21
Royal charters (John), ii	p. 40	p. 3	vas 5	p. 5 col. 1*	vas 9	CM XI/22
Royal charters (John), vi	p. 44	p. 3	vas 5	p. 5 col. 2*	vas 9	CM XI/11
Royal charters (John), xiii	p. 47	p. 3	vas 5	p. 5 col. 2*	vas 9	CM XI/12
Royal charters (John), xv	p. 48	p. 3	vas 5	p. 5 col. 1*	vas 9	CM XI/10
*Royal charters (John), Littere regis J. de fermacione pacis . . . post relaxacionem generalis interdicti Anglie	—	—	—	p. 5 col. 2	vas 9	[CM XI/7]
*Royal charters (Edw. II), Carta regis E. de mercatis et feriis . . .	—	—	—	p. 6 col. 2	vas 11	[CM XI/80]

*Royal charters (Edw. II), Carta de mercato et feria habendis apud Hargh	—	—	—	p. 6 col. 2	vas 11	CM XI/79
Non royal iv	p. 75	p. 5	vas 8	p. 11 col. 1*	vas 18	CM XI/50
Non royal xxx	p. 91	p. 5	vas 8	p. 8 col. 1*	vas 13	CM XI/15
Non royal xxxi	p. 91	p. 5	vas 8	p. 11 col. 2*	vas 19	CM XI/16
Non royal lix	p. 109	p. 7	vas 8	p. 10 col. 2*	vas 18	CM XI/37
Compositions iiii	p. 135	p. 11	vas 10	p. 8 col. 1	vas 13	CM XI/18
Compositions v	p. 136	p. 11	vas 10	p. 8 col. 1*	vas 13	CM IX/19
Compositions vi	p. 137	p. 11	vas 10	p. 8 col. 1*	vas 13	CM XI/17
Compositions xiii	p. 142	p. 11	vas 10	p. 9 col. 2*	vas 16	MS. 959 charter between pp. 190 & 191
Compositions xx	p. 163	p. 11	vas 11	p. 9 col. 2*	vas 16	CM XI/33
Compositions xxvi	p. 167	p. 11	vas 11	p. 9 col. 1*	vas 14	CM X/123
Compositions xxviii	p. 177	p. 11	vas 11	p. 9 col. 2	vas 15	CM XI/14
Papal bulls (Alexander III), v	p. 239	p. 226	vas 12	—	—	Papal documents no. 7
Papal bulls (Celestine III), i	p. 240	p. 227	vas 12	—	—	Papal documents no. 13
Papal bulls (Innocent III), v	p. 243	p. 227	vas 12	—	—	Papal documents no. 19
Papal bulls (Gregory IX), xv	p. 260	p. 229	vas 13	—	—	Papal documents no. 33
Papal bulls (Innocent IV), iii	p. 270	p. 230	vas 14	—	—	Papal documents no. 41
Papal bulls (Innocent IV), xvii	p. 277	p. 230	vas 14	—	—	Papal documents no. 53
*Miscellaneous, Certificatorium episcopi Exoniensis ... de baiulacione crucis	Reg. Winchelsey fo. 88	—	—	p. 12 col. 1	vas 19	CM XI/25
*Miscellaneous, Relaxacio interdicti in municipio Douorie ...	—	—	—	p. 14 col. 1	vas 21	CM XI/57
*Miscellaneous, Processus contra Leulinum principem Wallie	—	—	—	p. 15 col. 1	vas 24	{ MS. 959 charter between pp. 194 & 195 / †CM I/43
*Miscellaneous, Reformacio pacis inter Johannem regem Anglie et clerum comites ...	—	—	—	p. 15 col. 2	vas 29	MS. 959 charter between pp. 150 & 151

This schedule amalgamates material collected by A. J. Collins and I. J. Churchill, with additions. Documents which are bracketed together are duplicates. Square brackets denote uncertainty.

* Short title from 1330 list.
* Charters marked with an asterisk by Churchill in *Table of Canterbury Archbishopric Charters* to denote 'that the title is so far similar to one in MS. 1212 *Lambeth Palace Library* as to suggest a reference to the same charter'.
† Not included by Collins: probably belonged to Christ Church.

INDEX

A (?Adam), vice-archdcn Oxford: II 49
Acre: XI 197-9, 202-5, 207-8
Actor et reus: VII 75-81
Adria, Giles de, proct.: III 319, 329, 334
Adrian I, pope: IX 58
Adrian IV, pope: I 118; IX 57, 59-60
Aigueblanche, Peter d', bp Hereford: II 87; IX 69
Ailred, abb. Rievaulx: V 171-2, 175, 178
Alban, St: VI 178, 181, 193; IX 58, 71 & n
Albert, chanc. Milan: I 126
Albo Monasterio, R. d', proct.: IV 147, 149
Alexander II, pope: VI 180 & n
Alexander III, pope: II 51, 55; III 311, 313; V 24, 29; IX 62-4; XII App.
Alexander IV, pope: IX 57, 67-9
Alfred the Englishman, clk Ottobon: I 120
altercations: II 83-4
Amory family: X 135
Amphibalus, St: IX 58
Anagni, Petrus de, proct.: IV 151
Anglo-Norman school: II 45; VII 75
Anketil, Robert, proct.: IV 145, 160-1
Annibaldi family: I 122; Richard cdnl: I 118-21; nephews: (Richard subdcn, notary) I 120, 124; *and see* Surdus; great nephews: (John) I 120, 123; (Richard) I 120
appeal, to Rome: II 70, 90, 96-9; III 313n, 322; VII 78; tuitorial: II 96-8; VII 78
Aquamunda, Thomas de, proct.: IV 146-7
Aquila, Raynald de, proct.: III 345
archdeacons, monastic: VI 177-203
archives, storage: XII 95-7
Arezzo, Bonaguida of, *Consuetudines cancellarie*: III 312, 314n
Arfast, bp Elmham: VI 180
Arrouaise, St Nicholas, order: V 24-5
Ascibilis, Petrus de, proct.: IV 152, 156
Assisi, Bonaspes of: IV 146, 159n; Johannes of: IV 153; Petrus of: IV 145-6, 150; P. (Petrus, ? another): IV 148, 159n, 162
Aubigny, Richard d', abb. St Albans: IX 61
audientia litterarum contradictarum: II 55-8; III 311-45; IV 163n; auditors: II 56,

58; III *passim*; VI 200; *see* Després; Deux; Gerard; James; Novavilla; Somercotes; Roiardi
Augustinian order: I 120; V 24, 30-2
Aulanby, Richard de, r. Adisham: III 319, 322, 329, 334-5

Bacun, John, r. Eastry: III 319, 322, 333-4
Baldwin, abp Canterbury: XI 203; XII 104
Balliol family: XI 208-9, 212; Geoffrey de: X 208, 213; Gilbert de: XI 202, 208, 210; H. de: XI 208, 213
Barrio (Bari), Bernardus de, proct.: IV 145, 153
Barro, M. Robert de: IX 67
Barton, Philip de, proct.: IV 152, 153n
Bath, bp: *see* Reginald; marquess (Thynne): X 132, 135; Robert de, treas. abp Edmund: XII 106; Walter of, kg's clk: I 121
Bath and Glastonbury, bps: *see* Fitzgeldwin; Jocelin
Bath and Wells, bps: *see* Droxenforde; Harewell; Haselschawe; Shrewsbury
Battle, abbey: XI 207, 209-13; John of, proct.: IV 161
Beeleigh abbey: X 134-5
Bek, Antony, bp Durham: IV 151, 156
Belvoir priory: IX 60, 62, 69, 84; prior: (Richard Hall) IX 82
Benedictines: III 150; V 182; general chapters: V 30-2, 173
Berengaria, queen: XI 196, 207
Berkhamsted (Herts): I 125; John de, abb. St Albans: IV 149; IX 80
Bernard, bp St David's: V 170
Bernard, St: V 27, 170
Berton, John le, preb. Hereford: I 120
Bexhill (Sussex): XI 208-9; Barnhorne in: XI 207, 209-10, 213
Bicknacre priory: X 134
Bingham, Robert de, bp Salisbury: II 49
Binham priory: IX 62, 81, 84; priors: (William Dixwell; William Somerton) IX 82
Blockley, R. dean of: II 49-50

Meldona, Walter de, r. Chart by Sutton: III 326, 340-1
Meopham, Simon, abp Canterbury: III 330; IV 155; XII 100-1
Mere, W. de, proct.: IV 146
Merton, Walter of, bp Rochester: III 319
Middleton, William, bp Norwich: III 319
Milan, chapter: X 132
Molesme: V 26, 168
Monasterio, B. de, proct.: IV 148
Monington, Walter de, abb. Glastonbury: VI 189
Montfort, ct Simon de: V 182
Moote, John de la, abb. St Albans: IX 75, 80
Mortimer, Geoffrey de, archdcn London: III 319-20; Philip de, proct.: II 58; III 324-5, 327, 337
Morton, John, abp Canterbury: XII 107
Mota, William Arnaldi de: I 126
Mowbray, Nigel de: XI 202, 205; Roger de: XI 201, 205
Mussus, William son of: I 120

Nasinton, R. de, officl Worcester: VII 78 & n
Nazarenus, proct.: IV 157
Neuton, William de, proct.: IV 152
Neville, Hugh de: IV 154; Richard de, proct.: IV 144, 159
Newerk, H. (?Henry) de, proct.: IV 151-2, 156
Nicholas, archdcn Cambridge, Huntingdon and Hertford: VI 181
Nicholas IV, pope: IX 69
Nonant, Hugh, bp Coventry: I 122
Noreys, Robert le, chapl.: VII 77
Northampton, schools: II 51
Nortone, Roger de, abb. St Albans: IV 147, 156
Norwich, archdcns: see Burgh; Ferentino; bps: IX 83; and see Calne; Lyhart; Middleton; see at: VI 180
notaries, notarial copies: XI 196, 198-9, 204
Novaria, Guido de, proct.: III 345; IV 155
Novavilla, Guy de, can. Limoges, aud. litt. contr.: III 324, 340-1
nunneries: III 149; V 26n

oath of calumny: II 85-6
Odo, Master, the Spaniard (Hocco or Hoceo; Odo Pictaviensis): VII 76 & n
Offa, kg: VI 178; IX 58, 62
Olivetans: V 27
Ombersley ch. (Worcs): I 124-5; VII 77 & n, 80

Order of BVM of Mt Carmel: V 28
Order of hermits of St Augustine: V 28
Ordericus Vitalis, chron.: V 29
Orsini family: I 122
Orvieto, P. of, proct.: IV 147, 156
Osbert (the Roman), preb. London: I 123
Otto, cdnl, legate: I 120, 125; II 61, 85; III 325, 337; IV 144; XII 96
Ottobon (Fieschi), legate, pope Adrian V: I 116-21, 123-5; II 69
Oxford: II 49; archdcn: J. (?Master J. of Tynemouth) II 49 & n, 51n; and see Gravesend; vice-archdcn: see Adam; law school: II 43, 48, 52-3; monks at: IX 74, 79, 83; St Mary's ch.: II 49, 52-3n; university: III 328-9

Panormo, John de, r. Wandsworth: I 120
papal diplomatic: XI 198-9
Paris, Matthew, chron.: I 126; IX 59n, 70
Pascal II, pope: V 24
Patrick, St: VI 177-8
Peasants' Revolt (1381): VI 187n; IX 75; XII 106
Pecham, John, abp Canterbury: II 98; III 312, 322-3, 328; XII 98-9, 102-4, 106
Peling, Simon de, proct.: IV 152
Peter, Master, ?official of bp Lincoln: VII 77 & n
Peter the Venerable: V 29
Pictavens' (?of Poitiers), Master H.: VIII 206 & n, 207
Pictaviensis, Odo: see Odo
Pictor, Robert, of Abingdon: II 50, 88
Piperno, Peter de, papal chapl.: I 125
Pisa, Pisans: XI 197, 199-200, 203
Podiobonizi, Francus de, proct.: IV 149
Poitou, Philip of, kg's clk: 196-200, 212-13
Pomonte, Philip de, proct.: III 319-20, 323, 326-8, 332-4, 336, 338-40, 345; IV 161
Pontecurvo, Thomas de, proct.: IV 151
Portubus, James de, can. Syracuse: I 120
Poucyn, Robert, proct.: IV 161
Prato, Matheus de, proct.: IV 155
Premonstratensians: II 68; V 23-4, 32, 168, 172, 174, 179-81
Premontré, abb.: II 61; V 176
procedural books: II 42-7
procedure, judge delegate courts: II 42-99; VIII 201
proctors: I 117; III 311-45; IV 143-63; of laymen: IV 151-2, 156-7; of religious orders: IV 146-51; royal: I 116, 126; IV 144-5, 159-60
provision, papal: I 117, 122
Ptolemy, clk: I 124

INDEX OF RECORDS CITED